FOR THE PEOPLE, FOR THE COUNTRY

For the People, For the Country

Patrick Henry's Final Political Battle

JOHN A. RAGOSTA

UNIVERSITY OF VIRGINIA PRESS

Charlottesville and London

University of Virginia Press
© 2023 by John A. Ragosta
All rights reserved
Printed in the United States of America on acid-free paper

First published 2023

9 8 7 6 5 4 3 2 1

Library of Congress Cataloging-in-Publication Data

Names: Ragosta, John A., author.
Title: For the people, for the country : Patrick Henry's final political battle /
    John A. Ragosta.
Description: Charlottesville : University of Virginia Press, 2023. | Includes
    bibliographical references and index.
Identifiers: LCCN 2023012290 (print) | LCCN 2023012291 (ebook) |
    ISBN 9780813950228 (hardcover) | ISBN 9780813950235 (ebook)
Classification: LCC BV5294.W37 A4 2023 (print) | LCC BV5294.W37 (ebook) |
    DDC 152.9/4—dc24/eng/20230122
LC record available at https://lccn.loc.gov/2023012290
LC ebook record available at https://lccn.loc.gov/2023012291

For Sarah, and her special wonder

· CONTENTS ·

· PREFACE ·

As is often the case with a good tale, I came upon this story serendipitously. While doing research on other topics, I found myself reading George Washington's remarkable January 15, 1799, letter to Patrick Henry in which the former president warns that the nation is on the verge of disunion, possibly civil war. My curiosity piqued, I read further. When I discovered that the persons whom Henry and Washington believed were maliciously promoting their own political power at the expense of the nation were Thomas Jefferson and James Madison, I was hooked. Among the most intriguing aspects of all this is why this story was not better known, even among historians of early America. It was that story, related in the introduction, that launched me into this book project.

When I have the privilege of teaching, I often ask my students after reading a book why the author wrote it. More than a love of history or the author's craft is usually at work. Inevitably, the author has something to say.

Readers will undoubtedly have somewhat different takes on what this book "says," but I thought it important to explain Patrick Henry's transformation from the leading antifederalist in 1788—opposed to granting extensive powers to a new national government distant from the people—to a leading defender of the Constitution in 1799. His admonition that change must be achieved in "a constitutional way," at the ballot box or in court, spoke loudly in a nation suffering hyperpartisanship and threats to the still-fragile union, and speaks loudly today for many of the same reasons. Henry, having lost the battle over ratification of the Constitution, well understood that in a republic you don't always get your way, and you have to work within the system when you do not. Unfortunately, we must constantly learn and relearn the role of a loyal opposition and that, in our democracy, we must all live with the decisions of our co-citizens.

With that in mind, Henry's demand for "liberty, or . . . death" at Saint John's Church in March of 1775 is perhaps the best remembered and most misunderstood speech in American history. Too many modern advocates of conflict with the government invoke "liberty, or . . . death" as a call for obstinate, sometimes violent opposition to our government, but Henry was seeking to mobilize opposition to a government in which Americans had no vote and, as King George's refusal to even hear petitions from embattled American colonies demonstrated, no voice. Today, so much of the opposition to government is rooted in belligerent tantrums when some do not get their way because the majority have voted against them, when elected officials make laws with which they disagree. Sadly, the fragility of our nation in the 1790s, and whenever fundamental doctrines like a free press, resort to the ballot box, and acceptance of electoral results are seriously in jeopardy, is a lesson that we must learn again and again. It was a lesson sadly made real on January 6, 2021.

I started to think seriously about this project by 2010. In the intervening period, I have spent marvelous years teaching at Hamilton College, Oberlin College, and Randolph College, experiences that I thoroughly enjoyed and of which I am deeply proud, but the time preparing lessons and in the classroom certainly diverted attention from this project. In 2013, I was asked to prepare a short biography of Patrick Henry for the Routledge Historical Americans series; that project undoubtedly improved this volume, allowing me to steep myself more deeply in Henry's life and times. In early 2017, the Office of Lifetime Learning at the University of Virginia suggested that I prepare a MOOC (massive open online course) on Henry to be made available by UVA free online on the Coursera platform. That series of lectures has been viewed by hundreds of people all over the world. And for several years, I have worked as a historian at the Robert H. Smith International Center for Jefferson Studies at Monticello, spending time training guides, meeting with groups interested in Jefferson and early America, consulting on various historic issues, and assisting with publications.

Truth be told, however, none of these activities was the major impediment to finalizing this project. Rather, on and off for years I grappled with fundamental questions concerning what this book was about: Was this a story about Patrick Henry and how he grew into the 1799 election, a story with great implications for the early republic and our nation today? Alternatively, was this the story of politics in the 1790s and how the classic binary of "Federalist" versus "Democratic-Republic" missed a large group of the disaffected, with Patrick Henry being a useful literary device to explore that important topic? While these two projects would obviously be closely related, the latter would be a far more involved and longer project and, perhaps, one of more interest to scholars but perhaps less to the public generally. As the book came into its final form, I had to realize that the book was inevitably about both. I hope that the readers will conclude that I chose wisely in the topic and scope of the discussion. Certainly, there is, there is always, more research, analysis, and writing to be done.

I also grappled with Thomas Jefferson. He certainly treated Henry badly. Yet, as my research continued, and particularly as I engaged additional research by scholars such as Wendell Bird, Terri Diane Halperin, and others, I came to better understand how desperate things seemed to Jefferson and James Madison in 1798 as the free press was under attack and dozens of newspaper editors were jailed or silenced. This was Jefferson's "reign of witches." Jefferson chose a remedy very poorly—as Madison recognized quite early and Jefferson himself seemed to come to accept—and he unfairly attacked Henry, but perhaps his desperation and the grave risk posed by threats to the free press explain his reaction. In fact, as I grappled with Jefferson, I came to a new, more nuanced understanding of his term as president. I think that he understood as the eighteenth century ended that the hyperpartisanship of the 1790s had been very dangerous for the nation, partisanship that he had helped to feed (although perhaps that memory had faded by the 1820s when Jefferson reengaged some of his radical states' rights ideas in the face of a renewed threat to union in the rising regional conflict over slavery). What contemporary critics and historians have termed the hypocrisy of Jefferson's presidency may be more evidence of moderation, a recognition that things had gone too far and that our nation could be destroyed. Perhaps Jefferson quietly reconsidered his position, something that we hope our politicians will do.

However the results are evaluated, I know that this book owes much to many others who provided assistance, guidance, suggestions, and support. Chief among the institutions that helped to bring this project to fruition are the Robert H. Smith International Center for Jefferson Studies (ICJS) at Monticello, the Jack Miller Center and the Colonial Williamsburg Foundation, the Patrick Henry Memorial Foundation, and the Office of Lifetime Learning at UVA (and the remarkable Althea Brooks). Notably, Andrew O'Shaughnessy, formerly director of ICJS, and Leslie Greene Bowman, formerly president of the Thomas Jefferson Foundation, have made ICJS an extraordinary academic home as I completed my research and writing (while editing several volumes for Monticello, giving regular lectures, and otherwise participating in Monticello's important public history mission). Mark Couvillon (an interpreter at Colonial Williamsburg and a walking encyclopedia of Henry knowledge), Peter Onuf, Frank Cogliano, Paul Finkelman, Greg May, Alan Gibson, Sara Georgini, Johann Neem, George Cheek, Colleen Sheehan, Bill Barker, Hope

Marstin, Cole Poindexter (genealogist at the Patrick Henry Memorial Foundation and a font of knowledge on difficult Henry relations), Cody Youngblood, Caitlin Lawrence, Whitney Pippin, and Marianne Simpson, Lacey Hunter, and Bolling Izard (interns at ICJS) have each provided invaluable assistance. Then there are the librarians at Swem (William & Mary), Alderman (UVA), and especially Monticello's Jefferson Library (Anna Berkes and Endrina Tay), and dozens of other individuals whose aid has been invaluable. I also owe much to the wisdom and support of Nadine Zimmerli, my fine editor, and the rest of the dedicated staff at the University of Virginia Press. I can also say with both pride and humility that the recommendations of the various academic readers and my colleagues have made this a much better book as I tried, sometimes chafing, to reflect their varied wisdom. I thank them, too, for their assistance.

This book is dedicated to my daughter, Sarah, who can be restless and opinionated. She thinks that her father still sometimes sees her as the young child who held his hand for walks, laughed with him, snuggled close to read a book, and looked wide-eyed at new discoveries; perhaps I sink into the past when I refer to her as "my Sarah," something I now try to avoid. She is sometimes bemused with her father, when not annoyed. In fact, I know what a fine, successful young woman she has become and am very proud of her. What, perhaps, she does not fully understand is the reason that her father may sometimes seem to grasp at her younger self: A father hopes that he can be half the person that his young daughter thought him to be. I hope that I have been.

In quotations, original spelling, capitalization, emphasis, and punctuation have been retained without any other indication.

FOR THE PEOPLE, FOR THE COUNTRY

Introduction

"Every Thing Dear & Valuable to Us Is Assailed"

On January 15, 1799, despite the sunny and calm weather outside, a great storm was brewing inside Mount Vernon, George Washington's plantation home perched high above a wide bend in the Potomac River in northern Virginia. Living just miles from the bustling and sometimes frenzied construction of the new capital city that would bear his name, an aging Washington had hoped for a peaceful retirement after the rigors of a long war, nation-building, and eight years as the country's first president under the still recently adopted Constitution. He had envisioned spending his final years enjoying life, peace, and prosperity in the new nation that he had helped to birth and nurture, resting under his own "vine & fig tree" to use one of his favorite biblical metaphors. Instead, the arrival of 1799 found the former president consumed with events beyond his own estate and with fears for the future of the nation that he had led. One can almost see the towering Washington pacing the wide pine floorboards with a quickened step as he grew increasingly agitated.

Although the former president was never considered a scholar, he read widely in history, and he knew well that the past was littered with republics that had collapsed from internal discord. Conflict among political factions could bring strongmen to power and interfere with the virtuous commitment to public service that was so essential to undergird a republic. The United States was still an experiment in democracy, its political system fragile. European nations, anticipating the new nation's collapse into squabbling states or regional confederacies, lurked ready to absorb the fragmented pieces of the American republic into their own empires; some Americans were undoubtedly intriguing with foreign powers. The nation desperately needed time to mature; political leaders needed to become familiar with running a republic based on the consent of the governed; citizens needed to develop skills in political participation and oversight; political opponents needed to develop appropriate ways to act as a loyal opposition in challenging the government when it acted against their wishes, and the diverse states, still jealous of their own prerogatives, needed time to continue to knit themselves into a solid union. Unfortunately, the political landscape was far from quiet as the end of the eighteenth century approached, and time for the union to stabilize itself seemed to be slipping away. Anarchy, or worse, loomed.

Washington must have thought long and hard about what he could do to avert the threatening crisis on that crisp winter day in the waning year of the century. Finally, the general sat down at the desk in his study to write a difficult and important letter to a man with whom he had not communicated directly for going on four years. George Washington, the man known to history as the "Sword" of the American Revolution, took up a quill pen and a stack of paper and began a long and impassioned missive to Patrick Henry, the Revolution's "Trumpet," who was living in what he, too, had hoped would be a peaceful retirement at his Red Hill plantation, almost 200 miles southwest of Mount Vernon, a stone's throw from the North Carolina border.

Washington's anxiety poured out onto the page. The general wrote to his former compatriot and leader in the Revolution that the still-young nation to which Henry and he had devoted the better part of their lives was at risk from violent political and legal turbulence. A political faction, determined to fight its way to power regardless of the cost to the nation, took every opportunity "to disquiet the Public mind with unfounded alarms; to arraign every act of the [John Adams] Administration; to set the People at varience with their Government; and to embarrass all its measures," Washington railed. The national government was being directly challenged with credible and serious threats that states would simply ignore its authority (as they had done so often and so disastrously during the Revolution and under the now discarded Articles of Confederation), and they would try to nullify federal laws within their own borders. This was not a matter of mere political differences. Given the fragile state of the nation, the danger of such unbridled attacks on the integrity and authority of the people's own government was clear to Washington. Chaos beckoned if each state interpreted national laws for itself and threatened to ignore those with which it disagreed. States would take sides on every important federal matter; state would oppose state, and each undermine aspects of federal policy in its own territory. There would be no uniform national law; conflicts would snowball; states would join in regional groups in opposition to one another; federal authority would evaporate. Such attacks on the national government, welcomed and supported by foreign interests, threatened to ignite a civil war and to "destroy" the infant union, Washington warned.[1]

The former president did not believe for a moment that the attacks were the disinterested criticism of American patriots seeking to change government policies in a constitutional manner. His temper seemed to rise as his quill scratched across the pages; he insisted that ambitious and ruthless politicians had placed party over country and were at work trying to seize power on the dismembered corpse of the young nation. A dangerous hyperpartisanship was at work: "Measures are systematically, and pertenaciously pursued, which must eventually dissolve the Union or produce coertion." He feared that the federal government would have no choice but to use military force against its own recalcitrant people and its own states that had been whipped into a violent political frenzy by ruthless and myopic politicians seeking power, and the fabric of the nation would be torn apart when a U.S. army marched on American citizens. If something was not done soon to stop those who were sowing dissension and undermining the union, "vain it will be to look for Peace and happiness, or for the security of liberty or property."

Then came the specific point of the letter, the "ask" that caused Washington to write to his old revolutionary colleague, Patrick Henry, still the second most popular politician in Virginia (second only to Washington himself):

> at such a crisis as this, when every thing dear & valuable to us is assailed; when this Party hang[s] upon the Wheels of Government as a dead weight, . . . abetting the nefarious views of another Nation, upon our Rights; . . . I say, when these things have become so obvious, ought characters who are best able to rescue their Country from the pending evil to remain at home? rather, ought they not to come forward, and by their talents and influence, stand in the breach wch such conduct has made on the Peace and happiness of this Country, and oppose the widening of it?

Washington "express[ed] a hope, and an earnest wish" that Henry would "come forward" out of the sylvan repose of his own retirement, reenter the political fray as a candidate for Congress, and fight to save the union from a violent political faction ruthlessly seeking power through its reckless attacks on the national government, its institutions, and the constitutional settlement.[2]

Washington's call upon Henry was particularly poignant. The two leaders had worked together closely through the Revolutionary War. It was Henry who had defended the general against conspirators who sought to replace him in the so-called Conway Cabal, and Governor Henry had been a leader in the effort to supply Washington's troops at Valley Forge. But they had parted ways in 1787 shortly after the Philadelphia Constitutional Convention ended when Henry declared that he could not support the new Constitution for which Washington was a leading advocate. Henry feared that the new national government under the Constitution would be too powerful and distant from the people. Instead, much to Washington's consternation, he became the leading antifederalist in the unsuccessful effort to block ratification of the Constitution. While the two had become cordial again during Washington's presidency, from a distance, Henry had repeatedly declined Washington's offers of high political office, from Supreme Court justice to secretary of state, telling the president that he would only come out of retirement if the nation was actually at risk. Now, Washington felt that he had no choice but to try to enlist Henry to defend the country and, critically, the Constitution that he had opposed. Washington understood that no one else would have Henry's influence.

The retired Henry, raising a large brood of children and grandchildren with his second wife at his Red Hill plantation in south central Virginia, received Washington's letter three weeks later (a not unusual delay in the eighteenth century), and his temper, too, flared. Though Henry had not communicated directly with Washington for years—political enemies would later spread the canard that the two were hopelessly estranged and despised each other— he now warmly took up his pen. Echoing the former president's indignation over the efforts of the new and dangerous political faction, Henry also shared Washington's foreboding that the nation hung on the brink of a civil war. Turning on the politicians who were agitating the nation in a reckless search for power, Henry was concerned that "it may be doubted whether a Cure can easily be found for the Mischiefs they have occasioned. God grant it may be effected without coming to Extremity—yes my dear sir, I accord with every Sentiment you express to me." Henry realized that his retirement was at an end. Telling Washington that his children would "blush" were he to refuse such an urgent call from the father of his country, the aging patriot agreed to run for the Virginia legislature, adding apologetically that he was too old and ill to make the more arduous journey to attend Congress in Philadelphia, still the nation's capital.[3]

What was the danger to the union that so concerned Henry and Washington? What political actions threatened civil war? Who were the ambitious and unscrupulous political leaders putting personal ambition and party politics above country and endangering the legacy of the American Revolution and the U.S. Constitution, endangering the nation itself?

The threat was the radical states' rights agenda of the Kentucky and Virginia Resolutions and their authors, none other than Thomas Jefferson and James Madison.

An ailing Patrick Henry, feeling the infirmity that would lead to his death before four months passed, did reluctantly come out of retirement at Washington's behest and ran for office as a member of the Virginia House of Delegates. He easily won the spring election in Charlotte County—Henry always won his elections—but he died in June of 1799, never taking his seat in the Virginia assembly. Washington, too, was to pass away before the year was out. Had Henry lived, John Randolph of Roanoke (a leading Jeffersonian) later explained, Thomas Jefferson would have lost the election of 1800.[4]

Nonetheless, the forceful response of Henry, Washington, and others derailed, for a time, the active opposition by the states to federal authority. Jefferson and his allies were beaten badly in congressional elections in the South in 1799 as voters recoiled from the looming threat of disunion. Henry, returning to the public arena, played an important role, for example, in the election to Congress of Federalist John Marshall, soon to be Jefferson's nemesis as chief justice of the Supreme Court, and Henry "Light-Horse Harry" Lee, who would excoriate Jefferson's record as wartime governor in his early nineteenth-century history of the American Revolution in the South.

Significantly, Jefferson and Madison were chastened by both the opposition and the election results. They seemed to recognize belatedly the danger of the enflamed partisanship of the 1790s, knowing, too, that they had played a large part in feeding it. They and their Democratic-Republicans changed course. Instead of active opposition by states to federal laws with which they disagreed, Jeffersonians focused on the dangerous growth of federal power and suppression of the free press by the federal government. They took their legitimate grievances to the electorate, urging citizens to the polls in an effort to take control of the government and change federal policies.

Of course, Jefferson won the presidential election in 1800, and the United States became a Jeffersonian republic. The crisis of 1798–1799 was soon forgotten.

Critically for the nation, though, Jefferson's victory occurred not in state legislatures or by open resistance to federal power as initially urged by Jefferson and Madison but at the ballot box—exactly the place where Henry had insisted in his final political speech that the issues *should* be resolved. The peaceful transfer of power between political parties for which the election of 1800 is known was the result. But it was a result that had been thrown into doubt in the crisis and certainly had not been inevitable.

After his inauguration, Jefferson continued to temper his tone and sought as president to speak broadly for all of the American people. Madison, who had attempted to retreat from the radical states' rights agenda almost immediately, spent the rest of his long life attempting to paper over the most extreme of the proposals that Jefferson and he had made in the crisis. The moderation evident in Jefferson's presidency—a moderation that elicited cries of hypocrisy at the time and from historians ever since—was, in part, the result of their realization that the partisanship of the 1790s had almost destroyed the nation. President Jefferson, who had not been present for the Philadelphia Constitutional Convention or ratification, and who told one correspondent at the time that he was "nearly a Neutral" on the Constitution, also seemed to embrace a renewed and invigorated appreciation for the value of the constitutional union, and the need to protect it.[5]

The immediate crisis was over; civil war had been averted, but in some respects, the groundwork had been laid for active interference with the federal government by the states, for what would become disunion in the years ahead. The issues that drove the new nation to a precipice in 1799 would be submerged, quieted, and massaged until they were resurrected by southern secessionists in defense of the slavocracy and exploded sixty years later at Fort Sumter.

The crisis of 1799—pitting the Founding Fathers against one another in what they believed was a struggle for the nation's survival and its soul—is a story that has been largely forgotten. It is not only a story about the particular political crisis of the Alien and Sedition Acts and the Kentucky and Virginia Resolutions drafted by Jefferson and Madison in response, but also a story of enormous historic and political relevance about Americans in a still new and fragile nation grappling with how loyal citizens could effectively disagree with and oppose their own government's policies without undermining the republican system and endangering the nation. It is the story of the necessity of a free press in a functioning republic and the grave danger when politicians unhappy with what newspapers publish launch threats against the press. It is the story of the enormous influence of leaders and the struggle with whether they should be virtuous, disinterested servants of the republic or devoted party men. And it is the story of a struggle with how political change could be achieved, must be achieved, in "a constitutional way" to use Henry's term.

It is also the story of how Patrick Henry—the orator who compelled men forward into a revolutionary battle for liberty, the great antifederalist who opposed the U.S. Constitution for fear that it would create a government that was too powerful and distant from the people, the man who was the intellectual godfather of the states' rights philosophy of the new Democratic-Republican party that would be led to political hegemony by Jefferson and Madison—came out of retirement to enter his final political campaign defending the Constitution that he had opposed because his fellow citizens had ratified it and because he believed that the nation it created was at risk. Thus, it is a story of what it means to be a loyal opposition and Henry's role in developing that essential idea.

It is also the story of how Henry's populist commitment to his community and nation and belief in the rule of law drove his actions. Washington and he both believed that his 1799 campaign was necessary to save the nation threatened by partisanship. Washington, of course, was immortalized, almost deified in the new nineteenth century. In contrast, Democratic-Republicans labeled the ailing Henry an "apostate" (a term with religious connotations) for his efforts; he was denied honors upon his death, and his memory and legacy were viciously and successfully attacked for decades thereafter, undermining his historical legacy.

The story is fascinating, intriguing. The "Trumpet" and the "Sword" of the Revolution reluctantly abandoned their retirements to do battle with the Revolution's "Pen," Thomas Jefferson. This is the story of a constitutional and political crisis that threatened to divide the union a short ten years after the Constitution's ratification, and one which suggests that Patrick Henry—a founder who inhabits popular memory almost exclusively for seven words spoken in March 1775 at Saint John's Church in Richmond—"give me liberty, or give me death!"—was far more central to the history of the early republic than is generally remembered.

This book uses Henry and his role in the early republic as a lens through which this period and crisis can be better understood. Henry teaches us much about our nation and its people and the role of a leader, even today. His decisions demonstrate that in early American history, as now, political choices are rarely reduced to a binary—for or against the Constitution, Federalist or Democratic-Republican, with Hamilton or with Jefferson. He also warned his fellow citizens, and us, that if Americans cannot accept decisions by a majority of their fellow citizens with which they disagree and seek change in a productive, "a constitutional way," primarily at the ballot box, the republic cannot survive. Henry warned that the alternative is monarchy. How and why Henry, and the new nation, came to his final election and addressed the national crisis is the topic of this book.[6]

Henry's actions in 1799 have been described as a "puzzle," or largely ignored by analysts and biographers. Even his first biographer, a Jeffersonian, tread lightly on the topic. The reasons for this are myriad. Some, perhaps, did not understand why Henry acted as he did. Others did not want to understand because doing so meant questioning other assumptions and understandings, particularly about the triumphant Jeffersonians of the Revolution of 1800 and the states' rights agenda of 1798 that became a foundation for southerners and their support of slavery and Native dispossession in the antebellum period.[7]

Of course, each of the leading protagonists, Henry, Washington, Jefferson, Madison, . . . and many other founders, owned scores of slaves, and the policy debates in 1798–1799 that pitted them against each other were not immediately wrapped up in the tragedy of human slavery. Perhaps challenges to the terrible system of slavery still seemed so politically weak that they were not fixated on it. Soon, though, the issue of states' rights and the nation would be, and the implications of the policy debates of the 1790s became painfully clear. Similarly, the cry of "states' rights" would increasingly become a shield justifying Native land dispossession, and even in the 1790s was used to justify state actions against Native Americans. In any case, to make sense of Henry's campaign of 1799 is to challenge what became known as the "Spirit of '98," a bulwark of Jeffersonian loyalists and slavery apologists as the Civil War approached and still the basis of a radical states' rights philosophy up to this day.

Then there is our perception of Henry. If he was preaching moderation, support of the Constitution, and a dependence on the ballot box, his image as a belligerent opponent of the federal government, as someone who would choose "liberty or death" over obeying an increasingly powerful national government, must be questioned. Understanding this crisis, then, challenges much of the history about Henry that began to be formed almost before his body was cold in his grave. Far easier to dismiss Henry's actions in the late 1790s as evidence of senility or jealousy, or as a riddle, as the partisans sought to do. Properly understood, this story undermines the fire-breathing image of Henry that is so popular with government opponents today.

In rediscovering that story, this book challenges all of us to do as Henry did, to rethink our relationship with our government, even when we disagree with its decisions. Perhaps we have become too familiar and too comfortable with our nation's democracy, too complacent. Perhaps in an era that pundits define as fundamentally divided, we have become too willing to perceive our own government and political opponents as an enemy, to challenge the policies of our government through any means available, some even choosing violence. Henry, the firebrand of the Revolution, the leading opponent of the U.S. Constitution, understood that sometimes in a democracy, you lose; other voters and politicians decide in a manner that you do not approve. But if we fail to address our concerns and work with our co-citizens to improve our nation in "a constitutional way," we can yet lose the nation itself. We must do better.

Patrick Henry's Political Philosophy

The People's Right to Govern

P atrick Henry is remembered today primarily for his firebrand speeches and his all-consuming passion for individual liberty. People seem particularly fond of invoking Henry's most famous words—"give me liberty, or give me death!" Sometimes, his words are used to justify even violent opposition to government authority. But while it is true that Henry was devoted to freedom, his image as an antigovernment agitator devoted to liberty *über alles* is a caricature.

Henry was much more.

Perhaps the most obvious place to begin a discussion of Henry's political philosophy in an effort to understand his 1799 political metamorphosis would be in the 1780s, as his evolving views on the national government culminated in Henry's strident critique of, and opposition to ratification of, the new U.S. Constitution. Henry was America's leading antifederalist. Yet, to better understand Henry and his 1799 campaign, one should at least take a brief glimpse at an earlier episode that evidences his commitment to the people in his community and their democratic control of their own government, a commitment that would become even more apparent during the political turmoil of the 1780s and 1790s.[1]

The Parsons' Cause

Beyond his belief in personal liberty, Patrick Henry always believed in the people's collective right to govern themselves; his communitarianism was hiding in plain sight. A lawyer by profession, in his first famous legal case, the Parsons' Cause, Henry spoke out on the question of governance.

The Parsons' Cause involved colonial laws that supported the established church in Virginia, the Church of England. In colonial Virginia, each local parish (generally a county) had an Anglican priest, and all taxpayers, regardless of religion, paid a tax for the priest's salary. With gold and silver so scarce in the colony, tobacco served as a convenient currency for the church tax (and several other government obligations); thus, the people of each parish owed their Anglican priest 16,000 pounds of tobacco annually. Yet tobacco prices could fluctuate wildly depending on the annual harvest, resulting in similar fluctuations in priests' salaries in real, economic terms. When tobacco was plentiful and prices dropped, priests were effectively paid less; conversely, when tobacco was scarce and prices rose, Anglican priests gained a windfall.

In 1755, with a poor tobacco crop, Virginia's colonial legislature, the House of Burgesses, attempted to alleviate the strain on taxpayers by passing a law specifying that fees due in tobacco could be paid that year in cash at the average price of two cents per pound. Most of Virginia's Anglican priests grudgingly accepted the 1755 law; it was limited to one year and, based on actual tobacco prices that year, did not dramatically reduce their salaries. But in 1758, when the Virginia Burgesses passed a similar two-cents law for two years while tobacco prices soared to six cents a pound, many Anglican ministers challenged the "Two Penny" act in England, asking the king's Privy Council to invalidate the Virginia law. The ministers insisted that it was unfair that they effectively be paid less when tobacco was plentiful and prices low, but their congregants were unwilling to pay in tobacco when prices were high. After the Privy Council ruled that Virginia's two-cents laws were null and void, several ministers sued local tax collectors and their own vestries (local boards representing the people of each parish) for the difference between the two cents a pound they had been paid and what their salary would have been based upon the higher actual price of tobacco.

In the Parsons' Cause, the relatively unknown Patrick Henry defended the Louisa County tax collector and parish vestry against the claims of its priest, the Reverend James Maury (curiously, one of Thomas Jefferson's teachers), for the higher tobacco salary. While he technically lost the case (the law was clearly against him), after Henry's powerful appeal to the jury, Maury was awarded total damages of only one cent. The case is generally remembered for Henry's dramatic attack on the king, suggesting that he was a tyrant—seemingly portending the coming American Revolution. Henry's argument, though, is even more revealing of his political views and the coming crisis of the 1790s.

Henry was not attacking the monarchy generally. (Nor was he objecting that religious freedom was compromised by the requirement to pay an Anglican religious tax, an issue that he would revisit in the 1780s.) Henry focused on the monarch's decision (via the Privy Council) to overrule the Virginia legislature, that is, interference by the distant king and his aristocratic ministers in a local matter and local control by the community. The people's representatives in the House of Burgesses found the two-cents law both useful and necessary given the circumstances of Virginia in 1758. It had "every characteristic of a good law," Henry explained to the packed Hanover County courtroom. "It was a law of general utility," exactly the type of legislation that citizens had a right to expect from their government. It was simply misrule for the king, sitting over three thousand miles away and unfamiliar with conditions in Virginia, to usurp the people's judgment on a matter of enormous and very local concern. "A King, by disallowing Acts of this salutary nature, from being the father of his people, degenerates into a Tyrant and forfeits all right to his subjects' obedience," the young attorney explained as his argument was met with cries of "treason" from some of the assembled Anglican priests who had come to witness what was expected to be an easy victory. The tyranny was not that the king demanded support for the clergy, or that the American colonies owed allegiance to the king, but his decision to "disallow" the act of the duly elected local legislature. (In the same vein, the first grievance listed in the Declaration of Independence thirteen years later was that the king "has refused his Assent to Laws, the most wholesome and necessary for the public good.") Turning on the ministers, Henry (although a lifelong Anglican) continued: The clergy, by opposing the will of the people, became "enemies of the community."[2]

In this, one of his first and most important legal cases, Henry's commitment was to the people's collective will—the community—and their control of their destiny through representative government and law. He rejected control of the legislature by a distant king and aristocratic council for the benefit of an elite clergy. The same issues were at stake several years later when Henry, as a new member of the House of Burgesses, challenged the king's authority to tax unrepresented Americans with the Stamp Act.[3]

The same sense of community and the need for unity was at work as Henry led his neighbors, and the nation, into the Revolutionary War. In 1774, when representatives from twelve colonies spread across the eastern seaboard met at the First Continental Congress in Philadelphia to address Britain's intolerable response to the Boston Tea Party, many delegates had closer ties to London than to their sister colonies. But Henry, in his first speech on the national stage, sought a unity of purpose, mesmerizing members of the Congress as he proclaimed that "the distinctions between Virginians, Pennsylvanians, New Yorkers, and New Englanders, are no more. I am not a Virginian, but an American." (In fairness, Henry also hoped to promote Virginia's interests in this his first national appearance.) "It was Patrick Henry," explained Edmund Randolph, "awakening the genius of his country, and binding a band of patriots together to hurl defiance at the tyranny of so formidable a nation as Great Britain."[4]

It is important to note here that Henry did not extend his ideas of nation-building to enslaved African Americans. While he denounced slavery as vicious and unchristian, he enslaved people throughout his adult life, having at least ninety-eight enslaved at the time of his death. He neither manumitted enslaved men, women, or children during his life nor in his will, suggesting only that his wife might free several if she so wished.[5]

The Need for a Stronger Government

As Virginia's first wartime governor, like many of his compatriots, Henry feared that an imminent financial collapse threatened the Revolution. With inflation running rampant, he wrote to Thomas Jefferson, his successor in the governor's office, "I cannot forbear thinking, the present increase of prices is in great part owing to a kind of habit . . . which is fostered by a mistaken avarice." What was needed, Henry insisted, was "virtue and public spirit." These concerns were no less real after the war.[6]

After Yorktown, with the Revolution effectively won, Henry celebrated with the rest of the nation. But, with the rest of the nation, he quickly turned his thoughts to the critical problems facing the United States as it struggled to turn its wartime success into a stable and economically viable country. What was needed, from Henry's perspective, was a government that would be ruled by its own citizenry and a citizenry committed to making the government work.

Under the Articles of Confederation, the U.S. government was in many respects simply an alliance of independent, often squabbling states, essentially a compact or treaty between thirteen sovereign governments. During the war, their bickering often interfered with effective governance, but necessity forced the states to at least some level of cooperation. After the war, the challenge of governance loomed without the crisis-induced cooperation. Chaos seemed to threaten. The most obvious problem with the Articles of Confederation, and the one that is generally mentioned in histories, is that the Confederation could not impose any taxes itself; it could only ask each state to shoulder its share of expenses through a "requisition," requests that were more often than not ignored or met only in part, especially after the war was over and the revolutionary crisis had seemed to pass.[7]

By the end of the war, states were regularly failing to provide funds requisitioned by the national government, and as the 1780s continued, the situation got worse. By early 1787, states had paid only "two-thirds of the congressional requisition of October 1781, 20 percent of the September 1785 requisition, and only 2 percent of that of August 1786." And the rate of payments by each state varied enormously, ranging "from a high of 67 percent by New York and 57 percent by Pennsylvania to a low of 3 percent by North Carolina and 0 percent by Georgia," further heightening conflict among the states.[8]

By 1785, the United States was unable to pay even the interest on the foreign loans that had been critical to financing the war. By 1787, it was in default. A frustrated James Madison, one of Virginia's representatives to the Confederation Congress, bemoaned the situation in a letter to Virginia's governor, Edmund Randolph: "No money comes into the federal Treasury. No respect is paid to the federal authority; and people of reflection unanimously agree that the existing Confederation is tottering to its foundation."[9]

Henry was keenly aware of these problems, but also focused on the fact that the consequences of the government's financial collapse were often felt most severely by small farmers and tradesmen. Thousands of former soldiers and small farmers held government "IOUs" for their wartime service or supplies, IOUs that were beginning to seem worthless. Facing difficult economic circumstances as they tried to repair farms and shops after the long war, many of the former soldiers could not wait indefinitely in the hope of future payment and had to sell these "promises to pay" by the state and Confederation governments to speculators for pennies on the dollar of their face value.

This alone was a disaster in the making, but the problems with the national government's lack of authority went well beyond taxation.

The Confederation government also had no authority to regulate commerce, domestically or internationally, making commercial relations among the states tense as they vied for control with other states. States with large ports—such as New York, Pennsylvania, and Massachusetts—raised a large share of their revenue by imposing duties on imports, a system that effectively passed on a portion of their tax burden to citizens of other states who imported goods from overseas through their neighbors' ports. State laws discriminating against out-of-state merchants and debtors proliferated; some states even imposed the same (or even higher) restrictions and duties on goods from other states as they did on foreign goods.[10]

Less than two years after Yorktown, George Washington gave a dire warning about the lack of authority in the Confederation government: "If the powers of Congress are not enlarged, & made competent to all *general purposes,* . . . the

Blood which has been spilt [in the Revolution] . . . will avail nothing, and . . . the band, already too weak, wch holds us together, will soon be broken; when anarchy & confusion will prevail." Madison wrote despairingly to his father in early 1787 that Americans were "losing all confidence in our political System."[11]

The Congress under the Articles of Confederation was often unable even to obtain a quorum, and reforming the government to increase its power seemed impossible. Any amendment to remove the limitations embedded in the Articles would require the unanimous consent of the thirteen states; each independent state had a veto over any significant change that would increase the power of the national government, change which would inevitably compromise its own authority. Many thought that the Confederation would have to dissolve, and foreign leaders expected its imminent collapse.[12]

Henry was intimately familiar with the lack of necessary power in the national government, and it weighed heavily upon him as Virginia's governor again from 1784 to 1786 and as a member of the House of Delegates when not governor. He worked throughout the period to assist the small farmers and tradesmen who suffered, but he recognized that to address the underlying problem, the power of the national government must somehow be enlarged.

States Abusing Power

Many American leaders in the 1780s had a second group of concerns that contributed significantly to their view that a constitutional convention was needed: states were flexing their political muscles in ways that deeply troubled America's wealthy elites, although far less so Patrick Henry.

The Revolution contributed to a relative democratization of American politics and expansion of the right to vote and to participate in government (at least when it came to white men) as elites began to lose their previous exclusive control. Both Henry and Jefferson championed such changes, supporting broad rights of citizenship for white men and expanding voting rights. Many small farmers and tradesmen were taking an increasingly prominent role in politics, and they took an activist, progressive approach to the economic challenges facing their peers, the "middling and lesser sorts." As a result, debt and tax relief and restrictions on merchants became favorite causes of state legislatures. In spite of the massive inflation that had occurred during the war, some states adopted new "paper money" and "tender" bills, not only issuing more paper currency, but mandating that it be accepted as payment for all contracts when "tendered" (offered) by a debtor. Taxes, too, were postponed or made payable in Revolutionary War script of questionable value, further delaying payment of public debts and leaving state governments in precarious financial circumstances. Henry led efforts in Virginia in support of many of these progressive reforms.

While cheered by populists, these laws posed a serious risk to moneyed interests and threatened commercial relations. James Madison, George Washington, Alexander Hamilton, Robert Morris, and others were increasingly alarmed at what they saw as assaults on property and wealth and the dangers posed by a rising democracy. Complaining against "paper emissions, and violations of contracts," Madison struggled to convince the more progressive Jefferson that "the injustice of them [these state laws] has been so frequent and so flagrant as to alarm the most steadfast friends of Republicanism." Richard Henry Lee concluded that democratization had gone too far and that a change "from Simple Democracy seems indispensably necessary, if any government at all is to exist in N. America." (Of course, the irony of these complaints about excessive democracy is that women, enslaved, Native Americans, and, in most jurisdictions, propertyless men still had no right to participate in American government at all.)[13]

Stopping state interference with propertied interests became for Madison and many other elites another major reason to support development of a new constitution that would not only significantly increase federal power but also restrict state authority to issue paper money or otherwise to interfere with private contracts. For example, historians have often focused on the violent aspect of the protests known as Shays's Rebellion and their very substantial influence in encouraging independent-minded states to support the Philadelphia Constitutional Convention, but after that revolt was relatively quickly put down, angry taxpayers in Massachusetts elected a progressive state legislature that began to adopt laws providing much of the tax and debt reform that the protestors had sought. These progressive laws disturbed many elites as much as the protests. Madison was outraged, as were other conservative leaders. Any interference with the "sacred" right of property ownership or debt collection, even by laws adopted through the democratic process, was unacceptable. In April of 1787, after Shays's revolt was over, Madison warned Washington that "the discontents in Massts which lately produced an appeal to the sword are now producing a trial of strength in the field of electioneering"—in other words they were using the ballot box and democratic processes to obtain relief from the merchants and creditors. Less than a week later, the man who would be called the "father of the Constitution" was even more pointed in writing to Edmund Pendleton when he expressed concern that Shays's rebels might "muster sufficient numbers" in the election so that "their wicked measures are to be sheltered under the forms of the constitution."[14]

This response to progressive measures and to the relative success of the "middling and lesser sort" at the ballot box has convinced many historians that the U.S. Constitution was essentially a reactionary effort to reverse the trend toward empowering common people and to protect elite control of the government. After the Philadelphia Convention ended, Madison seemed to confirm those conclusions, confidentially telling Jefferson that state debtor and tax laws "contributed more to that uneasiness which produced the Convention, and prepared the public mind for a general reform" than "inadequacy of the Confederation to its immediate objects."[15]

Patrick Henry, more of a populist, had a much more nuanced view on these matters, and his opinions deviated significantly from those of Madison and other elite nationalists who were demanding a new constitutional convention. While he recognized the necessity of increasing the power of the national government on matters of taxation and commerce, his interest in reform was not fed by progressive state programs that had been adopted to benefit the common man.

In fact, Henry was deeply sympathetic to the economic crunch that faced yeoman farmers, and he supported many of the populist reforms that elites tended to vilify. For example, Henry took the lead in tax commutation and legislation that allowed deer hides to be accepted in payment of tax bills. In the 1790s, he would become famous for his defense of Virginian debtors against the effort of British merchants to collect prewar debts, another issue that upset conservative supporters of constitutional reform. Although Henry himself became a wealthy member of the gentry over the course of his career (enslaving almost 100 humans and owning over 50,000 acres at his death), he never found a reason to support a broad limit on state authority to enact progressive reforms like those of the 1780s.[16]

Patrick Henry: Moderate Nationalist

Faced with dim prospects both at the national and the state level, American leaders began to contemplate concrete measures to increase the power of the national government. Initially, Patrick Henry supported the proposed reforms.

Henry, like other prominent leaders, was dumbfounded and frustrated with the Confederation's inability to enforce its requisitions from the states and the apparent unwillingness of some states to cooperate in reform. In May

1784, Henry urged that Virginia should lead by supporting strong measures to strengthen the national government. In apparent exasperation, the Virginia House of Delegates—Henry again leading—unanimously advised the Virginia delegation to the Confederation Congress that requisitions on the states "ought to be enforced, if necessary, by such distress on the property of the defaulting States or of their Citizens, as by the United States in Congress assembled, may be deemed adequate and most eligible." In other words, regardless of the express terms of the Articles of Confederation, including Article II's reservation to the states of any powers not "expressly" granted, the Confederation should accept that it had implied powers to enforce its requisitions as if they were taxes, potentially seizing property. Several years later, George Nicholas, a Virginia politician and former ally of Henry, confirmed that this resolution was Henry's "child."[17]

William Short, a family friend and soon to be Jefferson's private secretary, wrote to the U.S. minister in France that Henry "saw Ruin inevitable unless something was done to give Congress a compulsory Process on delinquent States," that is, the power to force states to provide revenue, and that Henry would support a plan to give the central government "greater Powers." Henry was "strenuous for invigorating the federal Government," James Madison added, "though without any precise plan."[18]

Notably, Henry's concerns with the deficiencies in the Articles of Confederation went beyond increasing the fiscal integrity of the national government, permitting soldiers and creditors to be paid, and regulating international commerce. He also wanted the national government to take the lead in westward expansion, particularly in addressing conflicts with Indigenous nations and the removal of British troops from the forts in the Northwest Territories. With a gaggle of relatives having already moved across the Appalachian Mountains into the Kentucky territory, and with little apparent concern for Native sovereignty and dispossession, this was more than a passing interest for Henry. When a brother-in-law, Colonel William Christian, was killed in an attack by Natives near the Ohio River in April 1786, Henry, again governor of Virginia (in his fifth one-year term), demanded that the Confederation Congress "defend & protect our Frontiers." Ominously, he warned the Confederation Congress that people on "Western waters" might be forced to "abandon[] [settlements] or the present Confederation!" After all, in theory, treating with Native nations was "amongst the capital advantages of federal government to Virginia." It was essential for the federal government to have the ability effectively to protect the frontiers. While Henry had supported intermarriage to encourage Native assimilation into white society, one way or the other he saw western expansion, regardless of the cost to Natives, as fundamental for the nation. If the Confederation could not protect that western expansion, states would.[19]

By the mid-1780s, then, Patrick Henry saw a broad necessity for a significant increase in the power and authority of the national government. While he never embraced the antidemocratic efforts to restrict state legislative authority to adopt progressive regulations championed by many elites, he was poised to take an active role in expanding national government authority through constitutional reform.

Then something happened that fundamentally changed Henry's perspective and deeply influenced his political philosophy, something that would have a major impact on the coming battle over ratification of the U.S. Constitution.

The Jay-Gardoqui Treaty and Navigation of the Mississippi River

Henry was deeply committed to westward expansion and to the settler colonists who were driving the frontier west. After the Revolution, American families from across the thirteen new states poured over the mountains into western territory (with little regard for Native land ownership or the Native communities that had been ignored in the Treaty of Paris settling the war). The movement west was particularly strong from Virginia and other southern states, and initially the preferred destinations were the territories that would become Kentucky and Tennessee. By 1790, the trans-Allegheny region of Virginia had an American population estimated at over 100,000.[20]

While many western farmers were relatively "self-sufficient," even the most frugal needed to earn some hard currency for tools, gunpowder, taxes, and the like. If the western settlements were to prosper and grow, they had to have a convenient market for their agricultural produce. This, though, created a challenge: shipping goods by the rough trails back over the mountains to the east was prohibitively difficult, and expensive, leaving shipments downstream on the ubiquitous river network and through New Orleans as the practical alternative and as a critical element for future growth. The problem was that while Britain recognized American navigation rights on the Mississippi River as part of the 1783 treaty ending the Revolutionary War, Spain controlled New Orleans, and in July 1784, in an effort to strangle American westward expansion (and to encourage frontier settlers to switch allegiance to Spain), Spanish authorities prohibited shipment of American goods through their territory. Spain's action was a direct challenge to western settlement, and the impact of the restriction was only likely to increase over time.[21]

In 1785, the Confederation Congress entered into negotiations with Spain to address navigation on the Mississippi River and access to Spanish markets in Europe and the Caribbean. The former issue was essential to the South and West, but the latter topic was of particular interest to northern merchants and middle-state financiers. John Jay of New York, the Confederation's secretary of foreign affairs, was the U.S. negotiator, and Diego de Gardoqui represented Spain.

Initially, U.S. states were united on a negotiating position: The Confederation Congress unanimously instructed Jay that open navigation of the Mississippi was essential. Unfortunately, Gardoqui's instructions were exactly the opposite: Spain viewed limiting U.S. influence in the West as vital; the best way to do this was denying U.S. western settlers access to the Mississippi River. The possibility for internal American conflict hung over the talks, and American unity of purpose would not hold.[22]

The story of those negotiations is long and complex, but the end result is clear: Spain offered to open its overseas ports to American shipping (excluding tobacco—a commercial concession that might have appealed to some southerners), but Spain insisted on keeping the Mississippi River closed to American commercial traffic for at least twenty-five years. Jay, believing that he could achieve no more and supporting northeastern mercantile interests, urged the Confederation Congress to modify his negotiating instructions to permit sacrifice of Mississippi navigation and to approve the draft treaty.[23]

The proposed Jay-Gardoqui Treaty presented western frontiersmen with several highly unpalatable options. Long term, staying put and maintaining their allegiance to the United States while Spain restricted Mississippi navigation threatened poverty. One option, that Spain seemed to encourage, was for settlers to move to what is now Missouri (then still part of Spanish territory), declare allegiance to Spain, and strengthen Spain's grip on the Midwest. Alternatively, they could stay put and seek to join Spain, effectively declaring independence from the United States—an option that was both distasteful and highly speculative. Some suggested that westerners should renounce the Revolution, join British Canada, and rely on Britain to assert their rights to navigate the Mississippi River, an equally unpalatable option for most U.S. frontiersmen. Many westerners thought that they should simply pry the Mississippi open by force of arms. Any serious military action, though, would have caused an enormous problem with the Confederation government by effectively declaring war on a nation with which the United States was at peace, an informal Revolutionary War ally at that.

The risk for settlers and the young nation was real and serious. Henry Lee warned the Confederation Congress against sacrificing the West to eastern commercial interests; "if this measure was pursued farther," Lee insisted, "the people west of the moun[tains] would be severed from their brethren on the East, & either set up for themselves or put themselves under the protection of G[reat] B[ritain] or Sp[ain] and in either case become formidable enemies to the US." James Monroe, also a delegate to the Confederation Congress, agreed; if the Jay-Gardoqui Treaty was accepted, "we separate those people I mean all those *westward* of the *mountains* from the federal *government* & perhaps throw them into the hands eventually of a foreign power."[24]

When it became clear that John Jay was seeking to push the draft treaty surrendering rights of navigation on the Mississippi River through the Confederation Congress, it became a major national dispute. In a series of votes, seven northern and middle states voted to approve Jay's actions and the draft treaty; five southern states stood solidly against it. (Delaware did not vote as it did not have the requisite two representatives present in Congress at that time.) Since the Articles of Confederation required nine states to approve a treaty, it became clear that the proposed treaty would not be adopted, but the matter seriously frayed relations in the Confederation.

Advocates, both North and South, began to warn their opponents that perhaps the Articles of Confederation would be abandoned in favor of regional confederacies. Jefferson, watching from Paris, wrote to Madison that giving up the Mississippi would produce that result: "separation between the eastern and western country." James Monroe, reflecting real concern and some degree of paranoia, reported to Governor Henry in Virginia from the Confederation Congress that northerners seemed to be using the treaty to destroy the union and encourage a northern confederacy "east of the Hudson." Undoubtedly some officials did prefer regional confederacies. While the danger to the union may have been exaggerated, this view, this threat of regional confederacies, became a frequent topic of debate, and a source of fear, with both sides accusing the other of jeopardizing the still young and fragile union.[25]

Patrick Henry, like his western kinsmen and southern compatriots, unambiguously saw the proposed treaty as unacceptable: America's long-term interests were with westward expansion (regardless of Native claims), and Spain's restriction on use of the Mississippi River would stifle opportunity for tens of thousands of settlers. They feared that the Jay-Gardoqui Treaty would make the nation more commercial than agrarian. Not only the economic interests of the slavocracy were at stake, but its political interests as well. The treaty would be a debacle for western economic interests, and a death knell for southern, agrarian political interests, threatening what southerners saw as their eventual political ascendance. Monroe warned Henry of the "crisis" and that the treaty would "keep the States southw'd as they now are" (outvoted by the North) or encourage westerners "to separate from the Confederacy." In either case, it would keep southern interests a political minority. Foreign observers also saw the dispute in terms of the balance of sectional power.[26]

Beyond the immediate implications of the treaty, Henry and many other southerners were appalled at the willingness of a distant regional group to sacrifice so readily the essential local interests of a large group of co-citizens and what seemed like the nation's long-term interest for short-term commercial and political gain. For Henry, this dispute went to the fundamental nature of shared rights and responsibilities among the members of the union. Other southerners articulated the point well: The proposed treaty "would be a *voluntary barter* in time of *profound peace of* the *rights of one part of* the [American] *empire to* the *interests of another part*," Madison wrote to James Monroe; "can there be a more shortsighted or dishonorable policy"? Madison believed that such an effort should be "rejected with becoming indignation." Timothy Bloodworth, a member of Congress from North Carolina (and soon to be an antifederalist opponent of ratification of the Constitution), made the same point: "If seven states can barter any part of the Priviledges of the Different States, for any advantage whatsoever, there remains no security for any possession. It is wel known that the ballance of Power is now in the Eastern States, & they appear determined to keep it in that Direction."[27]

For Henry, such fundamental western (and southern) interests—going to the very viability of western settlement and western attachment to the union—should not be sold based on such a regional, short-term, commercial benefit. As in the Parsons' Cause so many years before, a distant government, now the Confederation Congress, urged on by elite, mercantile interests unfamiliar (or unconcerned) with local conditions, was threatening to interfere in a matter of enormous local import and ignoring the views of the local community. For Henry, the disagreement went to the heart of the Revolution and the Confederation. While in a republic a majority might always compromise minority interests, it was unjust for one region to do so on a matter of such importance to a different locality.

Nor could Henry, who had helped lead thirteen disparate, squabbling colonies into cooperation and revolution, accept the enormous pressure to dismember the union that would result if Jay-Gardoqui was adopted. While John Marshall claimed that Henry had declared that he "would rather part with the confederation than relinquish the navigation of the Mississippi," this was simply another way of declaring the necessity of unequivocally opposing the treaty. It was because a regional confederacy was so unacceptable to Henry and others that he was able to make this argument. Still, there was danger in such talk. Hearing similar arguments in Congress, Henry Lee bemoaned the fact that "gentlemen talk so lightly of a separation & dissolution of the Confederation," noting at the same time that he saw "no prospect" for the necessary enlargement of Congress's power if "this measure was pursued further."[28]

While the proposed treaty left Henry deeply suspicious of increasing the power of the Confederation government, for Madison and many other nationalists, the failure of the Jay-Gardoqui Treaty, and the rancor that the debate elicited, spoke to the need for a more radical increase in the powers of the national government. Only a strong central government would have the ability to force Spain to open the Mississippi (and force Britain to abandon the forts that it continued to hold in the American West). For nationalists, federal power would hasten the settlement of the West. John Jay made the point in testimony to Congress that the draft treaty was the best that could be obtained until the nation "shall become more really and truly a nation than it is at present."[29]

The efforts to adopt the treaty failed, but for our purposes, the critical point is that Henry and many southern colleagues were made deeply suspicious of increasing the power of the national government. Henry Lee saw the danger clearly and warned Washington that Jay-Gardoqui created "such a tent for popular declaimers, that the great object viz. bracing the foederal government may be thwarted." Certainly, Patrick Henry's perspective on national power was fundamentally changed. Rethinking his previous support for strengthening the national government, Henry became the strongest proponent of keeping power local and limiting the power of a distant national government.[30]

When proposals to increase the power of the national government finally moved forward, Henry was, to no one's surprise, elected to be a member of the Virginia delegation to the Philadelphia Constitutional Convention, but he declined the honor. Madison saw Jay-Gardoqui at work. The future "father of the Constitution" wrote to the "father of the country" that "I am entirely convinced . . . that unless the project of Cong[res]s [the Jay-Gardoqui Treaty] can be reversed, the hope of carrying this State into a proper federal system will be demolished." Madison added that "Mr. Henry, who has been hitherto the Champion of the federal cause, has become a cold advocate, and in the event of an actual sacrifice of the Misspi by Congress, will unquestionably go over to the opposite side." Edmund Randolph warned that it would be impossible to "secure Mr. H[enr]y to the objects of the convention at Phila." without an emphatic rejection of Jay-Gardoqui.[31]

Unfortunately for the nationalists, the damage had already been done. Henry, a moderate nationalist through 1785, became a nationalist skeptic and was becoming one of the biggest potential roadblocks to increasing the power of the national government.

British Debts and Economic Justice

Although the Jay-Gardoqui debacle was the primary cause of Henry's waning enthusiasm for increasing the power of the central government, a second issue also played a role in souring Henry on the movement to expand the power of the national government in the 1780s: the collection of pre-Revolutionary War debts owed to British merchants.

Before the Revolutionary War, Virginia's planters had run up a considerable debt with British merchants for any number of necessities and luxuries bought on credit over the years. By 1776, by one estimate, Virginians, including many yeoman farmers, owed a remarkable £1,500,000 to British firms (well over $250 million today). Others put the figure even higher. Given the number of Virginians who could share in the debt (approximately 300,000 whites), this was a very substantial financial burden. The war, of course, made it temporarily impossible for the British merchants to collect these debts, but that delay was not the real issue.[32]

During the war, facing a fiscal crisis, Virginia effectively sought to "confiscate" these debts. The idea was that during a war a government could confiscate property owned by citizens of the enemy. British troops often confiscated cattle, hogs, horses, blankets, grain, hay, and so forth owned by patriot farmers; American states often confiscated property of loyalists. Confiscation, however, was not normally applied to intangible property like debts.

Yet, in January 1778, in an effort to support its debtors and prop up its own failing paper currency, and in dire need of funds, Virginia passed a law that allowed its citizens who owed money to British creditors simply to pay the money to Virginia (using deeply depreciated paper currency) and in so doing to be relieved of the debt. The debt was sequestered by the Virginia government, essentially confiscated from the British creditors. In 1783, one Virginia newspaper directly linked the seizure of the debts to the seizure of loyalists' property and the British seizure or destruction of American property; the editor explained the situation this way:

the debts . . . of the British subjects [are] equally forfeited with their right to property amongst us, and [we] can never consent that the good citizens of this State shall lay *at the mercy of the British creditors on account of such debts;* neither do we think there should be any authority in the *laws* to *compel* the payment of such debts to British subjects, after our citizens have sustained such hardships and injuries within our own country by a mode of warfare unwarrantable, and by attempts upon their liberty unjustifiable.[33]

Unfortunately for Virginia's debtors, especially those who had already paid their British debts to Virginia under the sequestration law, the Paris Peace Treaty of 1783 ending the war expressly gave British citizens the right to collect their prewar debts (while only *recommending* that real property seized from loyalists be returned—a recommendation that was simply disregarded). Perhaps not surprisingly, Virginia initially ignored the treaty requirement permitting debt collection, and British creditors were unable to enforce the debts in Virginia's courts. As the 1780s went on, opposition to repayment grew—or at least was rationalized—based upon Britain's own violations of the treaty, for example Britain's refusal to evacuate western forts and the British military's (merciful) failure to return runaway slaves as required by the treaty. (Britain, of course, sought to justify its violations of the treaty based upon breaches by the United States.)[34]

When several Virginia leaders, including Madison, proposed a law requiring compliance with the terms of the treaty including payment of the British debts, Henry consistently blocked its passage in the General Assembly, or added "poison pill" terms, for example, requiring all the other states to pass similar laws and requiring Britain to vacate the western forts before Virginia would allow British debts to be collected.[35]

In the face of Virginia's intransigence, the weak Confederation government was hardly in a position to force compliance with the treaty provision. It was broadly understood, however, that increasing the power of the national government would change all that, and states would likely be compelled to open their courts to honor British debts.

This issue of British debts became particularly important to Henry. It was not that he personally owed an excessive amount. His debts were all paid by 1785, and he had not relied on the sequestration law. (Although, John Syme, his half-brother, paid more than £10,000 into the loan office under the law.)[36]

Rather, Henry, always concerned for the common man, thought that the treatment of British debts was fundamentally unfair and gave wealthy British merchants more rights than small farmers who had seen their livestock and produce seized by marauding Redcoats. After all, while guaranteeing the right of British creditors to collect their debts, the Paris Peace Treaty provided no remedy to American farmers and tradesmen whose property had been seized by British armies that had marched the length of America. If those seizures would not be compensated, he argued that the debts should likewise be void: "Wars between . . . nations [should] cancel every contract betwixt their citizens."[37]

The bottom line was that states could retain physical property confiscated from British subjects and loyalists; Britain did not need to compensate for the physical property taken by British and Hessian troops from thousands of American farmers and tradesmen, and Britain "stole" thousands of former slaves in violation of the treaty and was (thankfully) refusing to return them. Yet, by the terms of the agreement, British debts—money owed to wealthy merchants and bankers—had to be repaid.

Henry's opposition to these policies was well-articulated in the 1790s when he took the lead among the team of lawyers defending Virginia debtors against claims filed by British merchants after adoption of the U.S. Constitution. Initially, Henry and his co-counsel (including John Marshall) won the case, at least so far as crediting Virginians for debts "paid" to the Virginia treasury under the sequestration law (although that victory was later reversed by the U.S. Supreme Court after Henry retired from practicing law). Henry's defense relied upon a complex legal argument that even Jefferson had to confess was impressive. Those legal intricacies are addressed elsewhere and need not detain us. What is most interesting in terms of understanding Henry's political philosophy is the populist passion that Henry brought to the dispute. What he could not tolerate was the idea that property (intangible "debts") owed to wealthy people could not be confiscated in time of war but that farmers could lose the product of their lifeblood to rapacious armies without recourse. As in the Parsons' Cause, his argument was communitarian. He told the assembled courtroom crowd, "salus populi suprema lex" ("the public good is the supreme law"), going on to explain that this "is a maxim that ought to govern every community."[38]

Henry began his courtroom argument by calling upon American patriotism and noting the likely consequences had the patriots lost the war: "Had we been subdued, would not every right have been wrested from us? . . . Would it not be absurd to save debts, while they [the British] should burn, hang, and destroy?" Turning to address the argument that debts could not be confiscated like livestock, fodder, and other goods, Henry bellowed: "Debts are too sacred to be touched? . . . It is a mercantile idea that worships Mammon instead of God." ("Mammon," meaning riches or material wealth, is a derogatory biblical term.)[39]

The legal case, of course, did not occur until years after the Constitution was ratified, but everyone understood by 1787, and certainly Henry understood, that one consequence of increasing the power of the national government would likely be that the provision in the 1783 Paris Peace Treaty providing for the collection of British debts would suddenly become enforceable. With this problem in mind, when the proposed Constitution emerged from Philadelphia, Edmund Randolph explained to Madison that granting federal courts jurisdiction over such matters seemed to some "the most vulnerable and odious part of the constitution." Jefferson would later note that the "apprehension that the new government will oblige them to pay their debts" was a significant cause of opposition to the Constitution by Virginians. For Henry, this was grossly unjust and, like the proposed Jay-Gardoqui Treaty, gave great pause.[40]

Suffice it to say, while the issue did not come up often during the ratification debates (in part because of a disagreement on the question among antifederalist leaders), Henry was deeply concerned that empowering the federal government would increase the likelihood that British debts would be collected. This weighed on Henry as he contemplated the new and powerful government outlined in the Constitution.

Henry's dramatic shift in position from a moderate nationalist to a deep skeptic of a strong national government had enormous implications for the nationalists' plan to increase the power of the central government. When Virginia chose its delegation to the Philadelphia Convention, it surprised no one that Henry received the second highest number of votes (behind only Washington); he was, after all, the second most popular politician in Virginia. Henry, though, declined the position. At the time he told the governor, Edmund Randolph, that he faced financial difficulties and could not easily break away to join the convention. Perhaps true, as far as it goes. A later writer (known for some significant exaggerations) claimed that Henry declared his unwillingness to attend the Philadelphia Convention by insisting that "I smelt a rat" in the effort to increase the government's power. That particular story seems apocryphal; had Henry really feared such a power grab, he likely would have been the first to arrive in Philadelphia. Madison, though, noted that more than Henry's financial circumstances might be at play. Writing to Jefferson in Paris, Madison explained that "Mr. *Henry's disgust* [over Jay-Gardoqui] *exceeded all measure* and I am not singular in ascribing his refusal *to attend the convention to* the *policy of keeping himself free to combat or espouse the result of it according* to the result *of the Mississipi business among other circumstances.*" Henry's decision not to join the Virginia delegation in Philadelphia was multifaceted but rooted in his support for local self-governance, and he maintained a keen interest in the convention's outcome.[41]

· 2 ·

Patrick Henry, America's Leading Antifederalist

While Americans in the 1780s broadly agreed that something had to be done to improve the operation of the Confederation government, how to proceed was less clear, and hotly contested. Critical amendments had been proposed under the Articles of Confederation, for example allowing the Confederation to collect an impost (a tax) on imports. But by its terms the Confederation required unanimous consent of the thirteen states for any amendment, and essential changes had repeatedly been blocked by one or two states. Adding to the anxiety of many political and business leaders, a number of state legislatures, now with many small farmers and tradesmen as members, had acted to protect local debtors and farmers at the expense of elite creditors and merchants. With the nation suffering serious economic distress, tax collections were postponed or made payable in devalued Revolutionary War scrip, exacerbating states' inability to pay their debts. States were increasingly taking measures that struck at other states' commerce. U.S. trading partners continued to discriminate against American shipping without fear of retaliation by the impotent Confederation. Something had to be done.[1]

In 1786, Virginia invited the other states to send delegates to Annapolis, Maryland, to discuss possible reforms affecting interstate commerce, but even with that limited agenda, Virginia was careful to respect the Articles of Confederation's difficult mode of amendment. Virginia hoped that a broad group of delegates would "examine the relative situations and trade of the said States; to consider how far a uniform system in their commercial regulations may be necessary to their common interest and their permanent harmony; and to report to the several States, such an act relative to this great object, as, when unanimously ratified by them, will enable the United States in Congress, effectually to provide for the same." But after four days when only five delegations arrived, never achieving a quorum, the Annapolis convention adjourned (although several more delegations were en route). The problem of how to proceed loomed.[2]

The Philadelphia Convention

In spite of its failure, the Annapolis meeting provided an opportunity for the nationalists—led by James Madison and Alexander Hamilton—to seek a broader convention of the states in Philadelphia in 1787 that would look beyond the national government's authority over commerce. On September 14, 1786, twelve delegates from the five states present in Annapolis crafted a resolution asking their states to seek a convention of all of the states "to take into consideration the situation of the United States, to devise such further provisions as shall appear to them necessary to render the constitution of the Fœderal Government adequate to the exigencies of the Union; and to report such an Act for that purpose to the United States in Congress assembled, as when agreed to, by them, and afterwards confirmed by the Legislatures of every State, will effectually provide for the same." Notably, the delegates continued to declare their adherence to the unanimous amendment requirements of the Confederation.[3]

As states considered whether to send a delegation to the proposed Philadelphia Convention, political tensions continued to rise. By the end of 1786, open civil unrest had broken out in several states propelled by small farmers complaining bitterly about their tax burden, unequal representation in state legislatures, and court proceedings for taxes or small debts that often resulted in farmers and small landowners forfeiting land and property at a fraction of its value. In Virginia, debtors tried to shut down several county courts in the spring of 1787. Even more extensive protests in Virginia were likely prevented by the debt and tax relief adopted by the General Assembly under Henry's guidance.[4]

In the better-known Shays's Rebellion, hundreds of dissidents shut down courts in western Massachusetts, and a set battle was fought when armed rebels sought to take the Springfield Armory with its stores of muskets, cannon, and ammunition. Four protestors were killed and twenty wounded when, on January 24, 1787, a force cobbled together by the Massachusetts government and led by William Shepard unleashed cannon fire on poorly armed farmers, many of them Revolutionary War veterans. Revolutionary War general Benjamin Lincoln, with a military force paid for by private businessmen as state resources were exhausted, then arrested many and dispersed the rebels.[5]

Although Shays's Rebellion was relatively quickly defeated, it became a lightning rod for those seeking to strengthen the national government. "Our situation is becoming every day more & more critical," Madison lamented; people "unanimously agree that the existing Confederacy is tottering to its foundation." Washington wrote to his young friend from Orange, Virginia, about the danger of "anarchy & confusion!": "What stronger evidence can be given of the want of energy in our governments than these disorders? . . . Thirteen sovereignties pulling against each other, and all tugging at the fœderal head will soon bring on the ruin of the whole; whereas a liberal, and energetic Constitution, well-guarded, & closely watched, to prevent incroachments, might restore us to the degree of respectability & consequence, to which we had a fair claim, & the brightest prospect of attaining." After Shays's Rebellion, with few other options to address the evident deficiencies in the Articles of Confederation, states that had previously hesitated to endorse a reform convention because of fear of losing control began to embrace the idea of a meeting in Philadelphia to discuss how the Articles might be amended.[6]

The Confederation Congress also recognized the problems, but it still watched developments with a wary eye. Facing rising pressure for action, on February 21, 1787, Congress issued its own call for a meeting of the states, but it made the limited nature of the delegates' mandate quite clear: They would meet "for the sole and express purpose of revising the Articles of Confederation and reporting to congress and the several [state] legislatures such alterations and provisions therein as shall when agreed to in congress and confirmed by the states render the federal constitution adequate to the exigencies of Government & the preservation of the Union." The states, all but Rhode Island, responded favorably, and over the summer of 1787, twelve delegations joined the Philadelphia Convention for at least part of its deliberations.[7]

When the convention first obtained a quorum on May 25, no one was surprised that it elected George Washington to preside. Then, in a more controversial decision, the delegates agreed that their proceedings would be confidential; no one was to report on their discussions during the convention. Secrecy would encourage a willingness to contemplate bold schemes, and compromise would be far easier. Madison explained to a disapproving Jefferson (serving in Paris as U.S. minister) that secrecy "was thought expedient in order to secure unbiased discussion within doors, and to prevent misconceptions and misconstructions without."[8]

With the convention publicly silent as it went about its work for almost four long, hot summer months, the rest of the nation, Henry among them, watched with anticipation and some trepidation. A number of historians have provided excellent treatment of the negotiations at the Philadelphia Convention, examining everything from its division of authority to its class conflicts to its failure to address slavery. What was clear, though, was that when the convention concluded on September 17, 1787, and presented its proposal to a waiting, beleaguered nation, it had proposed the creation of a national government with new and expansive powers.[9]

The Nation, and Henry, React

The Constitution that emerged from the Philadelphia Convention met with a host of reactions. Some Americans were surprised at the breadth of the new plan in light of the guarded instructions from the Confederation Congress. Others were shocked. People were alternately angered, suspicious, or delighted with the result.

The convention did not propose amendments to the Articles of Confederation as expected; instead, it crafted a charter for an entirely new and powerful government to replace the Confederation. In sending the proposed Constitution to the Confederation Congress for transmittal to the states, the convention delegates explained that they had kept "steadily in our view" the necessity for "the consolidation of our Union." Elements of the states' "rights of independent sovereignty" had to be surrendered to the national government. The new Constitution, if adopted, would create a sovereign national government operating directly on the people, especially through its power to tax, to regulate commerce, to protect citizens' "privileges and immunities," and to guarantee the "supremacy" of federal laws and treaties.[10]

Pointedly, the convention did *not* transmit the Constitution for Congress's approval and the approval of the thirteen states as required for amendments to the Articles of Confederation (and by the instructions given to the convention), but only for Congress to "submit [it] to a Convention of Delegates, chosen in each State by the People thereof, under the Recommendation of its Legislature, for their Assent and Ratification." Even more portentously, the Philadelphia Convention ignored the Articles' unanimity requirement; the new Constitution would come into force when approved by conventions of nine states. Left unanswered was what would happen to a state that refused its assent to the new government and what would happen to the "perpetual" Confederation if not all the states ratified the new Constitution.[11]

Even Madison, credited as the document's chief architect, wrote to his friend and mentor Jefferson somewhat sheepishly given the breadth of the new Constitution and the revolutionary changes that it foreshadowed. Madison did not equivocate, though; the Constitution was designed to create a more powerful national government; nothing else would do. He explained to his senior colleague (whom Madison rightly expected to be skeptical) that a federal government endorsed by the people with authority to act independent of state action was needed.

> It was generally agreed that the objects of the Union could not be secured by any system founded on the principle of a confederation of sovereign States. A *voluntary* observance of the federal law by all the members, could never be hoped for. A *compulsive* one could evidently never be reduced to practice [under the current system], and if it could, involved equal calamities to the innocent & the guilty, the necessity of a military force both obnoxious & dangerous, and in general, a scene resembling much more a civil war, than the administration of a regular Government. Hence was embraced the alternative of a Government which instead of operating, on the States, should operate without their intervention on the individuals composing them: and hence the change in the principle and proportion of representation.

Certainly, the new government would be federal, with both the national and state governments continuing to operate in their own fields, but this was not to be a mere compact among sovereign states, a "league" among independent powers (to use the term from the Articles of Confederation). Unlike the Articles, the national government would be able to operate on its own authority and would not need state approval; indeed, its laws would be paramount to those of the states.[12]

As the delegates left Philadelphia, they understood that ratification of the Constitution would not be easy even without the requirement of unanimity. Having gone far beyond what the Confederation Congress had contemplated and having intruded substantially upon the authority of state governments, serious opposition was inevitable. Rhode Island had refused even to send a delegation to Philadelphia fearing such actions, but perhaps the smallest of states could be safely ignored, at least initially. Yet two of the three New York delegates had walked out of the convention based on its proposal for aggressive reforms that would create a powerful, sovereign national government, and two leading figures from Virginia's delegation—George Mason and Edmund Randolph, the governor—refused to sign the final document, as did Elbridge Gerry from Massachusetts. Many Americans were skeptical; they understood, as Henry would explain during ratification debates, that it was far easier to give up powers to a government than to get them back if abused.

No one doubted that the ratification of Virginia—still the largest, wealthiest, and most populous state—would be critical for the new nation. As one local newspaper reported, "Virginia is now about to decide perhaps the fate of millions, the future happiness or misery of remote posterity." And many delegates understood that Patrick Henry, the second most popular politician in the largest state and the most eloquent, would be one of the hardest, and most important, people to try to convince.[13]

In October, just weeks after the end of the Philadelphia Convention, James Madison bluntly told George Washington that "much will depend on Henry." The same refrain was taken up by Tobias Lear, Washington's personal secretary: "We have not yet been able to learn the sentiments of Mr. (formerly Governor) Henry upon this subject, & as he is a man of great popular influence in the lower parts of Virginia much will depend upon his *dictum*." Ten days after his first note on the subject, Madison warned Washington that "it appears that Mr Henry is not at bottom a friend." As Virginia's ratification convention approached, federalist Edward Carrington warned Thomas Jefferson's private secretary that "the popular talents of Mr. H—— is to be dreaded." The danger could not be minimized: If Virginia refused to ratify, it would, perhaps irrevocably, impair the Constitution's prospects, and Henry's influence could be decisive.[14]

With these concerns in mind, one of the first letters that George Washington wrote upon his return to Mount Vernon from Philadelphia was to his revolutionary colleague, Patrick Henry. This was an important letter. Henry had an enormous respect for Washington, even devotion, and the two had cooperated intimately during the Revolution. Very early in the war, it had been Henry who had played a role in relaying information from the newly appointed commander of the Continental Army to the Continental Congress, and Washington was extremely grateful after Governor Henry notified him in 1777 of the so-called Conway Cabal that sought to oust Washington as commander-in-chief. Henry also had reacted quickly when Washington appealed to state governors during the trying winter at Valley Forge. Both—one as governor, one as general—had experienced the grave danger that lack of authority in the central government had caused during the war. If anyone was going to move the forceful Henry to recognize the necessity of ratification, Washington had the best chance.[15]

Enclosing a copy of the proposed Constitution, and in almost a supplicant's voice, Washington reminded Henry of the "difficulty's" with reconciling different views when a gaggle of political leaders gathered each with the "local prejudices [that] pervade the states." With that in mind, Washington acknowledged that the Constitution was hardly perfect but urged Henry to support it as the best achievable at the time and, importantly, open to later amendments to correct any flaws (with amendment far easier than under the Articles of Confederation). Washington saw few options. He warned Henry that the nation was "suspended by a thread." Undoubtedly thinking about Shays's Rebellion, a war with Native Americans that threatened on the Georgia and North Carolina borders, and ongoing international conflicts over commerce, Washington feared the anarchy lurking if ratification failed.[16]

Henry must have struggled with his response. In his letter, one can almost feel the tension and Henry's deep discomfort in having to take a stand in opposition to the convention's president. Henry appreciated that Washington, who was certainly one of his heroes, had come out of retirement to suffer through the "arduous Business of the late Convention." Yet, Henry had to "lament" his inability to embrace the document; almost apologetically he added, "The Concern I feel on this Account, is really greater than I am able to express." Henry sought to soften the blow by noting that he would continue to consider the proposed Constitution and that deeper reflection might change his perspective, but they both understood that it would not. Ultimately, Henry concluded that the Constitution should not be ratified without first obtaining critical amendments limiting the national government's power and protecting individual and states' rights. He closed his letter by assuring Washington of his "unalterable Regard & Attachment." This was to be the last letter exchanged between the old friends and revolutionary comrades for eight years.[17]

Virginia's Ratification Convention

By the time that the Virginia ratification convention began on June 2, 1788, eight other states had ratified; only Rhode Island had refused to call a convention, and New Hampshire's convention (that met initially in February) had recessed with a plan to meet again in mid-June. Momentum was on the side of the federalists. Still, antifederalists saw an opportunity. When New Hampshire delayed, Washington worried that it "has entirely baffled all calculation upon the subject; and will strengthen the opposition here; the members of which are not scrupulous in declaring, that, the adjournment was with design to know the result of this [Virginia's] Convention." In fact, unbeknownst in Virginia, as its convention met and vigorously debated whether to launch the new nation, New Hampshire would become the ninth state to ratify on June 21, with Virginia's ratification vote not occurring until June 25.[18]

The mounting state ratifications had a powerful centripetal pull. What if the Constitution was ratified and Virginia was left out, even temporarily? Not only would Virginia have no official role in forming the new government, crafting the initial laws and any proposed amendments to the Constitution, but George Washington would be ineligible for the office of president—an office that everyone assumed would fall to the general were he eligible.

As he planned his battle against ratification, Henry feigned disinterest in what the other states did, bragging that he would hold firm even if "12½ states" had ratified. Henry argued that Virginia could stand alone, if necessary as an independent nation, even enter into foreign alliances. Giving credence to Henry's thinking, after Virginia set its convention for June 1788, North Carolina delayed its own convention until July, apparently wishing to evaluate options based upon Virginia's actions. New York, too, scheduled its convention for after Virginia's.[19]

In spite of Henry's bluster, the pressure swayed votes. Edmund Randolph, for example, initially hoped for a second convention to consider amendments before ratification, and he had continued to push that approach through 1787, telling Madison in December that "I verily believe, that the only expedient which can save the fœderal government in any shape in Virginia, will be the adoption of some such plan, as mine." But by Virginia's June 1788 convention, he had to "express my apprehension, that the postponement of this Convention, to so late a day, has extinguished the probability of the former [a second convention] without inevitable ruin to the Union," and he became a leader in support of ratification.[20]

In retrospect, the momentum for ratification proved to be a powerful weapon in the hands of the federalists. DeWitt Clinton, the leading antifederalist in New York, conceded after ratification that "it was a great error in policy that our convention was not called sooner."[21]

Still, even at that late date, if Virginia refused to ratify, it would have empowered New York's antifederalists. With Rhode Island and North Carolina refusing to ratify initially in any case, had Virginia and New York balked, the pressure on the new government to accept very substantial amendments or, possibly, a second convention would have been significant. "The new Government will exist more in name than in fact," if Virginia and New York refused to ratify, reported one foreign observer.[22]

In any case, for these purposes, the issue is not generally the complex and fascinating battle that ensued at the Virginia ratification convention—and we know the result: Virginia finally ratified the Constitution on June 26, 1788, after a close vote, becoming the tenth state to do so. What is at issue here is the nature of Patrick Henry's objections and how they reflected his political philosophy that would again be on display in the crisis of 1799.

Henry's opposition to ratification of the Constitution, in very broad terms, paralleled objections of other antifederalists, perhaps not surprising as Henry was the leading spokesman for antifederalist forces arrayed against ratification. Henry, though, had a somewhat different focus and emphasis than many of his allies.

What would prove to be the most powerful and successful objection lodged by antifederalists was that the draft Constitution lacked a bill of rights. Where was the protection for religious freedom? Free speech? The right to a jury trial in civil cases? What would prevent the new national government from violating core principles? This objection was made particularly poignant by the fact that George Mason—the primary author of Virginia's Declaration of Rights and a leading antifederalist—had asked the Philadelphia Convention to add a bill of rights near the end of its deliberations in the summer of 1787, but the convention declined, either through exhaustion or a belief that a listing of particular rights was not needed or was impracticable. Yet, while this was the most common objection, for Henry it was an important but in key respects secondary concern.[23]

Henry's most substantive concerns related to the extensive transfer of power from the people and the states to the national government. On its face, the Constitution's shift in power was breathtaking to many of the leaders of the Revolution. Under wartime necessity, they had cautiously agreed to the Confederation, but it only acted on and through the state governments, and those governments were controlled relatively closely by the voters. The draft Constitution embodied a new revolution. The proposed government would act directly on the people without the involvement (to Henry, the protection) of the states. The most obvious examples of the dramatically expanded national authority were the power of the new government to tax the people directly and the power over interstate commerce. The former meant that Americans would be subject to two taxing authorities that could be duplicative and potentially very burdensome; the latter might encompass broad areas of regulatory authority over particular sectors (e.g., tobacco or fisheries or, it was feared by many, slavery) and, thus, the possibility of sectional division. Direct restraints on states were also included, for example prohibiting their issuance of paper money even in an emergency or interference with private contracts, popular mechanisms that Henry and others had used to ameliorate economic pressures on the people.

The draft Constitution also vested the treaty-making power wholly in the president and Senate and made treaties the "supreme" law of the land. Divorcing the treaty power from the House of Representatives (the branch of government most closely aligned with the people) raised an immediate concern with the provision of the Paris Peace Treaty providing for collection of British debts. These concerns were fed by recollection of the failed Jay-Gardoqui Treaty that would have sacrificed navigation on the Mississippi. Distinctly local matters could be controlled by a distant government without the support of the people's directly elected representatives, exactly what had elicited Henry's ire in the Parsons' Cause twenty-five years earlier.

James Monroe, who initially supported the Constitution after the Philadelphia Convention, became increasingly concerned with the expansive power granted the federal government as the ratification convention approached. "It may now be asked are we reduced to this alternative either to subvert the state sovereignties or submit to these evils? . . . If the federal government has a right to exercise direct legislation within the states, their respective sovereignties are at an end, and a complete consolidation or incorporation of the whole into one, established in their stead." By the time of Virginia's convention, Monroe allied with Henry as an antifederalist.[24]

The draft Constitution's proposed awesome transfer of power to the new national government was made more problematic by the somewhat open-ended nature of the powers granted. Beyond the enumerated authority, the Constitution gave Congress the ill-defined authority to "make all Laws which shall be necessary and proper for carrying into Execution" any of the express powers granted. Congress, it seemed inevitable, would itself decide what was "necessary and proper." State authority could be consumed by such a provision. "It seams to me, if Congress, have a right to make all laws that may be necessary & proper," William Russell, a Revolutionary War general and member of the Virginia House of Delegates, wrote a friend, "that no inferiour Legislature, can be more than a Mitaphysical nothing."[25]

With prescience, Henry was deeply concerned with the "necessary and proper" clause and its likely unpredictable and even harder to control implications. Some federalists conceded that the clause would be a direct constraint on state power; to some extent that was intended. A federalist explained that "without it the different States might counteract all the laws of Congress, and render the Federal Government nugatory." Responding to Henry's argument that the clause provided almost unlimited power, Edmund Randolph insisted that it did not, but he had to concede that the provision could justify broad implied powers, arguing that this was essential with a constitution that merely provided a framework for the government. (The breadth of the "necessary and proper" clause would become apparent when, early in the 1790s, Alexander Hamilton relied heavily on that clause to justify creating a national bank regardless of the absence of any express provision authorizing the federal government to engage in banking.) The absence of a savings clause retaining to the states any authority not expressly transferred, a prominent clause in the Articles of Confederation, added to these concerns.[26]

Although Henry recognized the possible advantages of the Constitution, including how it would contribute to the growth of a powerful nation, he objected to the loss of sovereignty by the states and, with it, the loss of control by the people, the transfer of control to a governmental body far away both physically and politically. The Constitution, unlike the Confederation, was not a compact among sovereign states that were controlled relatively directly by the people. Federalists insisted that it was not a complete consolidation but a hybrid federal system. Henry scoffed at that idea. Since the new government would have the power of the purse and the sword, and all the implied powers that were "necessary and proper," he insisted that "this is a national Government. There is not a single federal feature in it." As Madison conceded during the ratification debates, the Constitution severely limited the authority of the states both directly and by creating a "supreme" national authority that could act without state approval (and, for Henry, potentially against the wishes and actions of the states and local citizens).[27]

Henry saw that the timeless tension between liberty and order (government power) would be at the heart of the Constitution's ratification debates. He asked delegates to consider the situation of Switzerland and France: "You will find the condition of the former far more desirable and comfortable. No matter whether a people be great, splendid, and powerful, if they enjoy freedom." Other antifederalists expressed similar concerns. "I see my Country on the point of embarking and launching into a troubled Ocean without Charts or Compass to direct them," Theodrick Bland wrote to Arthur Lee, "one half the Crew hoisting sail for the land of *Energy*—and the other looking with a longing aspect on the Shore of Liberty." Henry warned that one should be cautious in increasing the power of government in the hope for greatness. "It is easier to supply deficiencies of power than to take back excess of power."[28]

For Henry, at the center of the problem was not simply increased power in the national government, but the political distance of the new government from the people and the relative inability of citizens to control national officials. State governments could be controlled relatively directly by the people. A substantial farmer or tradesman likely knew a member of the state legislature personally; state representatives knew their districts well. This ensured a level of commitment and local accountability that provided strong protection against abuse of office. Most states also required annual elections, seen by many of the revolutionary generation as essential to prevent government abuse of power.

Not so with the proposed national government. Federal elections would be only every two (representatives), or four (president), or six (senators) years, and the relatively limited number of representatives meant that they would come from large districts, and likely few of their constituents would know them. Adding to the concerns, neither the president nor the senators were to be elected directly by the people. This problem of lack of local control and adequate representation lay at the heart of the colonists' rebelling against a formerly beloved British government. Similarly, the new government would be too distant from the people and therefore largely unaccountable, undermining the core foundation of a functioning republic.

All this offended Henry's sense of community localism; it risked distant congressional majorities acting against the fundamental interests of local people—exactly what had happened with the proposed Jay-Gardoqui Treaty and what Henry had denounced in the Parsons' Cause. While Congress's authority extended over many matters with a local impact (from taxes to commerce to treaties), even members of the House—much less senators and the president—would be too far removed from the common man and local concerns and were likely to be privileged elites. Reflecting concerns expressed by the great French political philosopher Charles-Louis de Secondat, Baron de La Brède et de Montesquieu, Henry believed that while republics were the hope of a free world, the ability of a republic to function effectively depended on elected officials having a real understanding of local concerns, meaning that small republics where officials knew their constituents and shared their interests (and vice versa) were likely to be more stable. "But sure I am that the dangers of this system are real, when those who have no similar interests with the people of this country are to legislate for us—when our dearest interests are left in the power of those whose advantage it may be to infringe them," Henry warned.[29]

Madison brilliantly responded to Montesquieu in *Federalist* #10, arguing that an expanded republic with a broad multiplicity of interests was less likely to allow a fixed majority to undermine the rights of a minority, but Henry understandably embraced a more traditional view that keeping the government closer to the people was likely to be most effective in protecting the community.[30]

These were the broad concerns that drove Henry through perhaps his most extended and important political discourse when, in the month of June 1788, he took to the floor of the convention in Richmond more often than any other delegate and dominated Virginia's ratification debates.[31]

Virginia's Convention: Patrick Henry Takes Charge

Beginning on June 2, 1788, 168 delegates gathered in Richmond to decide whether Virginia would ratify the Constitution. A great concourse of citizens gathered as well to hear the debates. Not only did the convention promise to be of enormous importance but it was also the "best show in town," with Henry's speechifying expected to headline the performances. With all this in mind, and perhaps intending a mild rebuke to the secrecy of the Philadelphia Convention, Virginia's delegates quickly decided to encourage maximum public exposure by moving their proceedings to the "New Academy," the largest building in the still village-like town of Richmond.[32]

As Virginia's convention got under way, there was a great deal of uncertainty. There were many devoted federalists and antifederalists, but there was also a substantial group of undecided delegates. Even among those "in opposition," there were distinctly different shades of opinion: Some were focused on the need for a bill of rights. Others shared Henry's broader concerns regarding the relative power of the federal and state governments, "the essence of the System," seeking "adherence to the principles of the existing Confederation," Madison warned. Some, including Henry, wanted specific amendments to be agreed to prior to ratification. Others sought a second constitutional convention to consider amendments proposed by the states. Even those who supported prompt ratification often agreed that amendments would then be needed; Washington had said as much in his letter seeking Henry's support of the Constitution. Many saw the decision in more overtly political terms: What could Virginia gain by holding out? How these differences would be resolved was uncertain and in flux. The leading federalists, however, were sure of one thing: "Mr. Henry is the great adversary who will render the event precarious."[33]

Henry's voice and rhetoric were compelling on the need for a bill of rights. Early in the Virginia debates he insisted that a bill of rights was "indispensably necessary." Having obtained a copy of a letter that Thomas Jefferson had sent to a Richmond merchant expressing concerns with the Constitution's lack of protections for key rights, Henry rose to a crescendo (one of many) reminding the delegates that the honored and patriotic Jefferson—Henry did not mind using Jefferson's prestige for his own purposes—"living in splendor and dissipation [in Paris], he thinks yet of Bills of Rights." Madison—who led the federalists in Virginia's ratification debates—was mortified to hear Jefferson's words used against ratification.[34]

To the argument that virtuous elected officials would protect the rights of the people, and, thus, a bill of rights was not needed, Henry lectured: "Shew me that age and country where the rights and liberties of the people were placed on the sole chance of their rulers being good men, without a consequent loss of liberty?" When federalists argued that individual states' bills of rights would protect the essential liberties of the people, removing the need for a federal bill of rights, Henry ridiculed the idea that existing protections against abuses by the states meant that none were needed against a new, powerful federal government. Accepting this argument would be to "arm yourselves against the weak and defenseless [state governments], and expose yourselves naked to the armed and powerful" national government. Based upon experience with Britain before the Revolution, Henry believed that an attack on individual rights was far more likely from a distant national government than a local one.[35]

Obtaining a bill of rights was the most popular demand of the antifederalists (supported by many federalists) and in key respects the most successful. In fact, some have argued that Patrick Henry, rather than James Madison, should properly be seen as the father of the Bill of Rights because it was his pressure that made the drafting and adoption of a bill of rights a political necessity.[36]

Henry did not, though, speak as often nor as passionately on the need for a bill of rights as he did about the growth of federal power at the expense of the states. The power of direct taxation was most frequently commented upon by antifederalists. (Of course, direct taxation was the power that Madison and other federalists viewed as a *sine qua non* for a functioning government.)

Giving the national government direct taxing authority, Henry explained, had broad implications for the growth and control of government power. Virginia's inability to control taxation by the federal government could effectively mean that the state would be taxed without its consent, the former revolutionary argued. Congressmen from other states could overbear the votes from Virginia and impose taxes on sectors of particular importance to the state, such as tobacco or slaves. Of course, this claim would become a convenient defense of slavery, demanding that the issue had to be resolved locally where people were more likely to share economic interests. The principle, though, had broader implications. "We fought then [in the American Revolution], for what we are contending now," Henry insisted, "to prevent an arbitrary deprivation of our property, contrary to our consent and inclination." Local community control was the key. Henry proposed that direct taxes not be imposed on any state without the federal government first being required to requisition the state for its contribution; if Virginia or any other state failed to meet its obligation it could be compelled to comply by the federal government taking control of its ports or the state even being in whole or in part expelled from the union until it met its responsibility. (He hastened to add, though, "but, Sir, the dissolution of the Union is most abhorrent to my mind: The first thing I have at heart is American *liberty;* the second thing is American Union.") While requisitions had a decidedly mixed record under the Articles of Confederation, antifederalists could argue that improved enforcement powers in the federal government would ensure reasonable compliance. The practicality of Henry's idea for requisitions need not detain us; the key point is his effort to maintain oversight of the purse in the states where it could be controlled by local representatives.[37]

One of Henry's most telling comments during the ratification debate was his warning that the president would be too powerful, distant from the people, and with an excessively long term of office. While the federalists were quick to note that the likely first occupant of the office (George Washington) could be trusted—a point with which antifederalists did not quibble—future occupants would lack his remarkable virtue. The office "squints towards monarchy," Henry thundered at the start of the convention. Whatever Washington's merits, Virginians would partake of a "folly in resting our rights upon the contingency of our rulers being good or bad." As the convention neared its end, he made the point that others might not be so trustworthy: "It will be an empire of men and not of laws—Your rights and liberties rest upon men—Their wisdom and integrity may preserve you—but on the contrary, should they prove ambitious, and designing, may they not flourish and triumph upon the ruins of their country?"[38]

Henry seemed even more personally passionate about the treaty powers and authority over interstate commerce proposed in the Constitution; these posed a possible threat to the navigation of the Mississippi River and presaged collection of prewar British debts.

It seemed that the battle over the Mississippi never ended. Almost immediately after the text of the Constitution was released from Philadelphia, southerners were analyzing its treaty provisions in light of the history of the Jay-Gardoqui dispute (in which the majority of the states in the Confederation Congress voted to surrender navigation of the river for twenty-five years). In November 1787, William Grayson, an antifederalist who soon would be one of Virginia's first senators under the Constitution, wrote that allowing a treaty to pass with two-thirds of the senators "present," with only half the senators needed for a quorum, and with no role for the people's House of Representatives, "will be the means of losing the Mississippi for ever."[39]

The issue was an important one for many southerners, but it could be pivotal in the decision of the twelve delegates from the Kentucky territory, delegates who might determine the result in a closely divided Virginia convention. Edmund Randolph warned Madison before 1787 was out that General James Wilkinson, an influential figure in Kentucky (and an opportunist, as his subsequent history with Aaron Burr and Spanish bribery would show), protested that if the Constitution was adopted "the surrender of the Mississippi would probably be among the early acts of the new congress." As the ratification convention approached, others warned the federalist leader of the danger. "One consideration only has any weight with them [Kentucky representatives]," George Nicholas reported to Madison: "a fear that if the new government should take place, that their navigation would be given up."[40]

The Constitution's provisions for treaties and the concomitant fear for the loss of the Mississippi became major targets of Henry's attack at the ratification convention: the particular issue of Mississippi navigation was important to a critical block of voters, and Henry was deeply committed to the western settlers. He was also motivated by the underlying possibility that a distant and relatively small coalition of uninterested and uninformed future senators (a group that threatened to be aristocratic) might sell out southern, western, Virginian interests. The Constitution "will involve in its operation the loss of the navigation of that valuable river [the Mississippi]," he warned before the convention's first week was out. He reminded the delegates that navigation of the Mississippi had almost been lost under the Confederation: "This new Government, I conceive, will enable those States who have already discovered their inclination that way, to give away this river."[41]

The "supremacy" of treaties over state laws provided by the Constitution was an important part of the problem. "Treaties were to have more force here than in any part of Christendom," Henry declared. "To make them paramount to the Constitutions and laws of the States is unprecedented." This was clearly not a mere compact of independent states that maintained their domestic sovereignty and could not be bound without their consent.[42]

Henry seconded George Mason's call for inclusion of the House of Representatives in the treaty-making process. The House, more attuned to the local interests of the people, "is the most essential part.—They ought to interpose in the formation of treaties. When their consent is necessary, there will be a certainty of attending to the public interest," Henry explained. His concern went to the exercise of political power by officials (senators and the president) distant from their constituents. Madison promptly responded, insisting that there was no danger, as the president would represent the American people as a whole and prevent any inappropriate sacrifice of local rights. (Henry and Madison would revisit this issue in the mid-1790s.)[43]

The issue was not simply control of the Mississippi, as important as that was for westerners and southerners. For many southern antifederalists, the danger in the long run was the control of the nation by a New England cabal, with potential implications for the "peculiar institution" of slavery. Obviously unconcerned with displacement of Native Americans, William Grayson warned that the eastern states (New England) actively wanted to give up the navigation of the Mississippi as a means to restrict the growth of the West (and the anticipated shift in political power to the agrarian West and South). With federalists urging on a most basic level that the danger was a national government that was too weak, Henry darkly reminded Virginians concerned about the Mississippi that "the southern parts of America have been protected by that weakness so much execrated." Henry was referring to the navigation of the Mississippi, but by the end of the ratification convention, he would remind his colleagues that a weak national government also protected the institution of slavery. (In time, southerners would realize that a weak national government also facilitated displacement of Natives, but in 1788 Henry had not abandoned his calls for the national government to address Native power in the West.)[44]

The issue of British debts, and the likelihood that federal courts created under the Constitution would entertain British suits against Virginia debtors, also weighed heavily on Henry. Before the ratification convention met, a

Virginia correspondent had reported to federalist Henry Knox that "Mr. Henry in his harangues respecting this question [British debts] attacked the constitution of the Union in the strongest terms and endeavored to sow the seeds of Jealousy against the federal court, the new-england States and the spirit of the Union itself." The issue did not attract vocal attacks during the ratification convention itself—with many antifederalists apparently having concluded that discussing the issue would only provoke a negative response from commercial interests and businessmen, including antifederalist George Mason, who supported payment of the debts to facilitate future trade—but opponents of paying the British debts were clearly aware of the issue, leading another federalist to declare during the debates that "the whole core of opponents to ye Paymt. of British Debts are against us."[45]

For many, the issue of British debts was another example of the broader issue: transfer of power from the states to the federal government and the "supremacy clause" in Article VI that would put federal policy in control. For Henry, it was another example of injustice that a distant government would impose upon local citizens who had been protected by their state governments.

While Henry, like any good advocate, pounded on specific issues, he and other antifederalists recognized that these were mere examples of the problem of a broad and potentially ill-defined transfer of power to the national government. Henry came back again and again to the uncertainty implicit in the Constitution's broad language. Over the past two centuries, this broad language—creating a structure for government but not seeking to legislate on specific issues—has proven to be the Constitution's greatest strength. But in 1788, it created uncertainty and that uncertainty fed a deep apprehension.

Federalists argued in response that the Constitution only gave the national government certain enumerated and defined powers and that the states would retain power in all other areas. Pointing to the potentially expansive necessary-and-proper clause, what he referred to as this "sweeping" clause, Henry wanted to embed federalist promises that the central government would have only limited, enumerated powers in the Constitution itself. Henry explained, "A general provision should be inserted in the new system, securing to the States and the people, every right which was not conceded to the General Government; and that every implication [implied powers] should be done away." George Mason reminded delegates that "there was a clause in the Confederation reserving to the States respectively, every power, jurisdiction, and right, not expressly delegated to the United States. This clause has never been complained of, but approved by all. Why not then have a similar clause in this Constitution, in which it is the more indispensably necessary than in the Confederation, because of the great augmentation of power vested in the former?"[46]

The ratification convention circled around this general question. By creating a national government that was independent of the states and enjoyed a broad list of enumerated powers and some relatively open-ended implied powers, how much independent power would be left in the states? In a critical sense, the question was about the source of power in the national government, because whoever gave the power could, in theory, control it. The Confederation had been created by the states and derived its power from the states; states controlled the Confederation. The Constitution went around the states to the people themselves; power in the federal government would come from the people, seeming to undermine the argument that the states would retain power to check potential federal abuses. How would "the people" exercise that power and control the national government? This issue led to one of Henry's most memorable and powerful outbursts. Turning on the delegates to the Philadelphia Convention, he demanded "what right had they to say, *We, the People* . . . instead of *We, the States?* States are the characteristics, and the soul of a confederation. If the States be not the agents of this compact, it must be one great consolidated National Government of the people of all the States." He returned to the point the next day: "Have they said, we the States? Have they made a proposal of a compact between States? If they had, this would be a confederation: It is otherwise most clearly a consolidated government. . . . Here is a revolution as radical as that which separated us from Great Britain." Henry never questioned the right of the people to create the new government, but he emphatically warned the delegates (and the people) that doing so would significantly limit their ability to control the new government through the states.[47]

Federalists insisted that the Constitution did not entail a complete consolidation, but they also recognized that it was not a confederacy of sovereign states (as under the Articles of Confederation). Responding to the argument that the Constitution is "a consolidated Government annihilating those of the States," Edmund Pendleton explained that "I should understand a consolidated Government to be that which should have the sole and exclusive power, Legislative, Executive, Judicial, without any limitation." Given the necessary role of the states in the new government, for example in the selection of senators and members of the Electoral College, and continued state governance over local matters, the government was not consolidated, according to Pendleton. The Constitution was a hybrid, which is what Madison argued in *Federalist #39*.

This, though, was at best a partial response to Henry's focus on the role of the states and how their ability to control abuses by the national government was being fundamentally compromised.[48]

In all of this, federalists had hoped to keep the debates at the ratification convention focused on particular clauses of the Constitution, but Henry's objections went to broad questions of how the government should be structured and control of government power. His rhetoric ranged equally widely, and, as so often had been the case in court or during the Revolution, his declamations seemed a torrent that could not be checked. However one characterized the national government, the concern with its ability to govern fairly over such a vast territory where representatives would be far removed from their constituents remained. Henry explained that "one Government cannot reign over so extensive a country as this is, without absolute despotism." This argument, though, was met with a rebuke: Was Henry suggesting that the nation should be torn into smaller, regional confederacies?[49]

The argument that antifederalists planned a devolution into regional confederacies became a major federalist weapon with which to browbeat opponents before, during, and after ratification, one that antifederalists sought to manage with care. Several months before the convention, Edward Carrington had told Henry Knox that, while he had not spoken with Patrick Henry, there was no way to explain Henry's position other than that "his views are a dismemberment of the union." Two months later, Carrington repeated his suspicion to Jefferson, himself still skeptical of the Constitution: "Mr. H—— does not openly declare for a dismemberment of the Union, but his Arguments in support of his opposition to the constitution, go directly to that issue." Madison was told the same by George Nicholas, also based on speculation:

> Mr. Henry is now almost avowedly an enemy to the union, and therefore will oppose every plan that would cement it. His real sentiments will be industriously concealed, for so long as he talks only of amendments, such of the friends to the union, as object to particular parts of the constitution will adhere to him, which they would not do a moment, if they could be convinced of his real design. I hope to be possessed of sufficient information by the meeting of the convention to make that matter clear, and if I am it shall not be withheld.[50]

These arguments, though, confused campaign rhetoric with reality. As Lorri Glover explains, "the allegation that Anti-Federalists planned to abandon the union and preside over a separate southern confederacy was as false as the claim that Federalists were conspiring to reduce Virginia to a 'state of vassalage.'"[51]

Henry tried to walk a fine line at the convention: He wanted a national confederacy. He recognized that a dissolution of the union would be a disaster, treason to the Spirit of '76 that had won the Revolution—a spirit that he had helped to form and lead. He remembered better than most the remarkable alliance between Virginia and Massachusetts that had driven the Revolution forward and understood how essential cooperation among the states was. It was he who had electrified the Continental Congress in 1774 when he declared "I am not a Virginian, but an American." During the ratification debates he agreed with Edmund Randolph that regional confederacies would "ruin us." He argued, however, that even the terrible result of regional confederacies would be better than what he perceived as the danger from a powerful, consolidated national government not subject to necessary restraints by the people. Such regional confederacies "are evils never to be thought of till a people are driven by necessity." He was cautious, though, neither to advocate nor to suggest a preference for regional confederacies. "But, Sir, I mean not to breath[e] the spirit nor utter the language of secession." While having recognized that devolution into separate regional confederacies "will ruin us," Henry and his supporters still believed that "compared to such a consolidation"—one that threatened tyranny, monarchy, no protection of individual rights, the impotence of the people to control their own government—"small Confederacies are little evils; though they ought to be recurred to, but in case of necessity." Edmund Randolph, somewhat kinder (or more honest) than some other federalists, specifically picked up on Henry's argument, noting that Henry had conceded that regional confederacies were an evil only to be accepted when the people had no other option. As Randolph recognized, but some historians have not, Henry's arguments about regional confederacies were so much political rhetoric to highlight the seriousness of his fear of a government that was too powerful, a power gained at the expense of the states.[52]

Of course, each side was attempting to make political points with its rhetoric, but in the often-hyperbolic comments rested a serious concern with the expansive power of the new national government. In its simplest terms, Henry was asking the people of Virginia, and the people of the United States, what they wanted from government. Did they prefer an empire or were they most committed to their own happiness and local control? And would the pursuit of the former cost the latter by undermining the liberties for which they had fought the Revolution? During his "Liberty or Death" speech at the beginning of the Revolution, Henry had famously argued that "I know of no way of judging of the future but by the past." He turned now to the historic demise of republics. "Those nations who have gone in search of grandeur, power and splendor, have also fallen a sacrifice, and been the victims of their own folly: While they acquired those visionary blessings, they lost their freedom." The fall of both the Roman and (first) British empires would have been on the minds of the delegates. "Look at the predominant thirst of dominion which has invariably and uniformly prompted rulers to abuse their power." Henry warned his colleagues that "if we admit this Consolidated Government it will be because we like a great splendid one. Some way or other we must be a great and mighty empire."[53]

For Henry, this was treason against the hopes of the Revolution. "When the American spirit was in its youth, the language of America was different," Henry declared. "Liberty, Sir, was then the primary object." Henry demanded answers. Would the more powerful government under the Constitution "constitute happiness, or secure liberty?" Over and over, Henry begged the convention's delegates to consider the dangerous tradeoff between national power and individual happiness. He admonished: "You are not to inquire how your trade may be increased, nor how you are to become a great and powerful people, but how your liberties can be secured; for liberty ought to be the direct end of your Government." He inspired: "Liberty the greatest of all earthly blessings—give us that precious jewel, and you may take every thing else." He lectured: "No matter whether a people be great, splendid, and powerful, if they enjoy freedom."[54]

Years later, Henry's argument about the tension between empire and happiness was still well-remembered by some. In the midst of the War of 1812, one newspaper editor wrote: "Ever since the Mania of conquest and war and extended territory has been visited on this Republic, as a punishment for its sins—that mania which the prophetic eye of Patrick Henry saw, through the smoke that was raised about us in the year 1788, and deprecated with all his mighty powers."[55]

Henry conceded that problems in the Articles of Confederation needed to be addressed, but he saw the greater danger in the Constitution. "Dangers are to be apprehended in whatever manner we proceed; but those of a consolidation are the most destructive." Addressing the problems with the Confederation did not require going so far as the Philadelphia Convention had been driven. "I know the absolute necessity of an energetic Government. But is it consistent with any principle of prudence or good policy, to grant unlimited, unbounded authority, which is totally unnecessary?"[56]

For Henry and his antifederalist colleagues, the critical element that seemed to portend doom to liberty in a republic was when the government became too removed from the people, incapable of understanding their particular concerns or, perhaps, not needing to. Removed from familiarity with and control by the common people, officials would focus on the welfare and power of the government and elites, their own wealth and power, more than that of the people. Yet, in the face of this truth, the Constitution signaled a dramatic movement away from local and community control. Senators and the president would not be directly elected by the people, and those officials would control both treaties and appointments to the judiciary and executive branch. Even the House of Representatives, ostensibly the people's representative in this new scheme, was far too removed. Not only was the term of office two years—annual elections were a necessity in a republic, many people insisted—but the districts for election of members of the House of Representatives were so large that representatives could not possibly understand or represent their constituents' interests well. For antifederalists, the House of Representatives of only the sixty-five members called for in the Constitution, representing such a vast and expansive nation, "afforded 'the mere shadow of representation,' 'a mere shred or rag of representation,' 'a mere burlesque.' 'Brutus' [an antifederalist essayist] charged that '[n]o free people on Earth who have elected person to legislate for them ever reposed that confidence in so small a number.' "[57]

The size of the House of Representatives became a recurring concern. Henry focused on this lack of accountability early in the ratification debates. Responding to federalist arguments that the people would be protected because they were "properly represented," Henry scoffed; citizens would know little of their representatives, and representatives less of their constituents:

> Remember, Sir, that the number of Representatives [for Virginia] is but ten, . . . Will these men be possessed of sufficient information? . . . They must be well acquainted with agriculture, commerce, and a great variety of other matters. . . . Virginia is as large as England. Our proportion of Representatives [under the new Constitution] is but ten men. In England [in Parliament] they have 530. . . . Will the few protect our rights? Will they be incorruptible? You say they will be better men than the English Commoners. I say they will be infinitely worse men, because they are to be chosen blindfolded.

With districts for members of the House of Representatives so large, and citizens relatively unfamiliar with candidates, representatives would be "chosen blindfolded," and any sense of local representation and control would be badly diluted. While the complaint that districts might include as many as 30,000 people now seems almost quaint, Henry understood that without local and regular control, government power was potentially dangerous. The connections between the people and their representatives would be, Henry insisted, stretched beyond their breaking point.[58]

Notably, this was the only substantive issue on which George Washington intervened while presiding over deliberations in Philadelphia. On the final day of the convention, Washington joined an objection to a provision specifying that the number of representatives should not exceed 1 for 40,000 citizens; he asked this to be changed to 1 for 30,000 to make representatives more attuned to local concerns: "The smallness of the proportion of Representatives had been considered by many members of the Convention, an insufficient security for the rights & interests of the people." The change was made, but for antifederalists it was a very minor concession. The episode does, however, highlight the nature and broad acceptance of Henry's concern.[59]

In fact, to some extent, limiting the direct influence of the people was exactly what the federalists had planned. During the convention, James Wilson argued that larger districts would ensure that "men of intelligence & uprightness" would be elected (by which he meant the gentry). Madison, who had supported a constitutional convention in part because of what he saw as the excess of democracy in the states, urged that larger districts would be a "defence agst. the inconveniences of democracy."[60]

Since the Revolution, most states had expanded substantially the number of representatives in their state legislatures at the same time they were expanding the voting franchise to permit more effective representation, albeit excluding women and African Americans.[61] The numbers anticipated for the House of Representatives stood in stark contrast to that trend. (While the Confederation Congress had a limited number of delegates, no one doubted that under the Articles the real power lay in the states in which much smaller electoral districts prevailed.) Seeking to address this problem of connection to the community would become one of Virginia's first proposed amendments to the Constitution. While Washington had supported the successful change that the House of Representatives would not have more than 1 representative per 30,000 in the district (permitting a somewhat larger house than the version permitting only 1 per 40,000), Virginia sought an amendment requiring *at least* 1 representative for 30,000 people until the House of Representatives had at least 200 members.[62]

Virginia Ratifies the Constitution

Henry's appeals had an impact. In the last days of the convention, under enormous pressure from the antifederalists and fearing that they might lose ratification, federalists abandoned their earlier position that no amendments were needed and agreed that they would support appropriate amendments *after* ratification was procured. This was the same position that federalists had taken when Massachusetts ratified the Constitution on February 6, 1788. The idea was that the various state ratification conventions would recommend constitutional amendments to be taken up by the first federal Congress, amendments that eventually became the Bill of Rights.

Henry, realizing that there was no guarantee that any amendment would be adopted, thought the idea was crazy: "I should be led to take that man to be a lunatic, who should tell me to run into the adoption of a Government, avowedly defective, in hopes of having it amended afterwards." As the proposal gained supporters, Henry sought more urgently to derail it, realizing that it might satisfy a few wavering delegates. He warned his colleagues that "tyranny submitted to, in order to be excluded by a subsequent alteration, are things totally new to me." These were ideas merely to "amuse" the convention, Henry argued. Yet, however crazy it may have seemed to Henry, as Washington concluded, this commitment to subsequent amendments likely swung enough votes to win ratification. It also demonstrated that a substantial majority favored amendments to the Constitution, before or after ratification.[63]

Without viable alternatives, the antifederalists seemed to sense that the convention was slipping away from them as the final vote loomed. Henry, a slave owner (as were many of the Virginia delegates), apparently in desperation, anticipating the conflicts that would lead to civil war in a little more than seventy years, unleashed an ugly attack premised on the idea that a national government would undermine the institution of slavery. While he acknowledged that "slavery is detested . . . we deplore it with all the pity of humanity," and insisted that there was an obligation to ameliorate the fate of the enslaved, Henry still sought to use slave owners' racism and fear to encourage opposition to ratification, arguing that a northern majority would eventually seek to undermine the foul institution. Henry's position again focused on local control; Virginia, after all, had dramatically liberalized its manumission laws in 1782 (and the number of free blacks in Virginia was rapidly increasing, albeit from a very low base). At the ratification convention, Henry focused on the fact that emancipation under the Constitution would affect primarily the South but might be supported by northern states that "have not the ties of sympathy and fellow-feeling for those whose interest would be affected by their emancipation." The danger was that "power was being put in the hands of those who have no similarity of situation with us." It was not Henry's finest hour. (Not surprisingly, federalists also used slavery as an argument for ratification. Edmund Randolph, for example, urged that slavery meant that a regional southern confederacy would be weakened by "an unhappy species of population.")[64]

Henry's long-running rhetorical battle against ratification came to a remarkable and dramatic climax at the New Academy on June 24, 1788. Henry began his speech that afternoon, one of his last at the convention, by responding to Madison's listing of the advantages that the Constitution could provide the nation and Virginia. "He tells you of important blessings which he imagines will result to us and mankind in general, from the adoption of this system," Henry began. The hoped-for benefits, though, were chimerical, at best only half of the story. "I see the awful immensity of the dangers with which it is pregnant.—I see it—I feel it." The danger seemed imminent in Henry's voice and mien as delegates were transfixed by his speech. Henry saw the battle in virtually apocryphal terms; "I see *beings* of a higher order, anxious concerning our decision." It seemed to the delegates and throng of public observers that Henry's appeal to higher beings had "addressed an invocation, that made every nerve shudder with supernatural horror." As Henry continued with his speech, as if in answer to his impassioned call to spiritual powers, an extraordinarily violent summer thunderstorm of the type that roll majestically off the Blue Ridge Mountains into Virginia's Piedmont erupted and "shook the whole building." As the lightning flashed and thunder crashed, Henry continued, and with the artistry of an orchestra conductor he seemed to "seize upon the artillery of Heaven, and direct its fiercest thunders against the heads of his adversaries," Judge Archibald Stuart reported.

> When I see beyond the horrison that binds human eyes, and look at the final consummation of all human things, and see those intelligent beings which inhabit the ethereal mansions, reviewing the political decision and revolutions which in the progress of time will happen in America, and the consequent happiness or misery of mankind—I am led to believe that much of the account on one side or the other, will depend on what we now decide. Our own happiness alone is not affected by the event—All nations are interested in the determination.

Henry's last impassioned appeal—"We have it in our power to secure the happiness of one half of the human race. Its adoption may involve the misery of the other hemispheres."—chorused by the roll of thunder, left delegates breathless.[65]

It was a fitting end to a bravura performance over more than three weeks, with no one having spoken as long or as often as Henry. Days after the convention's end, a French official who had been an observer wrote that "Mr. Patrick Henry, Leader of the Opposition Party, has displayed a popular Eloquence and an astonishing resource of Genius and abilities. He was always attacked, but never conquered."[66]

On June 25, 1788, Patrick Henry lost. The first important vote that day, often ignored in the histories, was a proposal to substitute for the resolution supporting ratification a Henry resolution calling for proposed amendments to be shared with and agreed to by other states prior to ratification. That was the critical vote, and it was defeated only eighty-eight to eighty. Then, with prior amendments having been rejected, the convention voted eighty-nine to seventy-nine to ratify the Constitution, the vote most commonly reported. Had five delegates switched their votes on the first resolution, history would have been dramatically different, but Henry's path was a road not taken.[67]

After the ratification vote, as the convention neared its end, with options limited, Henry and his allies were determined to at least seek Virginia's support for broad amendments going far beyond simply a recitation of individual rights. On June 25, a committee chaired by George Wythe and including Patrick Henry was formed to propose amendments. Two days later, the committee presented twenty amendments for a bill of rights and an additional twenty proposed structural amendments to the Constitution that paralleled the concerns of Henry and his antifederalist allies. The first three of these structural amendments suggested that states retained any power not delegated, that the number of representatives be dramatically increased (shrinking the size of districts), and that the federal government could not collect taxes directly without first giving a state the opportunity to raise the necessary funds itself. Other proposed amendments would have required a two-thirds vote of the entire Senate (not just those attending) for commercial treaties and an additional three-fourths vote of the House if a treaty sacrificed territorial or navigation rights (like the Jay-Gardoqui Treaty), restricted the president to two terms, and limited the federal government's ability to interfere in state elections of representatives.[68]

People understood that the amendments urging a bill of rights had a good chance of success; by early spring of 1789, Richard Bland Lee (the younger brother of Charles and Henry Lee) claimed that there was "little doubt that all the amendments tending to the greater security of civil Liberty will be obtained." Henry understood that the prospect for structural amendments was far worse. Although he knew that such proposals for later amendments were a very thin gruel since there was no promise that any of them would be adopted, it was the best that could be achieved at the time.[69]

Henry firmly believed that the majority of the American people actually opposed ratification of the new Constitution without amendments; "a great majority of the people even in the adopting States, are averse to this government." This was a significant point, and one not persuasively challenged. "If reports be true," he repeated, "a clear majority of the people are averse to it." Many historians agree. Jackson Turner Main said the antifederalists "probably had a very small majority" overall, including a majority in Virginia and Massachusetts and a commanding majority in New York and North Carolina (three to one) and South Carolina and Rhode Island (four to one). Richard Ellis refers to antifederalists as "perhaps even a majority of Americans." This, then, begs the question: If the majority of the American people were opposed to the Constitution, why was it ratified? How were the concerns of the majority so easily dismissed? Why was Henry not more successful?[70]

Federalists had several obvious advantages in the ratification fight. Dominating the business community, they controlled a large majority of newspapers. Prepared for ratification by the Philadelphia Convention, they effectively managed the process, and critically, they had the support of the political powerhouses—Washington and Benjamin Franklin, especially Washington.[71]

Perhaps an even more notable element in the federalists' success was simply that the antifederalists had no particularly viable alternative to the Constitution. Even the leading antifederalists recognized that some substantial changes were needed to the Articles of Confederation; during ratification, George Mason recognized the "defects of the Confederation and the necessity of reform." Henry, too, "acknowledge[d] the weakness of the old Confederation." The antifederalists' alternatives—negotiating prior amendments with other states or calling a second convention—were highly speculative and largely impractical answers to the admitted problems.[72]

Edmund Randolph had also supported a second convention as the Philadelphia Convention ended, but as Madison, Washington, and others observed, the idea of calling a second convention was a chimera: in a second convention, states would send delegations with strict instructions to take firm (and diametrically opposed) positions on critical issues from taxation to international commerce to slavery to the treaty power. Some delegates would come with the intent of preventing agreement, Madison warned, "men who secretly aimed at disunion." That objective could be achieved by making firm demands "on points popular in some parts, but known to be inadmissible in others." Delegates at a second convention would be far less willing to compromise than they had been in Philadelphia. (The question of convention secrecy, for example, would have immediately been a hotly contested issue.) Henry Knox explained to the Marquis de Lafayette that at a new convention "such an agreement could not again be produced even by the same men." The best that could be imagined was a deadlock.[73]

With antifederalist sentiment so strong throughout the nation, and with the angst of antifederalists rising daily, another absolutely critical issue came into play in Virginia in late June as antifederalists sensed the convention might be slipping away: How would Henry and other antifederalists react to a likely loss in the convention?

Antifederalists React, Henry Again Leads

Seeking to throw a final roadblock in the path of ratification, on June 23, George Mason made a remarkable speech in which he seemed implicitly to threaten violence if the Constitution was ratified. He warned the convention, "The adoption of a system so replete with defects . . . could not but be productive of the most alarming consequences. He dreaded popular resistance to its operation. He expressed in emphatic terms, the dreadful effects which must ensue, should the people resist; and concluded by observing, that he trusted Gentlemen would pause before they would decide a question which involved such awful consequences." Other delegates immediately took this as a threat. Federalist Henry Lee rose in determined and angry indignation.

> My feelings are so oppressed with the declarations of my honorable friend, that I can no longer suppress my utterance. I respect the Honorable Gentleman, and never believed I should live, to have heard fall from his lips, opinions so injurious to our country, and so opposite to the dignity of this Assembly. If the dreadful picture which he has drawn, be so abhorrent to his mind as he has declared, let me ask the Honorable Gentleman, if he has not pursued the very means to bring into action, the horrors which he deprecates? Such speeches within these walls, from a character so venerable and estimable, easily progress into overt acts, among the less thinking and the vicious.

Mason was forced into a tactical retreat, but the point had been made: ratification in the face of a populace that was opposed, guided by determined
and respected leaders, held untold and potentially dangerous consequences.
Madison wrote to Washington that evening that Mason's speech suggested that
the antifederalists despaired of success. Still, it was dangerous; Mason "held
out the idea of civil convulsions as the effects of obtruding the Government
on the people. He was answered by several and concluded with declaring his
determination for himself to acquiesce in the event whatever it might be."[74]

Where was Henry, the most popular antifederalist and one who had previously led the people into a revolution? How would he react? What would
he advise his supporters? If he supported active opposition, implementation
of the new government could be at risk even if the convention voted to ratify.
Much would turn on the answer to those questions.

The next day, June 24, the same day that Henry would later make his famous "Thunder Speech," he, too, warned of the dire consequences of forcing a constitution on a people fundamentally opposed, and while he cabined
his own likely response, his language seemed to some not far removed from
Mason's threats.

> I cannot conclude without saying, that I shall have nothing to do with
> it, . . . I conceive it my duty, if this Government is adopted before it is
> amended, to go home.—I shall act as I think my duty requires. . . .
> Previous amendments, in my opinion, are necessary to procure peace
> and tranquility. I fear, if they are not agreed to, every movement and
> operation of Government will cease, and how long that baneful thing
> *civil discord*, will stay from this country, God only knows. When men are
> free from restraint, how long will you suspend their fury? The interval
> between this and bloodshed, is but a moment. The licentious and wicked
> of the community, will seize with avidity every thing you hold.

Henry framed these concerns in terms of the necessity of prior amendments:

> You endanger the tranquility of your country—you stab its repose, if you
> accept this Government unaltered. How are you to allay animosities?—
> For such there are, great and fatal. He [George Wythe] flatters me, and
> tells me, that I could influence the people, and reconcile them to it. Sir,
> their sentiments are as firm and steady, as they are patriotic. Were I to
> ask them to apostatize from their native religion, they would despise me.
> They are not to be shaken in their opinions, with respect to the propriety

of preserving their rights. . . . Were I to attempt to persuade them to
abandon their patriotic sentiments, I should look on myself as the most
infamous of men. I believe it to be a fact, that the great body of yeomanry are in decided opposition to it. . . . it was not owing to me that
this flame of opposition has been kindled and spread. . . . Can you have
a lasting Union in these circumstances? It will be in vain to expect it. But
if you agree to previous amendments, you shall have Union, firm and
solid. . . . If you will in the language of freemen, stipulate, that there are
rights which no man under Heaven can take from you, you shall have me
going along with you:—Not otherwise.[75]

It was the next day, the day of the key vote, however, June 25, that Henry
had his final word on the topic in one of the most important speeches in the
entire ratification process in any state, a speech with profound implications
in American history. Perhaps he, too, was chastened. The day before he had
a bitter exchange with Edmund Randolph in which Henry insisted that he
was not advocating secession if the Constitution was ratified. On the 25th,
he seemed to sense that ratification was in the offing. Henry feared for his
country. He certainly did not abandon the principles that led him to dread the
powerful new government. He had not been convinced at all by the arguments
of the federalists. Henry believed the danger was real. What would he say as
the curtain seemed ready to fall? What would he do if the federalists won?

Henry rose one last time. This final speech spoke volumes as to what motivated Henry during ratification and what would continue to drive his views
for the next ten years until his death. It explained succinctly the role of a loyal
opposition in a functioning republic.

I beg pardon of this House for having taken up more time than came to
my share, and I thank them for the patience and polite attention with
which I have been heard. If I shall be in the minority, I shall have those
painful sensations, which arise from a conviction of being overpowered
in a good cause. Yet I will be a peaceable citizen!—My head, my hand,
and my heart shall be at liberty to retrieve the loss of liberty, and remove
the defects of that system—*in a constitutional way.*—I wish not to go to
violence, but will wait with hopes that the spirit which predominated in
the revolution, is not yet gone, nor the cause of those who are attached
to the revolution yet lost—I shall therefore patiently wait in expectation
of seeing that Government changed so as to be compatible with the
safety, liberty and happiness of the people.

While he could not openly acknowledge the antifederalists' impending loss, Henry grappled openly with one of the essential questions if a republic is to function: How to respond when "your side" loses a vote? Henry understood that this was a vital lesson for all Americans. He would continue the fight, in hope, but he was committed to doing so within the bounds of the government that the people adopted, seeking reform in "a constitutional way."[76]

Spencer Roane, later a leading Jeffersonian, and very recently having become Henry's son-in-law, wrote to a friend the next day concluding that Henry's effort in the convention had been profound, it "would almost disgrace Cicero and Demosthenes." The pathos and commitment in his speech of the 25th was among his most powerful. The critical importance of his vision would become clear within days and would continue to steer Henry for the rest of his life.[77]

All of this might have been mere political theater, except for the fact that in the evening of June 27, the day the ratification convention adjourned, George Mason organized a meeting of Virginia's antifederalists ostensibly to craft a resolution to take to the people to ensure their acceptance of the Constitution. The draft that Mason presented, although no copy survives, was apparently more consistent with his threats from June 23 and would have inflamed passions rather than cooled them. Mason's address would "tend . . . to irritate, rather than to quiet the public mind," one newspaper reported. Mason's proposal was a "fiery, irritating manifesto—which he would have sent out to divide the State," another wrote. With three states (New York, North Carolina, and Rhode Island) still having not ratified, and with antifederalists feeling slighted (for example, in Pennsylvania, Massachusetts, and South Carolina), the possibility of open, possibly violent, opposition to the implementation of the new Constitution was very real and seemed to be Mason's object. He had signaled as much four days earlier.[78]

Mason's meeting broke up when other antifederalists rejected his effort and urged legal compliance with the new Constitution. Among those urging restraint were Benjamin Harrison, John Tyler, and Robert Lawson.[79]

But, again, what of Henry? The few surviving newspaper accounts do not mention his presence, but he certainly would have been included in the meeting. The most thorough description of his involvement comes from David Meade Randolph, an ardent federalist and newspaper editor (and later federal marshal), mentioning that Henry was brought into the caucus late.

> General Meade and Mr. Cabell assembled the *discontents* in the old Senate Chamber; and after a partial organization of the party, a deputation

was sent to Patrick Henry inviting him to take the chair. The venerated patriot accepted. Understanding that it was their purpose to concert a plan of resistance to the operations of the Federal Government, he addressed the meeting with his accustomed animation upon important occasions; observing, "he had done his duty strenuously, in opposing the Constitution, in the *proper place,*—and with all the powers he possessed. The question had been fully discussed and settled, and, that as true and faithful republicans, they had better go home! They should cherish it, and give it fair play—support it too, in order that the federal administration might be left to the untrammeled and free exercise of its functions": reproving, moreover, the half suppressed factious spirit which he perceived had well nigh broken out. The impressive arguments of Mr. Henry produced the gratifying effect he had hoped for.

Unfortunately, Meade's account was probably not written until 1791 at the earliest.[80]

Some historians have dismissed this report, noting not only that it was not recorded immediately but that Randolph was not, himself, a delegate. Yet he was a newspaper editor and in a position to know what was happening. Moreover, Washington reported two days after the meeting of antifederalists that

> The Accts. from Richmond are, that the Minority will acquiesce with a good grace—Mr. Henry it seems having declared that, though he can not be *reconciled* to the Government in its *present* form, and will give it every *constitutional* opposition in his power; yet, that he will submit to it peaceably; as every good citizen he thinks ought; and by precept and example will endeavour, within the sphere of his action, to inculcate the like principles into others.

Another contemporaneous report from William Nelson Jr., a former member of the Virginia House of Delegates and future judge, squarely laid blame for the incendiary nature of the antifederalist effort at Mason's feet:

> Mr. Henry, with great talents & address, &, I verily believe, with views really friendly to liberty, stood forth, the opponent of the constitution—He was indefatigable, & more & more able day by day, for near three weeks, the convention continuing within one day of that term, & at last, when he discovered that there wd. be a majority agt him (tho' a small one) declared that "as far as he had influence there shd be good order."—Mr. Mason is said not to have behaved with so much temper.[81]

Perhaps most telling, in 1799, a widely reprinted newspaper article explained Henry's role at this conspiratorial meeting with antifederalists. This report, very consistent with David Randolph's, noted that Henry became deeply concerned when he heard proposals from some antifederalists of "rousing the people to oppose the work" of the convention and advised against disruptive behavior. "No, my friends, we must not do so—nor should we shew any ill nature or resentment at what has happened," he warned. "We are all brethren. We are one great family, embarked in the same vessel. . . . It has been ably, fully, and fairly discussed. A majority of our countrymen, having equal interests, and equal stakes with ourselves, have thought it their duty to accept of the instrument." Focusing on proposed amendments, Henry urged his colleagues to work to "make her [the Constitution] more perfect," but to do so "in the way pointed out by the workmen" who drafted it. This essay was reprinted throughout the country and notably was not contradicted at the time, even though many who had attended the key meeting were then living—many of whom found themselves opposed to Henry's politics in 1799 when the article appeared and would have had every incentive to challenge the account.[82]

It is sometimes said that Madison placed Henry at Mason's post-ratification meeting and identified him as one of the instigators, yet Madison's letters, while saying that Henry and Mason were likely to cause post-ratification problems, never directly claimed that Henry was supporting Mason's idea of encouraging dissent (and, in any case, Madison would not have been at the antifederalist meeting). Before the meeting occurred, Madison wrote to Alexander Hamilton:

> The minority will sign an address to the people. The genesis of it is unknown to me. It is announced as an exhortation to acquiescence in the result of the Convention. Notwithstanding the fair professions made by some, I am so uncharitable as to suspect that the ill will to the Constitution will produce [illegible] every peaceable effort to disgrace & destroy it. Mr. H—y declared previous to the final question that although he should submit as a quiet citizen, he should wait with impatience for the favorable moment of regaining in a constitutional way, the lost liberties of his country. My conjecture is that exertions will be made to engage 2/3ds of the Legislatures in the task of regularly undermining the government. This hint may not be unworthy of your attention.

Three days later, he reported to Hamilton, again without directly implicating Henry in the meeting, that "the intended address of the Minority proved to be of a nature apprehended by me. It was rejected by the party themselves when proposed to them, and produced an auspicious conclusion to the business." Later Madison told Jefferson that Henry and Mason would not support violent opposition to the ratified Constitution, but that they would continue to seek to make fundamental changes—Henry had said as much in his June 25th speech. The furthest that Madison went was to say that the effort to encourage dissent at the June 27th post-ratification meeting was under the "auspices" of both Henry and Mason. The irony may be that Madison's personal dislike of Henry may have blinded him to the greater danger that was emanating from Mason.[83]

As is the case with many of Henry's actions, the historical record is not without some complexity. Still, given Henry's speech on June 25 in which he vowed to live peaceably under the Constitution and work in "a constitutional way" for reform, and his subsequent actions to serve as a "loyal opposition," David Meade Randolph's account seems by far the most plausible explanation of Henry's involvement in that fateful meeting. The *Philadelphia Independent Gazetteer* reported a similar conclusion based upon an extract of Henry's speech in a letter from Richmond: "In all the stages of the business I have been an opponent, but being out voted, or defeated, I submit cheerfully, and will give every support to the system which I can, until I find errors like to take place. Mr. Henry has been powerful, but now appears to be content."[84]

Had Henry worked with Mason to enflame the public against the ratified Constitution, the consequences could have been dramatic.

Instead, Henry, as promised, went home after Virginia ratified the Constitution. But he did not abandon his effort to reform the new government and limit its power in "a constitutional way."

· 3 ·

The 1790s

A New Nation Takes Its First Steps

B y the end of July 1788, after New York became the eleventh state to ratify, the battle for adoption of the U.S. Constitution was effectively over. The battle for the soul of the new constitutional democracy, however, was just beginning.

Conventional wisdom has the 1790s as a period when two philosophies of government challenged each other and battled for supremacy in the United States. In time, the two groups became the first real U.S. political parties: Democratic-Republicans (often referred to as Republicans, eventually becoming Democrats) led by Thomas Jefferson and James Madison (supported by a large majority of antifederalists), and Federalists, nominally led by George Washington and John Adams but largely controlled for most of that decade by Alexander Hamilton and his allies. Jefferson "won" that battle when he was elected president in what he called the "Revolution of 1800," and America became a Jeffersonian republic, with avowed Jeffersonians holding the presidency for thirty-two of the next thirty-six years, ostensibly dedicated to individual liberty, democratic participation, small government, and strict construction of the still-young Constitution.[1]

Yet, that is a grossly simplified story, seeing the world in two-dimensions: Hamilton versus Jefferson, Federalist versus Democratic-Republican, large government versus small, strict construction versus implied powers. . . . The real history was much more complex.

Patrick Henry—still one of the most popular statesmen in the country throughout the 1790s—does not fit into that simple history, an important clue that the story is wrong or, at least, omits critical pieces. Henry certainly challenges the simplistic idea of a binary—Federalist or Democratic-Republican—as if two tightly framed groups stood in perpetual opposition and fully occupied the American political landscape of the 1790s.

In fact, the development of a two-party system did not proceed smoothly. One of the fundamental struggles in the 1790s was how those who disagreed with government actions would act in a republic: What would be the role of a "loyal opposition"? Was active opposition outside of the election cycle even legitimate? With a fresh memory of a Revolution in which British loyalists had been expelled or at least largely silenced, in early America, no one seemed prepared to embrace the idea of legitimate opposition to the new republican government. George Washington, for example, sharply criticized political meetings organized in opposition to his government. Henry, on the other hand, seemed to define the role of a loyal opposition as well as anyone while not easily fitting into the binary description of parties.[2]

Patrick Henry and the Challenge of the New Constitution

During and after Virginia's ratification convention, Henry made it clear that he thought the new Constitution and the government that it created were fundamentally flawed. He and almost certainly a majority of the American people agreed that the document needed to be significantly amended, the new government structured in a way that forcefully defined its limits and protected people's liberties. Yet, while there was a broad consensus that changes were needed, there was also great apprehension that a new campaign for change could hobble efforts to launch the recently adopted system. The nation seemed exhausted by political discord. Many were concerned that antifederalists would take the route promoted by George Mason after Virginia's ratification: encouraging divisions, impeding implementation, and stoking political battles. If opposition became pervasive and powerful, the untried nation might be stillborn or die in its infancy.[3]

Henry saw things differently. Though he stood firmly against efforts to encourage civil discord after Virginia's convention, Henry was consistent and emphatic that he would act in "a constitutional way" to try to address what he perceived as the Constitution's shortcomings and ensure that the new government was "compatible with the safety, liberty and happiness of the people." Now was the time for action, he insisted, before a flawed system became fixed or serious missteps were made.[4]

With a host of questions concerning implementation of the new Constitution pending, political opponents saw Henry's ability to direct developments in Virginia as almost unbounded. As the Virginia legislative session opened in the autumn of 1788, Washington grumbled to Madison that "the Edicts of Mr H—— are enregistered with less opposition by the Majority of that body, than those of the Grand Monarch are in the Parliaments of France. He has only to say let this be Law—and it is Law." Two days later, Henry Lee wrote to Madison with similar concerns: "Mr H is absolute, & every measure succeeds, which menaces the existence of the govt." Henry was the most powerful member of the Virginia assembly as it decided how it would implement key provisions of the Constitution, including organizing elections for the first federal Congress and appointing Virginia's first U.S. senators. (Until ratification of the Seventeenth Amendment to the Constitution in 1913, state legislatures appointed senators.)[5]

Henry and his antifederalist allies sought changes to the Constitution in two broad areas: First, they wanted to limit the power of the new national government and expressly reserve powers to the states, for example, by restricting the federal government's taxing power, limiting the power of the Senate and president to enter into treaties, making it far more difficult for Congress to regulate interstate commerce (requiring a supermajority to pass commercial legislation), increasing significantly the number of members in the House of Representatives (making representatives more accountable to local interests), and clearly restricting the government to enumerated powers. Second, specific rights needed protection—freedom of press, freedom of religion, jury trials in civil cases—"all the great essential and unalienable rights, liberties, and privileges of freemen," a Virginia House of Delegates Resolution explained. Initially, Henry and his allies sought to achieve these goals by calling a second constitutional convention.[6]

The Constitution provides that Congress must call a convention if two-thirds of the states submit a formal request. Given the depth and breadth of concerns expressed during ratification from North and South, a convention seemed the simplest means to address the Constitution's many perceived shortcomings. Edmund Randolph, Virginia's governor and a delegate to the Philadelphia Convention, began calling for a second convention shortly after the first convention ended. While Randolph became a key vote for ratification in Richmond because he feared what would happen if the Constitution was rejected with no immediate alternative, after ratification, a second convention seemed a real possibility, with amendments always an option.

Anticipating these efforts, Madison wrote to Washington immediately after Virginia's ratification that Henry's plan would be "to engage 2/3 of the Legislatures in the task of undoing the work [with a second convention]; or get a Congress appointed in the first instance that will commit suicide on their own

Authority [with amendments]." Washington urged Madison to run for office to counter Henry's potential mischief in the upcoming House of Delegates session. "To be shipwrecked in sight of the Port," Washington lamented, "would be the severest of all possible aggravations to our misery; and I assure you I am under painful apprehensions from the single circumstance of Mr H——'s having the whole game to play in the Assembly of this State, and the effect it may have on others—It should be counteracted if possible."[7]

If a second convention had been called, Madison and Washington would undoubtedly have been proven correct. Squabbling representatives from various states with entrenched positions would have been unable to compromise on fundamental changes, much less to draft a modified constitution adopted by three-fourths of the states. Furthermore, the rancor that a failed convention would cause to the toddling nation—cementing faction against faction and state against state—might have been irreparable. Henry and his allies, though, saw things differently.

To Henry and other antifederalist leaders, a second convention seemed the most effective means to make fundamental changes. They had repeatedly been defeated in state ratification conventions by the momentum for ratification and the Hobson's choice of voting for the Constitution or facing the prospect of anarchy (or a state's exclusion from the new nation if nine other states ratified). Yet, calls for important changes to the Constitution had come from almost every quarter. With the Constitution ratified, a second convention seemed a safe alternative; after all, the Constitution would be implemented while the necessary changes were debated and agreed upon before being returned to the people for approval. In the late summer of 1788, Beverley Randolph, soon to be Virginia's new governor, reported that Henry "is much pleased at the idea of a new convention." Undoubtedly, Henry would not have missed a second convention.[8]

With Rhode Island not ratifying the Constitution until May 1790 (with North Carolina ratifying in November of 1789), for the first year of the federal government's operation, only eight states would have been needed to meet the two-thirds requirement for a second convention. New York indicated its plan to call for a second convention as part of its ratification on July 26, 1788, and sent the other states a circular letter on the same day soliciting their support. On February 7, 1789, New York's legislature passed the formal resolution calling on Congress to summon a convention, still months before the new Congress first sat.[9]

Henry promptly embraced New York's proposal, declaring to Virginia's House of Delegates that "he should oppose every measure tending to the organization of the government unless accompanied with measures for the amendment of the Constitution for which purpose he proposes that another General Convention of deputies from the different states shall be held as soon as practicable." In the fall of 1788, Virginia, led by Henry, joined New York in calling for a second convention. In early December 1788, Governor Beverley Randolph sent requests to the other states that they join Virginia and New York in petitioning Congress for a convention.[10]

But then, unexpectedly, this effort fell flat, very flat. With the new nation having barely taken a first step, and with the memory of the contentious and bitter ratification fight still fresh, it was impossible to engage broad support for launching into a new and divisive second constitutional convention. This was especially true given the option of amending the Constitution directly, a procedure that had been urged by seven state ratifying conventions by 1788 (and Rhode Island subsequently). In spite of the pleas for support from New York and Virginia, no other state filed a request for a second convention.[11]

For Henry, all was not lost. Under his leadership, Virginia's ratification convention had proposed twenty structural amendments and an extensive bill of rights and instructed Virginia's representatives to the first federal Congress to seek these reforms through Article V's amendment process. Virginia proposed to increase dramatically the number of members of the House of Representatives, to permit states to avoid federal taxes by imposing their own and transferring requisitioned funds to the national government, to restrict the treaty-making power, to require a two-thirds vote of Congress for any law affecting commerce, and to limit the national government's authority in a host of other areas. Other states, too, had ratified the Constitution based upon an understanding that there would be amendments.[12]

Yet if amendments were to have a chance, electing antifederalists to the first federal Congress would be critical. The *Virginia Centinel* explained, "The election of a President, and Delegates from each state to form the first Congress, are matters of the utmost importance to every free citizen. On the choice of these persons depends our future well-being and prosperity.—Men of approved talents and strict integrity should be sought for to fill those important stations—men who would sacrifice everything at the shrine of liberty."[13]

The first task for Henry was to convince the Virginia legislature to appoint two antifederalist senators. With former antifederalists controlling the House of Delegates, and Henry's influence ascendant, this should have been easy, but the challenge was to exclude James Madison, whom many people thought would be, should be, one of Virginia's first senators. A somewhat reluctant

Madison was convinced to stand for the position when Edward Carrington, on Washington's advice, urged that he was the only federalist in Virginia with a chance of being elected to the Senate.[14]

Henry, though, was having none of it, warning that "no person who wishes the constitution to be amended should vote for Mr Madison to be in the senate." Since Madison had argued during ratification that no amendments were needed, and since Henry reasonably believed that most Virginians (and Americans) wanted important amendments, this was hardly a radical position. But according to Henry Lee, the former governor went further, saying that Madison was "unworthy" and that election of someone so opposed to amendments would result in "rivulets of blood throughout the land." In a more moderate tone, Henry explained to Richard Henry Lee that "the universal cry is for amendments," and only those showing the requisite "solicitude and zeal" for "public liberty" should be elected. Efforts at amendments would be "to no purpose . . . if one of her [Virginia's] senators had been found adverse to that scheme."[15]

With Henry's dominance in Richmond, Madison was denied a seat in the Senate. Madison, barely disguising his disgust and chagrin, insisted (with only a little less drama than Henry's alleged barbs) that the "destruction of the whole System" was the "secret wish of his [Henry's] heart." The first two Virginia senators were Richard Henry Lee and William Grayson, antifederalists and partisans dedicated to support Henry's call for structural amendments.[16]

Elections to the House of Representatives were equally important and here too Henry attempted to mobilize antifederalists but with mixed success. The most famous, or infamous, of Henry's machinations to promote an antifederalist Virginia delegation in the first House of Representatives was his unsuccessful effort to exclude Madison even from the House, correctly perceiving that he would be a critical opponent of amendments that fundamentally restricted the power of the new government. Under Henry's direction, the General Assembly gerrymandered the congressional district that included Orange County (where Madison's home, Montpelier, sits) to include several antifederalist counties, and Henry reportedly handpicked a serious antifederalist opponent for Madison—James Monroe.[17]

As late as October 1788, Madison, who strongly disliked electioneering, sought to avoid campaigning, hoping "that the arrangements for the popular elections may secure me agst. any competition which wd. require on my part any step that wd. speak a solicitude which I do not feel, or have the appearance of a spirit of electioneering which I despise." This was not to be. Instead,

Madison found himself locked in a heated contest against the man who would years later serve as his secretary of state and successor in the White House. Madison won the election, but only after he made a commitment to constituents, particularly evangelical Baptists and Lutherans deeply concerned about religious freedom, that he would champion amendments in Congress to protect their rights. While Henry welcomed the idea of a bill of rights, this obviously fell far short of a commitment to the structural amendments that he sought and that had been supported by the ratification convention.[18]

Of course, the composition of the rest of Virginia's House of Representatives delegation was also critical. Unfortunately, it is much more difficult to assess the impact that Henry had on other elections to the first federal Congress in part because "party" affiliation was less than clear in this period before firm political parties were formed. Further complicating matters, affiliations tended to change as the new federal government expanded its power and reach under the influence of Alexander Hamilton, with many federalists becoming Democratic-Republicans later in the 1790s. In the end, Henry's efforts to ensure a House delegation that would support fundamental changes to the U.S. Constitution had some success but far less than in the case of Virginia's first federal senators.

Various sources categorize Virginia's first ten members of the House of Representatives into different political categories. Five of Virginia's first representatives attended the ratification convention, and three of those (Madison, Andrew Moore, and Alexander White) voted in favor of ratification. Of the remaining representatives, two voted against ratification (Theodorick Bland, Isaac Coles), and at least one other representative (Josiah Parker) was seen by Madison as an antifederalist. Several other sources list the majority of Virginia's delegation as "anti-administration," but these classifications can be misleading. Many who favored the Constitution or appeared "pro-administration" were in fact strong supporters of amendments. John Randolph's biographer concluded simply, "[a] majority of the members in that body [the first Congress], from Virginia, belonged to the political school of Mason and of Henry."[19]

The discrepancies and confusion need not delay us. However one classifies individual members, Henry's efforts tended to encourage election of representatives who favored substantive amendments. And however one measures Henry's success in Virginia, unfortunately for the antifederalists, his efforts were not matched elsewhere.

Looking at the issue beyond Virginia more closely shows an interesting pattern vis-à-vis Henry's efforts to encourage a first federal Congress committed to amendments. Using the House of Representatives' Office of History,

Art & Archives guide, the share of each state's delegation to the first Congress classified as "pro-administration" can be compared to the share of each state's votes in favor of ratification at their own ratification convention. In every state north of the Mason-Dixon Line, the share of pro-administration federalists in the initial House of Representatives delegation was higher, often much higher, than the share of the vote in those states in favor of ratification; in every state south of Mason-Dixon, the opposite is true. While one might argue about classification of some individuals, the pattern is rather stark.[20]

What is clear is that antifederalist leaders in other states were not nearly as energetic nor as successful in electing antifederalists to the first federal Congress as Henry, especially vis-à-vis the Senate. New York, Massachusetts, and New Hampshire, each of which had a very strong antifederalist vote during ratification, elected overwhelmingly federalist congressional delegations to the first federal Congress. New York, for example, chose federalists for four of its six House seats and both of its senators. By any measure, when the Senate is included, Virginia's delegation was the most antifederal. Had antifederalists in other states been more successful in their campaigns for the first federal Congress, the pressure for the type of broad structural amendments that Henry sought would have been much greater.[21]

The result: while antifederalists outnumbered federalists at the time of ratification, antifederalists were not equally represented in Congress. The reasons for this are complex and worthy of further study. Perhaps antifederalists were simply disillusioned after their lack of success in blocking ratification. Equally important, many federalists were now promising to support amendments to the Constitution, although perhaps, as in the case of Madison, continuing to oppose structural amendments while supporting a bill of rights. Other impediments stood in the way of antifederalists. In Virginia, property ownership requirements for voting that had been suspended for elections to the ratification convention were again in force, and electoral politics tended to return to their old patterns in which the wealthy, well-known, well-born leaders—most of whom were federalists—tended to win elections. And some antifederalists simply decided to allow the system to operate without their participation, effectively abandoning active involvement in national politics. Whatever the reasons, the result was both remarkable and enormously important, and for Henry, deeply frustrating.[22]

Had Henry's allies in other states been as successful in electing antifederalist senators and representatives, the consequences for the young republic would have been dramatic. For example, Alexander Hamilton's plans for the federal government's assumption of states' Revolutionary War debts and for the Bank of the United States—both of which antifederalists saw as exceeding the authority granted in the Constitution—would likely have required substantial changes. The Bill of Rights would have more dramatically limited federal authority. It is also likely that at least some of the structural amendments to limit the power of the national government that antifederalists had supported during ratification would have been adopted by Congress and approved by the states. The result would have been a very different America, and Henry could have more comfortably retired from politics.[23]

Ironically, James Madison, the federalist leader who insisted during the ratification debates that a bill of rights was not needed, became the leader in the campaign for amendments, often facing opposition from other federalists who insisted that Congress had more pressing responsibilities. Congressman Madison, though, carefully circumscribed what was to be changed.

The Constitution Is Amended and Henry Reacts

By 1789, Madison had several reasons for changing his position and championing amendments: First, both before and after ratification, Madison was battered by allies and opponents demanding a bill of rights. In December of 1787, Jefferson wrote Madison from Paris urging that "a bill of rights is what the people are entitled to against every government on earth . . . and what no just government should refuse, or rest on inferences." During Virginia's ratification convention, Madison had been vexed by Henry's quoting a letter from Jefferson demanding a bill of rights. And, of course, antifederalists had hammered on this issue. As Madison's opposition seemed to waver, Jefferson urged a series of arguments; interestingly given later developments, he told Madison that "in the arguments in favor of a declaration of rights, you omit one which has great weight with me, the legal check which it puts into the hands of the judiciary" to strike down unconstitutional congressional action. During congressional debates over the Bill of Rights, Madison echoed the argument in favor of judicial review.[24]

After Virginia ratified, Madison began to temper his position, telling Jefferson that he never really opposed a bill of rights, "provided it be so framed as not to imply powers not meant to be included in the enumeration" of federal authority. Madison was not being disingenuous. When ratification was still in doubt, he did not want a search for consensus on a bill of rights to derail the effort to ratify. Equally important, Madison's constituents, especially Baptists and Presbyterians, were demanding protection for religious freedom and a separation of church and state, and as part of his hotly contested campaign for a position in the new House of Representatives, Madison committed to seek such protections.[25]

Madison also belatedly began to be concerned that the Constitution's "necessary and proper" clause could be used to increase federal power beyond what he had initially imagined. As Henry had warned during ratification, this invitation to implied powers could become an almost blank check for federal authority if interpreted broadly. If that occurred, a bill of rights could take on an even greater importance.[26]

The pressure from Henry and his antifederalist allies also undoubtedly influenced Madison's decision to embrace a bill of rights. After ratification, Madison, always a clever politician, saw political advantage in seeking a bill of rights that omitted structural changes limiting the power of the new federal government but satisfied many of its opponents on individual rights. This would weaken opposition to the new government—defanging many antifederalists and encouraging ratification by the hold-out states, North Carolina and Rhode Island. Amendments concerning individual liberties, Madison explained to Jefferson, would "separat[e] the well meaning from the designing opponents" to the Constitution, that is, opponents who, like Henry, wanted structural changes in favor of the states. Madison had no intention of seeing "a door opened for a reconsideration of the whole structure of the Government, for a re-consideration of the principles and the substance of the powers given." In the same vein, Henry Lee advised Washington to "disarm them [antifederalists] by complying with the rational views of the advocates for amendments spontaneously."[27]

Thus, Madison, sometimes referred to as the Father of the Bill of Rights, took control of the campaign in Congress for amendments, pushing them through in spite of the apparent indifference of most members of Congress—in fact opposition from many federalists and weak support from a small, poorly organized antifederalist contingent. Some have argued that Patrick Henry might be more accurately described as the Father of the Bill of Rights. After all, it was his actions—including forcing Madison to commit to a bill of rights as part of his campaign for a seat in the House of Representatives—that made the Bill of Rights a political necessity for Madison. "It was to his [Henry's] foresight and persistency that we are mainly indebted for the important safeguards for our liberties, which were engrafted on the instrument soon after its adoption," a grandson and biographer wrote. Yet, whoever claims the moniker "Father of the Bill of Rights," the changes that Madison sought and that Congress approved fell far short of those sought by Henry and his allies.[28]

Henry was not fooled by Madison's new-found interest in amendments. Before Congress convened, he warned Senator Richard Henry Lee that the "universal cry is for amendments, and the Federals are obliged to join in it; but whether to amuse, or conceal other views seems dubious." When he saw the amendments that passed the federalist-controlled Congress in September 1789, he knew that antifederalists' hopes for structural reform had been dashed. The amendments proposed would do little to limit essential federal power and protect the states. No structural changes were made affecting taxation, the president's power, commercial regulation, or the treaty power, the types of changes that antifederalists sought.[29]

Even the protections for civil rights fell short of Henry's hopes. Other antifederalists agreed. George Mason called the proposed Bill of Rights "a farce," referring to it as a "tub to a whale" (a device used by seamen to distract a whale when it approached a ship). While Mason later expressed "much Satisfaction" with the changes that had been made, he, like Henry, continued to insist that additional changes were necessary.[30]

Most notably, Madison was able to sap the strength of the one amendment that ostensibly restricted federal power and protected the states by specifying that powers not delegated to the federal government were reserved to the states. What became the Tenth Amendment is often cited by historians, political scientists, and lawyers as a significant early restraint on federal power but, tellingly, it is rarely relied upon by courts for that purpose, as they see it as "but a truism."[31]

Antifederalists sought an amendment mirroring Article II of the Articles of Confederation: "Each State retains its sovereignty, freedom, and independence, and every power, jurisdiction, and right, which is not by this Confederation, expressly delegated to the United States, in Congress assembled." The goal was to make clear that the national government only had powers expressly delegated in the Constitution, and other powers were retained by the states. Federalists had repeatedly argued as much during ratification debates in an effort to assuage concerns about expansive governmental powers. Antifederalists hoped that such an amendment would protect the power of the states and prevent the federal government from assuming new powers that it could argue were "implied" by the Constitution. This became a "repeated theme of the eulogies of those, who oppose the new constitution," Hamilton explained. Massachusetts, the first state to recommend amendments, sought a provision limiting federal powers to those "expressly delegated." New Hampshire wanted the amendment to limit federal powers "expressly & particularly delegated." New York and Rhode Island agreed that only powers "clearly delegated" should be available to the federal government.[32]

In any case, Madison had no intention of including such a clear restriction on federal power. As Justice John Marshall wrote in *McCulloch v. Maryland*, 17 U.S. 316, 406–7 (1819), "The men who drew and adopted this amendment had experienced the embarrassments resulting from the insertion of this word ['expressly'] in the Articles of Confederation, and probably omitted it, to avoid those embarrassments." What emerged from Congress after Madison's work was the current Tenth Amendment: "The powers not delegated to the United States by the Constitution, nor prohibited by it to the states, are reserved to the states respectively, or to the people." Commentators realized immediately, and history has demonstrated, that the failure to include the term "expressly" or to link the amendment with other restrictions on federal power (as Virginia proposed) seriously limited its impact. The clear implication of dropping "expressly," especially given language in the Articles of Confederation and proposed amendments from several states, was that the federal government had implied powers that were not specifically laid out in the Constitution. Identifying those powers would depend upon Congress, the president, and the federal courts. Later, ignoring the change, Democratic-Republicans would insist, perhaps hopefully, perhaps disingenuously, that the Tenth Amendment was central to maintaining state power. Spencer Roane may have been trying to convince himself when he declared that "it is not easy to devise stronger terms to effect that object." This was simply brave rhetoric.[33]

Henry, an experienced lawyer and politician, realized the Tenth Amendment did little, and there was a second serious problem with the amendment: Unlike Article II of the Articles of Confederation or the provisions proposed by Massachusetts, South Carolina, New Hampshire, Virginia, and North Carolina, all of which provided that the *states* retained power not delegated to the union, the proposed amendment specified that retained powers were left "to the states . . . , or to the people." Only New York had suggested such a formulation. (After the amendment was adopted by Congress, Rhode Island did as well.)[34]

On its face, this addition seems reasonable—after all, in a republic, in theory all power originates from and can be exercised by "the people." Yet, Henry realized that this formulation further undermined the power of the states and their ability to control federal overreach by creating a serious question as to whether any particular nondelegated power was vested in the states or the people, thus making enforcement of retained powers far more difficult.

Edward Fontaine, one of Henry's great-grandsons, related how Henry reacted when he saw the proposed language: "My father [who was then studying
law with Henry] said he threw the pamphlet upon the table with an expression of much dissatisfaction and distress; & turned to him and Mr. Dandridge
& remarked with such solemnity: that Virginia had been outwitted, & her
reserved rights sacrificed by the ingenious wording of the amendments which
had been adopted." Referring to Virginia's proposed restriction on federal
power, Henry explained

> they have . . . changed it into this equivocal thing . . . & they have tacked
> to it the objectionable & dangerous clause: "or to the people." . . . Why
> did they add: "or to the people"? They determined from the first that it
> should be a strong consolidated government. They inserted this amend-
> ment *guilefully* as something guarding the reserved rights of the States to
> induce North Carolina, Rhode Island & others to adopt it. It would guard
> them effectively if it ended with the word "*respectively.*" But the words,
> "or to the people," are added *insidiously,* not to be used *now,* but which,
> he said, those who inserted them would construe at "some *future time* to
> suit their own purpose." They will construe them so as to neutralize the
> amendment of Virginia, & sweep away the sovereignty of the States.

So long as "the people" retained some unspecified powers, it was more difficult
for states to use the amendment to enforce their own power. To Henry, the net
effect was clear: the amendment improved neither the states' nor the people's
ability to control the federal government.[35]

A disgusted Patrick Henry wrote to Senator Richard Henry Lee that the
proposed amendments "tend to injure rather than serve the cause of liberty."
Henry insisted that a single amendment restricting the federal government's
authority to tax would have been more effective than all of those offered. Lee
agreed and bemoaned that the Constitution had been adopted based upon
the chimerical commitment to unspecified later amendments. This was "little
better than putting oneself to death first, in expectation that the doctor, who
wished our destruction, would afterwards restore us to life," Lee complained.
"Good for nothing" was how Virginia's other senator described the amendments. It was not that the proposed amendments were, themselves, harmful,
but they did not include the structural changes that Henry and his supporters thought essential, and Henry correctly perceived that the pressure for
other reforms would evaporate with the passage of the Bill of Rights—as Madison intended.[36]

Recognizing that the useful aspects of the amendments, especially religious and press freedom, would diminish pressure for more reform, Henry tried to delay consideration of the proposed amendments in hopes of forcing Congress to accept some structural reform. In the fall of 1789, there was an influx of federalist members into the Virginia House of Delegates, apparently in response to Congress's adoption of the proposed Bill of Rights and Henry's efforts to delay the amendments. Henry's supporters tried to force through the House of Delegates a vote demanding that Congress consider all of Virginia's proposed amendments, but after three attempts that effort ultimately lost on a 62–62 vote when the speaker, Thomas Matthew, voted against it (after Henry had left the House in some disgust at its inaction). A milder version asking Congress to reconsider the proposed Virginia amendments was then passed without division.[37]

Initially, Henry's view prevailed in Virginia's Senate. After the House of Delegates approved the amendments (urging Congress to consider others), the Senate rejected them. After the House again approved all the amendments, the Senate disapproved the third, eighth, eleventh, and twelfth (what we now know as the First, Sixth, Ninth, and Tenth Amendments). With no agreement, the amendments failed in conference. But when North Carolina and Rhode Island (the last of the original thirteen states to ratify the Constitution) accepted the amendments, Henry's effort to delay was effectively undermined, and Henry's opposition waned. Virginia finally approved the amendments in the fall of 1791, with which they had the requisite approval of three-fourths of the states and became part of the Constitution.[38]

Anxious about what the new federal government might do, with some trepidation, Henry and other antifederalists were reduced to watching closely the implementation of the Constitution by the new government.

Patrick Henry versus Alexander Hamilton

Despite antifederalists' fears, in the first years under the Constitution the new national government operated relatively well, and there were no obvious attacks on individual liberties nor excessive taxation or regulation. (Initially, most revenue came from import duties, allowing the federal government to collect revenue without taxing citizens directly.)[39]

Citizens, even many antifederalists, seemed prone to give the government the benefit of any doubts and to let it develop. Henry, never a dogmatist, agreed, to a point. In late 1790, after a year and a half under the Constitution, Henry conceded that "Truth obliges me to declare that I perceive in the

Federal characters I converse with in this country an honest and patriotic care of the general good." Earlier, knowing that his battle for structural amendments faced an almost insurmountable obstacle, Henry began to "advise . . . all his partisans to support the Constitution, and if they wish to be secured against its supposed ill tendency, to get into the government." Prudent elected officials were needed, and changes could best be made from within.[40]

Yet, Henry's efforts to restrict the power of the government "in a constitutional way" did not end with congressional elections and constitutional amendments. He also believed that the states had an important role to play in monitoring federal actions and, when necessary, responding to specific abuses of power. In the first several years of the new constitutional republic, no clearer example of this type of "loyal opposition" to governmental policies exists than Virginia's reaction to Alexander Hamilton's plan for the national debt.

As the new government took shape, Hamilton, the first secretary of the treasury, had an ambitious plan to build support for the federal government among elites in the business community and expand its power. Having studied Britain's financial system carefully, in particular how finance played a major role in Britain's eighteenth-century successes over the larger but fiscally backward France, Hamilton sought to replicate Britain's success in the United States. To achieve this, he proposed a national bank and full repayment, at face value, of the deeply depreciated outstanding debt from the Revolution, including a proposal for the federal government to assume outstanding debt owed by the states. This plan was explained in Hamilton's Report on Public Credit sent to Congress in January of 1790. As legislation to implement the plan was introduced, former antifederalists, and many former federalists now concerned with this unforeseen expansion of federal power, argued that the federal government had no authority to assume state debts or to charter a bank; the Constitution certainly never expressly granted such power. Hamilton, though, argued successfully to Congress and President Washington that such power was implied and "necessary and proper" to get the new nation's financial house in order.[41]

Hamilton's plan to pay all debts owed by the former Confederation at face value was a significant decision. After all, given the virtual bankruptcy of the Confederation, its debts had deeply depreciated, and a large share of the paper instruments (government IOUs) had been bought by speculators at well below face value. Under Hamilton's plan, these speculators would gain a windfall when the debts were paid in full. Hamilton, though, insisted that establishing American credit and future fiscal strength depended upon the government fully supporting outstanding financial commitments, regardless of who benefitted. Full repayment of the debt would breed confidence in both the domestic and international financial and business communities. Hamilton also understood that creating a creditor class of wealthy merchants who depended upon the solvency of the federal government to ensure that they received regular payments on government debt would guarantee their support of the new government, support that could be crucial in a crisis.

While Hamilton was correct about the new nation's finances, to former antifederalists it smacked of corruption: wealthy merchants would profit by buying and selling government securities while necessity had forced the original recipients—often soldiers or farmers who had supplied the army during the Revolution—to take pennies on the dollar when they had sold their debts to these speculators. Farmers, small shopkeepers, and soldiers are estimated to have sold over 90 percent of their debt by this point. Beyond the injustice to those who fought and supported the war, with a merchant class of speculators owning debt being paid by the federal government, they would have a financial interest in supporting government policy, further insulating the new and powerful government from the people at large. Henry and Mason had warned during the ratification debates that exactly this might happen.[42]

Hamilton also wanted the federal government to assume responsibility for all outstanding state debts from the Revolution and guarantee those debts at face value as well; this would further increase the federal government's power and influence. But this was a massive undertaking, meaning that in addition to the over $50 million in debt owed by the Confederation directly, the federal government would take on an additional $25 million in state debt. Moreover, while many antifederalists thought that paying the Confederation's debts at face value was bad policy, assuming state debts raised a more fundamental, constitutional concern: Where in the Constitution did the federal government receive authority to assume state debts, much less effectively increase the cost of those obligations to taxpayers by guaranteeing them at face value? The proposal was even more politically explosive since some states, including Virginia, thought that they had managed their own debts well and paid off a substantial portion, but if the federal government assumed all of the state debts, they would now be effectively responsible for debts from states that had not practiced sound fiscal policies. (History would show that Virginia was wrong about this and still owed a very substantial share of its own debt, but at the time, many Virginians believed otherwise.) Given the plan for assumption of state debts and the huge windfall for speculators, even Madison, a leading federalist and Hamilton's ally during ratification, now agreed with the concerns about unfettered federal power expressed by his former antifederalist opponents.[43]

In spite of the objections, funding of the national debt and assumption of the state debts was approved by Congress in August 1790. The national bank was authorized in February 1791, over the same constitutional objections by antifederalists. President Washington signed both bills, the latter over Jefferson's constitutional objection. Many people were unhappy with Hamilton's plans, but George Washington was still so universally revered as to temper any opposition. Henry's biographer grandson concluded that the vote over assumption of the state debts signaled the beginning of distinct political parties, "having given rise to the political parties subsequently known as 'Federalist' and 'Republican.'"[44] The question is, how did Patrick Henry react?

While Hamilton's plan for assuming state debts evidenced financial genius, it also struck Henry as a great usurpation of state authority. The federal government might well guarantee Confederation obligations, but the Constitution did not expressly provide it with authority to assume state debts, much less to charter a national bank. Both tended to diminish the power of the states. In spite of all the promises made during ratification that the federal government would have only those powers that were specifically delegated, Hamilton was reading the Constitution to provide implied powers to the new government, exactly what Henry and antifederalists had warned against. Now, Congress and President Washington had accepted his arguments. Hamilton's financial plan also benefited the wealthy and powerful at the expense of common taxpayers, something Henry had fought against his whole career. What were opponents of such a policy to do? How could one resist in "a constitutional way"?

By April of 1790, Henry Lee, a leading federalist during the ratification debates, reported despondingly to Madison on the effect Hamilton's financial plan was having in Virginia. "[Patrick] Henry already is considered as a prophet, his predictions are daily verifying." Especially troubling was the way that Hamilton's plan worked to benefit the wealthy at the expense of the people; Henry's "declarations with respect to the division of interests which would exist under the constitution & predominate in all the doings of the govt. already has been undeniably proved." Lee was deeply disturbed by the apparent dominance of commercial interests in the new government, referring to "the mad policy which seems to direct the doings of Congress." While recognizing that "we are committed" to the new Constitution and "we cannot be relieved I fear only by disunion," he warned Madison in language

hauntingly similar to that for which Henry had been berated during the ratification debates that "to disunite is dreadful to my mind, but dreadful as it is, I
consider it a lesser evil than union on the present conditions." Almost taunt-
ing, he concluded with a question for Madison: "How do you feel, what do you
think, is your love for the constitution so ardent, as to induce you to adhere to
it tho it should produce ruin to your native country [Virginia]. I hope not, I
believe not." Within a year, Lee would turn on Hamilton's plan and be elected
governor of Virginia based upon opposition to the actions of the new government that he (and Madison) had helped to create.[45]

Faced with this new expansion of federal authority, former antifederalists,
led by Henry, pushed through both houses of the Virginia legislature resolutions denouncing Hamilton's plan. By this time, many of Virginia's former federalists had developed deep suspicions of the federal government and joined
Henry's efforts. The resulting state petition that the federal government trim
its sails, "the first of any Legislature against an act of Congress, was the work of
the advocates, as well as of the opponents, of the Constitution," Henry's biographer noted. The precise nature of the protest, though, was very important,
particularly in light of subsequent events and the development of an ideology
of states' rights.[46]

On November 3, 1790, as the new session of the General Assembly got
under way, Henry introduced a resolution condemning Hamilton's plan and
declaring that assumption of state debts was "repugnant to the constitution of
the United States, as it goes to the exercise of a power not expressly granted
to the General Government." Many of Henry's opponents in the ratification
debates, chastened by the apparent expansion of the new federal government's
power so soon, joined his opposition. Federalists who continued to support the
administration sought to weaken the resolution by removing the assertion that
assumption was unconstitutional, but that effort failed miserably, forty-seven
to eighty-eight. Henry's resolution was then approved, seventy-five to fifty-
two. Significantly in light of subsequent developments, while Virginia's House
of Delegates denounced aspects of Hamilton's plans as unconstitutional, there
was not even a suggestion that the state retained power to block the federal
government or nullify its laws, or that in ratifying the Constitution the states
had merely joined a new confederacy, a compact among sovereign states that
they could effectively control.[47]

After the House of Delegates adopted the resolution, it drafted a remonstrance to Congress against Hamilton's plan. Henry, of course, was put on the
drafting committee. The resulting memorial began by noting that it was agreed
at ratification that "every power not expressly granted, was retained," and

concluded that "as guardians then of the rights and interests of their constituents, as sentinels placed by them over the ministers of the Federal Government, to shield it from their incroachments, or at least to sound the alarm, when it is threatened with invasion," the legislature would not silently acquiesce to what it saw as unconstitutional actions. By December 16, the House adopted the address declaring the "censure of the General Assembly" against the federal actions. But beyond the rebuke of Hamilton's constitutional theory, the action taken by the Virginia legislature (and the action not taken) were equally important: "The General Assembly of the Commonwealth of Virginia confide so fully in the prudence and wisdom of Congress upon the present occasion, as to hope that they will revise and amend the aforesaid act generally" and repeal the federal assumption of state debts. Less than a week later, the Virginia Senate agreed with a minor amendment.[48] This Virginia challenge to the federal program was widely reported in the press.[49]

As with the House resolution, the General Assembly's memorial did not refer to the Constitution as a "compact" nor was there any suggestion that the state could take direct action to interfere with federal law. Nor did the protests against the constitutionality of Hamilton's plan by Jefferson, or Randolph, or Madison, or any other leader of the future Democratic-Republican party, suggest that the state could unilaterally interfere with federal actions. While recognizing that "the state legislatures have at least as good a right to judge of every infraction of the constitution as Congress itself," John Taylor (a leading Jeffersonian and later a proponent of radical states' rights) suggested only that the states could remonstrate and act against such laws through their choice of senators. In the case of the General Assembly's protest, as he had promised at the ratification convention, Henry was seeking to redress the perceived infringement "in a constitutional way."[50]

An argument in the General Assembly's remonstrance based upon the debt clause in the Constitution, Article VI, has led some historians to suggest that Virginia argued in 1790 that the Constitution was merely a compact among sovereign states with continuing authority to control the federal government. However, what the Virginia memorial said was:

> This provision is—"That all debts contracted and entered into, before the adoption of this constitution, shall be as valid against the United States, under this constitution, as under the confederation;" which amounts to a constitutional ratification of the contracts respecting the state debts; in the situation in which they existed under the confederation; and resorting to that standard, there can be no doubt, that in the present question,

the rights of the states, as contracting parties with the United States, must
be considered as sacred.

Virginia was arguing that the state debts could not be changed without the
state's approval. In this context, reference to states as "contracting parties" was
not to argue that the Constitution was a mere compact to which each state
was a party; rather, the states were parties to their debt contracts (as the
United States was to its debts) and could claim the protection of the Constitution that shielded such contracts from modification.[51]

Historian Richard Beeman suggests that Virginia's objection, fashioned by
Henry, paved the way for the Virginia and Kentucky Resolutions of 1798 and
the doctrine of state "nullification" of federal actions. Virginia's Address to
Congress "would serve as a practical guidebook for anyone wishing to attack
the federal government in the future," Beeman concludes. Yet, the difference
between the Henry-endorsed address of 1790 and future states' rights actions
in opposition to federal laws is striking. Only by projecting backward from the
Virginia and Kentucky Resolutions and subsequent battles over nullification
leading up to the Civil War can one conclude that Virginia legislators in 1790
"were taking a step toward a general constitutional principle upholding the
right of the states to exercise authority in cases where the policies of the state
and national governments conflicted." A state's declaration that the federal
government was acting unconstitutionally and a request that offending laws
be repealed by federal authorities is entirely different than asserting a right
of each state to interfere with the operation of a federal law within the state.[52]

Still, even though the Virginia resolutions were quite tempered (especially
in light of subsequent states' rights efforts in support of nullification), in an era
when an appropriate manner of expressing opposition to government policies
was still being formed, the resolutions were seen by many as an unduly harsh
criticism of the Washington administration. Hamilton, enraged by Virginia's
rebuke and reverting to deeply partisan language, wrote that "this is the first
symptom of a spirit which must either be killed or will kill the constitution of
the United States." Yet, as one Henry biographer noted, it was Hamilton who
"had urged the adoption of the Constitution on the ground, 'that the State
Legislatures would act as sentinels in sounding the alarm if anything improper
should occur in the conduct of the national rulers, and prove the proper and
sufficient security against invasions of public liberty by the national authority.'"
Nonetheless, federalist newspapers echoed Hamilton's outrage with sarcasm
heaped on Virginia and Henry (who was understood to be the "instigator" of
the resolutions):

The resolution of the Virginia Assembly respecting the Assumption of the State Debts . . . exhibits a very curious phenomenon in the history of the United States. The majority who voted in favor of the resolution, it seems, fell asleep in September 1787, (just before the rising of the Federal Convention) and did not awake till a few weeks ago; during which time the Federal Government was adopted and established throughout all the States. Their vote therefore must be ascribed to *ignorance* of what passed during their long sleep. The *Resolution* is calculated only for those years of anarchy [under the Confederation], which preceded the general ratification of the present HAPPY NATIONAL GOVERNMENT. It is now nugatory and ridiculous. . . . the *well known* instigator of it [Henry], who never sleeps when there is "mischief afloat," . . . will be treated with universal contempt.[53]

It is worth noting that Henry, while on the committee that drafted the remonstrance, left the House to return to his plantation before it was introduced, but he did not "drop his opposition" to federal assumption of state debts, as some have suggested. Having introduced the original resolution and managed drafting of the remonstrance, he was confident of its adoption before family obligations required his taking the long road home.[54]

After Henry left Richmond in December 1790, he would not again sit in a government assembly. That spring, he declined reelection. Yet, he did not lose interest in the important issues facing the new nation.

Rather than surrendering his opposition to the expansion of federal powers, Henry's motives in leading opposition to Hamilton's financial system and then retiring seem to be better explained by a letter he wrote several months later to Virginia's newest senator, James Monroe, noting that resistance to programs of the new federal government should be addressed with caution. While Henry still supported reforms to the constitutional structure, he was firmly opposed to any action that threatened to destroy the government. Henry told Senator Monroe that

alto' The Form of Govern^t into which my Country men determined to place themselves, had my Enmity, yet as we are one & all imbarked, it is natural to care for the crazy Machine, at least so long as we are out of Sight of a Port to refit. I have therefore my Anxietys to hear & to know what is doing, & to what point the State pilots are steering, & to keep up the Metaphor, whether there is no Appearance of Storms in our

Horizon? . . . all I can promise you is, that I will be sparing of Complaints ag^t. the Government, & find Fault as little as my fixed Habits of thinking will permit. . . . The little Stock of good Humour which I have towards them, is increased by reflecting that some Allowances ought to be made, & some Hopes indulged of future amendment.

Rather than an ideologue who would do anything to sabotage the federal government as Madison angrily insisted after ratification, Henry seemed to work constantly and carefully to remedy what he saw as defects in the Constitution but also to work within its form.[55]

Henry and Virginia were confronting a crucial question, one that lingered in the new republic for decades and continues to challenge today (although the novelty of the problem in the 1790s is difficult for modern readers to appreciate fully): If a person or a state believed that the federal government exceeded its constitutional power, what was to be done? Certainly, the courts had the authority to strike down unconstitutional laws, but in the 1790s the entire federal judiciary was Federalist and not disposed to limit the power of Congress. Henry took what he thought was an emphatic stance against federal usurpation, but he did not suggest that the state refuse to abide by federal authority. Henry and his supporters urged other states to join in their protest against what they saw as Hamilton's usurpation, and they hoped the federal government would, under political pressure from constituents, change course. Henry was acting, and urging others to act, as a loyal opposition.

Henry's plan for Virginia to protest Hamilton's actions stands in stark contrast to Jefferson's almost delirious, albeit private, attack on Hamilton's plan. Secretary of State Jefferson warned President Washington that Hamilton's plans confirmed the worst fears of southerners and could lead to calls for secession. In late 1792, Jefferson wrote to Madison suggesting that any Virginian who went to work for the Bank of the United States (including its Richmond branch) should be "adjudged guilty of high treason and suffer death accordingly." While Jefferson was prone to hyperbole, even by his standards this was extreme. The difference in Henry's approach and Jefferson's is notable, particularly in light of what was to come.[56]

Henry's leading role in Virginia's denunciation of Hamilton's financial plan is significant for another reason. Years later, after Henry's death, in an effort to explain Henry's "apostasy" in his campaign against a sweeping states' rights movement in 1798–1799, Jefferson argued that Henry became wealthy because of Hamilton's debt assumption plan and that, as a result, "Hamilton became now his idol." This was simply not true at several levels. Henry, still the most popular politician in Virginia bar Washington, took the lead in denouncing Hamilton's funding scheme, a political battle that rallied opposition to expansive federal power and played an important role in creation of the Democratic-Republican party that Jefferson would come to lead. While Henry profited when national and state debts were made payable at face value, as did many others, this did not change his opposition to what he understood to be an unconstitutional plan. In fact, in 1790, as Virginia's legislature debated the Hamilton financial system, Jefferson himself suggested that Henry, "an implacable" foe to federal authority, opposed state debt assumption because of "disaffection to the government." It was only years later, after Henry came out in opposition to Jefferson's radical states' rights agenda and after Henry's death, that Jefferson argued that Henry became a supporter of the federal government because of the Hamilton financial plan.[57]

Overall, after the Constitution had taken effect, developments in the federal government were confirming Henry's concern about the loss of local control that he had expressed throughout the ratification debates. By 1792, a newspaper story reiterating Henry's concerns about ratification was widely reprinted: "The following prophecy of St. Patrick (alias Patrick Henry) taken from the debates of our state convention, may be very aptly applied to our present situation:—'When oppressions take place, our Representatives may tell us, we contended for your interest, but we could not carry our point, because the Representatives from Massachusetts, New Hampshire, Connecticut, &c. were against us.'" Notably, Henry was broadly seen as the intellectual godfather of the states' rights movement and the nascent Democratic-Republican party, with John Randolph's biographer declaring that "it is certain that they [Democratic-Republicans] took their origin in those principles which on the one side he [Henry] so eloquently defended."[58]

Henry's Retirement

Henry, retired from political office, continued as a trenchant observer of federal action and states' rights and maintained his position as "loyal opposition" to unnecessary expansion of federal powers while, at the same time, voicing that opposition in measured ways.

Even out of office, Henry's political influence continued. For example, Jefferson had hoped to modify Virginia's constitution since its 1776 inception, but he saw Henry's support of the document as a serious impediment. At the end of 1791, Jefferson wrote to Archibald Stuart, a well-connected politician, asking that he sound out Henry on the possibility of rewriting Virginia's constitution. Jefferson wrote: "I have understood that Mr. Henry has always been opposed to this undertaking: and I confess that I consider his talents and influence such as that, were it decided that we should call a Convention for the purpose of amending, I should fear he might induce that convention either to fix the thing as at present, or change it for the worse." In September 1792, Jefferson was still seeking Stuart's assistance in approaching Henry on the topic of Virginia constitutional reform.[59]

Three additional incidents during this period are notable both for demonstrating Henry's continued popularity and engagement with critical political issues and how Henry framed his continuing opposition to undue expansion of federal power: the British debts case, formation of Democratic-Republican Societies, and the Jay Treaty of 1795 with Britain.

British Debts Case

As Henry anticipated (and as discussed earlier), adoption of the U.S. Constitution created opportunities for British merchants to go to court to enforce pre-Revolutionary debts. Henry, with co-counsel John Marshall, sought to have the federal lawsuits dismissed and was initially successful in part (before the Supreme Court reversed the lower court decision after Henry retired from the practice of law). Henry argued that protecting the intangible debts of British merchants and bankers while farmers and tradesman had lost inventory and supplies to marauding troops was unjust: "It is a mercantile idea that worships Mammon instead of God."[60]

The case demonstrated again Henry's great legal skill (even Jefferson conceded as much) and his continued popularity. Edmund Randolph wrote to Washington that after the British debts case, Henry's "ascendancy has risen to an immeasurable height." Randolph went on to tell the president that Henry "has been loud in reprobating the decapitation of the French king," referring to the rising radicalism of the French Revolution, but assured Washington that he "is a friend to peace and the steps pursued for its security."[61]

Democratic-Republican Societies

In 1789, as the new government under the Constitution was being formed, the French Revolution erupted across the Atlantic Ocean. Initially, most Americans rejoiced; it appeared that a fellow republic would join the United States on the world stage. Jefferson, U.S. minister to France at the time, was particularly hopeful that the French Revolution presaged a wave of progressive political reform across Europe and the world.

Unfortunately, it was not long until the excesses of the French revolt dashed those hopes. In the meantime, the French Revolution posed a major challenge for the United States and Washington's administration. While France had provided essential aid during the American Revolution, the forces that seized power from Louis XVI (America's former ally) were increasingly radical. The beheading of Louis on January 21, 1793, the revolutionary government's attacks on other European nations, and even more seriously to many Americans, its attacks on religion dramatically increased these concerns. In 1793, Britain went to war with its historic enemy; the two nations would be at war for most of the next twenty-two years (until Napoleon's final defeat at Waterloo in 1815).

American leaders believed that the still fragile new nation could easily be destroyed by a renewed war with Britain or a war with France. So, on April 22, 1793, George Washington declared American neutrality in the European conflict with the unanimous support of his cabinet officers—although Jefferson and Hamilton embraced the proposal with different degrees of warmth and their positions on the French Revolution would rapidly diverge. In particular, Jefferson and his supporters increasingly believed that Federalists were treating France, the United States' former ally, unfairly and were far too entangled with British interests.

In the midst of these heated political debates, and as opposition grew to the Washington administration's 1791 excise tax on whiskey, local groups began to form to voice opposition to governmental policies and support for France and to communicate with like-minded citizens. By July 4, 1792, the *National Gazette*—published by Philip Freneau with the support of Jefferson and Madison—observed approvingly that political clubs had been formed in England supporting opposition politics and "promoting an enquiry into, and asserting the natural and civil rights of the people" so as to be "safe from the encroachments of any administration whatsoever." Similar organizations in America became known as Democratic-Republican Societies or Clubs (building blocks for the emerging Democratic-Republican party).[62]

There was no precedent in the United States for a formal organization opposing the government, and many—especially Hamilton and his supporters—saw these Democratic-Republican Societies as disloyal. When the Constitution was drafted, founders hoped that formal parties would not emerge in the United States. In fact, there was a view, especially prevalent among conservative leaders, that citizens participated in setting the direction of the nation at elections but otherwise there should be "a firm reliance of the people on the wisdom and integrity of those authorities which they have themselves constituted to manage their public concerns, and [give] a chearful acquiescence in the decisions of the rulers."[63]

When Democratic-Republican Clubs erected "liberty poles" to rally opposition to the whiskey tax, supporters and opponents rushed to claim the legacy of the American Revolution. "Federalists argued that an elected Congress had passed the whiskey excise, making the tax a reflection of the popular will. In their view, the pole-raisers were rebels who challenged the administration of representative government and so threatened the Revolutionary legacy. 'How nearly do the opposite extremes of toryism and anarchy approach each other?' observed the *Baltimore Daily Intelligencer*, as the rebellion spread into Maryland, 'Are they not twin brothers?'" Federalists insisted that pole-raisers threatened the "chaos of the 1780s" (a reference to Shays's Rebellion). They were "hypocrites 'who boast of being republicans, while they violate the most essential principle of republicanism, which is obedience to the laws passed by the consent of the majority.'" In contrast, Democratic-Republicans claimed that assaults on political expression, including removing liberty poles, was "more apt to excite the people to insurrection and raise them against their government, than to enforce obedience and peaceable quietness." Open conflict broke out over some liberty poles, with one young boy killed in a riot in Carlisle, Pennsylvania.[64]

George Washington was incensed by these new organizations. He always had a bit of a thin skin, but in these growing protests he heard rumblings of the mob anarchy that he had feared during Shays's Rebellion and that seemed to be metastasizing in France as the Reign of Terror took hold. He thought the Whiskey Rebellion the "first *ripe fruit* of the Democratic Societies . . . a self-created, *permanent* body" (although he conceded that "no one denies the right of the people to meet occasionally, to petition for, or remonstrate against, any Act of the Legislature"). Washington did little to hide his disdain, referring derisively to "certain self-created societies." Other Federalists denounced the societies as encouraging anarchy, ruling by "tar and feathers." As he prepared to leave office in late 1796, in perhaps his most famous political address, Washington continued his attack, warning that such societies could "become potent engines by which cunning, ambitious, and unprincipled men will be enabled to subvert the power of the people, and to usurp for themselves the reins of governments; destroying afterwards the very engines which have lifted them to unjust dominion."[65]

Jefferson, on the other hand, saw these groups as patriots continuing the tradition of protest against ill-founded government policy evident in the Spirit of '76. He and his supporters were deeply disturbed by Washington's attacks on the societies, "friends of general freedom." In late 1794, Jefferson denounced the societies' opponents as "those who wish to confine that freedom [of speech and press] to the few." Seeking to shift the blame for Washington's denunciation of the societies to Hamilton, Jefferson wrote of his surprise that the president "should have permitted himself to be the organ of such an attack on the freedom of discussion, the freedom of writing, printing & publishing." Yet, in attributing the administration's opposition to Hamilton, Jefferson underestimated Washington's real concern for what such organizations—political factions—might become.[66]

Henry had a more moderate position on the societies. He thought that they (like modern political parties) often exaggerated their conflicts with the Washington administration to foment partisan political support; he was suspicious of such efforts to politicize every issue. At the same time, he thought that the societies should not be suppressed. He wrote to Henry Lee, "Although a democrat myself, I like not the late Democratic Societies." Yet, "as little do I like their suppression by law." Henry would have found the societies' own defense persuasive: "they never did attempt to substitute their wishes for law, and never expected that their opinion would have more weight than their intrinsic merit demanded. They felt themselves, as a portion of the People, bound by the acts of the legal representatives of the whole, and ready with their lives and fortunes to maintain obedience to the laws, but the observance of this duty did not deprive them of the right of questioning their policy." Henry concluded, "Silly things may amuse for a while, but in a little time men will perceive their delusion." Here, as elsewhere, Patrick Henry's thinking failed to conform to the simple binary of Hamiltonian Federalists versus Jeffersonian Democratic-Republicans.[67]

Jay Treaty

The 1795 Jay Treaty provides another good example of Henry's measured response to federal action in the 1790s and his role as loyal opposition. It also demonstrates Henry's growing frustration with Democratic-Republican efforts to recast the Constitution in ways that Henry might have preferred in 1788 but that were inconsistent with the Constitution as adopted.

The Jay Treaty between Britain and the United States was part of the Washington administration's effort to remain neutral in the British-French wars that

erupted after the French Revolution. Each belligerent sought to obtain supplies from the United States while denying their enemy access to the same,
threatening U.S. neutrality. Each seized U.S. ships "trading with the enemy";
Britain also impressed U.S. sailors who it claimed were British citizens.

The Jay Treaty, while preventing war with Britain, was broadly seen
as deeply flawed; it did not prevent Britain from seizing U.S. ships trading
with France (although it provided the prospect of compensation) nor did it
eliminate the threat of impressment by the British navy. At the same time, by
maintaining peace with Britain, it was seen by partisans of France—especially
Jeffersonian Democratic-Republicans—as a threat. (The French response to
the Jay Treaty and efforts to reach a treaty with France are discussed in the next
chapter.) Important to Henry, the treaty did require Britain finally to vacate
forts in the Northwest Territories (forts that Britain had agreed to vacate at
the end of the Revolution); since Britain had used the forts to supply Native
Americans fighting U.S. expansion, U.S. control of the forts would encourage
western settlement, something that Henry had consistently supported (and
increase pressure on Native lands). But beyond the forts, the treaty seemed
otherwise to provide few benefits to the United States—other than preventing
a shooting war with Britain. Southern Democratic-Republican opposition to
the Jay Treaty also often stressed its failure to obtain compensation for the
previously enslaved whom the British army had evacuated after the peace in
violation of the Paris Treaty of 1783.[68]

After the Jay Treaty was ratified by the Senate and signed by Washington,
Democratic-Republicans in the House of Representatives, led by Madison,
threatened to block its implementation by refusing to appropriate funds necessary to bring it into force.[69]

Henry was disgusted with Madison's effort. Although he thought the Jay
Treaty granted far too much to Britain, he saw the effort to block the treaty
in the House of Representatives as equally ill-advised and disingenuous. Once
the Senate and president ratified the treaty, the United States had an international obligation; to violate that obligation would have consequences. As
Madison had argued during the ratification debates, "if they [treaties] are to
have any efficacy, they must be the law of the land." A treaty "bound the public
faith and could not be violated without national disgrace and personal dis-
honor," Theodore Sedgwick, a Federalist congressman, argued. "They might
require Legislative provisions to carry them into effect; but this neither implied nor authorized the exercise of discretion, as to refusal."[70]

Recognizing the danger of delayed implementation or a breach of the Jay
Treaty resulting from the actions of the House of Representatives, Washington

bristled. House opponents of the treaty "resolved to . . . render the Treaty making power a Nullity without their consent . . . worse, to render it an absolute absurdity," he fumed. Their obstruction "not only brought the Constitution to the brink of a precipice but the Peace, happiness & prosperity of the country into imminent danger." Vice President Adams agreed, believing the dispute presented a fundamental choice as to "whether National Faith is binding on a Nation"; he denounced the Democratic-Republicans as having "no National Pride—no National sense of Honor."[71]

Henry pointed out that during the ratification debates antifederalists had objected strongly to giving the president and the Senate exclusive authority over the treaty power. Excluding the House of Representatives, the part of the federal government closest to the people, was dangerous, he had insisted. With the failed Jay-Gardoqui Treaty clearly in mind, antifederalists had argued during ratification that without oversight from the popular branch of government, treaties could undermine the people's interests in the areas of trade, regulation, even territory.[72]

Yet, during ratification, Madison and his federalist colleagues had insisted that authority over such treaties was appropriately, and safely, invested exclusively in the president and the Senate. Having rejected Henry's warnings during ratification, Madison now, recognizing without saying so the legitimacy of those warnings, was ignoring his own ratification arguments. While Henry had firmly objected to granting this authority, and post-ratification sought an amendment to involve the House in the treaty-making process, he had lost both of those debates. The Constitution, which laid out the treaty-making power clearly, was adopted after a full debate and vote, and the proposed amendment had been quashed by Madison and Congress. For Henry, Madison's efforts to deny that authority were inconsistent with the understanding he and his federalist colleagues had advocated during ratification; Henry understandably believed that Democratic-Republicans had abandoned principle for political gain. Moreover, efforts to block a treaty only recently negotiated and ratified threatened an open rupture, likely war, with Britain.[73]

Henry was well aware that his views on operation of the government under the Constitution, including the Jay Treaty, were causing some nervous Democratic-Republicans to claim that he had changed his political position. He flatly denied it; while objecting to provisions of the Jay Treaty, he pointed out that he was maintaining the understanding at the time of ratification (although he had not liked the treaty provision, it had been approved by his co-citizens) and warned against violating the United States' international obligation. Henry explained that "he disliked it [the Jay Treaty], and if he had been in the *proper place* [the Senate], he might have voted against it. *But, after it was signed and sealed by the constituted authorities, to have said or done any thing against carrying it into effect, would have been an act too base to think of without horror.*" Writing to Betsy Aylett (a favorite daughter), Henry dismissed claims about his own change in views and, obviously referring to Madison, denounced how others had changed their positions:

> As to the reports you have heard of my changing sides in politics, I can only say they are not true. I am too old to exchange my former opinions, which have grown up into fixed habits of thinking. True it is, I have condemned the conduct of our members in congress, because, in refusing to raise money for the purposes of the British treaty, they, in effect, would have surrendered our country bound, hand and foot, to the power of the British nation. . . . The treaty is, in my opinion, a very bad one indeed. But what must I think of these men, whom I myself warned of the danger of giving the power of making laws by means of treaty, to the president and senate, when I see these same men denying the existence of that power, which they insisted, in our convention, ought properly to be exercised by the president and senate, and by none other?[74]

Another aspect of Democratic-Republican opposition to the Jay Treaty is interesting in this regard. Hoping to encourage a substantive review by the House of Representatives, the Virginia General Assembly thanked its senators for their opposition to the treaty, and proposals were floated for constitutional amendments to prevent adoption of such treaties in the future, much like the amendment that had been proposed by Henry and his supporters in 1788. At the time, while some questioned the constitutionality of the Jay Treaty, there was again apparently no suggestion that the Constitution was a mere "compact" among the states or a confederation over which the states had binding authority, permitting the states to block the treaty.[75]

The reasons for Henry's seeming moderation in the 1790s are multiple. Certainly, his normal disposition was to prefer democratic solutions to problems, to win battles at the ballot box when possible. Moreover, while he objected strenuously to the overreach of Hamilton's financial plan, the federal government had not abused its power as seriously as he had feared during ratification. Similarly, although the Bill of Rights failed to restrict federal power and promote that of the states in the manner that he had hoped, it did promise protection of religious freedom, freedom of the press, the right to jury trials, and so forth, all of which had been areas of concern during the ratification debates.

Beyond these factors, as the 1790s progressed, Henry's politics were influenced by the growing excesses of the French Revolution and his own sincere,
conservative religiosity. Henry, like most Americans, watched the outbreak of
the French Revolution in 1789 with great hope. Yet, when Louis XVI, America's
staunch and essential ally during the Revolution, was beheaded in early 1793,
even the most Francophile Democratic-Republicans had to pause. Henry was
"loud in reprobating the decapitation of the French King," Edmund Randolph
reported, and saw this as a powerful reason to reject France's appeals for the
United States to enter the war against Britain. When the Reign of Terror out-
lawed public worship in late 1793, after the French revolutionaries had de-
frocked or killed hundreds of Catholic priests, religious Americans, including
the deeply religious Henry, reacted with horror. His grandson and biographer
wrote that "Mr. Henry, who was deeply pious, and who realized as few men
did the danger to the republican institutions of his country from the undermining influence of French infidelity, set himself to counteracting its baneful
influence by every means in his power. This fact will prove to be a key to
much of his subsequent political course." Whatever the cause, Henry's initial
support of the French Revolution had turned into deep suspicion and with it
a growing concern over the embrace of France by Democratic-Republicans.[76]

In the late 1790s, as Napoleon became a military leader in France, many
Democratic-Republicans warmly embraced his growing string of battlefield
successes; perhaps the French Revolution could yet succeed in bringing reform to Europe, and Napoleon's victories dampened the perceived anti-French
leanings of Federalists. Yet, by 1798, Henry warned that Napoleon would follow the path of Caesar, taking power for himself. Given the long history of repression in France, with a citizenry "debased by a long despotism," the French
people in the 1790s were "incapable of forming a correct and just estimate of
rational liberty," Henry explained. As the end of the decade neared, he cautioned: "I should not be surprised, if *the very man* at whose victories you now
rejoice [Napoleon], should, Caesar-like, subvert the liberties of his country."
Long before most Democratic-Republicans acknowledged the excesses of the
French Revolution and the danger of a rising Napoleon, Henry did.[77]

While retired to southwestern Virginia, Henry was still well informed on
national and international affairs. Henry's growing concerns with the excesses
of the French Revolution moderated his apprehensions over the Constitution and inclined him against the Democratic-Republicans. Combined with
deep concerns over Hamilton's financial plans and aggrandizement of federal
power, Henry was increasingly alienated from "parties." As Washington's second term neared its end, Henry, in the first letter that he had written to his

former compatriot since ratification, assured Washington that while he had "bid adieu to federal & Antifederal" he was increasingly concerned with the serious threat posed by rising partisanship and how rising political factions could destroy the nation.[78]

Offers of Political Office: Henry and Washington

In 1796, Patrick Henry was again (for a sixth time) elected governor of Virginia by a very Democratic-Republican General Assembly. Feeling his age and with a bevy of young children for whom he hoped to provide a sound financial legacy, Henry declined the honor. The election is noteworthy, however; Henry had clearly not lost his political standing because of his alleged Federalist "apostasy" and support for Alexander Hamilton, as some later claimed.[79]

In fact, throughout this period, Henry remained remarkably popular and influential. President Washington and then President Adams repeatedly tried to entice Henry to join the federal government. Henry was offered a position on the Supreme Court, the office of secretary of state, and ambassadorships to France or Spain. In addition to offering him the governorship, Virginia's legislature offered Henry the position of U.S. senator after his retirement, with a Philadelphia (Federalist) newspaper reporting, "No measure of Government could have been more popular, than the appointment of this Veteran Defender, of the rights and liberties of the people."[80]

In 1796, there was serious talk of making Henry a vice-presidential candidate with John Adams (who, himself, was unpopular with high Federalists like Hamilton). An Adams-Henry ticket would have been unbeatable. "Henry was one of the few figures with the potential to win something close to a Washington-like national consensus victory," a historian of the 1796 election notes. The talk was serious enough that Henry wrote public letters urging voters not to waste votes on him as he had no intention of serving as vice president. In his effort to undermine Adams, Alexander Hamilton even had Henry sounded out on his willingness to run for president, but John Marshall reported that he was "unwilling to embark on the business."[81]

These offers of office provide several significant insights into Henry's thinking as well as the politics of the 1790s. First, they speak to Henry's political significance during the early republic. Very few other Americans were so ardently solicited for such a plethora of high positions (by interests across the political spectrum). Second, they demonstrate Henry's continued political popularity. Even in the 1790s, he was the most popular politician in Virginia (Washington excepted). Federalists sought to trade on that popularity, even if, as some Democratic-Republicans grumbled, their efforts were cynical. Finally, the efforts by Washington to solicit Henry's support put the lie to Jefferson's later claims that Henry and Washington loathed each other, a lie that Jefferson conveniently promoted after the 1799 deaths of both in an effort to taint their memories. These latter two points are worth considering in more detail.[82]

Federalists were not the only ones who sought to trade on Henry's popularity. Jefferson had despised Henry since the abortive 1781 investigation into Jefferson's governorship, an investigation that seemed to question Jefferson's competence, bravery, and honor and for which Jefferson blamed Henry. The injury cut especially deeply; Jefferson confessed to James Monroe that the investigation "had inflicted a wound on my spirit which will only be cured by the all-healing grave." In 1785, Jefferson snubbed Henry's effort to reconcile. Yet, in the mid-1790s, Jefferson also thought that the emerging political parties were engaged in a virtual battle-to-the-death for the soul of America. Not only was the republic at stake, Jefferson believed, but republicanism itself. In that battle, Jefferson was willing to swallow his considerable pride. In 1795, he wrote to a political supporter who was on good terms with Henry and asked his correspondent to "satisfy him [Henry] if you please that there is no remain of disagreeable sentiment towards him on my part. I was once sincerely affectioned towards him and it accords with my philosophy to encourage the tranquilizing passions." Henry, perhaps remembering Jefferson's snub in 1785, did not respond. Still, Jefferson bristled, later writing to Monroe suggesting that Federalist efforts to recruit Henry were intended to create a schism among Virginia Democratic-Republicans, obviously a very real fear. "Most assiduous court is paid to P.H. He has been offered every thing which they knew he would not accept. Some impression is thought to be made, but we do not believe it is radical. If they thought they could count upon him they would run him for their V.P. their first object being to produce a schism in this state." Little did Jefferson know that there was an abortive effort to enlist Henry as vice president.[83]

Jefferson also told Henry's biographer that

> Genl Washington flattered him by an appointment to a mission to Spain, which however he declined; and by proposing to him the office of Secretary of state, on the most earnest sollicitation of Genl Henry Lee, who pledged himself that Henry should not accept it. for Genl Washington knew that he was entirely unqualified for it; & moreover that his self-esteem had never suffered him to act as second to any man on earth. I had this fact from information; . . . because, after my retiring from the

office of Secretary of State, Genl Washington passed the papers to mr Henry through my hands.

After their deaths, Jefferson claimed that Henry had a "thorough contempt & hatred of Genl Washington," but Jefferson did so at the same time that he argued (fancifully) that Henry had become a great supporter of Alexander Hamilton, Henry's "idol." This claim was accompanied by the effort to associate Henry with the fraudulent land sales surrounding the Yazoo controversy, another canard. In fact, the correspondence between Henry and Washington demonstrates that Jefferson was fabricating for political effect—and history.[84]

Rather than offering Henry only positions that he knew the former governor would not accept, the evidence suggests that Washington was genuinely trying to bring Henry into his administration. In 1794, Washington wrote to Henry Lee that he felt a "strong inducement on public & private grounds, to invite Mr. Henry into any employment under the General Government to which his inclination might lead."[85]

For his part, it is true that Henry was concerned by early reports of "court" practice in the Washington administration, for example Washington's rather formal levies and John Adams's aborted effort to have "royal" titles used for the president and vice president. More importantly, though, Henry became concerned with reports that Washington—whom he had idolized since the Revolution—had been personally critical of him. This malicious political gossip had caused any temporary alienation that did exist. Before efforts to enlist Henry in the Washington administration had any hope of success, lingering suspicions had to be addressed, and in doing so, the great respect that the two revolutionaries had for each other again became apparent.[86]

In 1794, Henry Lee wrote Washington that he had spoken to Patrick Henry at length in an effort to enlist him in Washington's administration, but Henry was apparently somewhat cool to the idea, being particularly concerned with reports that Washington had called him a "a factious seditious character." Lee wrote Washington, "assured in my own mind that his opinions are groundless I have uniformly combated them, & lament that my endeavours have been unavailing—He seems to be deeply & sorely effected." Lee continued, "It is very much to be regretted, for he is a man of positive virtue as well as of transcendent talents, & was it not for his feelings above expressed, I verily beleive he would be found among the most active supporters of your administration—Excuse me for mentioning this matter to you, I have long wished to do it in the hope that it will lead to a refutation of the sentiments entertained by Mr H."[87]

Washington wrote back promptly avowing his respect for Henry at length, and assuring Lee, and Patrick Henry, that reports that he had criticized Henry were false:

> With solemn truth then I can declare, that I never expressed such senti- ments of that Gentlemen, as from your letter, he has been led to believe. I had heard, it is true, that he retained his enmity to the Constitution; but with very peculiar pleasure I learnt from Colo. Coles (who I am sure will recollect it) that Mr Henry was acquiescent in his conduct, & that though he could not give up his opinions respecting the Constitu- tion, yet, unless he should be called upon by official duty he wd express no sentiment unfriendly to the exercise of the powers of a government which had been chosen by a Majority of the people; or words to this effect. . . . It is evident therefore, that these reports are propogated with evil intentions—to create personal differences. On the question of the Constitution Mr Henry & myself, it is well known, have been of dif- ferent opinions; but personally, I have always respected and esteemed him; nay more, I have conceived myself under obligations to him for the friendly manner in which he transmitted to me some insiduous anony- mous writings that were sent to him in the close of the year 1777, with a view to embark him in the opposition that was forming against me at that time.

(The reference to Henry's support during the Revolution related to the Con- way Cabal, when some military officers and politicians sought, unsuccessfully, to have Washington replaced as commander-in-chief. Henry forcefully sup- ported the general at that time, sending Washington a nominally anonymous letter from Benjamin Rush supporting the conspiracy.)[88]

Later that year, declining Washington's proffered appointment as minister to Spain, Henry was quick to note, "I cannot forebear to express my highest obligations to the president for his favorable sentiments."[89]

Henry Lee, though, continued to solicit Patrick Henry's involvement in the Washington administration. Henry assured Washington's confidante that "since the adoption of the present constitution I have generally moved in a narrow circle. But in that I have never omitted to inculcate a strict adherence to the principles of it [the Constitution]." Rejecting the offers, Henry assured Lee nonetheless that Washington's confidence was "highly flattering indeed." Still, he insisted that the only thing that could draw him forth from retirement was if his service was "necessary for the safety of the country." He concluded by asking Lee to convey his "best respects and duty to the President."[90]

Henry's continued reverence for Washington and anger at factions that attacked the president were quite public. In 1796, newspapers reported that Henry had said that

> if anything could make him execrate and damn a republican government,
> it would be the abuse of, and the ingratitude with which one of the greatest
> characters the world ever saw, has been treated.—And if he should
> outlive that *great* and *good man,* he would once more come into the Assembly
> of Virginia, on purpose to have a *monument* erected at *Mount
> Vernon,* inscribed with a summary of the virtuous deeds performed by
> as pure a patriot, and as true a friend to the liberties of mankind as ever
> lived, to which the students of the country, should be bound to make annual
> pilgrimages, in order that their minds might receive just impressions
> of the true history of the founder of their liberties, to the end, that they
> may be stimulated to *emulate* his *uncommon talents and virtues.*[91]

The discussion in 1795 when Washington offered Henry the position of secretary of state is particularly interesting. After Jefferson retired as secretary of state in 1793, Washington had difficulty filling the position. At the same time, Washington was also seeking to fill the position of attorney general (after Edmund Randolph resigned in disgrace in the face of accusations that he had sought a bribe from France), and he did not want to offer both positions to Virginians. Hoping to expedite the process, Washington entrusted Edward Carrington and John Marshall with several letters requesting that James Innes accept the position of attorney general and, if he declined, that Henry be delivered a letter asking him to be secretary of state. Having consulted with Marshall, Carrington wrote Washington that they decided to approach Henry first, although they thought that "his non-acceptance, from domestic considerations" likely. Still, they thought making the offer could only redound to the government's, and Washington's, benefit. This was not a case of offering him a position only because they knew that he would not accept it; rather, they suspected that he would not accept the position because of his familial obligations, but would have been thrilled if he had, assuring Washington that "a more deadly blow" could not be delivered to opponents in Virginia than Henry's joining the administration.[92]

Washington's October 1795 letter to Henry evidences real warmth and support:

> It would be uncandid not to inform you that this office has been offered to
> others; but it is as true that it was from a conviction in my mind that you

would not accept it (untill tuesday last in a conversation with General, late Govr, Lee, he dropped Sentiments which made it less doubtful) that it was not offered first to you. I need scarcely add that, if this appointment could be made to comport with your own inclination, it would be as pleasing to me, as I believe it would be acceptable to the public.

Washington openly commiserated with Henry about challenges facing the government in an increasingly partisan environment: "I persuade myself, Sir, it has not escaped your observation, that a crisis is approaching, that must, if it cannot be arrested, Soon decide whether order and good Government Shall be preserved, or anarchy and confusion ensue." Washington concluded, "I am Satisfied that these Sentiments cannot be otherwise than congenial to your own—your aid therefore in carrying them into effect would be flattering and pleasing to Dear Sir your most obedient and very Humble Servant."[93]

Henry responded with even more warmth, assuring the president that his letter made "a deep Impression on my Mind." He apologized for his inability to accept the position: "To disobey the Call of my Country into Service when her venerable Chief makes a Demand of it, must be a Crime, unless the most substantial Reasons justify declining it." Recognizing that their relationship had been strained by Henry's opposition to ratification of the Constitution, Henry was heartened by "the friendly & unreserved Sentiments you have been pleased to express towards me." Henry told Washington that he would agree to serve only in a crisis and explained when and why he, the great antifederalist, would defend the constitutional government:

> [I]n the Circle of my Friends [I] have often expressed my Fears of Disunion amongst the States from Collision of Interest; but especially from the banefull Effects of Faction—In that Case the most I can say is, that if my Country is destined in my Day to encounter the Horrors of Anarchy, every power of Mind & Body which I possess will be exerted in support of the Government under which I live & which has been fairly sanctioned by my Country men. I should be unworthy the Character of a Republican or an honest man if I withheld my best & most zealous Efforts, because I opposed the Constitution in its unaltered Form.

As the majority of the people had "fairly sanctioned" the government, Henry felt obligated to defend it; a republican government demanded no less of a loyal opposition. Noting that he understood that Washington was grappling with "Uneasiness" over political events, Henry assured the president that "I did hope & pray that it might be your Lot to feel as little of that, as the most favour'd condition of Humanity can experience." He sent his former Revolutionary War colleague "best Regards which are due to a well spent & long Life. . . . With the most sincere Regard & the highest Esteem."[94]

All of this is important context for seeking to understand the coming crisis of 1798–1799 and Henry's treatment in subsequent history, especially efforts to characterize Washington and Henry as foes. It is true that there was some temporary alienation between Henry and Washington after their 1787 exchange concerning the proposed U.S. Constitution; ratification battles left some hard feelings. This was the nadir of their personal relations. Mostly, though, their work took them in different directions for much of the 1790s but did not result in a personal animosity, much less hatred.

If further evidence of the excellent relationship between Henry and Washington was needed, one could look to the latter's statement shortly after Henry's untimely death in June of 1799, noting that political machinations had been made against their friendship:

> My breast never harboured a suspicion that Mr. Henry was unfriendly to me, although I had reason to believe that the same Spirit which was at work to destroy all confidence in the Public functionaries, was not less busy in poisoning private fountains and sowing the seeds of distrust amg men of the same Political sentiments. Mr. Henry had given me the most unequivocal proof whilst I had the honor to command the Troops of the United States in their Revolutionary struggle, that he was not to be worked upon by Intriguers; and not conscious that I had furnished any cause for it, I could not suppose that without a cause, he had become my enemy since.[95]

Henry had continued to act in "a constitutional way" to seek reform, and he abided by that commitment throughout the 1790s. Failing to obtain the reforms that he had sought, he continued to protest what he perceived as unconstitutional expansions of federal power. Even after he left political office, he was an active, observant, and, importantly, moderate commentator on the leading political controversies of the day, from the Democratic-Republican Societies to the Jay Treaty. Eschewing a disruptive party politics that put party over country, he hoped to live in a peaceful retirement. He repeatedly declined appointment to some of the highest offices in the land, but at the same time repeatedly indicated that he would again enter public service if his country, "fairly sanctioned" by his co-citizens, needed him.

4

The Alien and Sedition Acts

Jefferson's Dilemma and Radical Response

T he infancy of the new American republic was shaped in critical respects by factors beyond its borders, in particular, the French Revolution and the resulting almost constant conflict between Britain and
France that culminated with the conquests of Napoleon Bonaparte and his
ultimate defeat at Waterloo in 1815. Despite Washington's neutrality proclama-
tion, both France and Britain demanded supplies from America, vehemently
objected to U.S. merchant ships supplying their enemy, and sought the new
nation as an ally. Both tried to block American ships from delivering supplies
to their enemy's ports by seizing ships and supplies. Tensions rose as President
Washington struggled to maintain his seemingly simple policy of neutrality. To
do so, he sought to negotiate treaties with each nation that would allow U.S.
trade to continue and keep the United States out of the war.

These conflicts created the conditions for the rise of American political
parties and for Henry's final political battle to defend America's constitutional government.

The Quasi-War with France and the XYZ Affair

A Federalist Senate ratified the 1795 Jay Treaty to keep the peace with Britain; nevertheless, the treaty was wildly unpopular. John Jay quipped that he
could travel the length of the country lighted by his burning effigies. Jefferson,
a private citizen again after resigning from Washington's cabinet in 1793 and
before being elected vice president in 1796, denounced the treaty, calling it
an "infamous act, which is nothing more than a treaty of alliance between
England and the Anglomen of this country against the legislature and people

of the United States." Riots erupted; Alexander Hamilton, himself recently re-signed as secretary of treasury, was actually bloodied in one riot when hit by a thrown rock.[1]

France saw the Jay Treaty as an insult. It had supported the United States in its struggle against Britain when the American Revolution hung in the balance, and from France's perspective, its 1778 treaty with the infant nation required U.S. support for France's war with their old enemy. More viscerally, revolutionary France operated on the principle that the "friend of my enemy" must be an enemy. By 1796, France started seizing U.S. ships trading with Britain, taking well over 300 by the end of 1798. Beyond direct losses in lives, ships, and cargo, marine insurance rates skyrocketed and commerce was seriously impaired. In the midst of these heightened tensions, France refused even to receive Charles C. Pinckney, President Washington's ambassador sent to negotiate a treaty to maintain the peace.[2]

When John Adams was sworn in as president on March 4, 1797, this "Quasi-War" with France presented an immediate national security crisis. A shooting war threatened. President Adams hastily called the first ever special session of Congress for May 1797 to seek authorization for a military buildup in response to French aggressions and to prepare America's very weak defenses for a possible war, a move heartily endorsed by Federalist leaders and denounced by Democratic-Republicans.

At the same time, over the objection of many in his own party, and notwithstanding the affront to Minister Pinckney, Adams decided to send a special, bipartisan peace delegation to France. Naively, the new president initially hoped that James Madison, a leader of the emerging Democratic-Republican party, would head the delegation. While that hope proved unpopular with both parties, and with Madison, Adams continued to buck his own party and push for a bipartisan peace delegation, in July 1797 sending Elbridge Gerry from Massachusetts (a Democratic-Republican) and John Marshall of Virginia (a Federalist) and reappointing Pinckney of South Carolina who had remained in Europe awaiting further instruction.

Unfortunately, when the three U.S. ministers sought to present their credentials to authorities in France, they met a series of roadblocks and insults from a French government newly emboldened by the victories of the young General Napoleon Bonaparte against the Austrian Empire. For five months, the U.S. delegation was prevented from even meeting officially with the French foreign minister, Charles Maurice de Talleyrand-Perigord. Finally, in late 1797, Talleyrand's agents presented the commissioners with three demands if they wanted negotiations to proceed: the diplomats had to denounce President

Adams's May 16, 1797, speech to Congress calling for preparation for a possible war; France had to receive a large loan to assist its war with Britain; and a personal bribe of £50,000 had to be paid.

Each of these demands was an insult to American honor, particularly the demand that the United States pay a bribe to enter negotiations. The U.S. diplomats, flabbergasted, were assured that such payments were common in Europe, but that hardly assuaged their boiling anger. The American delegation pointedly refused to meet any of the conditions, and negotiations on broader issues never really began. After John Marshall sent several detailed dispatches to President Adams outlining France's perfidy, and after a final contest of wills with French officials who threatened to detain them in France, Marshall sailed for home in April 1798 and Pinckney left Paris. Against their advice, Elbridge Gerry, the sole Democratic-Republican member of the delegation (and one of the great gadflies of early American history), succumbed to French pressure to remain in hope of salvaging negotiations, a decision for which he was strongly criticized (although his presence may have played a role in resolving the crisis several years later).[3]

The French insult met a violent patriotic reaction in America. Upon his return, Marshall was feted as a hero; at one dinner, he was greeted with the toast, "Millions for Defense, but Not a Cent for Tribute!"—the slogan became a Federalist rallying cry. Democratic-Republicans downplayed the controversy, believing that Federalists, including President Adams, were exaggerating the dispute for political gain. They demanded official documents explaining what had happened. In April 1798, when Adams published the diplomatic correspondence from Marshall and Pinckney, rather than calming the waters as Jeffersonians hoped, it further inflamed passions. The insult to the U.S. ministers and offense to American honor became known as the XYZ Affair—Talleyrand's three agents who conveyed French demands to the U.S. ambassadors were initially simply referred to as X, Y, and Z in the diplomatic correspondence. Evidencing the extent of partisan rhetoric engulfing the country, Madison wrote to Jefferson that "no one who has not surrendered his reason can believe them [John Adams and the Federalist Senate] sincere in wishing to avoid extremities with the French Republic." (History would prove Madison wrong, at least with respect to John Adams.)[4]

With American ships still being seized in the raging Quasi-War and American peace negotiators having been insulted and threatened, Federalists believed that the country faced a likely war with France and Napoleon's seemingly unstoppable armies. While Congress had balked at military preparations a year earlier, in March 1798, legislators responded forcefully to Adams's new request, authorizing a dramatic increase in the size of the U.S. army and navy, including funding thirty-seven warships (several of which, ironically, were instrumental in Jefferson's war against Barbary pirates years later). Trade was embargoed, and attacks on French ships striking U.S. merchants authorized. George Washington agreed, reluctantly, to come out of retirement to command the army should France invade but only on condition that he could choose his own subordinates. When Adams equally reluctantly agreed, Washington chose Alexander Hamilton as second-in-command, a decision that annoyed Adams (who despised Hamilton) and scared Jefferson and Madison (who believed Hamilton favored a British system, perhaps monarchy).[5]

The threat of war and military preparations left Americans deeply divided. Federalists insisted that, in such a foreign policy crisis, anyone challenging government policy lacked "loyalty, religion, conscience, or any other honorable motive." Many Federalists believed that once the people elected a government, it was the duty of responsible citizens to accept government decisions, especially in a crisis, at least until the next election; this was the only way to guarantee majority rule, they argued. Benjamin Rush, for example, had claimed during the ratification debates that while sovereign power is derived from the people, "they possess [that power] only on the days of their elections. After this, it is the property of their rulers, nor can they exercise or resume it, unless it is abused." Only this understanding would lead "to order and good government." In a national crisis like the Quasi-War with France, these obligations became overwhelming, Federalists believed.[6]

Democratic-Republicans, on the other hand, struggled with how to express opposition appropriately. To some extent, the Democratic-Republican party owed its existence to opposition to just the type of quiet obedience to government policy preached by some Federalists, from the lifting of liberty poles to Democratic-Republican Societies formed in the early 1790s. Yet, with limited experience on how to oppose administration policy during a crisis, they struggled with how a "loyal opposition" should behave. Some went too far. Several Democratic-Republican militia officers reportedly threatened that they would fight for France were an invasion to occur (a story reprinted in newspapers). A Philadelphia printer told Daniel Morgan, Federalist congressman from Virginia, that Democratic-Republican Senator Littleton Walker Tazewell of Virginia had blurted out that France would be justified in landing an army; the editor added that he would not fight for an Adams administration. A Democratic-Republican newspaper in Kentucky suggested that if war struck Americans should not support the administration, a greater threat to freedom than France, and flee to the west. In other instances, Democratic-Republicans protested Federalist policies but pointedly affirmed that they would support the United States in the event of war (implicitly suggesting that earlier threats by some of their colleagues were taken seriously).[7]

While some of this was undoubtedly political hyperbole—another member of Congress insisted that Tazewell was joking, for example—this threatened opposition roused righteous indignation, and paranoia, among Federalists; Democratic-Republicans were threatening treason as the risk of war loomed. John Quincy Adams, serving as ambassador in the Hague, wrote to his father in April of 1797 that "from the present conduct of the [French] Directory, it cannot be questioned but that they are determined upon a war with the government of the United States. There are also numerous proofs that in the prosecution of this war they are preparing to derive support from a part of the American people." A "southern republic . . . in alliance with France" was allegedly contemplated. The notorious "Y" from the XYZ Affair boasted about a "French party" in America that would "throw the blame" of any failure in negotiations upon the Federalists. Such attacks and reports fed an escalating fear among Federalists.[8]

In 1798, political disputes played out in the streets. There were riots. Fist-fights between Democratic-Republicans and Federalists proliferated. Watching violent protests and an estimated 10,000 people taking to the streets of Philadelphia, President Adams feared for his life and had arms brought to his home as an estimated 1,000 people gathered there to protest Federalist actions. (Adams gathered with friends inside the house, later reporting that he was prepared to fight and sacrifice his life if need be.) While Adams was prone to grandiose statements, there was a real fear of a war at the same time when civil discord seemed to threaten the government and some members of the political opposition spoke treason. The Democratic-Republican press contributed to the agitation (or caused it, in many people's minds). Abigail Adams (reflecting perhaps the not uncommon tendency of a spouse to respond angrily to attacks on a partner) referred to the "vile incendaries" of the press, "most wicked and base, voilent & caluminiating abuse" of Federalist officeholders.[9]

The Alien and Sedition Acts: Prosecuting Political Opposition

France had insulted America's peace negotiators; war threatened, and do-mestic dissent increased the danger—the latter made real in the streets of the nation's capital and by an alleged "French party" in the country. The threat from foreign agents seemed particularly serious in Philadelphia where French nationals (many having fled to the United States after the French and Haitian revolutions) accounted for as much as 10 percent of the population. Federalists insisted that something had to be done.[10]

In the summer of 1798, the Federalist-dominated Congress passed several laws intended to respond to the danger from possible foreign agents operating in the United States, the Naturalization and Alien Acts (called the Alien Acts). These laws made it more difficult for immigrants to become citizens (increasing the residency period from five to fourteen years, for example) and gave the president unilateral power to expel any alien, without benefit of trial, whom he believed was dangerous.

While the Alien Acts were roundly denounced by Democratic-Republicans, gauging their impact is more complex. No one was actually deported under the acts. But over a score of prosecutions/deportations were contemplated, especially of aliens working on Democratic-Republican newspapers; several deportations orders were signed by Timothy Pickering, Adams's secretary of state, although not executed. The laws certainly had an *in terrorem* effect, and a large number of Frenchmen—fifteen boatloads by one account—voluntarily left the country after the laws' adoption.[11]

Even more portentously, Congress adopted the Sedition Act of 1798, making it a crime to publish or speak anything "false, scandalous or malicious" against the president or Congress or to "unlawfully combine or conspire together, with the intent to oppose any measure or measures of the government." In essence, the Sedition Act made it a crime to criticize the president or Congress (but, tellingly, not the vice president, now Thomas Jefferson). While the law made truth a defense against a claim of sedition, the "truth" of most political criticism simply was not readily subject to proof; opinions could be prosecuted. Those in opposition could literally be silenced with fines and incarceration.[12]

Today, the Sedition Act is broadly understood to have violated the First Amendment's protections for freedom of speech and of the press, but in the early republic, the scope of free speech and press was less clear. In Britain, freedom of the press generally only prevented prior restraint of a publication; sedition could be prosecuted, and sedition was actionable in many U.S. states under the common law. During debates over adoption of a Bill of Rights, Jefferson himself had argued that "a declaration that the federal government will never restrain the presses from printing any thing they please, will not take away the liability of the printers for false facts printed." Even in that vein, the Sedition Act ostensibly liberalized the common law since truth was not a defense against a charge of sedition in Britain.[13]

In any case, with the XYZ Affair fresh in mind, and the very real fear of war with Napoleonic France, the Adams administration and Federalists had support for aggressive action to restrain what was seen as dangerous dissent. In fact, these laws were initially very popular. President Adams, perhaps for the only time in his political career, became personally popular. (A surly character at the best of times, he was intoxicated with his newfound popularity and took to wearing a military uniform, complete with sword, to public events.) In fairness, President Adams did not propose the Alien and Sedition Acts, but his secretary of state, Timothy Pickering, with Adams's apparent approval, used the laws actively, personally "scann[ing] the columns of numerous Republican newspapers to detect possible material for sedition cases" and advised district attorneys to do the same.[14]

For many years, historians reported that the Sedition Act resulted in only fourteen indictments, to which three common-law indictments for sedition are often added. One historian termed those prosecutions "paltry." This suggests a significant but hardly earth-shattering "reign of witches," to use Jefferson's term. All of which begs the question: Why such alarm?[15]

More recent scholarship, however, has shown that the Sedition Act posed a far more serious threat than historians had seen. Beyond the fourteen commonly reported cases, at least twenty-five additional sedition cases were filed. Over 120 individuals were indicted. Dozens of Democratic-Republican newspaper editors were targeted, many jailed, more fined. Scores more were arrested for conspiracy to violate the act (mostly in the context of Fries's Rebellion, a rather ineffective 1799 tax revolt that included protests against the Sedition Act and arrests targeted at newspaper editors). Federalists planned as many as an additional dozen indictments of selected newspaper editors.[16]

Of course, newspapers were not pursued at random. At the time, almost all newspapers were firmly affiliated with either the Federalists or Democratic-Republicans. (Jefferson, for example, while secretary of state, had enticed Philip Freneau to open the *National Gazette* in Philadelphia by providing a State Department printing contract and otherwise encouraging the new publication.) Enforcement of the Sedition Act targeted communities where Federalists needed protection and rising Democratic-Republicans needed to be suppressed. In 1798, editors of leading opposition newspapers in Philadelphia (*Aurora*) and New York (*Time Piece*)—the nation's two largest cities—were arrested and charged with seditious libel. (Benjamin Franklin Bache, Benjamin Franklin's grandson, was the editor of the *Aurora*.) Pickering often intervened with local officials to suggest indictments to promote Federalist political aims.

Jefferson—vice president and leader of a political party—was so concerned that he might be caught in the web of indictments that he told some correspondents that he could not communicate freely in writing and urged Elbridge Gerry to burn part of a letter after reading it (a letter to which Jefferson would not sign his name). While Jefferson could be paranoid, Pickering and Secretary of Treasury Oliver Wolcott Jr. did in fact intercept some of his mail.[17]

Once indicted, defendants faced a very high likelihood of conviction; in only one case was a defendant acquitted, that being in a jury trial. Yet, Federalist judges managed to convince many defendants, without legal counsel, to waive their right to a jury trial. Those prosecuted faced prison sentences, fines (and forced sale of property or indefinite imprisonment if fines could not be paid), and the necessity of obtaining financial sureties against future "sedition." In many cases, newspapers were forced to close.[18]

Federalists also brought state sedition cases against Democratic-Republican newspapers. While those state cases did not raise the same constitutional objections as federal cases, since the First Amendment did not apply to the states at the time, they fed the threat to free political discussion and heightened the fears of Jefferson and the political opposition.[19]

These prosecutions left Democratic-Republican leaders with deep foreboding. The threat to free communication of ideas and public oversight of the government struck at what Jefferson understood to be the foundation of any free nation. Citizens must have access to information and the ability to criticize government action if they are to control the government and prevent abuses. Elections would be meaningless if people could not openly debate government policies and officials. Newspapers were essential. In 1798, as Congress planned the Sedition Act, Jefferson warned Madison that if Democratic-Republican newspapers fail "republicanism will be entirely brow-beaten." Madison agreed; free exchange of ideas was central to building public opinion and government oversight, including "a circulation of newspapers through the entire body of the people." Jefferson rhapsodized to one supporter that "to preserve the freedom of the human mind . . . & freedom of the press, every spirit should be ready to devote itself to martyrdom." Confirming Democratic-Republican fears, a new wave of prosecutions was launched in late 1799 to silence newspapers before the 1800 election. Jefferson bemoaned that "this onset on the presses is to cripple & suppress the republican efforts during the campaign which is coming."[20]

With the government less than a decade old, freedom of the press was under direct assault by a partisan administration seeking to silence political dissent and maintain its power by indicting scores of newspaper editors. This was a real crisis, Jefferson's "reign of witches." With the nation still in its infancy, the attack on the press put the democratic process itself in danger. Jefferson and his supporters feared for the republic. Outrage, though, was not action.

What to Do?

With Democratic-Republican newspaper editors facing arrests from Virginia through New Hampshire (Federalists did not attempt any prosecutions in the Deep South or west of the Appalachians), Jefferson and his followers were left with complicated and difficult choices.

Normally, in the face of such government abuse of power, opponents would mobilize the electorate, kick those who adopted such policies out of office, change the laws. . . . As Jefferson wrote a few years later, "Should things go wrong at any time, the people will set them right by the peaceable exercise of their elective rights." This, though, posed a problem in 1798: First, with the Quasi-War and threat of even more active conflict with France adding to the insult of the XYZ Affair, public opinion was in high dudgeon. Criticizing the government seemed unpatriotic. This was neither the first nor, unfortunately, the last time that a foreign crisis would permit a government to abuse power. As Madison had warned in the early 1790s, foreign policy dangers could support a government assault on liberties: "fear & hatred of other nations, the greatest cement, always appealed to by rulers when they wish to impose burdens or carry unpopular points."[21]

There was an even bigger problem. Jefferson and Madison feared that serious restrictions on a free press fundamentally threatened the ability of Democratic-Republicans to conduct a fulsome political campaign and enjoy a free and fair election. With each Democratic-Republican editor indicted, and with the threat of more to come, Federalists were attacking the electoral process itself. The problem was not unanticipated. In debates over the Sedition Act, John Nicholas of Virginia admonished the House of Representatives that restrictions on newspapers undermined "the elective principle, by taking away the information necessary to election." In essence, "there would be no difference between it [press restrictions] and a total denial of the right of election, but in the degree of usurpation." John Fowler, congressman from Kentucky, warned that "the conduct of the public servants has been screened from that public investigation" by the Sedition Act; without a free press, "it is impossible that we, my fellow citizens, can exercise our high privilege of voting." Madison, too, noted that "the right of electing the members of the government, constitutes more particularly the essence of a free and responsible government.

The value and efficacy of this right, depends on the knowledge of the comparative merits and demerits of the candidates for public trust; and on the equal freedom, consequently, of examining and discussing those merits and demerits of the candidates respectively."[22]

Although the Sedition Act was scheduled to expire in March 1801 (conveniently after President Adams's first term ended), there would be two congressional elections and a presidential election while it was in force. And, if the Federalists won, the act could be extended, or even more repressive laws adopted. This fear gripped Jefferson and Madison. Although Jefferson had a great faith in the wisdom of the electorate, *if* it was informed, with elections tainted by press restraints, relying solely on the electoral process seemed dangerous. It also required patience as arrests proliferated and more and more Democratic-Republican editors were jailed.

Adding to their anxiety, while juries, provided for in the Constitution and the Sixth Amendment, were intended to be a bulwark against violation of citizens' rights in criminal cases, in 1798, the choice of jurors was controlled by political appointees in most states, and perhaps it was no coincidence that most prosecutions occurred in states where judges could hand-pick juries. Albert Gallatin, a Pennsylvania Democratic-Republican leader, asked: "when the supposed crimes to be punished were a libel against the Administration, what security of a fair trial remained to a citizen, when the jury was liable to be packed by the Administration, when the same men were to be judges and parties?" Jefferson prepared a petition seeking to eliminate court control over jury selection in Virginia convinced that if Virginia adopted this reform "either Congress will agree to conform their courts to the same rule, or they will be loaded with an odium in the eyes of the people generally which will force the matter through," but nothing came of it. (This is why Jefferson's first inaugural address promoted the importance of "trial by juries impartially selected.")[23]

An alternative to electoral victory or jury trials for Democratic-Republicans was to file a lawsuit to have the Alien and Sedition Acts (or at least the latter) declared unconstitutional. After all, Jefferson, Madison, Henry, Marshall, and other leaders argued before and after ratification that the courts would strike down unconstitutional exercises of congressional power to protect American freedoms. Gouverneur Morris had made the point at the Philadelphia Convention, reminding delegates that "a law that ought to be negatived will be set aside in the Judiciary department." Jefferson had insisted that a Bill of Rights was needed in the first place because it would put a "legal check" against congressional abuse "in the hands of the judiciary." Patrick Henry had made the same argument during ratification: "I take it as the highest encomium on this country that the acts of the Legislature, if unconstitutional, are liable to be opposed by the Judiciary."[24]

Unfortunately, in 1798, when arguably an independent judiciary enforcing the Bill of Rights against congressional usurpations was most needed, a host of problems advised against a lawsuit to have the acts declared unconstitutional. At a practical level, every one of the sitting federal judges had been appointed by Federalists; the tradition of judicial independence had not been firmly established, and a bevy of Federalist judges had already urged convictions under the Sedition Act—some in quite an outrageous manner. While the Sedition Act was never directly tested in the Supreme Court, by the end of 1800, seven federal judges affirmed its constitutionality and, if one includes all of the recently rediscovered prosecutions, five of the six Supreme Court justices presided over Sedition Act cases without questioning its constitutionality. Samuel Chase, the most notorious Federalist partisan on the Court (and the only U.S. justice ever impeached—albeit not convicted by the Senate), "turned his circuit tour into a search and destroy mission for sedition," one historian concludes.[25]

Democratic-Republicans probably correctly concluded that bringing a case to challenge the constitutionality of the Alien and Sedition Acts would be a waste of time. Even worse, if they lost, as they almost certainly would, it would appear to legitimate the laws.[26]

What, then, were opponents of the Alien and Sedition Acts to do as editors were arrested and newspapers quashed?

In 1798, Democratic-Republicans saw few options. They felt that the nation was at a critical crossroads and if Federalist attacks on the free press were allowed to continue, the nation—and everything that the patriots of 1776 had fought for—would fail. The threat imagined by a beleaguered Jefferson was that Federalist hegemony, supported by the Alien and Sedition Acts and backed by a standing army (with Alexander Hamilton in command), would empower an aristocracy, if not a monarchy.[27]

Jefferson was a politician entangled in a very real crisis in 1798, and a desperate one. With other avenues of redress seemingly foreclosed, in the summer of 1798, Jefferson and Madison and their allies settled on a third option: encouraging states to challenge the laws and the federal government.

In broad terms, this approach had been used before. Patrick Henry had led Virginia in protest against Hamilton's assumption of the states' Revolutionary War debts, for example. This time, however, with the stakes high and the situation dire, Jeffersonians concluded that a mere protest was not enough. Rather, they decided that the states should threaten open resistance to federal authority. How far they intended to go with this strategy is not clear; some of their correspondence suggests that it was not clear to them, and they maintained a careful ambiguity. Perhaps they were floating a political trial balloon. Perhaps they felt that they had no other choice. Perhaps, confronted by a very real threat to freedom of the press and to the electoral process, and with few other options, they overreacted in fear and desperation. Regardless of the reason, Patrick Henry, George Washington, and others saw the Jeffersonians stoking a fire that could raise a conflagration that would consume the union. The Democratic-Republicans' actions brought the nation to a precipice, a crisis that was narrowly averted and that would be revived in the antebellum era only to explode sixty years later at Fort Sumter.

Since ratification of the Constitution, it had been argued that the states possessed a "powerful check" on Congress. In *Federalist #44*, Madison wrote that successful congressional usurpation of power was virtually impossible; if the executive and judiciary did not check it, the states "will be ever ready to mark the innovation, to sound the alarm to the people, and to exert their local influence in effecting a change of federal representatives." That was what Henry and Virginia had done in response to Hamilton's debt assumption and the Jay Treaty. The emphasis was on a state "sound[ing] the alarm," publicizing abuse of power, encouraging "change of federal representatives" in the next election, and asking other states to join a protest.[28]

But could a state's check on federal power be applied more forcefully? Was the check political or legal? Could a state go beyond remonstrances and resort to the ballot box, and instead seek to interfere with or block federal actions?

On several prior occasions, Jefferson had spoken in broad, sweeping terms about a state's ability to respond to perceived federal overreach. Madison later sought to excuse his apparent radicalism by acknowledging that there was "a habit in Mr J. as in others of great genius, of expressing in strong and round terms impressions of the moment," but his pronouncements in this particular area were remarkable. In 1792, Jefferson suggested that Virginia should not only declare Hamilton's financial plan unconstitutional (as the General Assembly did under Henry's guidance), but it should also announce that anyone using the new national bank branch in Virginia or working there, by recognizing a "foreign" authority within the state, should "be adjudged guilty of high treason and suffer death accordingly." He told Madison that "this is the only opposition worthy of our state, and the only kind which can be effectual." While one might well doubt that Jefferson really intended to hang employees of the Richmond branch of the national bank, in light of events in 1798 and 1799, his advocacy of an extreme intervention by the state to undermine a federal law should not be blithely dismissed.[29]

In 1797, Jefferson's ire was likewise raised when a federal grand jury in Richmond entered a "presentment" against Democratic-Republican congressman Samuel Jordan Cabell—the Charlottesville area representative—at the suggestion of Federalist Supreme Court Justice James Iredell because Cabell had criticized the Adams administration in a letter to his Virginia constituents. (The foreman of the grand jury that attacked Cabell was John Blair, a retired Federalist Supreme Court justice.) While the Sedition Act had not yet been adopted, Iredell believed that the letter was common law sedition. Nothing came of the presentment; it was essentially the grand jury expressing a grievance and not an indictment. Still, Jefferson thought strong action by the state was needed to stop any possible effort by federal (Federalist) judges to prosecute common law crimes not specified in the Constitution, especially when they sought to silence a member of Congress. Such suppression of political opposition would "leave [the people] indeed the shadow, but . . . take away the substance of representation."[30]

Scrambling for some type of action beyond simply protest, Jefferson argued to James Monroe and James Madison that the federal grand jurors should be impeached by the state. When Monroe expressed concern that federal officials should not be, "by a code of crimes and punishments, amenable to state tribunals" and suggested that the proper remedy was for Congress to act, Jefferson angrily shot back that seeking a remedy in Congress would be deferring to a "foreign jurisdiction." The federal government was engaged in a "scramble" for power, Jefferson lectured, "seiz[ing] all doubtful ground. We must join in the scramble, or get nothing." Jefferson's overheated rhetoric hid political reality; Jefferson was probably more concerned that Congress's Federalist majority might vote to approve the presentment. Still, the idea of state impeachment of federal officials serving in Virginia, even grand jurors, was radical. Jefferson went so far as to draft a petition to the Virginia House of Delegates urging action. After consultation with Madison, Monroe, and Wilson Cary Nicholas, Jefferson deleted the reference to impeachment, merely asking the legislature to address the matter.[31]

In May of 1798, John Taylor warned Jefferson that if federal actions continued, "the southern states must lose their capital and commerce—and . . . America is destined for war—standing armies—and oppressive taxation." Before spring was out, Taylor told a mutual correspondent (in a letter shown to Jefferson) that "it was not unusual now to estimate the separate mass of

Virginia and N. Carolina, with a view to their separate existence." The suggestion of secession initially seemed to surprise Jefferson who, in his own way,
was a nationalist. He lectured Taylor that "if on a temporary superiority of the
one party, the other is to resort to a scission of the union, no federal government can ever exist." Still, as Federalist attacks on the free press and his own
desperation mounted, he would find himself recurring to the idea of secession
in less than a year.[32]

Faced with the Alien and Sedition Acts and burgeoning arrests of
Democratic-Republican newspaper editors, Jefferson's patience with mere
state remonstrances against what he believed were dangerous federal grabs
for power had worn thin. Jefferson turned to the states, as had Henry, but this
time Jefferson was determined to do more than merely register a complaint
as Henry and Virginia had done before.

Initially Jefferson and his colleagues planned to draft resolutions against the
federal laws and have them adopted by the state legislatures in North Carolina
and Virginia, but Federalist electoral gains in North Carolina in 1798 resulting
from the XYZ Affair and Quasi-War with France caused the conspirators to
switch their focus to Kentucky. Jefferson prepared the first draft of resolutions
for Kentucky, and Madison drafted resolutions for Virginia. Although the two
leaders exchanged drafts, the texts were significantly different.[33]

Both Jefferson and Madison seemed intentionally to retain some studied
ambiguity in their drafting. As Jefferson explained, "I think we should distinctly affirm all the important principles . . . , so as to hold to that ground in
future, and leave the matter in such a train as that we may not be committed
absolutely to push the matter to extremities, & yet may be free to push as far as
events will render prudent." Both leaders recognized that they were engaged
in a high-stakes game of political chess in which plausible deniability might be
critical. This was not a theoretical political science exercise in which perfect
clarity was the goal—and historians who seek such clarity and consistency
from Jefferson, Madison, and others can tend to miss the very serious concern
as they struggled with these partisan battles.[34]

Kentucky (and Jefferson) Claim the Constitution
Is Merely a Compact of Sovereign States

Jefferson's draft of the Kentucky Resolutions was the strongest statement of the
Democratic-Republican position and helps to explain why so many feared that
the nation was rapidly descending into a crisis, open conflict among the states,
disunion, potentially civil war.

Jefferson began by insisting that the Constitution was a "compact" to which "each state" was "an integral party." Today the term sounds obscure, perhaps benign, but its implications in 1798 were widely understood. The Articles of Confederation—with all their problems: national incompetence, state control, and threat of collapse in the 1780s—had been a compact among sovereign states. A compact was like an international agreement among independent nations. If the Constitution was a mere "compact," Jefferson explained that each state "has an equal right to judge for itself" the legitimacy of federal actions as well as the "mode & measure of redress"; a state could block federal actions with which it disagrees—at least block their application in the state's own territory—and withdraw from the compact at will based upon any self-identified "breach" by another party. During the Philadelphia Convention, Madison had focused on this point in explaining the essential difference between a constitution created by the people and one created by the states (like the Articles of Confederation): "He considered the difference between a system founded on the Legislatures only, and one founded on the people, to be the true difference between a league or treaty, and a Constitution. . . . The doctrine laid down by the law of Nations in the case of treaties is that a breach of any one article by any of the parties, frees the other parties from their engagements. In the case of a union of people under one Constitution, the nature of the pact has always been understood to exclude such an interpretation."[35]

In fact, during the ratification debates antifederalists had complained that the Constitution was abandoning the compact of the Confederation. This was the essence of Patrick Henry's famous complaint: "who authorised them to speak the language of, *We, the People* instead of *We, the states*? States are the characteristics, and the soul of a confederation. If the States be not the agents of this compact, it must be one great consolidated National Government of the people of all the States." The antifederalist leader had expressly asked: "Have they made a proposal of a compact between States? If they had, this would be a confederation: It is otherwise most clearly a consolidated government." Henry, though, lost that debate. Notably, although federalists during ratification had every incentive to mollify antifederalists by insisting that the new Constitution was only a compact and maintained a confederacy, they abjured doing so.[36]

In 1798, in desperation, believing that the nation itself was at risk, Jefferson resurrected the idea of a compact that had effectively been abandoned and made a reactionary argument harking back to the Confederation about a state's ability to interfere with federal authority. (It's worth remembering that Jefferson was not present for drafting or ratification of the Constitution and was quite surprised at the time by the extent that it limited the power of the states, as a result telling Edward Carrington that he was "nearly a Neutral" on the new charter.) This was a radical, arguably revolutionary, idea. It raised the real possibility of federal laws being interpreted differently in every state and conflicts among the states and between the federal government and states arising as a result. Such conflicts could generate serious actions or leave the new nation hamstrung (as they had under the Confederation). In a compact, when faced with a national law that a state thought violated the agreement, secession would be a right of each state, and a real possibility.[37]

Madison also adopted "compact" language in his draft of the Virginia Resolutions (although, as explained below, he would later try mightily to redefine the term to limit its application or to ignore the term as he focused on ambiguities in his own resolutions). Previously, Madison had insisted that the Constitution was not a compact among sovereign states and that a mere compact could not hope to address the problems facing the nation. Before the Philadelphia Convention, he had explained that "as far as the Union of the States is to be regarded as a league of sovereign powers, and not as a political Constitution by virtue of which they are become one sovereign power . . . a breach of any of the articles of confederation by any of the parties to it, absolves the other parties from their respective obligations, and gives them a right if they chuse to exert it, of dissolving the Union altogether." Shortly after the convention, he wrote to Jefferson explaining that "it was generally agreed that the objects of the Union could not be secured by any system founded on the principle of a confederation of sovereign States. . . . Hence was embraced the alternative of a government which instead of operating, on the States, should operate without their intervention on the individuals composing them."[38]

In *Federalist* #43, Madison explained some of the infirmities of a Confederation "compact" created by the states rather than the people: "A compact between independent sovereigns, founded on ordinary acts of legislative authority, can pretend to no higher validity than a league or treaty between the parties. It is an established doctrine on the subject of treaties, . . . that a breach of any one article is a breach of the whole treaty; and that a breach, committed by either of the parties, absolves the others, and authorizes them, if they please, to pronounce the compact violated and void." In *Federalist* #15, the idea that states retained sovereignty to ignore federal mandates was referred to as "a principle which has been found the bane of the old" Confederation. Alexander Hamilton warned that a "compact between the States" would be subject to dissolution because any state that felt aggrieved "would not long consent to remain associated." Other federalists agreed that a compact was rife with dangers for the union: "The great object which we had in view when we first called for the assistance of a convention, was, the strengthening the hands of the UNION; and if there are to be left in the hands of the different states sufficient powers to supersede those of Congress, little after all has been effected."[39]

During ratification Madison explained, "that as far as the articles of Union were to be considered as a Treaty . . . among the Governments of Independent States, the doctrine might be set up that a breach of any one article, by any of the parties, absolved the other parties from (the whole) obligation." Invoking his extensive study of the history of republics, he warned, "If we recur to history . . . I undertake to say, that no instance can be produced by the most learned man, of any Confederate Government, that will justify a continuation of the present system; . . . instead of promoting the public happiness, or securing public tranquility, [confederacies] have, in every instance, been productive of anarchy and confusion; ineffectual for the preservation of harmony, and a prey to their own dissentions and foreign invasions." The furthest that Madison would go was to say that the new government was a hybrid evidencing some characteristics of a national consolidation and some of a "federal" system. Later, Madison renewed this point; the Constitution was neither a "simple Gov't" nor "a mere League of Govts.," that is, a compact. Even Madison's "hybrid" equivocation elicited Henry's rebuke as the new government controlled the purse and the sword: "To all the common purposes of Legislation it is a great consolidation of Government."[40]

At the time of ratification, Jefferson recognized as much, writing to one friend that "our new constitution . . . has succeded beyond what I apprehended it would have done. I did not at first believe that 11. states out of 13. would have consented to a plan consolidating them so much into one. A change in their dispositions, which had taken place since I left them, had rendered this consolidation necessary, that is to say, had called for a federal government which could walk upon it's own legs, without leaning for support on the state legislatures." Jefferson recognized that the role of the states was heavily circumscribed from what would exist under a compact. For example, as Noah Webster explained when the compact theory was used by southern slave owners opposing federal authority in the 1830s, the Constitution provided for amendments being binding upon states even if a state had not itself endorsed them, something impossible with a compact of sovereign states.[41]

Former governor Henry Lee understood the term as Jefferson used it to mean "a mere alliance, dependant for its preservation on the will of each state, . . . subject to all those casualties, to which contracts between independent nations have ever been exposed." In 1798, the idea that the nation was a mere compact was broadly understood to invite a clash among the states and possible disunion. (Tellingly, in the antebellum period, compact theory would become foundational for secessionists who sought to protect the institution of slavery and who claimed the mantle of Jefferson. In the 1830s, relying on Jefferson's Kentucky Resolutions, South Carolina nullifiers argued: "The constitution of the United States, as is admitted by contemporaneous writers, is a compact between sovereign states. . . . the constitution is a confederacy." Abraham Lincoln would later conclude that by providing an alleged constitutional basis for secession, the compact argument was essential for convincing many Americans that secession was legal, without which it could not have occurred.)[42]

In reality, after ratification, the compact theory largely disappeared from political discourse until Jefferson, almost in despair, resuscitated it in 1798. Notably, neither the 1790 Virginia protest against Hamilton's financial plan nor the 1796 protest against the Jay Treaty even intimated that the Constitution was a mere compact or that states could unilaterally interfere with federal actions. John Taylor, who would become a devotee of radical states' rights, never mentioned the theory in his 1794 attack on Hamilton's financial system, arguing only that states' authority consisted of appointing senators, protesting federal actions, and if two-thirds agreed, pursuing amendments under the Constitution. Nor did Madison mention it in his early 1790s *National Gazette* essays urging limits on federal power. While the issue continues to be argued by academics, many of the arguments fail to distinguish between what was said in the 1780s during ratification and the ten years thereafter from what was said by Democratic-Republicans (and nullifiers) after 1798 and Jefferson's inventive, desperate use of the term. The compact argument propagated in the Kentucky and Virginia Resolutions and then embraced by states' rights conservatives (later taking precedence in efforts to protect slavery) has been projected back ten years. "While federalism had received ample attention before the [Kentucky and Virginia] resolutions, only after they were issued did state-based constitutional challenges to federal laws take a prominent place in American political culture," Jonathan Gienapp notes.[43]

Semantics aside, it was clear before 1798 that under the Constitution, as opposed to the Confederation, no single state could block or undermine federal action. In 1798, Henry, Washington, and others rightly saw the new, reactionary theory propagated by Democratic-Republicans as unjustified by the terms of the Constitution or the history of its drafting and ratification; in any case, they understood that it was dangerous for the union.

Jefferson Proposes Nullification

Jefferson's resolutions focused on several federal laws alleged to be unconstitutional: the Alien Acts, an act punishing fraud against the Bank of the United States (which, of course, Jefferson also thought was unconstitutional), and the Sedition Act.

With respect to aliens, Jefferson insisted that once a person was admitted to the country, he or she was "under the jurisdiction and protection of the laws of the state," entirely beyond the criminal jurisdiction of the United States. Jefferson argued that the Constitution's ban on prohibiting importation of people before 1808 (intended to protect the slave trade) meant that the federal government could not deport even dangerous aliens once they arrived. Jefferson's inclusion of the bank fraud act was equally vacuous. His argument was that the Constitution expressly provided for only a discrete group of federal crimes: piracy, counterfeiting, treason, and offenses against the law of nations; thus, any additional federal criminal laws were, ipso facto, unconstitutional. Yet, if the Bank of the United States was constitutional, most would concede that punishing bank fraud was well within the "necessary and proper" federal powers. (Tellingly, Madison omitted both claims from his Virginia Resolutions.)[44]

Jefferson's attacks on the constitutionality of the Sedition Act (expanded upon by Madison in the Virginia Resolutions) were on much firmer ground.

These claims, though, were mere groundwork for the more significant issue: proposed actions in response to the allegedly unconstitutional federal laws. If there was any doubt about what Jefferson intended by claiming that the Constitution was a compact, he removed it with his proposals. Jefferson argued that laws that the state believed to be unconstitutional were "altogether void & of no force." Conceding that normally the response to "abuse of delegated powers" would be for people to vote against responsible legislators in the next election, Jefferson argued that if a state determined that the powers exercised were "not within the compact," then "every state has a natural right . . . to *nullify* of their *own authority* all assumptions of power by others within their limits." In other words, each state could (and should) ensure that federal laws that it unilaterally concluded exceeded delegated powers were not enforced in the state, creating a potential inconsistency in application of laws in different states and a direct confrontation with federal officials. While the Kentucky Resolutions called for consultation among the states, the declaration of a unilateral right of "each state" to take action, accompanied by the rhetoric of the times, made the danger clear.[45]

Tellingly, before the Philadelphia Convention, Madison had urged that just this type of state interference with national laws was one of the "Vices of the Political System of the United States" under the Articles of Confederation that the Constitution was intended to remedy. He wrote, "Whenever a law of a State happens to be repugnant to an act of Congress, particularly when the latter is of posterior date to the former, it will be at least questionable whether the latter must not prevail; and as the question must be decided by the Tribunals of the State, they will be most likely to lean on the side of the State." (As others note, Madison apparently transposed "former" and "latter" in this draft.)[46]

Regardless, Jefferson's draft calling for nullification was relayed to John Breckinridge who introduced the resolutions in the Kentucky legislature on November 8, 1798. While the term "nullify" was removed from the draft during ensuing debates, Breckinridge insisted that "if, upon the representations of the States from whom they derive their powers, they [federal officials] should nevertheless attempt to enforce them [laws declared void], I hesitate not to declare it as my opinion that it is then the right and duty of the several States to nullify those acts, *and to protect their citizens from their operation.*" In an effort to obfuscate, perhaps maintain plausible deniability, Breckinridge then said more cautiously, "We do not pretend to set ourselves up as censors for the Union, but we will firmly express our own opinions and call upon the other States to examine their political situation." In any case, while the term "nullify" was removed, the Resolutions insisted that the challenged federal laws were "unauthoritative, void, and of no force" in Kentucky and, relying on the compact theory, that "each state" could act unilaterally to determine "the mode and measure of redress." And, as the press reported, supporters threatened nullification in public statements. Pleas by some members that the state legislature had no authority to "repeal or declare void the laws of the United State" were dismissed by Breckinridge's insistence that the Constitution was merely a compact among sovereign states. Public meetings in Kentucky in opposition to the Alien and Sedition Acts openly discussed secession.[47]

George Nicholas, a Jeffersonian in Kentucky's legislature, made the same threat of action while insisting that no action was, at least for the time, planned. He wrote that Kentucky viewed the referenced federal laws as "absolute nullities . . . dead letters, and therefore that we might legally use force in opposition to any attempts to execute them, yet we contemplate no means of opposition . . . but an appeal to the *real laws* of our country." Jefferson sent Nicholas's pamphlet to Monroe and urged its distribution. (Ironically, George Nicholas, at the time a supporter of Patrick Henry, had introduced the resolution calling for an investigation into Jefferson's governorship in 1781 that so outraged the future president.)[48]

Opponents of the Resolutions dismissed this flip-flopping obfuscation with scorn: "say if he [Nicholas] can, that they [the Kentucky Resolutions] do not tend, directly, to the dissolution of the union, . . . for, when any member of the union refuses obedience to the laws of the union, it can no longer be considered as a component part; and by declaring the laws of the union void, they leave no choice to the rest, but either to compel them to obedience or to abandon them." The power Kentucky claimed was "absolutely inconsistent with the union, and involves its destruction."

> If instead of this rash resolution, which violates the constitution, and virtually annuls the union, the government had remonstrated against the laws . . . in as strong terms as they thought proper, and *demanded,* if they thought that the best way, that they should be referred to the supreme court, for their determination . . . ; instead of the condemnation their conduct has generally met with, it would have been approved by all their fellow citizens in every part of the United States, and they would have evinced that, altho' they did not feel, in all cases as they do, they equally regarded the constitution and constituted authority of the nation, both of which have been wounded by the manner in which they have proceeded.[49]

Jefferson seemed to be playing a complicated game intended to keep options open. After the Kentucky Resolutions were adopted, he wrote John Taylor, "I would not do any thing *at this moment* which should commit us further, but reserve ourselves to shape our future measures or no measures, by the events which may happen." Nonetheless, the Kentucky Resolutions clearly threatened state interference with federal laws based upon a unilateral state determination.[50]

For Patrick Henry, George Washington, and others who were concerned about the union, the argument that a state could declare a federal law void and ignore federal authority in its own territory—creating the possibility of different interpretations of the Constitution and different applications of federal law in each state—took on critical importance. Under Jefferson's theory articulated in the Kentucky Resolutions, "there seemingly could be in principle no collective decision binding an individual state," Jefferson Powell concludes. As Madison conceded years later, "that to have left a final decision, in such cases, to each of the States, . . . could not fail to make the Constitution and laws of the United States different in different States, . . . that this diversity of independent decisions, must altogether distract the Government of the Union, and speedily put an end to the Union itself." This is what frightened Henry and Washington.[51]

The Kentucky Resolutions were adopted on November 10, 1798.

Madison and Virginia Act

Democratic-Republicans sought to bolster the Kentucky Resolutions with a parallel protest from Virginia. That, though, proved more complicated than was hoped. On the one hand, while the Virginia Resolutions were somewhat more moderate than Kentucky's, they still served to increase the anxiety of Henry, Washington, and other observers that the union was on the verge of collapse as states threatened to interfere with federal actions. As one Federalist newspaper concluded, "Virginia will have either a majority in Congress or a separation of the states!" At the same time, Virginia's and Madison's moderation tended to show how extreme was Jefferson's position in the Kentucky Resolutions.[52]

In October 1798, Madison visited Monticello and was almost certainly shown Jefferson's draft Kentucky Resolutions. But, reflecting Madison's often more cautious, less doctrinaire approach, his draft of the Virginia Resolutions was quite different than Jefferson's resolutions. For starters, Madison dropped entirely the tenuous reference to the bank fraud act and the argument that the Alien Act violated the prohibition on restricting slave importation.[53]

Madison's draft agreed that the Alien and Sedition Acts were unconstitutional. The Virginia Resolutions were particularly forceful on the danger of such interference with the free press. The Sedition Act, Madison wrote, violated the express terms of the First Amendment; this "ought to produce universal alarm, because it is levelled against the right of freely examining public characters and measures, and of free communication among the people thereon, which has ever been justly deemed, the only effectual guardian of every other right."[54]

Madison echoed Jefferson's insistence that the Constitution was merely a compact among the states (regardless of what he had said during the Constitution's drafting and ratification and what he would write later when nullification became a favorite device of the slavocracy and secessionists). Historians and political scientists have grappled with Madison's position on this point for years.

Even with his embrace of a compact theory, though, Madison was much more circumspect about appropriate action in the face of a perceived unconstitutional federal law. Madison's resolutions stated that the "states" (plural) were "duty bound, to interpose for arresting the pro(gress) of" such usurpations. This somewhat undefined call to cooperative state action is spelled out in the seventh of the Virginia Resolutions: While insisting that the people of Virginia feel "the most scrupulous fidelity to that Constitution, . . . the General Assembly doth solemnly appeal to the like dispositions of the other States, in confidence that they will concur with this Commonwealth in declaring, as it does hereby declare, that the acts aforesaid are unconstitutional; and that the necessary and proper measures will be taken by each for co-operating with this State, in maintaining unimpaired the authorities, rights, and liberties reserved to the States respectively, or to the people."[55]

Madison's use of "states" rather than "state" (as in Kentucky's Resolutions) suggests that concerted action of the states is necessary to block federal action. Over thirty years later, responding to slave state calls for nullification, Madison stressed this distinction: "the plural number 'States', is used in referring to them; that a concurrence & co-operation of all might well be contemplated, in interpositions for effecting the objects." It is not entirely clear what this cooperative action would entail. Yet, if the Constitution was a true compact of the states as understood at the time of ratification, any single party could block action in its own territory or withdraw (as Kentucky made clear). Alternatively, one could argue that since the Constitution required over two-thirds (nine) of the states to ratify for the government to come into existence, at least a comparable decision would be necessary for any collective dissolution or secession. (Perhaps with a wry sense of humor, Madison's resolutions called on other states to take all actions "necessary and proper" to maintain the people's rights.)[56]

Here, too, though, Madison left some ambiguity, suggesting that the states could take action to "maintain[] within their respective limits, the authorities, rights and liberties appertaining to them." Yet, to assert a right to act within the states' "respective limits" implied individual action.[57]

Madison also did not define what was intended by his assertion of the states' right to "interpose" (rather than "nullify"). He might have hoped to argue later that he was only suggesting that the states should act politically to rouse opposition to federal overreach and call upon congressional representatives to reverse the policy (or face their constituents). As he had urged in Federalist #44, states could "sound the alarm to the people, and . . . exert their local influence in effecting a change of federal representatives." By 1825, this is how Madison characterized his actions in 1798: "to rouse the attention of the people, and a remedy ensues thro' the forms of the Constitution." Some modern analysts, seeking to find consistency between Madison's declarations in 1798 and his later express opposition to nullification, interpret his language in this manner. Yet, such doctrinal consistency is often the pursuit of latter-day academics at the expense of real-world political controversies; at the time, such post hoc rationalizations were not available.[58]

Other forms of clearly legitimate state cooperative protests were contemplated by other Democratic-Republicans; John Taylor, for example, suggested that if Congress did not repeal the offending laws after state protests, states could request a convention under Article V of the Constitution, which was certainly their right. This, though, was not the remedy called for in either the Kentucky or Virginia Resolutions.[59]

When Jefferson saw Madison's draft, he was deeply disappointed. He wrote to Wilson Cary Nicholas, a member of Virginia's House of Delegates, "The more I have reflected on the phrase in the paper you shewed me, the more strongly I think it should be altered. suppose you were to instead of the invitation [to other states] to cooperate in the annulment of the acts, to make it an invitation: 'to concur with this commonwealth in declaring, as it does hereby declare, that the said acts are, and were ab initio—null, void, and of no force, or effect.'" This, then, was not intended by Jefferson to be merely an objection to the laws, a declaration that they were unconstitutional, or even a call for collective action by the states, but to offer direct defiance of federal authority by a single state, as had Kentucky. Nicholas took Jefferson's advice, and the modified resolutions were introduced on December 10, 1798, by John Taylor of Caroline.[60]

The "null, void, and of no force" language, while accepted in Kentucky, caused a strong pushback even in Virginia's heavily Democratic-Republican assembly. To call federal laws null and void was "dangerous and improper; inasmuch as they had, not only a tendency to inflame the public mind; . . . but they had a tendency to sap the very foundation of the government, by producing resistance to its laws," one legislator insisted. After an intense debate, the House of Delegates removed Jefferson's inflammatory language (apparently not aware of its origin) leaving the resolutions essentially as Madison drafted them.[61]

Whether Madison played a direct role in watering down Jefferson's language in the Virginia Resolutions is not perfectly clear, although several historians conclude that he "almost certainly" did. If so, it is a fascinating example of Jefferson and Madison engaged, through surrogates, in an important argument on the nature of constitutional authority.[62]

In the face of the later nullification crisis that gripped the nation in the 1820s and 1830s, Madison pointed to this removal of the "null, void" language as clear evidence that Virginia had not adopted the nullification doctrine. Madison emphatically rejected the idea "that the States (perhaps their Governments) have, singly, a constitutional right to resist & by force annul within itself, acts of the Government of the U.S. which it deems unauthorized by the Constitution of the U.S." (Of course, his denial again demonstrated the radical nature of the Kentucky Resolutions.) In a later letter, Madison would argue that even the inclusion of this language would not have meant that an individual state could "annul the acts or sanction a resistance to them," and at least one commentator has urged, using the same strained reasoning, that neither Madison's Virginia Resolutions nor Kentucky's Resolutions declaring the laws "void and of no force" should be interpreted as doing so. Yet, even in that letter, Madison conceded that his "memory" could not decide if the language had been included in his draft, and he had obviously forgotten that the language was inserted by Jefferson to strengthen his draft and the battle in Virginia to have the language removed.[63]

In the end, in terms of their call for action by the "states" and use of the ambiguous notion of interposition, Madison may have wished the Virginia Resolutions to model the response to "unwarrantable" federal action that he had discussed in *Federalist #46*.

> The means of opposition to it [unwarranted federal action] are powerful and at hand. The disquietude of the people; their repugnance and, perhaps, refusal to co-operate with the officers of the Union; the frowns of the executive magistracy of the State; the embarrassments created by legislative devices, which would often be added on such occasions, would oppose, in any State, difficulties not to be despised; would form, in a large State, very serious impediments; and where the sentiments of several adjoining States happened to be in unison, would present obstructions which the federal government would hardly be willing to encounter. But ambitious encroachments of the federal government, on the authority of the State governments, would not excite the opposition of a single State, or of a few States only. They would be signals of general alarm. Every government would espouse the common cause. A correspondence would be opened. Plans of resistance would be concerted. One spirit would animate and conduct the whole.

Ten years after writing *Federalist #46*, Madison may have seen his suggested "legislative devices" as referring to just the type of protest in the Virginia Resolutions.[64]

Henry, Washington, and others saw the dangerous possibility of nullification and secession in the Kentucky and Virginia Resolutions. While the final Virginia Resolutions were ostensibly milder, they were undoubtedly read in light of the more rabid, earlier Kentucky Resolutions. Moreover, the possibility of secession was implicit in the claim, promoted by both Kentucky and Virginia, that the Constitution was only a compact. Henry Lee—a federalist in the ratification convention, a former Virginia governor, and a confidante of both Henry and Washington—was aghast at the Virginia Resolutions and made clear that they were no mere protest that the Alien and Sedition Acts were unconstitutional. Recognizing the right of a state legislature to declare its views on the constitutionality of federal action (what Virginia had done under Patrick Henry's guidance with respect to Hamilton's financial plan and, later, the Jay Treaty), Lee

> begged the Assembly to confine itself to a petition for repeal of the Alien and Sedition Laws, or at most to refer the issue to the federal judiciary. To declare the laws null and void was to invite civil disobedience and chaos. He predicted that "if the principle of obeying the will of the majority was once destroyed, it would prostrate all free government." . . . Daniel Morgan predicted that "Instead of an extensive, united nation, respectable among all the powers on the Globe, we shall dwindle into a number of petty divisions, an easy prey for domestic Demagogues and foreign Enemies."

Morgan—Virginia Federalist member of Congress and former Revolutionary War general—wrote one correspondent, "In the name of heaven! . . . are their Views honest? . . . does it not appear that these people—disappointment at not being elevated in the Genl. Government, wish to cut it to pieces, in order that they may rule & tyrannize over a part." Lee published a pamphlet warning that the Resolutions had "a tendency to dissolve the union." The compact theory, he wrote, "is believed to be untrue in fact, and dangerous in principle." Reminding people of the Confederation's failure, he explained that "it will scarcely be contended that, under such a state of things, the government of the whole can be preserved." States were not parties, Lee wrote, but agents in carrying the Constitution into effect. "The people, and the people only, were competent to these important objects." While the states were parties to the Confederation, history demonstrated "the inability of such a government to preserve the Union." Lee's pamphlet was serialized. Patrick Henry endorsed Lee's protests, calling the Resolutions a "system that leads, by the shortest cut, to perdition."[65]

To no avail. The Virginia Resolutions were adopted on December 21, 1798, almost a month and a half after Kentucky's.[66]

Newspaper Reports, Threat of "Civil War," and Arming the Militia

Newspaper accounts of the Kentucky and Virginia Resolutions fed a festering public angst. The Kentucky Resolutions were printed in Virginia at least by December 4 and were broadly reprinted elsewhere. On December 11, the *Times and District of Columbia Daily Advertiser* printed a summary of the Kentucky Resolutions, emphasizing that "several acts of congress particularly the alien and sedition laws are condemned as unconstitutional and declared *utterly void and of no force,* in that state." Kentucky's strong language with the threat of direct interference with federal laws and secession tended to be the focus. On December 13, aware of efforts to adopt resolutions in Virginia, the *Federal Gazette and Baltimore Daily Advertiser* reprinted the full Kentucky Resolutions with a warning: "We can not omit observing, however, that should they be concurred in, the suspicion that a coalition has been formed between that State and Virginia, for ceceding from the federal government, will then be confirmed. In the old dominion, a spirit of ambition and domination has too long been its distinguishing feature." The *Bee,* from New London, Connecticut, quoted Kentucky's "*unconstitutional and void*" language, noting that "the Virginia legislature are now in session, and will probably pass similar resolutions."[67]

As fate would have it, the Virginia Resolutions were first published as Taylor introduced them, including Jefferson's more aggressive "null, void, and of no force" language. This more strident version was reprinted elsewhere, for example in the *Aurora* (Philadelphia), December 22, 1798, *Claypoole's American Daily Advertiser* (Philadelphia), December 25, 1798, the *Commercial Advertiser* (New York), December 27, 1798 (Americans must read the Resolutions with "honest indignation"), the *Spectator* (New York), December 29, 1799, the *Bee* (Norwich, CT), January 2, 1799, and the *Maryland Herald and Hager's-Town Weekly Advertiser,* January 3, 1799. For readers throughout the nation, including Henry and Washington, it appeared that Virginia was following the radical agenda of Kentucky, an agenda threatening direct opposition to federal authority while warning of "blood." On December 25, the *Virginia Argus* (Richmond) printed the final version of the Virginia Resolutions as adopted on

December 21 with the more extreme language expunged (although including the claim that the Constitution was a mere "compact"), but other states had already begun to react to the Virginia draft declaring federal laws "unconstitutional and void." As the editors of the *Papers of James Madison* observe, "Whatever political benefits J[ames] M[adison] had anticipated from casting his arguments in temperate and conciliatory language were lost by the coupling of his resolutions with those adopted in Kentucky." If Madison's more moderate tone was not entirely "lost," it was certainly compromised.[68]

In this milieu, the Kentucky and Virginia Resolutions appeared very serious threats to the new nation. A letter from a Richmond resident, reprinted across the country, explained the machinations of the Virginia General Assembly as "passing an appeal to the People, in the shape of an address, fraught with the most direful sentiments to the government of the United States. Times are alarming—civil dissensions, if not actual civil war, may be expected." "Civil War!" was picked up as a newspaper headline. The report warned that Virginia would not hesitate to force the issue. "The government of the United States must protect itself or yield to the force of Virginia." Other papers insisted that the Kentucky and Virginia Resolutions "look[] like the prelude to a civil war."[69]

For some Federalists, the Virginia and Kentucky Resolutions were on their face a call to arms. John Lowell, a member of the Massachusetts legislature, insisted angrily during debates over the Resolutions that "we were solemnly called upon, by the State of Virginia, in *artful,* but *intelligible* language, to arm against the Federal Government!" Federalist newspapers agreed, warning Virginia that "an allusion to *force* in *discussing* questions of government, is an improper precedent." The New England newspaper editors went on to advise (threaten) Virginia and Kentucky that they would find the other states "as able in the field as in the cabinet."[70]

As the Virginia Resolutions were circulating, reports began to emerge that Virginia was also funding a new armory and a large purchase of arms for its militia. The heavily reprinted letter from Virginia asked portentously: "Another project is before the house [of Delegates], for arming en masse all the militia of the commonwealth—this is also the scheme of [John] Taylor and his party—and who can doubt the object?"[71]

Was there a real threat of military conflict? Were states really arming for a potential battle with the federal government? These are surprisingly complicated questions.

Virginia was building an armory, and there were at least some reports that the state was arming for a possible conflict with the federal government. In early 1799, as Patrick Henry was launching his final political campaign, John Nicholas, a former member of the Virginia House of Delegates (not to be confused with the John Nicholas, a Democratic-Republican member of Congress), published several essays in which he renounced his Democratic-Republican affiliation, lamenting that the Kentucky and Virginia Resolutions portended "the destruction of the bonds of society by which alone rights may be permanently secured, . . . Every thing dear and valuable to the citizens [is] . . . evidently and clearly in a train to be destroyed." Like Henry Lee, Nicholas explained that Kentucky and Virginia were effectively seeking to undermine majority rule by opposing a majority acting in Congress. He warned that while Virginia bemoaned the alleged threat of "the direct and common application of force," this was an excuse to justify its own action, "making preparations of a military kind. . . . A destruction of the government and union, and not a correction of the administration, must be the object of such an opposition." Nicholas, running for Congress himself, specifically urged that any grievances be taken to the ballot box: "a change of public servants when the time of election comes about, is at last in our power. Any other method would be contrary, not only to the letter and spirit of our constitution, but to every principle of liberty." Virginia and Kentucky's actions put at risk "every principle upon which it [the Constitution] is really established, and along with those principles the union, and, of course, the peace, happiness and safety of the states, . . . unless the good sense, moderation and independence of the citizens should interfere" and elect those opposing the Resolutions. Wilson Cary Nicholas, John Nicholas's brother and a leading Democratic-Republican, was so outraged by the essays, what he saw as treason to the party, that he urged his brother to change his name so as not to disgrace the family (and hurt Wilson Cary's own political career). But "considerable credence was given Nicholas's declaration, especially since the Virginia legislature of 1798–1799 that passed the Virginia Resolutions also reorganized the militia, purchased additional arms, provided funds to build an armory in Richmond, and increased taxes by 25 percent" to do so.[72]

Years later, John Randolph, another Democratic-Republican leader who was just entering politics in 1799, seemed to confirm Nicholas's claim. During congressional debates, Randolph explained that Virginia's 1799 decision to build an armory was "not so much because of the badness of the arms, as because it was proper for the State of Virginia to keep in her possession the means of arming the militia, rather than depend for her supply on contracts that the United States might stop." Randolph acknowledged that the threat of "civil war" hung over the decision, admitting in 1817 that "there was no longer any cause for concealing the fact, that the grand armory at Richmond was built to enable the State of Virginia to resist, by force, the encroachments of the then Administration upon her indisputable rights." William Giles, another Democratic-Republican, also linked the armory to Virginia's being threatened by federal government actions in 1798. For years, historians gave these claims that Virginia was arming for a possible conflict with the United States some credence. Robert Howison, in his mid-nineteenth-century *History of Virginia,* concluded that construction of Virginia's armory and collection of arms in 1798–1799 was in apprehension of a possible conflict with the federal government.[73]

Alexander Hamilton, still effectively leader of the Federalists, took these threats seriously. After adoption of the Virginia Resolutions, William Heth, a Revolutionary War officer, wrote to Hamilton warning that Virginia was purchasing arms to support its opposition to federal laws. Hamilton wrote to Jonathan Dayton, youngest member of the Philadelphia Convention and Federalist member of Congress in 1799, that

> The late attempt of Virginia & Kentucke to unite the state legislatures in a direct resistance to certain laws of the Union can be considered in no other light than as an attempt to change the Government. It is stated, in addition, that the opposition-Party in Virginia, the head Quarters of the Faction, have followed up the hostile declarations which are to be found in the resolutions of their General Assembly by an actual preparation of the means of supporting them by force—That they have taken measures to put their militia on a more efficient footing—are preparing considerable arsenals and magazines and (which is an unequivocal proof how much they are in earnest) have gone so far as to lay new taxes on their citizens.

In early February 1799, Hamilton went so far as to write Theodore Sedgwick, soon to be speaker of the U.S. House of Representatives, that even if peace with France was achieved, the federal government should maintain its expanded army (which Hamilton effectively commanded) for a possible conflict with Virginia. A federal military force might be "drawn toward Virginia, for which there is an obvious pretext—& then let measures be taken to act upon the laws & put Virginia to the Test of resistance." Sedgwick wrote to Rufus King in November of 1799, warning that Virginia and Kentucky seemed determined to change government by force and that Virginia was driven by "an anxiety to render its militia as formidable as possible, and to supply its arsenals & magazines, and for those purposes it actually imposed a tax on its Citizens."[74]

Several historians insist that the claim that Virginia was arming for a conflict was "totally unfounded," although conceding that "it enjoyed wide currency." They argue that Virginia had planned a new armory and arms purchase for several years, but this misses the complexity of the situation, suggesting an either/or conclusion—either Virginia had independent reasons to upgrade its armory (which it did) or it was arming for a potential conflict with the federal government. It may have been both. After all, Virginia had repeatedly delayed upgrading its armory in part because of the expense, but as Hamilton noted, in 1798–1799, tax-averse Virginians increased taxes to do so. More reasonable is the conclusion that "although some historians have denied it, there are a number of indications that the Virginians were also arming for a possible military showdown by quietly building up their state's defenses in the event the political conflict were to turn violent and its citizens were to need defending." At least some in Virginia bandied about the idea of arming for a possible conflict with the federal government.[75]

What is clear is that those concerned with the future of the union in 1799 were surrounded by reports of possible military conflicts between the states and the federal government. Even those reports increased the risk that the nation might slip into conflagration.[76]

By the spring of 1799, in this heated environment, the tax revolt known as Fries's Rebellion broke out. With hindsight, Fries's is seen as a relatively small, even insignificant protest, but at the time the nation was a powder keg; Fries's revolt could not so easily be ignored given the riots of the 1790s, the Quasi-War with France, ongoing European wars, and threats of violent opposition to federal authority. Some Fries's rioters were openly attacking the Sedition Act (seeming to support the Kentucky and Virginia Resolutions). At the time, Fries's added fuel to the growing concerns that Virginia and Kentucky, and the Democratic-Republicans, were fomenting a crisis and possible dissolution of the union.[77]

In addition to building a new armory and buying arms, Virginia legislators proposed a law threatening direct judicial interference with any prosecutions under the Sedition Act. "The Legislature of Virginia is about appealing to the people, against the general government.—A bill is ordered to be bro't into the House, arraying the state judges against those of the United States, in cases that may occur under the Sedition act; the avowed object of the bill is, to set at liberty any person who may be prosecuted under the act." William Heth warned Hamilton that if Virginia passed the habeas corpus law empowering state judges to release federal prisoners, "the next moment, some of those of the opposition, who are panting to become Martyrs in the *holy cause,* will throw themselves in the way of the Marshal, or of some officer of the government whom they may supposed bound by oath & duty, to notice seditions, or treasonable expressions. And thus, the signal of Civil War will be given." Kentucky also seemed to be itching for a fight and threatening that any Sedition Act prosecutions in Kentucky would be met with open defiance.[78]

The very real threat was heightened (in perception and reality) because the nation was still new, its structures still gelling, settling itself on a foundation that still seemed shaky. Rather than several centuries of constitutional evolution, the nation had a history of revolution and rapid, almost violent change. Critically important, in the late 1790s, political leaders and citizens still struggled with the question of what was the legitimate role of a loyal opposition, and radicals seemed committed to going beyond vocal protests. Some of this, undoubtedly, was political hyperbole, but "in the absence of a legitimate system of opposition," Joanne Freeman explains, "Federalists and Republicans alike assumed that there was only one answer: They must unite temporarily to eliminate opponents who seemed bent on destroying constitutional order." Given the conflicts of the 1790s and reports of militia officers threatening to join a French invasion, the Resolutions elicited grave concern.[79]

This, then, was the crisis of union that haunted both Patrick Henry and George Washington in 1798 and early 1799. This is why Washington was convinced that the challenge to the federal government launched by Jefferson, Madison, and their supporters would "dissolve the Union or produce coertion," domestic military intervention by the U.S. army against citizens, and possible civil war.

5

"A Constitutional Way"

L ooking back over more than two hundred years of growth and success for the United States, it is, perhaps, easy to discount the seriousness of the crisis of the late 1790s.

At the time, Americans could not.

The nation had already seen several armed rebellions since the end of the American Revolution—most notably the Shays's and Whiskey Rebellions—and while those revolts might be dismissed as relatively small matters, they did not draw upon support from state governments and high-ranking officials, nor did they involve the threat of significant foreign interference that pervaded the late 1790s. Still, the fact that those rebellions occurred at all fed the rising concern of Americans facing a much greater danger at the end of the eighteenth century.

Political disputes were igniting riots in major American cities, with the president of the United States gathering with trusted and armed allies in his Philadelphia home in fear of an attack by the mob. The former secretary of the treasury was bloodied in a political street brawl in New York City. The vice president so feared arrest for sedition that he did not sign some letters and refused to record some concerns in writing.

Through most of 1798, war with France appeared a real danger; hundreds of American ships were being seized and skyrocketing marine insurance rates were crippling trade. Many feared an invasion by Napoleon's seemingly invincible armies. Portentously, some Democratic-Republican militia officers, unable to express opposition to government policy in a loyal manner, vowed treason, a willingness to fight for France if an invasion occurred, even threatening to enlist enslaved men in the cause. In late June 1798, Washington's former secretary of war, Henry Knox, warned President Adams that France could easily transport an army of 10,000 Caribbean Black soldiers to America's undefended shores where the enslaved and others were likely to rally to the French flag. Knox sent a similar warning to Washington. (While modern armchair analysts can dismiss this as highly unlikely—enslaved people supporting slaveholding states against the federal government—it could not be so easily dismissed at the time.) The risk of a slave uprising against the federal government in concert with Kentucky and Virginia was discussed in print as late as the spring of 1799, "employ[ing] the force of the country in its own destruction." Other accounts reported, "There is reason to believe that the French have determined on an invasion of some of the Southern States. It is not to be supposed that their designs are to be effected by any great armament from France, but by the more sure and fatal operations of secret emissaries, who will combine the slaves with the enemies of government in Virginia, Kentucky, &c. and thus employ the force of the country in its own destruction."[1]

Newspapers filled with dire warnings. In early 1799, with the nation still trying to digest the significance of Kentucky's and Virginia's threats, Fries's Rebellion flared in Pennsylvania; the protest against a new federal tax to fund military preparation for a possible war with France seemed to portend armed resistance to government power. "They are already in arms in Pennsylvania," a Boston newspaper warned, "and Virginia holds forth all possible encouragement to their rising by revolutions [sic] and remonstrances calculated to excite civil war, and to infuse in to the bosoms of the factious all the fury with which such wars are carried on." There were reports of states gathering arms for a possible conflict with the federal government, and a massive federal military expansion—effectively commanded by deeply partisan Alexander Hamilton—lurked in the background. Newspaper editors were being prosecuted and jailed for criticizing the Federalist administration. The nation seemed to many to be dividing into two camps on the verge of open, armed conflict.[2]

Patrick Henry Is Called Back into the Political Arena

Of course, Washington's letter to Patrick Henry of January 15, 1799, calling the retired patriot back into the political fray, the story with which this book began, did not alone precipitate Henry's anxiety; it fell on fertile ground. Even after his formal retirement, living in a string of rural homes across south central Virginia, Henry kept up with key national and international developments, and the news did not encourage a peaceful retirement. He was keenly interested in the negotiations with England and France, the machinations of the Democratic-Republican Societies, the Jay Treaty, the insult to the United States of the XYZ Affair, and the Quasi-War with France. The Kentucky and Virginia Resolutions fed a growing alarm.

It may be true, as Democratic-Republicans later alleged, that living in retirement far from the centers of political and commercial activity Henry did not fully appreciate the gravity of the attack on the free press and the extent of convictions under the Sedition Act. Perhaps few did. Historians have also missed the extent of that threat. While some of the individual prosecutions were reported, the scope of the problem may have been clear only to party leaders at the time. Henry himself lamented that "the wide extent to which the present contentions have gone will scarcely permit any observer to see enough in detail, to enable him to form any thing like a tolerable judgment of the final result." Perhaps, like Washington, he was less concerned with prosecutions of sedition, but in Henry's defense, most of the Sedition Act convictions occurred in 1799, *after* adoption of the Kentucky and Virginia Resolutions and Henry's final campaign. In early 1799, though, as Washington beseeched Henry to come out of retirement, it is simply too facile to dismiss his views as based on ignorance, as political opponents later did in an effort to undermine Henry's judgment and actions.[3]

With the Alien and Sedition Acts adopted by Congress in the shadow of the nationalist fever generated by the XYZ Affair, and the Kentucky and Virginia Resolutions further riling political waters, elections for the Sixth Congress, scheduled to convene in December of 1799, gave the first opportunity to test public opinion at the polls, and Henry would play a role. One hotly contested campaign in Virginia is particularly informative concerning Henry's political influence and his reluctant return to politics: In 1798, John Marshall, one of the envoys to France during the XYZ Affair, was summoned to Mount Vernon and convinced by George Washington to run for Congress as a Federalist from the Richmond district against an entrenched incumbent Democratic-Republican, John Clopton. Representative Clopton had been a vocal opponent of the administration and was also a target of the grand jury that had produced the presentment against Representative Samuel Cabell that so enraged Jefferson. During the campaign, friends of Clopton spread a false report that Patrick Henry supported their candidate, urging people not to vote for Marshall, a friend of "Scottish merchants and old tories." Given Henry's history as the leading antifederalist and a strong advocate of states' rights, the claim seemed plausible. Still, Federalist Archibald Blair, longtime clerk of the Virginia Council of State, was surprised by the claim and wrote to Henry directly about this effort to capitalize on his continuing popularity. Blair included with his letter a copy of the recently adopted Virginia Resolutions.[4]

On January 8, 1799, one week before Washington would call on Henry for his aid, the former governor responded angrily in a letter to Blair that was clearly understood to be for public distribution and which Blair handed about the district freely. Henry began by noting that Virginia's Resolutions gave "cause for lamentation," and he openly accused "certain leaders" of the Democratic-Republicans of "meditat[ing] a change in government" possibly through "dissolving the confederacy." Henry's anxiety erupted on the page. Whatever their intent, Henry thought the strident attacks on federal authority by Kentucky and Virginia could lead to disunion: "I am free to own, that in my judgment most of the measures, lately pursued by the opposition party, directly and certainly lead to that end." (The letter, circulated heavily, had such an effect that Archibald Blair later had it published in response to claims that he had misrepresented its contents.)[5]

Turning to the Marshall-Clopton contest, Henry praised Marshall, his co-counsel in the British debts case: "He ever stood high in my esteem. . . . his talents and integrity unquestioned. These things are sufficient to place that gentleman far above any competitor in the district for congress." Referring to Marshall's role in the XYZ Affair, Henry concluded, "Tell Marshall I love him, because he felt and acted as a republican, as an American. . . . I really should give him my vote for Congress, preferably to any citizen in the state at this juncture, one only excepted, and that one [George Washington] is in another line." Not knowing that within a week Washington would be calling the old patriot back to the field, Henry concluded, "I am too old and infirm ever again to undertake public concerns."[6]

Henry's letter in favor of Marshall "turned the guns of Clopton's friends against them." When the votes were counted, Federalists flipped the district; Marshall won that election by just over 100 votes of a total of over 2,000. "Henry's letter saved Marshall," the future chief justice's biographer concluded. Fortuitously, within months of his taking his seat in the House of Representatives, Marshall would be appointed secretary of state by John Adams and, a few months later, after Jefferson's election but before his inauguration, be appointed to the Supreme Court as one of Adams's "midnight appointments." Patrick Henry, then, was responsible for Marshall's illustrious and prominent three-decade career on the Court.[7]

Henry also assisted Henry "Light-Horse Harry" Lee in his election campaign for Congress that year, a campaign won by only thirty-five votes. In a May 1799 letter, Henry expressed "gratitude" for Lee's efforts to oppose the

Virginia Resolutions in the House of Delegates, telling Lee, "I can no longer remain a silent spectator of a system that leads, by the shortest cut, to perdition." When Lee won his election, Jefferson was undoubtedly nonplussed by the success of another ardent political foe (a foe who, in the early nineteenth century, would write scathingly about Jefferson's "timidity and impotence" as governor during the American Revolution). Jefferson grumbled to one supporter "that Lee should have been elected . . . marks a taint in that part of the state which I had not expected." To another, he lamented that "the Virginia congressional elections have astonished every one." (Henry's support of two of Jefferson's most despised political opponents, placing both in Congress at a critical moment, may well have also encouraged Jefferson's longstanding enmity for Henry.)[8]

Adding to his own mounting fear for the state of the nation, Henry received a second letter from Archibald Blair in early 1799. Blair began by thanking Henry for the letter in support of Marshall that "completely gives the lie to the base insinuation" that Henry supported Clopton, the Democratic-Republican candidate. But Blair continued, voicing his deep concerns that the "youth" of America had "imbibed the poison" of a "mad philosophy . . . born to liberty without knowing how they came by it." Henry would understand that drinking freely of intoxicating individual liberty, untempered by a commitment to the law, to civic responsibility, and to a concern for the community and its people, was a dangerous draft. Reflecting that "mad philosophy," the Democratic-Republican party was riddled with "ambition," putting parochial and personal interests over national concerns. Turning on the Virginia Resolutions, Blair lectured ("preaching to the choir" as it were): "The present [Virginia] assembly has gone further than any other to loosen the bonds of union—their resolves declaring certain laws of congress unconstitutional I make no doubt you have seen. It is thought they will go still further. . . . I cannot believe that the good sense of the people will suffer a dissolution of the confederacy, but I apprehend, if the opposition party are permitted to go much further, a civil war with all its fatal consequences must ensue." Blair's predictions must have sent a chill down Henry's spine, especially given rumors that Virginia was arming for a possible conflict with the federal government. In spite of Henry's insistence several weeks earlier that he was too old and infirm for a return to public life, Blair urged him to reenter politics. "You would speak truths, and the people would believe."[9]

Henry was still ruminating on Blair's letter when he received the urgent plea from George Washington asking that he reenter politics to help save the union. Now, the general's fears and entreaties added to Blair's and confirmed

Henry's stewing anxiety. "It would be a waste of time," Washington wrote, "to attempt to bring to the view of a person of your observation & discernment, the endeavors of a certain party among us, to disquiet the Public mind with unfounded alarms." Washington regretted that Virginia, or at least its legislature, was taking a lead in igniting and fueling the conflagration, but he was most deeply concerned about its possible fatal consequences.[10]

The actions of opposition leaders, especially the Virginia and Kentucky Resolutions, could "destroy" the nation, Washington lamented. Those Resolutions and their supporters were threatening disunion, the collapse of the new nation for which the revolutionaries of 1776—led by Henry and Washington—had risked everything. "At such a crisis as this," Washington insisted that it was essential for Henry to reenter the political fray and defend the nation that he had helped to create against disunion and the "Civil discord" of anarchy. Expressing his belief that Virginia's state legislature and congressional delegation did not well represent most Virginians' devotion to the union, Washington was confident that Henry's "weight of character and influence in the Ho[use] of Representatives would be a bulwark against such dangerous Sentiments as are delivered there at present." As it had been in years past, Henry's presence "would be a rallying point for the timid, and an attraction of the wavering. In a word, I conceive it to be of immense importance at this Crisis that you should be there; and I would fain hope that all minor considerations will be made to yield to the measure."

While Jefferson (and Jeffersonians) would later insist on the canard that Washington and Henry despised each other, Washington's correspondence with Henry demonstrates extraordinary respect and regard. Here, Washington concluded: "With great, and very sincere regard and respect, I am—Dear Sir Your Most Obedt & Very Hble Servt" (a warm and personal ending even in the era of overly sentimental closings).

The old patriot at Red Hill was genuinely touched by Washington's letter. When Henry received the general's plea that he reenter politics to arrest the imminent danger of the Kentucky and Virginia Resolutions, the sixty-two-year-old Henry was feeling his age (apparently suffering from some of the medical problems and pain that led to his death from a bowel blockage within five months). Only weeks earlier, he had insisted that he could not return to the public arena; he was "too old and infirm." Now, Henry likely remembered that in refusing Washington's offer of high office several years earlier, he had told Henry Lee that he would only return if "necessary for the safety of the country." Even more to the point, in his last direct communication with Washington when the president offered to make him secretary of state, Henry then insisted that he would only come out of retirement if disunion was threatened. If "my Country is destined . . . to encounter the Horrors of Anarchy," he had written in 1795, then "every power of Mind & Body which I possess will be exerted in support of the Government under which I live & [referring to ratification of the Constitution that he had opposed] which has been fairly sanctioned by my Country men." In the winter of 1799, with Washington's plea in hand, Henry decided it was that time.[11]

Henry had often expressed great respect for the sacrifices that Washington made for the country, during the war, the Constitutional Convention, and his presidency. Now, Henry wrote warmly in reply to the former president's entreaty, "I am ashamed to refuse the little Boon you ask of me, when your Example is before my Eyes." He went on: "My Children would blush to know, that you & their Father were Co[n]temporarys, & that when you asked him to throw in his Mite for the public Happiness, he refused to do it." While succumbing to the former president's pleas to reenter politics, Henry told Washington that he could not agree to run for Congress. Although the federal government would move in 1800 from Philadelphia to the new district rising on the Potomac River (and to be named for the father of his country), even that location was too distant for the ailing Henry. With the immediate risk of disunion coming from the state capital, Henry was hopeful that his intervention in Richmond might arrest the danger. Still, "it may be doubted whether a Cure can easily be found for the Mischiefs they [Democratic-Republicans] have occasioned," but Henry concluded expressing confidence that "the Friends of Order, Justice, & Truth will once more experience the Favor of that God who has so often & so signally bestowed his Blessings upon our Country."[12]

Patrick Henry, the "Trumpet" of the American Revolution, the great antifederalist of the ratification debates who had worked so tirelessly (and almost successfully) to block adoption of the Constitution, the intellectual godfather of the states' rights movement, was coming out of retirement during a crisis of union in what would certainly be his last political campaign. Now, though, Henry was defending the Constitution, "fairly sanctioned by [his] Country men," and the still fragile nation from what he perceived to be dangerous and unfounded opposition of a radical agenda propagated by ambitious politicians insisting on a state's right to interfere with federal actions.

Henry's Final Speech

When it was announced that Henry was again running for office, promising a campaign speech at Charlotte County Court Day in March, people took notice. Henry's last major public political efforts had been ten years earlier when he defended states' rights against what he perceived to be the potential danger of a distant and powerful federal government, but times had changed.

Democratic-Republicans in 1799 had no doubt that Henry's campaign promised trouble, and they quickly grew nervous with the news of his decision to reenter politics. Jeffersonians were virtually abuzz with foreboding. Spencer Roane, one of Henry's sons-in-law but a dedicated Jeffersonian, warned James Monroe, soon to be Virginia's governor, that Henry had committed "to arrest the progress of the State legislature in opposing the measures of the General Government; which is, as I conceive, to attack the republican Cause in it's last Citadel." It was essential for the party to use "every means tending to defeat his schemes," Roane advised. "It appears to me advisable to notify the above Circumstance to some of my republican friends," and Roane entreated Monroe that "I hope & trust, that yourself & your illustrious friend Madison, will not hesitate in coming into the legislature, on such a momentous occasion." (Madison did run for election to the Virginia House of Delegates, in part to try to constrain Henry, from which fact Jefferson took much comfort.)[13]

While Jeffersonians plotted how to counteract the dramatic, explosive force of Henry, people in Charlotte and surrounding counties waited for Henry's speech with anticipation. With Henry scheduled to appear at the Charlotte County Courthouse in the small town then known as Marysville (now Charlotte Court House), people flocked from surrounding farms and villages. Hampden-Sydney College was almost twenty miles away in Prince Edward County—a significant distance in days of poor roads and horse-drawn buggies—but students and faculty abandoned classes and gathered for what they sensed would be a historic event. John Miller, a Hampden-Sydney student at the time, later reported to Patrick Henry Fontaine, Henry's eldest grandson, that "every student that could borrow, or hire, anything to ride, went to the Courthouse, and many of them walked." On the morning of March 4, a large crowd gathered around the courthouse in anticipation of Henry's appearance.[14]

Accounts of the speech at the Charlotte Courthouse, Henry's last, are fairly extensive, which was not always the case with Henry's speeches. In fact, while Henry is remembered in history primarily for his compelling oratory, his most famous speeches—"liberty, or . . . death," "Caesar had his Brutus"—were not recorded until many years after they were delivered, leaving historians with serious questions about the remembered texts. But in the case of the March 1799 speech, there are several detailed accounts, including one from John Randolph of Roanoke, a rising star in the Democratic-Republican party whose political career began that day at Charlotte County Courthouse as Henry's approached its finale. Randolph recorded his recollections at the time. The speech was also later reported by Dr. John Miller, a student at Hampden-Sydney at the time of the speech; while his recollections were not reported until 1838, they were confirmed "in every particular" by Nathaniel West Dandridge, who studied law as a clerk under Henry, was present for the speech, and later married Henry's granddaughter, Martha H. Fontaine. As with other famous Henry speeches, the precise words can well be questioned, but the outline of the argument and some of the more memorable phrases can reasonably be relied upon.[15]

On March 3, Henry, now unable to ride horseback comfortably, took a carriage from his home at Red Hill to a friend's home several miles from Marysville. Making his way into town the next morning, Henry rested on the porch of a local tavern across the road as a large throng of folks gathered on the courthouse lawn. When it seemed that enough people had arrived, Henry slowly, it seemed painfully, rose to deliver his remarks. It was often reported, even when Henry was in his prime, that he began his speeches with a deceptively reserved character before his composition rose to an oratorical crescendo, but this time, if reports are credited, his hesitancy was not a device for effect. "At length he arose, but stooped a little from age, and seemed feeble," the former Hampden-Sydney student recalled. His face seemed gray—it "had a Scotch cast," his countenance worn, and "when he commenced his exordium, his voice was slightly cracked and tremulous." But once Henry launched into his oration, a "wonderful transformation of the whole man occurred. . . . He stood erect; his features glowed with the hue and fire of youth; his face shone with an expression that seemed almost supernatural, and his voice rang clear and melodious, with all the intonations of some grand musical instrument . . . and fell distinctly upon the ears of the most distant of the thousands gathered before him." Echoing Miller's recollections, an early historian wrote that Henry, "enfeebled by age and ill health with a linen cap upon his head, . . . mounted the hustings, and commenced with difficulty; but as he proceeded, his eyes lighted up with its wonted fire, his voice assumed its wonted majesty; gradually accumulating strength and animation, his eloquence seemed like an avalanche threatening to overwhelm his adversary." As was so often the case with Henry's speeches, observers were almost stunned by the power of his voice and arguments. One observer said years later that "many of its passages were indelibly impressed upon his memory," a common reaction to a Henry speech.[16]

Given the centrality of Henry's final speech to the crisis of union, it is worth quoting the most comprehensive account at length:[17]

He told the people that the late proceedings of the Virginia Assembly [the Resolutions] had filled him with apprehension and alarm; that they had planted thorns upon his pillow; that they had drawn him from that happy retirement which it had pleased a bountiful Providence to bestow, and in which he had hoped to pass, in quiet, the remainder of his days.

Having justified his own campaign as the disinterested work of a patriot who would rather enjoy his retirement, Henry launched into the dangers that Virginia and the nation faced, and he directly confronted the Virginia Resolutions' call for action against the federal government and the compact theory that Jefferson and Madison were seeking to revive:

The State had quitted the sphere in which she had been placed by the Constitution; and in daring to pronounce upon the validity of Federal laws, had gone out of her jurisdiction in a manner not warranted by any authority, and in the highest degree alarming to every considerate man.

This was not merely a matter of conflicting theoretical arguments among lawyers and politicians. The claim that a state could interfere with execution of a federal law created a real danger:

Such opposition on the part of Virginia to the acts of the General government must beget their enforcement by military power; that this would probably produce civil war; civil war, foreign alliances; and that foreign alliances must necessarily end in subjugation to the powers called in. He conjured the people to pause and consider well before they rushed into such a desperate condition, from which there could be no retreat.

With an aside to the dramatic expansion of the U.S. military apparatus that had accompanied the Quasi-War with France,

He painted to their imaginations Washington, at the head of a numerous and well-appointed army, inflicting upon them military execution. "And where (he asked) are our resources to meet such a conflict? Where is the citizen of America who will dare to lift his hand against the father of his country, to point a weapon at the breast of the man who had so often led them to battle and victory?"

This, though, was an eighteenth-century political gathering, and as was common at such gatherings, some in the crowd had been drinking, heavily. When Henry asked rhetorically who would dare to oppose Washington, "A drunken man in the crowd, John Harvey by name, threw up his arm and exclaimed, that 'he dared do it.'" But this boozy outburst only fueled Henry's fury as he turned a withering gaze on Harvey.

> "No," answered Mr. Henry, rising aloft in all his majesty, and in a voice most solemn and penetrating; *"you dare not do it; in such a parricidal attempt, the steel would drop from your nerveless arm!"* "The look and gesture at this moment," said Dr. John H. Rice, who related the incident, "gave to these words an energy on my mind unequalled by anything that I have ever witnessed."

While political hyperbole was no less common in 1799 than today, Henry's warning of civil war and of potential alliances with foreign governments that would control America if called upon to support a domestic political faction against the federal government seemed a very real concern as citizens divided between Francophiles and Anglophiles, Democratic-Republicans and Federalists.

Henry, a far more accomplished lawyer than Jefferson ever gave him credit, appealed to the people to reject any notion of state sovereignty in a mere compact among sister states, explaining the issue in terms that would make sense to the gathered farmers and tradesmen:

> Mr. Henry, proceeding in his address, asked, "whether the county of Charlotte would have any authority to dispute an obedience to the laws of Virginia["]; and he pronounced Virginia to be to the Union what the county of Charlotte was to her. Having denied the right of a State to decide upon the constitutionality of Federal law, he added that perhaps it might be necessary to say something of the merits of the alien and sedition laws, which had given occasion to the action of the Assembly. He would say of them, that they were passed by Congress, and Congress is a wise body. That these laws were too deep for him, they might be right and they might be wrong.

Henry's views on the Alien and Sedition Acts were apparently more complex than this account may suggest and, as discussed below, what he said in this regard was contested over time. Henry, though, focused on what he thought was a more fundamental question: What was the proper role of a loyal opposition that disagreed with government policy? Where and how should the people voice disapproval to a government with which they disagreed and how should they exercise control over the government?

> But whatever might be their [the Alien and Sedition Acts'] merits or demerits, it belonged to the people who held the reins over the head of

Congress, and to them alone, to say whether they were acceptable or otherwise to Virginians; and that this must be done by way of petition. That Congress were as much our representatives as the Assembly, and had as good a right to our confidence.

With his voice rising to its crest, Henry reminded his audience of his own opposition to ratification of the Constitution for fear that it would create a government too powerful and distant from the people. He had warned that such a government might compromise the people's rights, exactly what was now happening.

He had seen with regret the unlimited power over the purse and sword consigned to the General government, but that he had been over-ruled, and it was now necessary to submit to the constitutional exercise of that Power.

He echoed his admonition from 1788 that any opposition to that government must occur in "a constitutional way." When Henry was later accused of inconsistency between his position in 1788 and 1799, one of his grandson's replied in the same voice: "The change was in his opponents who, having forced upon him the system of Government, after being warned of its powers, and confessing them, afterwards denied the very powers they had first admitted." Henry was endorsing, and bowing to, the community's right to decide.[18]

In terms remarkably like those that he now used at Charlotte Courthouse, during the ratification debates Henry had warned that if the Constitution was adopted, "Virginia cannot controul the Government of Congress no more than the county of Kent can controul that of England." But Virginia *had* ratified the Constitution, and with that action by the majority came important consequences. Since the majority of the people had "fairly sanctioned" the government, Henry felt obligated to defend it; a republican government demanded no less from its loyal citizens. In a republic, one would not always win or get one's way. Rule by the majority necessitated that minorities accept their losses and redress them "in a constitutional way." As he had written to Washington when agreeing to come out of retirement, "I should be unworthy the Character of a Republican or an honest man if I withheld my best & most zealous Efforts, because I opposed the Constitution in its unaltered Form." Henry—lawyer and communitarian—was adamant: the decisions of properly constituted authorities needed to be obeyed or the lawgivers and laws properly changed. This was foundational for any "Republican or . . . honest man"; the central point: the appropriate redress to ill-advised governmental action is in petitioning (as he had led the Virginia General Assembly in 1790) and at the ballot box—this is the proper role of a loyal opposition.[19]

Henry did not question the sovereign power of the people to act in extremity.

> "If," said he, "I am asked what is to be done when a people feel themselves intolerably oppressed, my answer is ready: *Overturn the government.* But do not, I beseech you, carry matters to this length without provocation. Wait at least until some infringement is made upon your rights which cannot be otherwise redressed."

Only a very serious problem that could not be resolved through remonstrance, a court challenge, or a change made at the ballot box might justify revolution. Unlike 1776, Virginians now elected their own representatives; democratic mechanisms to address problems, "to set us right," existed. Elections were pending. None of these options were available in 1776: petitioning had been exhausted (the king even refusing to hear petitions); colonists were unrepresented in Parliament; no mechanism for the community to redress the grievances remained in 1776. In 1799, the situation was entirely different and could not justify revolution, and he warned of the dire consequences of opposition to properly constituted authority in terms that continue to speak loudly today.

> "For if ever you recur to another change, you may bid adieu forever to representative government. You can never exchange the present government but for a monarchy. If the administration have gone wrong, let us all go wrong together." Here he clasped his hands and waved his body to the right and left, his auditory unconsciously waving with him. "Let us," said he, "trust God and our better judgment to set us right hereafter. United we stand, divided we fall. Let us not split into factions which must destroy that union upon which our existence hangs. Let us preserve our strength for the French, the English, the Germans, or whoever else shall dare invade our territory, and not exhaust it in civil commotions and intestine wars." He concluded by declaring his design to exert himself in the endeavor to allay the heart-burnings and jealousies which had been fomented in the State legislature; and he fervently prayed, if he was deemed unworthy to effect it, that it might be reserved to some other and abler hand to extend this blessing over the community.

Henry's final warning was powerful, and spoke brilliantly to Washington's fears, and his own, that had brought him out of retirement. If the people could not live within the Constitution that they had themselves written and ratified, and when necessary make changes in "a constitutional way," the republic that

Jefferson would call the "world's best hope" in his first inaugural address would fail; democracy would fail. If citizens could not be trusted to rule themselves, which included abiding by government decisions with which they disagreed, if revolution and disunion were the only responses from those opposing government policy in the United States, monarchy, tyranny, would be the undoubted result.

This warning was particularly poignant at the time. The audience understood that Jeffersonians were raising an insistent hue and cry that Federalists threatened monarchy. On March 8, the *Aurora*, the leading Democratic-Republican newspaper, printed an extended attack on the "monarchical party" that continued to seek to strengthen the federal government. Reminding its readers of the dangers of monarchy, and before the contents of Henry's Charlotte County speech were known, the paper cited Henry's "unconquerable and unanswered arguments" from the ratification debates concerning the potential abuse of power by the federal government. At least one report on the Charlotte Courthouse speech relayed Henry specifically defending George Washington and John Adams against claims that they favored a monarchy. "He said that they were not monarchists, although they, & many other pure patriots had been from the foundation of the Republic in favor of a much stronger government that he thought the wisest & safest for Virginia."[20]

Henry did not stop with a defense of Washington and Adams against the claims that they were monarchists, however; he turned directly on Jefferson and Madison and how their position had shifted dangerously since the ratification debates.

> He then exposed the inconsistency of Jefferson, Madison & others who after inducing the people to adopt such a government [the Constitution] in spite of his strenuous opposition, & solemn warnings, were now urging Virginia to destroy it *suddenly* at the risk of immediate Civil War & foreign invasion.

In one account, he could not resist chiding Jefferson for his aristocratic ways, telling the assembled citizens that "they should beware of this man, who . . . lived in Paris till he had so Frenchified himself, that he could no longer eat the vittles they were all fetcht up on."[21]

Turning again to the role of a loyal opposition and the necessity of making changes at the ballot box, Henry

> exhorted the people to be patient for a while; and promised if elected to use every effort to secure a peaceable repeal of *the odious & tyrannical*

laws which had alarmed Virginia; & to cast oil upon the waters of strife; & save the Union of the states.[22]

As with most of Henry's speeches, what was recorded was obviously just the main points and most memorable lines of what was a lengthy oration. Dr. Miller remembered that as Henry finished, almost collapsing into the crowd from exhaustion, he was stunned to look at his watch and find that Henry had spoken for an hour; he had been spellbound, as so many were, by the "Trumpet" of the Revolution.[23]

As any echo of Henry's voice faded, the gathered throng sensed that they had seen the final act of a great public servant. "The sun has set in all his glory," declared Dr. John H. Rice as Henry finished and was mobbed by an adoring crowd.[24]

John Randolph, the young Democratic-Republican candidate for Congress who supported the Kentucky and Virginia Resolutions, rose then to answer Henry, although much of the crowd had dispersed and nothing could diminish praise for the old governor's speech. Randolph, a noted speaker and important politician in his own right in the early nineteenth century, had always thought very highly of Henry and said so, but he defended the Resolutions as necessary. If reports are accepted, when Randolph finished, Henry told the rising politician, "*Keep truth*—and you will live to think differently," but that story may be apocryphal.[25]

Henry and the Alien and Sedition Acts

Even with the relatively good reporting on the Charlotte Courthouse speech, one critical issue concerning Henry's views was contested from early on: What exactly did Henry say about the Alien and Sedition Acts? Did he see them as unconstitutional? Ill-advised?

Unfortunately, the question is muddied by political bias. Democratic-Republicans, particularly after Henry's death in June of 1799, insisted that Henry supported the Alien and Sedition Acts; this was an effective means to undermine his criticism of the Kentucky and Virginia Resolutions and the party's leaders. This claim was also undoubtedly intended to undermine Henry's reputation in Virginia when he was no longer able to answer the attack and after the "Spirit of '98" reflected in the Resolutions became southern gospel.

Three stories concerning Henry's position on the Alien and Sedition Acts emerge: While John Randolph, a devoted Democratic-Republican, had every political reason to attribute support of the Alien and Sedition Acts to Henry, his account of the Charlotte Courthouse speech (the most heavily reported and the primary source relied upon here) has Henry demurring, saying that "these laws were too deep for him." Randolph's account suggests some ambivalence on the acts but that Henry did say that their fate should be resolved by the people in the political process. A similar, but more nuanced position is attributed to Henry by a Mr. Moulton; according to Henry Howe's account, Moulton reported that Henry said, "The alien and sedition laws were only the fruits of that constitution, the adoption of which he opposed. . . . If we are wrong, let us all go wrong together." Since Henry had made clear his fear that the Constitution would result in the federal government aggrandizing itself and violating the rights of the people, this was a backhanded way of expressing dissatisfaction with the Alien and Sedition Acts while stressing the need for a loyal opposition to work within the law.[26]

A more accusatory position was taken by William Wirt, also a rising star in the Democratic-Republican party and a firm Jeffersonian who did not attend the speech. In his biography of Henry published in 1817, Wirt did not directly challenge most of Randolph's account of the Charlotte Courthouse speech, indeed largely relying upon it by his own admission, but on the issue of the Alien and Sedition Acts, he wrote that Henry's "private opinion was, that they were good and proper." Wirt did not provide a source for this statement (although Jefferson had a major influence on Wirt's biography of Henry). Wirt's report has broadly made it into other histories, with a biographer of Light-Horse Harry Lee, for example, concluding that Henry "ended his days damning French infidels, supporting the Alien & Sedition Acts, and winning election to Congress as a Federalist."[27]

Others who witnessed the Charlotte Courthouse speech were adamant that Henry made clear his opposition to the Alien and Sedition Acts while insisting that the matter ultimately had to be resolved at the ballot box. John Miller, the former Hampden-Sydney student, recalled that Henry gave a "severe denunciation" of the laws. If elected, Henry pledged to "use every effort to secure a peaceable repeal of the odious & tyrannical laws which had alarmed Virginia." When asked what to do if Congress would not repeal the laws, he responded, "Then Sir, we must overturn the government: but we should use all peaceable remedies first before we resort to the last argument of the oppressed,—Revolution—and avoid as long as we can the unspeakable horrors of Civil War."[28]

Others weighed in on the controversy after Henry's alleged support for the Alien and Sedition Acts was published. In 1837, William Spotswood Fontaine (one of Henry's many grandchildren) published reports from several sources who heard Henry's Charlotte Courthouse speech and disagreed with Wirt's characterization of Henry's position on the laws. Robert Morton, at the time of the speech a teenager living with the clerk at the Charlotte County Court-house, remembered that

> the great object Col. Henry seemed to have in view, in his speech, was to keep the people together under the grievances of the General Gov-ernment, of which they complained, until constitutionally they could remedy the evils. . . . And I remember Col Thomas Read [the clerk of court], with whom I lived until I arrived to over twenty-one years of age, say that he was gratified, as much as he differed with Colonel Henry on some political topics of the day, that they agreed in opposition to the Alien and Sedition Laws.

Clement Carrington, on the other hand, seemed to agree with John Randolph on some equivocation by Henry: he "neither approved nor condemned those Laws, but said they were beyond his comprehension. . . . He decidedly con-demned the Virginia Resolutions as tending to civil war. He said 'Let us all go together, right or wrong.'" The Reverend Clement Read directly challenged Wirt's account that Henry believed the laws to be "good and proper," saying that "I did not hear it; as I now recollect. My own opinion is, that Mr. Henry was opposed to those laws, judging from some expressions that fell from him, before he made his speech and from his known political opinions. I lived in the same county . . . and if Mr. Henry had altered his political creed, I had an op-portunity of knowing it." (Read's suggestion that Henry had made comments in opposition to the laws before his speech might account for some of the con-fusion in the various accounts.) Reverend Read added that Henry's "only ob-ject, as it appeared to me, was to quiet the minds of the people and to prevent them from resorting to unconstitutional methods to remove any grievances." George Woodson Payne, a brother-in-law of Henry's second wife, reported "of his own knowledge, that Mr. Henry thought those Laws unconstitutional, particularly the Sedition Law, that he believed there were aliens who ought to be sent out of the country; but that the [Alien] Law, if not unconstitutional, operated unjustly and hard in many cases."[29]

Another great-grandson reported that he had discussed the matter with his father who "has often told me that he [Henry] never made any such assertion" in support of the Alien and Sedition Acts as claimed by Wirt. Using the same language recollected by John Miller, John Smith Fontaine, Henry's grandson, in conversing about the matter . . . generally lost his patience, and said most emphatically that the statement [that Henry thought the Alien and Sedition Acts were "good" laws] was false; on the contrary he said in his speech that they were *odious and tyrannical laws;* and that they ought to be repealed but at the same time he complained that he had warned Mr. Madison, who was then endeavoring to induce Virginia to secede from the Union, in the Convention of 1788 that if Virginia adopted the constitution of 1787 she would place herself in the power of a Federal Government which would claim the right under the constitution to pass such laws.[30]

The record is simply not perfectly clear on the question. Based on the various accounts, it appears most likely that Henry expressed opposition to the acts, during or before his speech, but focused on what he believed to be the nub of the issue at the time: citizens needed to take their opposition to the ballot box. Henry's object was to maintain the unity of the people, and the union, and to address the Alien and Sedition Acts in a constitutional manner—that is, by electing those who would change the laws to Congress, as he committed to do according to Miller. While Henry may have demurred on aggressively criticizing the laws in his speech (as Randolph and at least one other listener reported), he apparently believed that the laws were ill-advised and, especially in the case of the Sedition Act, unconstitutional. Wirt's unsourced argument to the contrary seems to be Democratic-Republican political propaganda.[31]

Importantly, both the Democratic-Republican and Federalist parties took a position that *either* the Alien and Sedition Acts were bad *or* the Virginia and Kentucky Resolutions advocated a terrible and dangerous remedy, but such a simple binary approach to the issues confronting the nation was a party position. Henry, among the moderates or what today would be called "independents," rejected that simplistic approach and thought that both were true.

Henry and a Loyal Opposition

Looking beyond opposition to the Alien and Sedition Acts, the general import of Henry's campaign is clear: Henry emphatically reminded the gathered throng that he had led the opposition to ratification of the Constitution because he believed that the new federal government would be too powerful and distant from local communities and the people, that it would be prone to abuse of power. He had counseled that, expanding on its own power, the federal government would invade the rights of the people. But (and this was the critical point) the Constitution had been properly adopted by conventions of the people nonetheless. When Virginia antifederalists, led by George Mason, gathered the evening after the ratification vote in 1788 and some sought to undermine the newly ratified Constitution, Henry had denounced extralegal efforts, insisting that reform must occur in "a constitutional way." In a republic, one had to accept the decision of the majority, even when not agreeing with it and even as one worked to change it. Washington had made this point in his famous Farewell Address: "The basis of our political systems is the right of the people to make and to alter their Constitutions of Government—But, the Constitution which at any time exists, 'till changed by an explicit and authentic act of the whole people, is sacredly obligatory upon all. The very idea of the power and the right of the people to establish Government presupposes the duty of every individual to obey the established Government." In 1790, Jefferson had said much the same: "the will of the majority, the Natural law of every society, is the only sure guardian of the rights of man. Perhaps even this may sometimes err. But it's errors are honest, solitary and short-lived."[32]

Now, Kentucky and Virginia were arguing that they had authority to nullify or bypass federal laws, contrary to the Supremacy Clause in Article VI of the Constitution. Equally troubling, they were justifying their arguments based upon a compact theory that had been rejected when the Constitution was drafted and ratified because the history of the 1780s demonstrated that a mere confederation or league of independent states that could unilaterally interfere with federal authority was both ineffectual and unstable. Encouraging such behavior and suggesting that the fabric of the nation was so flimsy was dangerous to the nation; it courted civil war. Such efforts to undermine legitimately constituted governmental authority had never been part of Henry's opposition.[33]

Revolution always remained an option for a people tyrannized by their government, but it should only be used in the most dire of circumstances: when redress through political means was unavailable. Henry, who had led the country into its war with Britain in 1776—when Americans had no right to vote for British government officials and their petitions had been unceremoniously dismissed—concluded that 1799 was not a time for revolution. After the Whiskey Rebellion, the former firebrand of the Revolution, Samuel Adams, had similarly explained the limitations to the right to revolution, arguing that "our Constitution provides a safe and easy method to redress any real grievances. . . . What excuse can there be for forcible opposition to the laws?"

Now, as the world watched the infancy of the first modern constitutional republic, if political means did not work, revolution would inevitably lead to
collapse of the republic and to monarchy.[34]

Henry's role as the leading antifederalist in the Constitution's ratification
debates was critical in giving his message legitimacy. In the 1790s, a conservative estimate was that one-half to two-thirds or more of the Democratic-
Republicans had been antifederalists during the ratification debates. Thus,
a majority of the people driving the Kentucky and Virginia Resolutions had
likely opposed ratification of the Constitution. Henry's denunciation of their
new effort was particularly powerful, and pointed, and the cause of deep consternation among many of his former supporters and devotees. Even after his
death, some remembered his opposition to the Virginia and Kentucky Resolutions in this context: "Virginia may boast, that she gave birth to one of the
greatest Orators of the present, if not of any age, and to a statesman, whose
prophetic mind fore saw, and pointed out, those evils in our Constitution,
attached to the executive power, against which we now complain. If any are
disposed to censure Mr. Henry for his late political transition, if any thing
has been written upon that subject, let the Genius of American Independence
drop a tear, and blot it out forever!"[35]

An early nineteenth-century report on the episode recognized the centrality
of Henry's opposition to ratification of the Constitution to his new argument.

> Believing that the democratic party in Virginia were yielding to passion,
> and advocating principles hostile to the safety of the country, and op-
> posed to the constitution of the United States, Mr. Henry espoused the
> cause of that instrument which he had so strenuously resisted. The Vir-
> ginia resolutions of 1798 filled him with alarm, and although subsequent
> events have shown that the authors of them did not harbor intentions
> hostile to the union, Mr. Henry firmly believed that he saw in their train
> the most ruinous consequences. . . . at the county of Charlotte, . . . in an
> eloquent address to the people [he] expressed his alarm at the conduct
> of the party opposed to the national administration, his belief that their
> measures were not in accordance with the constitution, and his determi-
> nation to support that instrument. He reminded them of his opposition
> to it on the very grounds that the powers they were then condemning,
> were conferred, denied the right of a state to decide on the validity of
> federal laws, and declared his firm belief, that the destruction of the con-
> stitution would be followed by the total loss of liberty.[36]

After his speech at Charlotte Courthouse, Henry renewed his criticism of the Virginia Resolutions with the same message less than a month before his death. Writing to Henry Lee, whom Henry assisted in his election to Congress, he explained, "Although my health and strength are very much impaired, I can no longer remain a silent spectator of the progress of a system which leads, by the shortest cut, to perdition.—I have offered my service to the country as a Delegate, but have not been able to go out." Foretelling the personal attacks that he would face from former political allies, Patrick Henry predicted that "every effort, of course, will be made against me, having made public my detestations of the late proceedings of the Assembly, and thereby provoked an opposition to my Election." Still, his faith in the people remained strong; the opposition "would have been very feeble indeed if I had seen the people generally, for the bulk of them seek after truth, which a little attention only, would discover in the present contest."[37]

The implications of Henry's speech at Charlotte Courthouse were profound. Fundamentally, Henry was not simply addressing the Kentucky and Virginia Resolutions and the Alien and Sedition Acts. At a very basic level, Henry was grappling with the complex, vexing, and unresolved question of how, in a republic, and a new and fragile republic at that, one should act as a loyal opposition. How should one voice disagreement with and oppose government policy such as the Alien and Sedition Acts without wrongly challenging or undermining the legitimacy of the government itself? How could states object to federal policy without—illegitimately and dangerously—interfering with federal authority?

Some saw immediately that these were the issues at stake, and Henry's message was broadly circulated. In an essay titled "Lesson to Men of All Parties" issued shortly after Henry's Charlotte Courthouse appearance, the anonymous author commended Henry for his patriotic efforts to support the Constitution that he had originally opposed because it had been endorsed by the people. Such support depended upon a profound sense of the responsibility that citizens owed to the democratic process. The essay began, "Patrick Henry, of Virginia, opposed, with the utmost of his abilities, the constitution of the United States, as submitted to the state conventions, because he tho't it destructive in *some parts*. The moment however it was adopted by a majority of his countrymen, he, like a good citizen, and a man of great and magnanimous mind, most peaceably and quietly *acquiesced*." The author reminded readers of Henry's denunciation of efforts to undermine the Constitution after it was ratified; when some antifederalists, led by George Mason, urged continued opposition after the June ratification vote, Henry objected: "No, my friends, we must not do so—nor should we shew any ill nature or resentment at what has happened. We are all brethren. We are one great family, embarked in the same vessel. . . . It has been ably, fully and fairly discussed. A majority of our countrymen, having equal interests, and equal stakes with ourselves, have thought it their duty to accept of the instrument." Henry urged his colleagues to work to "make her [the Constitution] more perfect," but to do so "in the way pointed out by the workmen" who drafted it.[38]

This essay was very broadly reprinted throughout the country, its dissemination seemingly only arrested by news of Henry's death in early June. Even then, reports of Henry's death picked up on the message that Henry, having opposed the Constitution, insisted that citizens live within its terms, reprinting part of the article. "When the majority decided against him, he not only peaceably, and like a true republican, acquiesced, but recommended acquiescence to others." Henry was widely seen as exemplifying a loyal opposition standing between two radical political parties that had engulfed the 1790s in a hyperpartisan battle.[39]

Reaction to Henry's Campaign

The mudslinging that Henry anticipated began even before he sat down at Charlotte Courthouse. The president of Hampden-Sydney College, the Reverend Dr. Archibald Alexander, was at Henry's speech and reported with some disgust that "Creed Taylor, then an eminent lawyer and afterwards a judge; who made remarks to those around him during the speech, declaring among other things that the old man was in his dotage. It is much to be regretted that a statement so untrue should be perpetuated." (Creed Taylor was a member of the Virginia Senate and correspondent of John Taylor of Caroline who introduced the Virginia Resolutions, including Jefferson's "null, void" language.) In February, the leading Democratic-Republican newspaper, the *Aurora,* had praised Henry: "Mr. Henry's reputation is alike pure, and his talents conspicuous. . . . Of his patriotism any more than his talents there can be no question." The *Aurora's* praise of Henry continued in early March, invoking his "unconquerable and unanswered arguments" against monarchy. But when the editors heard that Henry decided to run for office, the *Aurora* called his earlier appointment by Adams as a peace commissioner to France a "mere mockery on the people." After the Charlotte Courthouse speech, the *Aurora* claimed that "his mind [was] no longer quick to the apprehension of worldly deceit, the insuspicious temper of his dotage, or second childhood has made him a dupe." Such claims of Henry's senility—disproved by the speech itself—and other attacks would continue long after Henry's death. The point here is that these vicious attacks evidenced deep political concern.[40]

Democratic-Republicans reacted violently to Henry's campaign and electoral victory. Jefferson and his allies were absolutely enraged. "His apostasy must be unaccountable to those who do not know all the recesses of his heart," Jefferson railed to Archibald Stuart, a former law clerk of Jefferson's. (Apostasy is a religious term for betrayal; its use in this context is an indication of the vitriol that the Democratic-Republicans heaped on Henry.) Jefferson's letter signaled one reason for his violent reaction: fear that the press might be undermined by the Sedition Act. He assured Stuart that "our citizens may be decieved for a while, & have been decieved; but as long as the presses can be protected, we may trust to them for light."[41]

John Taylor raged that Henry was supporting just the type of "measures he so lamentably deprecated and foretold in the [ratification] convention." Unable to distinguish the legitimacy of objections before and after ratification and struggling to find some explanation for Henry's behavior other than the obvious—the Virginia and Kentucky Resolutions had gone too far and, taken to their logical extreme, threatened the union—Taylor rationalized to Madison that Henry's "apostasy" was driven by "personal enmity to Mr: Jefferson and yourself." Refusing to recognize the danger of the Resolutions, or to countenance opposition to them, it was essential for Jeffersonians to describe Henry's actions as unfathomable or petty: "What other motive can he have, but a desire to gratify hatred or ambition," Taylor sniped.[42]

Of course, Jeffersonians' anger barely disguised their grave concern. In the mid-1790s, when the possibility of Henry joining the Washington or Adams administrations seemed real, there had been great handwringing among Democratic-Republicans. In discussing Washington's offer to make Henry secretary of state, Edward Carrington, recognizing the relationship between the antifederalists of 1787–1788 and Democratic-Republicans in the 1790s, wrote the president that "so much have the opposers of the Government held him [Henry] up as their oracle, even since he has ceased to respond to them, that any event demonstrating his active Support to Government, could not but give the party a severe Shock." Henry's apparent support of the Federalists in 1799 (although it might more accurately be labeled opposition to the Democratic-Republicans) struck directly at the political strategy of the Jeffersonians. The Democratic-Republicans had been effectively labeling Federalists as monarchists and tories, and sought to rally political support around the "Spirit of '76." This strategy was highly effective: When Federalists turned to the Revolution, Jeffersonians insisted that the Democratic-Republicans were truer to its principles; if Federalists appealed to obedience to the postwar government as the protector of American liberty, they sounded like the "tories" who had been denounced in 1776. Patrick Henry, though, was nobody's tory, and his commitment to the Spirit of '76 was unquestionable. That was what made his political campaign against the Kentucky and Virginia Resolutions so dangerous to the Jeffersonians.[43]

Democratic-Republicans really believed that the fate of the union was at issue and that Henry's election could seriously interfere with their efforts to save the country. John Taylor invoked the upcoming presidential election and warned Madison that Virginia "is the hope of republicans throughout the union." Taylor was almost desperate with anxiety, worried that Henry in the legislature would end Virginia's "resistance" to what he termed "monarchical measures." If this were to occur, he counseled Madison, "the whole body will be dispirited and fall a sudden & easy prey to the enemies of liberty." Begging Madison to run for a seat in the General Assembly to oppose Henry's still-dominant popularity, Taylor concluded, "if you will not save yourself or your friend—yet save your country. The public sentiment of Virginia is at a crisis—at the next assembly it will take a permanent form which will fix the fate of America."[44]

While Jefferson feigned confidence that Henry's ability to control the Virginia General Assembly would be much diminished with Madison present, he still expressed concern for Henry's "intriguing & cajoleing talents," his ability of political persuasion, "for which he is still more remarkeable than for his eloquence"—high praise indeed.[45]

Interestingly, as Democratic-Republicans were contorted by his political campaign, Henry's patriotism and competence were again brought to the attention of the American people in a different manner. Early in 1799, President John Adams confounded the war hawks in his own party, and the skeptics among the opposition, and decided to send a second peace delegation to France to see if open conflict, still brewing in the Quasi-War, could be avoided. Adams appointed Henry to the delegation, an appointment quickly confirmed by the Senate and broadly embraced by the public before the old patriot could decline the honor; his health would simply not permit an overseas trip. Yet, in spite of Adams's effort to appoint a bipartisan delegation, Henry's appointment seemed to confirm to the hyperpartisan Jeffersonians that he had become an enemy and posed a threat. In the heat of the political crisis of 1798–1799, they simply seemed incapable of understanding a politician who had always opposed excessive government authority but who insisted, even in the face of the Alien and Sedition Acts, that the problem be addressed at the ballot box.[46]

Of course, Henry won his April election "by his usual commanding majority"—Henry always won his elections—and a fearsome and consequential battle in the Virginia General Assembly seemed inevitable.[47]

But the epic Virginia legislative battle over the proper scope of states' rights led by Patrick Henry on one side and James Madison as a surrogate for Jefferson on the other was not to be. (What a historic battle that might have been.)

In early June, a melancholy scene overtook Henry's home at Red Hill. Months before Henry was scheduled to take office in Richmond, he was incapacitated by pain. He had a bowel blockage; the pain struck him "like the gravel" (kidney stones), Henry said. His doctor, Dr. George Cabell, had little to offer other than some pain relief, probably laudanum (an opium derivative). Finally, in early June, with no other options, Dr. Cabell offered Henry a vial of liquid mercury, telling the stricken patriot that it would either relieve his problem, clear the blockage, or . . . the doctor was unable to finish. Henry, understanding the options, turned to the doctor, and said: "You mean, doctor, that it will give relief or will prove fatal immediately?" Knowing that he had few options, Henry gathered with the members of his large extended family who were present and gave them his blessing, said a prayer, drank the mercury, and died on June 6, 1799.[48]

Henry's death was politically explosive. Those concerned that the Virginia and Kentucky Resolutions threatened disunion were devastated. Having heard of Henry's illness (although prematurely reporting his death), Ralph Wormley wrote to George Washington that "he is surely a great loss; at *this crisis* and with *this* disposition, what mighty good, would not such a man, with his great powers of Oratory and his known character of integrity, have wrought! but alas! he is gone, leaving behind him few who excel him as an Orator, or, as a Patriot." Washington, hearing of Henry's death, lamented that "at any time I should have received the account of this gentleman's death with sorrow. In the present crisis of our public affairs, I have heard it with deep regret." (Washington himself would face an untimely death, also pregnant with political implications, before the year was out.) Within days, General William Davie, one of Adams's peace commissioners to France awaiting passage to Europe, wrote presciently to Federalist James Iredell of North Carolina that the Democratic-Republicans would seek to obscure Henry's final campaign: "The death of P. Henry, at this critical moment, is much to be lamented. Had he lived, I am persuaded he would have convinced the people of Virginia, that it was the conduct of their Legislature, not any change in his opinions that was the proper subject of regret, over which the patriot would wish to drop a tear, that might blot out its memory forever. Thus the Jacobins affect now to treat his last political opinions." In South Carolina, a story reprinted from Petersburg, Virginia, lamented "the loss of such a man would, at any time, be deeply felt; but now, when the national safety is endangered, and the public mind so much agitated, it is absolutely irreparable."[49]

Had Henry Lived . . .

Of course, the full implications of Henry's untimely death cannot be known with certainty; such "what-ifs" always involve some speculation. Yet, John Randolph's conclusion that had Henry lived Jefferson would not have been elected president in 1800 deserves some careful consideration. "Had Patrick Henry lived, . . ." he explained, "the electoral votes of Virginia would have been divided and Mr. Jefferson lost his election!" Others agreed. Writing after Jefferson's suggestion of nullification, the "Spirit of '98," had been fervently embraced by southern secessionists defending the institution of slavery, Edward Johnston, an essayist who knew the Jeffersons well, wrote "If the great PATRICK . . . had lived a little longer, the story of Ninety-eight and the whole Jeffersonian history would probably have been a very different one."[50]

Understanding the likely effect of Henry's serving in the Virginia House of Delegates in the fall of 1799 requires some familiarity with the Electoral College. This archaic device that determines who wins the presidency (and continues today to sometimes confound the will of the majority of the American people) was still in its infancy in 1799, but states were experimenting with how it could be manipulated to their political advantage almost from its inception. The heated political environment at the end of the 1790s supercharged that process.

When the Constitution was adopted in 1788, it was generally assumed that presidential electors would be chosen in districts in each state. James Madison explained that "the district mode was mostly, if not exclusively in view when the Constitution was framed and adopted." Under a district system, a state's electoral vote could be split with one candidate winning in some districts, another candidate in different districts, not unlike the common split in party affiliation among a state's congressional delegation. In 1797, Jefferson referred to the splitting of the electoral vote in a state as "the more free and moral agency." (A constitutional amendment to require electors to be chosen by districts, a proposal that Madison favored, absent gerrymandering, would reduce the chance of someone winning the popular vote but losing in the Electoral College.) States realized quickly, though, that the Constitution does not specify how electors must be chosen and that various options, with varying political ramifications, could be used. In addition to district elections, state legislatures could choose electors (awarding all a state's electoral votes to a preferred candidate); a statewide ticket could be used (also a "winner-take-all" system—now essentially the system in all but two states, Maine and Nebraska), or a hybrid system could be used.[51]

The possibilities came into focus after 1796 when Jefferson lost three electoral votes in strongly Democratic-Republican states, Virginia, North Carolina, and Pennsylvania, due to those states using districts to choose electors. By the end of the 1790s, as partisan politics became more heated, states were trending toward awarding all their electors to the state's preferred candidate, increasing the political clout of the state. Virginia, the most populous state, and the one that benefitted most from the three-fifths clause awarding additional electors and members of Congress based on the population of the enslaved, had 21 of 138 electoral votes in 1800. Fearing a repeat of 1796, Virginia's Democratic-Republicans introduced a statewide ballot system (essentially a winner-take-all system) in 1799—the bill was introduced into the legislature to which Henry had been elected but in which he did not serve because of his untimely death.[52]

While the Jeffersonians had an overwhelming majority in the House of Delegates, the highly partisan nature of a winner-take-all system with a hotly contested presidential election looming meant that it only squeaked by the Virginia House of Delegates in early 1800 in a seventy-eight to seventy-three vote, carried by only five votes. That some Democratic-Republicans were uneasy with this change even after it was made is evident in a letter to Jefferson from James Barbour, a supporter in the House of Delegates. Barbour sought to defend the partisan result with a semantic diversion: under the new law "there shall be one elector from each District," but the designation of districts would be meaningless to the result with the statewide ticket requiring voters to vote for the entire ticket. "This law excited the opposition more sensibly than any measure which has obtained this Session," Barbour conceded. Democratic-Republicans could only try to justify the law by arguing that other states were engaged in similar machinations and that "it is necessary to fight an adversary at his own weapons."[53]

Henry would almost certainly have prevented that result. As John Randolph explained,

I leave you to judge, sir, who knew the man, what chance the general ticket law would have stood, had Patrick Henry lived to have taken his seat. Five votes! . . . Patrick Henry was good for five times five votes doubled, in that body. Patrick Henry, said Mr. R, arrayed himself on the side of what he called the Constitution. I heard the last speech he made. He told the people they had, against his voice, made over the purse and the sword. He was a practical politician, and knew, that where these were given away, very little was retained. He saw and depicted, in clear and vivid colors, the dangers of a civil war.[54]

Henry would have opposed the electors bill not only because it was an obvious partisan ploy to elect Jefferson, but on principle as well. During the ratification debates, Henry had opposed creation of large districts because they tend to prevent local citizens from having a personal connection with their political leaders. "It has been said by several gentlemen," Henry noted, "that the freeness of elections would be promoted by throwing the country into large districts. I contend, Sir, that it will have a contrary effect. It will destroy that connection that ought to subsist between the electors and the elected. . . . This, Sir, instead of promoting the freedom of elections, leads to an aristocracy." After Henry's death, as states sought to manipulate the Electoral College to their advantage, Henry's views were remembered. In Virginia, an extract from a Henry speech from the ratification convention was reprinted explaining that Henry would not have supported the new Electoral College law: "The sentiments of such wise and good men as Mr. Henry cannot be too often laid before the public. They may call us back to the standard of true republican principles, which party spirit is banishing from our land. What would this patriotic gentleman have said to the law passed at the last session, changing the mode in Virginia, of choosing Electors of President and Vice President!" Emphasizing the political nature of the change, the writer concluded: "By whom has this monster been produced in Virginia?—By a description of people who misname themselves republicans; who, pretending to be friendly to our republican system, have struck a blow at the root of republicanism. . . . In the language of the American orator [Henry], they are an *aristocracy*, who produced the law." Another newspaper insisted sharply, and ironically, that Democratic-Republicans were seeking to subvert the Constitution by a "liberal construction" of its terms.[55]

The highly likely defeat of Virginia's Electoral College reform had Henry lived led Randolph to conclude that Adams would have won a significant number of (district) electoral votes in Virginia, and Jefferson (who won the Electoral College seventy-three to Adams's sixty-five) would not have been elected president in 1800.

Not surprisingly, it is all a bit more complicated than that.

Even if Virginia had retained the district voting system, it is not self-evident that in 1800 four of Virginia's twenty-one electoral votes would have been turned from Jefferson to Adams, throwing the election into the lame duck Federalist House of Representatives and procuring the latter's election. That was the fear of the Jeffersonians; after all, in the 1799 elections as many as eight of the Virginia congressional districts had returned Federalist representatives. Given that Virginia would have had two more electoral districts than House congressional districts, one might conclude that at least four electoral votes would have shifted to Adams. Political allies were writing to Madison that "it seems agreed that the fate of the election will depend upon the regulations [on the Electoral College] which Virg[ini]a may adopt." Charles Pinckney added, "pass the [electoral] act. I tell you I know nothing else will do & this is no time for qualms." On the other hand, the Federalists fared far more poorly in the congressional elections in Virginia in 1800–1801 than they had in 1799 (holding only one seat), suggesting some caution before concluding that retaining Virginia's old electoral law alone would have cost Jefferson the election.[56]

Yet, looking only at the congressional results in 1801 is as misleading as looking only at the 1799 results. Had Henry lived, not only would he have likely successfully opposed adoption of the winner-take-all Electoral College system in Virginia, but he would have more directly opposed Jefferson's election and supported Adams (an ally since 1774), not to mention assisted in congressional elections as he had done in 1799 (to the benefit of John Marshall and Henry Lee). As before, Henry would have undoubtedly had a substantial impact on voting in Virginia (not to mention Henry's significant influence in North Carolina and Kentucky, states that still had district systems for presidential electors).[57]

In fact, even with Henry's death and after Virginia's adoption of a statewide ticket, a quixotic effort was made to use Henry's opposition to the Kentucky and Virginia Resolutions to encourage Virginia's electors chosen under the new system to oppose Jefferson's election. Henry's January 1799 letter to Blair expressing the view that the Resolutions could lead to dissolution of the republic was quoted in an anonymous article reminding electors that "this text may be deemed infallible in point of authority, as falling from the pen of one of the first and ripest sages in the country, residing in the midst of the intrigue which he deplores, and writing a mere private letter." Henry's actual participation would have had a much larger impact.[58]

The speculation has continued for years. As late as 1809 a Federalist newspaper stated bluntly "Patrick Henry, unfortunately for the country died . . . or probably his talents [and] weight of character would have been [able to] crush that Virginia faction which afterwards succeeded in exalting Jefferson to the Presidency." Jefferson himself told Benjamin Rush in 1799 that if Henry and Washington were to die, the rise to power of the Jeffersonians would be more *"speedy,* as well as *certain."* In the end, while somewhat speculative, one can agree with John Randolph with reasonable confidence that had Henry lived (or, for that matter, had Washington lived past 1799), Thomas Jefferson would not have been elected president in 1800.[59]

In any case, Henry's death stopped neither the political battles and campaigns, nor the march of history.

Did Henry Plant the Seeds of the Kentucky and Virginia Resolutions?

At Charlotte Courthouse, John Randolph insisted that Henry had sown the seeds of the principles in the Kentucky and Virginia Resolutions. Another nineteenth-century historian, describing the rising states' rights movement and maturation of the Resolutions, wrote that the "Virginian of Virginians, Patrick Henry, who so strenuously opposed his State's adoption of the Constitution, struck the keynote, when he objected that it was 'We, the people,' and not 'We the States,' that made the government."[60]

Historians have also sought to argue that the Virginia protests against the Hamilton financial plan, led by Henry, contained the germ of Jefferson's and Madison's Kentucky and Virginia Resolutions. Richard Beeman, for example, asserts that while Henry's *"Address of 1790* did not pronounce the assumption law null and void, it did hint at a way in which the constitutionality of an act could be determined and prepared the way for the doctrine of nullification expressed eight years later in the Kentucky Resolutions." Beeman argues that Virginia's protests harked back to the state's authority to block actions of the national government under the Articles of Confederation—as if Virginians (and Henry) did not understand that the Constitution dramatically limited states' authority compared to that held under the Confederation.[61]

The view that Henry was the progenitor of the Kentucky and Virginia Resolutions would have been seen by the protagonists in 1798–1799 as deeply revisionist. Henry certainly understood that Virginia's protest against the Hamilton plan in 1790 was fundamentally different from the Resolutions of 1798.

Peter Onuf hits closer to the mark when he notes that Jefferson and Madison in 1798 were adopting the concerns that Henry had voiced at the ratification debates, debates that Henry lost and that were effectively rejected in the vote in favor of ratification.

> In the context of deepening partisan division in the 1790s, that collaboration [between Jefferson and Madison] moved them both closer to positions staked out by Henry in the Virginia debate over ratifying the Constitution. The threat Henry discerned to Virginia's vital interests and very existence from an all-powerful, neoimperial central government now became manifest in the consolidationist designs of the faction of High Federalist courtiers who gathered around the new president and dominated his administration. . . . Henry feared that their mobilization against the Washington and Adams administrations would jeopardize national unity at a critical juncture in the great geopolitical crisis unleashed by the French Revolution. Now it was the Jeffersonians who rallied around the states'-rights flag, putting Virginia first and risking the union.

Yet, Henry's insistence that these concerns must be addressed in "a constitutional way" was a very great distance from urging that the states could interfere with federal actions or that states were somehow independent parties to a mere compact from which they could block federal action in their own territory or withdraw from the union. Henry supported the rule of law and decisions by the majority, even those with which he disagreed. This is the essence of a loyal opposition. Jefferson took Henry's concerns and, in his desperation, applied a radical, unconstitutional remedy.[62]

Linking Henry's 1790 protest that Hamilton's financial plans were unconstitutional and the Virginia and Kentucky Resolutions is to misread history, teleologically to project back the actions of 1798 and beyond onto 1790 and Henry's actions. Only by equating these two fundamentally different actions can one declare that Henry's denunciation of the Virginia and Kentucky Resolutions was a "puzzle." Rather, Henry had been consistent in his fears of a powerful federal government that would interfere with the people's liberty, but he was equally consistent, and even more emphatic, in demanding that changes be made in "a constitutional way." As one of his biographers (and a grandson) wrote: "Mr. Henry, in his last speech in the Virginia convention which adopted it [the Constitution], said he would live under it a peaceable citizen. He redeemed his pledge, nobly."[63]

Henry died in June of 1799. Washington died in December. Jefferson was elected president in 1800, and all the "what-ifs" are mere speculation.

With Henry's and Washington's deaths and Jefferson's election, the crisis that had gripped Henry, Washington, and the nation died as well. The election of 1800 presaged a new seemingly bright future in the nation's history.

Was there, then, no crisis?

6

The Crisis Dissolves

"The Earth Belongs . . . to the Living"

From a distance, with Henry's June death (and that of Washington in December), it may seem as if the crisis simply evaporated like dew in the morning sun on top of Jefferson's little mountain. The election of 1800, what Jefferson would later term the "Revolution of 1800," promised a new day, and many welcomed the opportunity to forget the partisan battles of the 1790s.

Of course, resolution of the crisis was far more complex, filled with contingency, irony, good luck, pathos, and lessons for the still new nation. Jefferson and Madison were deeply affected. Understanding the crisis requires careful consideration of how its worst possible consequences were avoided and what happened to allow the nation to move forward.

As 1798 came to an end, no one was quite sure how far the constitutional challenge and the partisan battles would go. Jefferson and Madison seem to have intended as much with their studied ambiguity. Yet, with the Kentucky and Virginia Resolutions and threats of active state opposition to federal laws adding to the already simmering political cauldron, the possibility of violence against the government became so great that even Jefferson feared it might become a reality, with a backlash and potentially devastating political consequences for Democratic-Republicans, and the nation. The threat of disunion no longer seemed a mere rhetorical ploy.

Abandoning the desperate rhetoric of only a few months earlier, Jefferson wrote Archibald Stuart in February of 1799 with a much more moderate and hopeful message:

> A wonderful & rapid change is taking place in Pennsylvania, Jersey & N. York. Congress is daily plyed with petitions against the alien & sedition laws & standing armies. several parts of this state are so violent that we fear an insurrection. this will be brought about by some if they can. it is the only thing we have to fear. the appearance of an attack of force against the government would check the present current of the middle states & rally them around the government; whereas if suffered to go on it will press on to a reformation of abuses.

Jefferson wrote another old friend and ally the next day, "nothing could be so fatal. any thing like force would check the progress of the public opinion." Jefferson, perhaps contemplating the deep unease with the Resolutions that was percolating from multiple sources, including Madison, now wanted to focus on the need to "bear down the evil propensities of the government by the constitutional means of election & petition. if we can keep quiet . . . the tide now turning will take a steady & proper direction."[1]

In fact, the damage—fomenting a strong political backlash—had already been done.

Political Fallout: Federalists' Political Victories

Did the Alien and Sedition Acts hurt the Federalists electorally? Did the Kentucky and Virginia Resolutions help the Democratic-Republicans? Conventional wisdom is a resounding "yes" to both, although conventional wisdom also seems to see these questions as two sides of the same coin. In fact, they are distinctly different questions.

Richard Ellis concludes that the Kentucky and Virginia Resolutions "were issued for political effect to rally the Republican opposition, to reaffirm the Revolutionary tradition whereby the defense of personal and civil liberty was joined to states' rights, and to offer a theory of the origins and nature of the national government that undercut the constitutional basis for the Federalist program of centralization. In this sense the resolutions were an enormous success, as they played an important role in helping Jefferson obtain the presidency in 1800." Akhil Amar agrees, declaring that "in their first opportunity to weigh in on the matter, American voters sided with Madison, vaulting his mentor and fellow free-speech champion Thomas Jefferson into the executive mansion and sweeping the Jefferson-Madison party into congressional power." Other historians make the same leap directly from the Resolutions to Jefferson election: "The victory of that year [1800] may, in this sense, be accounted not only a Southern victory, but Virginia's and Kentucky's particular victory."[2]

These conclusions miss the actual historic progression. After the Kentucky and Virginia Resolutions were adopted, there was an election for Congress in 1798–1799 in which the Democratic-Republicans suffered losses across most of the South and the Federalists continued to expand their congressional majority. Jud Campbell rightly responds to the argument that the Resolutions were an electoral success for Democratic-Republicans that "for those keeping score, Americans' first electoral opportunity to weigh in on the Sedition Act was the election of 1798—a tidal wave Federalist victory."[3]

Beyond the election of John Marshall and Henry Lee, assisted by Patrick Henry, Federalists doubled their share of Virginia's delegation in the U.S. House of Representatives in 1799—from four to eight of the nineteen-member delegation, and Federalists made significant gains in congressional delegations elsewhere in the South—from three representatives in South Carolina, one in North Carolina, and none in Georgia to five in South Carolina, five in North Carolina, and two in Georgia. The substantial Federalist majority in the Senate was unchanged. After passage of the Kentucky and Virginia Resolutions, Federalists also made inroads in several state legislatures controlled by Democratic-Republicans; for example, they increased their representation in the Virginia House of Delegates from fifty to sixty. While Democratic-Republicans made some minor gains in the middle states, the election results overall "startled and unsettled the Republicans, who were particularly dismayed by the success of Federalism in the very citadel of opposition." Democratic-Republicans had their chins "hanging on their breasts—and their countenances depicted with fear and terror," the *Virginia Gazette* reported. Contrary to the myth that the Resolutions begat electoral success, their implicit "disunionist" threat and their compact theory were firmly rejected at the ballot box.[4]

A young Joseph Carrington Cabell, who would become Jefferson's greatest ally in the fight to build the University of Virginia twenty years later, wrote to a friend that the Resolutions led to the Federalists' victories. "Do you agree with me in opinion that the proceedings of the last assembly have caused the change?" Cabell could not accept the claims of Henry, Washington, and others that the Democratic-Republicans were wantonly threatening the union; "I have no doubt that the objects of the Members in adopting the Resolutions and addresses were perfectly pure," he insists. "But whether the Measures they adopted to effect these objects were the most *prudent* and *politick* I doubt very much." Cabell specifically noted that concern over disunion and conflict generated by the Resolutions trumped the rising concern over the Alien and

Sedition Acts: "The handle that was made of the Measures of the last assembly [Virginia Resolutions] had had its desired effect in alarming the people. The federalists have excited a belief that the legislature intended, and that their measures, led to, disunion. The people fearing disunion as the worst of evils have therefore thought it better even at the risk of bad laws, to elect men who would never consent to a dissolution of the federal compact." As Cabell recognized, the political fallout from the Kentucky and Virginia Resolutions actually tended to obscure the serious concerns with the Alien and Sedition Acts. This was not, though, an unmitigated Federalist success; Myron Wehtje explains that "political moderation, not Federalism, was endorsed at the polls in Virginia." Henry's election was part of that result.[5]

During the election of 1798–1799, even some of Jefferson's supporters seemed to distance themselves from the more radical views expressed in the Resolutions. When Jefferson asked the aging Edmund Pendleton, a respected Revolutionary leader (and, interestingly, a leader who had often clashed with Patrick Henry), to write about the XYZ Affair to support Democratic-Republicans in the upcoming election, Pendleton obliged by insisting that the affair had been blown out of proportion. Yet, in an apparent rebuke to the Resolutions, he advised (like Henry) that redress of grievances must take place at the polls and cautioned the people:

> I cannot conclude without earnestly recommending to my fellow-citizens, the forbearance of all force or violence, *to obstruct the execution of the laws,* or disturb the peace of society; relying, to effect the desirable reforms, upon the ordinary and proper modes of petition and remonstrance; and above all to be peculiarly cautious, and attentive to that object, in their suffrages at the various Elections, which, in a representative government, cannot fail of restoring things to their first principles, if the people are not deceived or cajoled, nor in a state of apathy or inattention to the importance of these suffrages.

After election to the presidency, Jefferson recognized the extent of the backlash in 1799, writing to Monroe, "we gained the victory in Nov. 1800. which we should not have gained in Nov. 1799."[6]

Beyond 1799, the political role of the Kentucky and Virginia Resolutions becomes more complicated, but they likely did not play a critical role in the presidential election of 1800. Primarily, they can be seen as efforts to energize Jefferson's "base" and may have been partially effective in that regard. Of course, the problem with motivating a party's political base is that it can alienate the middle, and that is apparently what happened with the Resolutions in 1799, with a dramatic impact.

The Alien and Sedition Acts were another matter. They certainly served as a drag on the Federalists, especially in 1800. As prosecutions under the Sedition Act increased in 1799 and into 1800, so did local petition campaigns against the acts, as did, ironically, the total number of Democratic-Republican newspapers. As time went on, rather than effectively quashing the press, even in states that firmly rejected the arguments of the Resolutions, newspapers in opposition to the Federalists proliferated. This dramatic increase in the Democratic-Republican press (from thirty-seven in 1798 to eighty-five in 1800) combined with the taxes imposed to fund the Federalist-supported military buildup likely had a far greater impact on the election of 1800 than the Resolutions. As Jefferson said in May of 1799, "our citizens may be deceived for a while, & have been deceived; but as long as the presses can be protected, we must trust to them for light: still more perhaps to the tax gatherer."[7]

Importantly, though, while opposition to the Kentucky and Virginia Resolutions by Henry and others led to sweeping Federalist victories in 1798–1799, over time, the Resolutions became very popular as a foundation for the South's increasingly radical embrace of states' rights, particularly as a defense of slavery after 1820 and the conflict over the Missouri Compromise. While slavery had not been prominent in the public defense of the Kentucky and Virginia Resolutions in the eighteenth century—at the time, slave owners seemed to believe the institution of slavery was effectively protected from serious challenge, and even among Virginia's slave-owning leaders, there was obviously a split on the Resolutions—protecting slavery became the foundation for states' rights arguments, including nullification and compact theory, in the nineteenth century. Similarly, while state sovereignty and opposition to federal judicial authority would also become pivotal in supporting the displacement of Native Americans in the nineteenth century, there is little evidence that Native land dispossession was a significant argument in favor of the Kentucky and Virginia Resolutions in 1798. Over time, however, as John Marshall explained, opposition to the "Spirit of '98" became "political sacrilege" for southerners in the antebellum period. Long term, the Virginia and Kentucky Resolutions helped the Democratic-Republicans (later Democrats) in the antebellum period to earn "a reputation as the party of limited federal authority and freedom of expression," a reputation that the party maintained through the Civil War and used in the defense of the slavocracy and Native dispossession.[8]

Other States Reject the Kentucky and Virginia Resolutions

Beyond the elections, much to Jefferson's surprise, and Democratic-Republicans' chagrin, a strong majority of the other fourteen states did respond to Kentucky and Virginia, but not in the manner hoped. Ten emphatically rejected the Kentucky or Virginia Resolutions or both. No other state acted to support Kentucky and Virginia as they had expected.

Of the ten states that rejected the Resolutions, each condemned the idea that states could unilaterally interfere with a federal law. Each saw grave danger if this policy was pursued. The governor of Delaware set the tone when, on January 7, 1799, he transmitted the Kentucky Resolutions to his state's legislature declaring that if Kentucky was correct, "as well may the Legislature of Kentucky or of any other State decide upon all and every other law of Congress"; such an application of the compact doctrine would inevitably "terminate in our utter ruin." The Pennsylvania Senate concluded that "a declaration by a state legislature that an act of the federal government is void and of no effect is a 'revolutionary measure' as dangerous as unwarranted." Referring to the compact theory, the legislature of Rhode Island argued that such an approach to the Constitution risked the "peace of the states by civil discord, in case of a diversity of opinions among the several state legislatures; each state having, in that case, no resort for vindicating its own opinions, but to the strength of its arm." Massachusetts's legislature noted that the "union of the states" was based upon the "consent of the people," but it could not "admit the right of the state legislatures" to intervene in this manner as they had under the Confederation. The Connecticut General Assembly, while noting its support for the Alien and Sedition Acts, focused on the constitutional theory espoused by Kentucky and Virginia, concluding that it "views with deep regret, and explicitly disavows, the principles contained in the aforesaid resolutions." As the new year dawned, newspapers began to report other states' rejections of the Resolutions; Kentucky's approach, in particular, was "highly *improper*" and "unwarranted by the constitution" according to Maryland's legislature.[9]

It is true that there was significant opposition to the Alien and Sedition Acts even in several states that rejected the Kentucky and Virginia Resolutions. This, though, does not diminish the rejection of the Resolutions; rather, it demonstrates the strength of the objection to the compact theory. Even when other state legislators, like Henry, questioned the wisdom or constitutionality of the Alien and Sedition Acts, they condemned the resurrected idea of state control of the federal government through the compact theory proposed by

Kentucky and Virginia, and it was the proposed remedy and theory of federalism that took center stage in the constitutional crisis (and those to follow). Maryland's response, for example, focused on the insistence that federal laws were "void"; when an effort was made to remove that term (suggesting that a state should not even declare a federal law unconstitutional) that motion was overwhelmingly defeated. The effort of an individual state to "void" federal law was the crux of the danger. The fear of disunion pervaded the responses, and none of the other states saw either set of resolutions, much less the Kentucky Resolutions, in the relatively benign manner in which Madison and others would later seek to rationalize them.[10]

Several other state legislatures that did not formally protest the Resolutions were sympathetic with objections to the Alien and Sedition Acts, much as Henry had been at Charlotte Courthouse, but they still saw Kentucky's and Virginia's actions as highly problematic. For example, Tennessee adopted resolutions opposing the Alien and Sedition Acts—taking the path that Henry had marked in objecting to Hamilton's financial plan—but pointedly not endorsing Kentucky's or Virginia's Resolutions. While Georgia's legislature took no official action, a Georgia Senate committee declared that while it disapproved of the Alien and Sedition Acts, it "hope[d] that they will be repealed without a necessity for the legislature of Georgia to enter into violent resolutions against them," apparently seeing the Resolutions as threatening violence.[11]

The radical nature of nullification and the principle of a compact among sovereign states is further demonstrated by other aspects of the states' responses. Several responding states made a point to note that states do have a specific authority under the Constitution to address alleged federal overreach, for example, by proposing amendments, but there was no authority for states to nullify or otherwise actively interpose between federal actions and the people. Years later, Madison would insist that the Resolutions were benign by, in part, pointing to the right of amendment. But Vermont's legislature rightly explained that "there is a wide difference between proposing amendments to the constitution, and assuming, or inviting, a power to dictate and control the General Government." Massachusetts agreed; while states seeking directly to undermine federal authority was dangerous, amendment was "an amicable and dispassionate remedy . . . for any evil which experience may prove to exist, and [through amendment] the peace and prosperity of the United States may be preserved without interruption." It was simply revisionist to suggest that either set of resolutions was simply seeking constitutional amendments.[12]

Seven of the responses—those from Maryland, Massachusetts, New Hampshire, New York, Pennsylvania, Rhode Island, and Vermont—expressly noted that it was the role of the federal judiciary to resolve constitutional questions presented by the Alien and Sedition Acts. New Hampshire's legislature was clear: "the state legislatures are not the proper tribunals to determine the constitutionality of the laws of the general government; that the duty of such decision is properly and exclusively confided to the judicial department." Vermont listed various alternatives for possible federal abuse: "right of election, the Judicial courts . . . and, in a jury of our fellow citizens."[13]

It is noteworthy that none of the states that affirmatively rejected the Resolutions are located south of Maryland, but even in the South, other states declined to support the Resolutions. "In North Carolina, the lower house passed a resolution favoring the laws' [Alien and Sedition Acts'] repeal, but the state senate rejected it. . . . Georgia agreed that the laws were unconstitutional but refused to endorse nullification. Tennessee called for the laws' repeal," but, as noted, pointedly did not endorse the Resolutions.[14]

At the time, it was well understood that the other states had offered a strong rebuke to Kentucky's and Virginia's radical resolutions. Newspapers reported that "the vigorous, decided and almost unanimous opposition which the legislatures of the several states have manifested to the spirit of revolt and disaffection in the States of Virginia and Kentucky, forms an important epoch in the political history of the United States, and it is presumed, will effectually restrain such open hostility against the principles of our constitution."[15]

While political discourse in the late 1790s had been marked with violent hyperbole, other states seemed to conclude that the Kentucky and Virginia Resolutions confirmed the Federalists' worst fears. The *Federal Gazette* warned that "a revolt from the Union" was being promoted by French spies and that "the revolt has at length been bro[ugh]t about in the state of Kentucky." Altogether, the other states issued a resounding rejection of the Resolutions. While modern academics can parse the Resolutions (especially Virginia's) in an effort to find them innocuous, that is not how they were perceived at the time.[16]

Madison Reconsiders

As 1798 came to an end, even before receiving any of the other states' responses, James Madison was deeply concerned with the Resolutions. Setting aside Kentucky's assertion that a state could declare federal laws null and void, he still worried that the much milder Virginia Resolutions (that he had drafted) had gone too far with their reliance on the newly reanimated compact theory and ambiguous claim that states should "interpose" between a federal law and the people, "arresting the pro[gress] of the evil . . . within their respective limits." Referring to the 1798 debates in the Virginia General Assembly over his own resolutions, and only two weeks before Washington would entreat Henry back into action because of the danger posed by the Resolutions, Madison suggested privately to Jefferson that "it is to be feared their [Democratic-Republican legislators'] zeal may forget some considerations which ought to temper their proceedings."[17]

Attempting post hoc to insert ambiguity and nuance into the Virginia Resolutions, Madison now for the first time suggested to Jefferson that while it could be said that the "state" was a party to the "federal pact," perhaps that did not mean the state government (or legislature) had authority to ignore or interfere with federal laws. "On the supposition that the former [the state] is clearly the ultimate Judge of infractions, it does not follow that the latter [the legislature] is the legitimate organ especially as a Convention [of the people] was the organ by which the Compact was made." Rather, Madison finagled, the "state" could mean the "people" of the state. Recognizing that the people of the state held sovereignty, rather than the state government, Madison now argued, might lead other states to look more kindly on the Resolutions and "would shield the [Virginia] Genl. Assembly agst. the charge of Usurpation in the very act of protesting agst the usurpations of Congress."[18]

This was a remarkable declaration by Madison, essentially conceding that action by the state governments to interfere with federal legislation—which both the Kentucky and Virginia Resolutions were—could be seen as usurpation. Madison understood, privately, that they had gone too far.

As Madison's letter makes clear, he understood that this new interpretation—"state" means "people"—was a very different position than what had been articulated in the Resolutions and certainly a very different position than that taken by Jefferson and Kentucky. After all, in both Kentucky and Virginia, it had been the state legislatures, not the people, that had acted. In retirement, Madison would insist that this was the only possible meaning of the compact of the states: The Resolutions of 1798 "proceed[ed] from the Legislature only wch. was not even a party to the Constitution," he wrote. In fact, the Virginia General Assembly had modified Madison's draft that claimed the "states alone" were parties to the compact; the term was removed because the people, in addition to the states, were alleged to be parties. Obviously, then, when the Resolutions referenced the "state," they were not talking about the "people." (Notably, Washington's January 15 letter to Henry specifically claimed that the legislature was underestimating the people's commitment to the union.) Similarly, Jefferson's draft of the Kentucky Resolutions stated that the "people" should respond at the ballot box when the federal government took action abusing an authority that was provided for in the Constitution, but that "every State" should nullify federal laws outside of delegated authority. Here, too, the "state" was clearly understood to be something very different from the "people." Madison's new theory was simply revisionist.[19]

Contra Madison's newfound distinction, the other states reasonably read the Resolutions of 1798 not as resting on the sovereignty of the people (a largely uncontested point), but the alleged sovereignty of states as governmental units and parties to a claimed "compact" with other states, an argument that Madison now eschewed. Massachusetts, for example, distinguished the "consent of the people" from the "right of the state legislatures." Eight of the ten states that responded to the Kentucky and Virginia Resolutions expressly saw the danger as the authority of state governments to interfere with federal actions— "legislatures of the . . . states," "State legislatures," "state government"—not the "people." The sovereignty of the people was never at issue, as was clear, for example, in Federalist #49. Addressing Madison's change of heart, Jack Rakove concludes that "Madison knew how far he had come since 1789, and . . . the dangerous conclusions to which the positions of 1798 led." Rakove, though, suggests that Madison's reconsideration related solely to the Kentucky Resolutions and the threat that "a state legislature could nullify any act of Congress," realizing that this was "a formula not for opposition but for disunion," a possibility that Jefferson "hinted" at in August of 1799. In fact, Madison's concern that they had gone too far went to both the Virginia and Kentucky Resolutions. In any case, when they evaluated the Virginia and Kentucky Resolutions of 1798, neither Henry nor Washington nor other states had the benefit of Madison's post hoc, hand-wringing parsing of terms in an effort to rework the Resolutions and defang the threat posed by the compact theory.[20]

In fact, some Federalists, in rejecting the Kentucky and Virginia Resolutions, specifically recognized that "the people, to be sure, had the ultimate right, in extreme cases." Madison's effort to redefine the "state" was "virtually to eliminate any difference between (his version of) state compact theory and the nationalist view that the Constitution was created by 'the people.'" That is, sovereignty and the ability to respond to a violation of the Constitution ultimately lay with the people, but, in spite of Madison's later contortions, that was not what was being argued, not what was being threatened, in the Kentucky and Virginia Resolutions of 1798. At Charlotte Courthouse, Henry had concluded with exactly this point, recognizing the possibility of the people, in extremity, rejecting government actions, but he understood how different this was from what the state legislatures had done in the Kentucky and Virginia Resolutions.[21]

Kentucky and Virginia Defend the
Resolutions, and Muddy the Waters

Faced with the strong rebukes from other states, many Democratic-Republicans were initially hesitant to reopen the issue. By the end of the summer of 1799, though, Jefferson, seemingly angered by the emphatic rejection of his Resolutions, urged his colleagues that silence might be seen as surrender. "That the principles already advanced by Virginia & Kentucky are not to be yielded in silence, I presume we all agree," he wrote (and cajoled) Madison. As his ire rose, Jefferson suggested even stronger language, threatening secession, telling Madison that the states might say that they were "determined, were we to be disappointed in this, to sever ourselves from that union we so much value, rather than give up the rights of self government which we have reserved, & in which alone we see liberty, safety & happiness." William Branch Giles, a devoted Jeffersonian and member of the House of Representatives through 1798, declared affirmatively for secession. Realizing that in the 1798–1799 election cycle political opponents had warned with some effect that the Kentucky and Virginia Resolutions portended disunion, Madison firmly cautioned against any hint of secession.[22]

Admonished, again, by Madison, Jefferson wrote to Wilson Cary Nicholas that any threat of disunion should await "repeated and enormous" violations by federal authorities. Still, he "thought something essentially necessary to be said in order to avoid the inference of acquiescence." Seeming to equivocate, obfuscating, Jefferson called for an "affectionate" embrace of the union but, at the same time, "making firm protestation against the precedent & principle, & *reserving* the right to make this palpable violation of the federal compact the ground of doing in future whatever we might now rightfully do, should repetitions of these and other violations of the compact render it expedient."[23]

Recognizing that he had lost this nullification battle, and having been sharply admonished about talk of secession, Jefferson was still deeply concerned. What if persecution of newspapers editors continued? (In fact, arrests under the Sedition Act accelerated in 1799 and into 1800.) What if citizens did not react against the Alien and Sedition Acts at the polls as he hoped? Omitting the threat of secession that he had floated with Madison two weeks earlier, he projected confidence, but sought to preserve his position for a possible future political war:

> not at all disposed to make every measure of error or of wrong a cause of scission we are willing to look on with indulgence & to wait with patience

till those passions & delusions shall have passed over which the federal government have artfully excited to cover it's own abuses & conceal it's designs, fully confident that the good sense of the American people, and their attachment to those very rights which we are now vindicating, will before it shall be too late rally with us round the true principles of our federal compact.[24]

Taking up Jefferson's challenge to respond to the other states, Kentucky's legislature drafted a second set of resolutions. The legislature now went out of its way to insist that it would "submit to a candid world" (echoing language from the Declaration of Independence) that it was "unconscious of any designs to disturb the harmony of that Union" in its previous effort. The Kentucky legislature then adopted resolutions that, in some particulars, were even more strident than those adopted in 1798 and in other respects introduced a confused ambiguity.[25]

In 1799, Kentucky expressly embraced Jefferson's initial language and a state's alleged right to "nullify" federal laws with which they disagreed. States "have the unquestionable right to judge of its [the Constitution's] infraction; and that a nullification, by those sovereignties, of all unauthorized acts . . . , is the rightful remedy." A right to nullify was unanimously supported in Kentucky's House before meeting some opposition, eventually overcome, in Kentucky's Senate. This language of nullification would become central to southern arguments in the run-up to the Civil War.[26]

While Kentucky's 1798 Resolutions clearly focused on the right of each state acting on its own behalf, some analysts argue that Kentucky's 1799 resolutions speak to collective action by the states. If so, while that action may still be ill-defined, that would certainly compromise their radical nature, but this may be too kind. The 1799 resolutions argue that "the several states . . . , being sovereign and independent, have the unquestionable right" to nullify actions that they judge to violate the compact. This formulation seems to contemplate action by a single state, although the draftsmen may have intentionally sought some ambiguity.[27]

Virginia also sought to respond to other states' rejection of the original Resolutions. Not surprisingly, Madison, having been elected to the Virginia House of Delegates scheduled to meet in the fall of 1799 (in part to respond to Patrick Henry's anticipated presence), was chosen to author a report from the House responding to other states' rebuke of the 1798 Resolutions. In Madison's Report, Virginia sought to assert some continued oversight of the federal government without exceeding a state's authority under the Constitution, exactly the concern that Madison had expressed in his December 1798 letter to Jefferson. Of course, as Harry Jaffa notes, "prudence forbade that he comment openly upon the differences that we know he perceived between the resolutions he had drawn, and those that Jefferson had secretly drawn for Kentucky."[28]

In fact, among the most striking things about Madison's Report in 1799 is how opaque and, at times, internally inconsistent it is. Given the clarity with which Madison usually wrote, Virginia's 1799 report is a model of ambiguity and misdirection, and people recognized as much at the time. One contemporary, a Pennsylvania judge and member of the American Philosophical Society, wrote, "it may be doubtful whether it be the work of a candid mind ingeniously endeavouring to impress on others its own convictions; or the work of an ingenious mind uncandidly endeavouring to persuade others to believe what it believes not itself." Years later, Madison seemed cautious about even embracing his own Report. He

> never claimed the "Address" [the Report] as his own. As his letters to Edward Everett in August 1830 reveal, JM approved of the content of the "Address" insofar as it provided evidence that the Virginia protest of 1798 did not furnish a historical sanction for the doctrines of nullification which were being propounded by John Caldwell Calhoun and others after 1828. But JM seems to have been careful to say no more than this, and he may even have intended to distance himself from the document [which he wrote] in other respects.[29]

Responding to attacks on the 1798 Resolutions' compact theory, Madison's Report firmly asserted that the federal government was a government of limited powers, . . . but no one really contested that point. Madison's Report also introduced the revisionist semantic argument that he had belatedly made to Jefferson after the 1798 Resolutions were adopted, urging that the term "states" (still plural) was sometimes used to represent the geographic territories, sometimes to refer to the political institutions of the state governments, and sometimes "the people composing those political societies." That understanding was important to the new rationalization; in this latter "sense the States ratified" the Constitution, that is, through conventions of the people. Recognizing the danger of allowing state governments to interfere with federal authority, and ignoring the language and history of the 1798 Resolutions to the contrary, Madison concluded that this narrower understanding of the term "states," that is, the people, "must be" what was intended. Thus, Madison (and Virginia's legislature) now insisted that the 1798 Resolutions made by the legislature were mere "declarations . . . , expressions of opinion, unaccompanied with any other effect, than what they may produce on opinion, by exciting reflection." Madison seemed now to be invoking the position that he had taken in *Federalist* #44 and #46 (and that Virginia had taken under Henry's guidance in 1790): states could remonstrate with the federal government, seek amendments, and change their elected federal officials. Of course, it is evident in the 1798 Resolutions themselves that "state" did not mean "people," and if the 1798 Resolutions were merely declaratory, there would have been no reason to raise the issue of "interposition," much less nullification.[30]

Still, in terms of resolving conflicts over state and federal authority, Madison's Report now argued that "where resort can be had to no TRIBUNAL SUPERIOR TO THE AUTHORITY OF THE PARTIES, THE PARTIES THEMSELVES MUST BE THE RIGHTFUL JUDGES IN THE LAST RESORT, WHETHER THE BARGAIN MADE HAS BEEN PURSUED OR VIOLATED." Madison concluded that judicial review would not be the "last resort," therefore, "in relation to the rights of the parties [presumably now meaning the people] to the Constitutional compact." This seems rather circular. While *Federalist* #39 explained that "it is true that in controversies relating to the boundary between the two jurisdictions [state and national], the tribunal which is ultimately to decide, is to be established under the general government" (i.e. the Supreme Court) and that "some such tribunal is clearly essential to prevent an appeal to the sword," to the extent that the "parties" who are "rightful judges" are the sovereign people, once again, no one questioned Madison's conclusion. Confusion and obfuscation may have been Madison's goals.[31]

Madison scholar Drew McCoy provides a good overview of Madison's Report of 1799, concluding that he used "such cautious and guarded terms" that it was evident that nullification had been rejected. In fact, McCoy concludes, Madison was seeking to respond "to the doctrinal ambiguities and excesses" that Jefferson had introduced, excesses that Madison now regretted.[32]

Notably, Madison's complicated and convoluted Report resulted in an extended minority report, written by John Marshall. Most importantly, Marshall reminded citizens that the "constitutional corrective, which you annually dispense" to perceived government overreach occurred at the ballot box. The minority report also rejected the injured cries of innocence that the 1798 Resolutions were merely a remonstrance or declaration, insisting that if the Resolutions had been limited to peaceable objections to the law, "no opposition would have been made by those who now address you." The minority report, reprinted around the nation, went on to argue that the Alien and Sedition Acts were constitutional, albeit ill-advised.[33]

Years later, Jefferson included Madison's Report of 1799 in the law curriculum at his new University of Virginia over Madison's mild objection that it might be perceived to place the university under "Party Banners" and, furthermore, that the document was "not, on every point, satisfactory to all who belong to the same party." UVA's curriculum also required students to read Washington's Farewell Address that had forcefully attacked hyperpartisanship and vigorously warned against disunion. Notably absent from the proscribed curriculum were the Kentucky and Virginia Resolutions of 1798.[34]

Having been chastened by the vigorous rejection of their Resolutions and the claims that they were supporting disunion, Jefferson and Madison seemed to recognize belatedly that the best response lay in what Jefferson now described as the "constitutional means of election & petition" to make things right. Unfortunately, regardless of Madison's and Jefferson's reconsideration, the Resolutions became foundational for secessionists and states' rights advocates since.[35]

And, of course, none of these post hoc rationalizations and reinterpretation of the 1798 Resolutions, by Madison or academics, were available to Henry or Washington, to the other states responding to the original Resolutions, nor to the electorate that firmly rejected their disunionist tendency.

A New Electoral Strategy

Faced with a broad rejection of the theories advanced in the Kentucky and Virginia Resolutions and the electoral losses of 1798–1799, Democratic-Republicans made significant changes in their electoral strategy as the election of 1800 approached. Madison began to rethink the approach almost immediately in December 1798, Jefferson soon thereafter.

In 1798, Jeffersonians were seeking a direct confrontation over enforcement of the Alien and Sedition Acts in the South or the West, perhaps permitting those prosecuted, or those who would interfere with federal prosecutions, to become "Martyrs in the *holy cause,*" Federalists alleged. Kentucky made clear that it would not permit the laws to be enforced in the state. When Virginia adopted its initial resolutions, it also proposed a law that would have permitted state judges to invoke habeas corpus in support of anyone seized in a federal prosecution, something that undoubtedly would have precipitated a confrontation between state and federal officials. By 1800, however, the Democratic-Republicans realized that their assault on federal authority with the threat of disunion embodied in nullification and compact theory was alienating citizens who were deeply committed to the union. As a result, rather than threatening to interfere with Sedition Act prosecutions, or to authorize state judges to invoke habeas corpus against federal prosecutions, it was more politically sound to allow Federalists to prosecute newspaper editors and then to use the prosecutions as political fodder, to focus on interference with free speech rights rather than alleged compact theory, state sovereignty, or state control of the federal government.[36]

Perhaps the change in the Democratic-Republican approach was nowhere clearer than in their treatment of the spring 1800 Sedition Act prosecution of James Callender—the muckraking journalist who would become better known to history for spreading the story about Thomas Jefferson and his enslaved mistress, Sally Hemings. In 1800, Callender was prosecuted for publication of "The Prospect before Us," a favorite pro-Jefferson pamphlet of Democratic-Republicans. By the time that Callender was jailed for sedition (for which President Jefferson would later pardon him), Democratic-Republicans had learned their lesson. They did not call for nullification or even interposition. No one demanded that the conviction be treated as "null, void, and of no force, or effect." A state judge was not called upon to issue a writ of habeas corpus against the federal prosecution. Rather, in words that stood in stark contrast to the violent language of 1798 and that seemed to echo Henry's admonition from Charlotte Courthouse, Democratic-Republicans focused on the necessity for change through the electoral process.

> Let us now show our calumniators, by a perfect obedience to this law, which we believe not only to be unconstitutional, but inexpedient; that republicans, while they oppose by every constitutional effort, obnoxious systems of administration and unpopular laws, are always willing to be governed by the acts of a majority. Virginia has too much respect for the Constitution of the United States, and too much property and happiness at stake, ever to gratify her enemies by hazarding confusion and licentiousness. She will patiently expect the return of reason, truth, and liberty; and with them, that confidence which should forever subsist throughout the United States. The same majority which will elect the PATRIOT JEFFERSON to the Chief Magistracy of United America, will relieve us from those laws which we bear for the sake of philanthropy and Union.[37]

The change from the heated rhetoric of 1798 was palpable. James Monroe, now governor of Virginia, warned Jefferson that no radical response to a Federalist enforcement of the Sedition Act should be made. Then, "deprived of a plausible pretext" and apparent threat of disunion, the attack on the free press would "become a burden to themselves," Federalists, in the upcoming election. Madison agreed with Monroe that caution and electoral action, rather than a direct confrontation with the federal government or federal laws, was called for. Then, use of the Sedition Act would "be turned agst. its authors" and result in the Federalist party "co-operating in its own destruction."[38]

A similar pattern accompanied Thomas Cooper's sedition conviction in Pennsylvania. Once again, nullification, habeas corpus, interposition, null and void . . . were not the focus. Instead, Democratic-Republican papers wrote that "all we shall say at present is Republicans should rest compleatly assured, that they will have every reason to be satisfied with the effect of this most singular trial on the mind of the public." As prosecutions increased with the electoral campaign in 1800, another Democratic-Republican newspaper recognized that "it is a happy circumstance for the republican cause, that such firm, undaunted characters as *Duane* and *Cooper* should be selected as victims for immolation. They will pass through the fiery ordeal of persecution with that resolute spirit which has at different times rendered the persecuted assert-ers of civil rights, the saviours of freedom."[39]

Generally, after the electoral debacle of 1798–1799, and rebuke of Kentucky and Virginia by most of the other states, Democratic-Republicans, and their rhetoric, focused on the rights of free speech and freedom of the press in the campaign of 1800, rather than on states' rights. This was a major shift from 1798, and it was hoped that this would be a winning campaign issue, but all was dependent upon the election of 1800.[40]

The change in the Democratic-Republican response was evident even when Fries's Rebellion threatened violence in early 1799. As Fries's simmered, Jefferson wrote to Edmund Pendleton that, in Pennsylvania, "we fear the ill-designing may produce insurrection. nothing could be so fatal. anything like force would check the progress of public opinion & rally them round the er-rors of the government. this is not the kind of opposition the American people will permit. but keep away all shew of force, and they will bear down the evil propensities of the government by the constitutional means of election & pe-tition." When Fries was put on trial, "great stress was laid on the Sedition Law, which has been so abused and vilified by these very people." By focusing on the Sedition Act prosecutions, Democratic-Republicans made Fries's a politi-cal liability for the Federalists.[41]

The new electoral moderation was evident in other ways as well. With Pat-rick Henry out of the way, and George Washington dying in December of 1799 of a sudden illness (or, more accurately, his doctor's repeated bloodletting that accompanied his sudden illness), and with the Democratic-Republican presidential campaign pitting Jefferson against the incumbent Federalist John Adams under way, Democratic-Republicans now found it convenient to stop their vilification of Henry. Instead, they shamelessly sought to co-opt his memory in support of Jefferson's 1800 election campaign (another indicator of Henry's popularity and influence).

Even before his Charlotte Courthouse speech, Democratic-Republican newspapers had enlisted Henry's memory against Federalists. With the presidential campaign in mind, readers were reminded of the "intrigues of a monarchical party in the convention that established our constitution" under the influence of Federalist Alexander Hamilton and the "unanswerable argument of Patrick Henry" at Virginia's ratification convention against such a powerful executive.[42]

While favorable characterizations of Henry had disappeared from Democratic-Republican newspapers for a period after his 1799 campaign, efforts to co-opt Henry again accelerated in 1800 after his death. With Jefferson's most prominent 1799 adversaries unable to speak for themselves, James Callender was more than willing to use Henry's name to promote Jefferson's candidacy. Indicting Adams's "imperial" presidency, Callender published the widely distributed "The Prospect before Us" (for which he was prosecuted under the Sedition Act as noted above). On the cover of this election pamphlet, he quoted Henry's warning during Virginia's ratification convention: The presidency "has an awful squinting! It squints to monarchy!" Callender invoked Henry throughout his partisan attack on Adams's presidency. Jefferson, seeing the draft (that he helped to fund) with Henry's name on the cover and throughout, assured the author that it "cannot fail to produce the best effect."[43]

Not only were these political manipulations of the dead man's words inconsistent with Henry's wishes for the 1800 election, but they ignored his most recent statements concerning Adams. For example, in early 1799, when Adams sought Henry as a peace commissioner to France, Henry declined the offer in a letter to Timothy Pickering, Adams's secretary of state, but added that "nothing short of absolute necessity could induce me to withhold my little aid from an administration, whose abilities, patriotism and virtue, deserve the gratitude and reverence of all their fellow citizens." (Pickering leaked the letter to the press; it was broadly reported in northern and middle states.) One report has Henry at Charlotte Courthouse specifically rejecting claims that Adams had monarchist tendencies. None of which stopped Jeffersonians from embracing his words when they could do so to broaden their electoral appeal.[44]

With the election in South Carolina expected by many to hold the balance in the coming presidential election, an interesting twist on this effort to co-opt the now-deceased Henry and Washington appeared in the *City Gazette* of Charleston on August 18, 1800. Acknowledging that Henry and Washington had opposed the Jeffersonian policies of 1798, the author insisted that they shared Jefferson's political sentiments but had been driven by "envy" (although the author never explained exactly what Henry and Washington were envious of). Doctrinally, the editor assured his readers that Washington and Henry "wished success to his [Jefferson's] political sentiments."[45]

In 1799, Jefferson told Madison and others that "firmness on our part, but a passive firmness is the true course. any thing rash or threatening might check the favorable dispositions of these middle states & rally them again round the measures which are ruining us." Belatedly, Jefferson seemed to recognize that the Alien and Sedition Acts and the taxes that had been imposed to pay for the military buildup themselves would tend to undermine support for the Federalists. Aggressive state action against the national government was not only a lightning rod for opposition to Democratic-Republicans and a possible threat to the union but was not likely to be needed. In late January he told Elbridge Gerry that "the alien & sedition acts have already operated in the South as powerful sedatives of the XYZ. inflammation. . . . the tide is already turned and will sweep before it all the feeble obstacles of art. the unquestionable republicanism of the American mind will break through the mist under which it has been clouded, and will oblige it's agents to reform the principles & practices of their administration."[46]

Jefferson and the Revolution of 1800

Thomas Jefferson was fond of reminding people that the earth belongs to the living. The past—whether calcified laws, land titles passing only to eldest sons, customs and traditions standing in the way of progress, or even a constitution worshipped with "sanctimonious reverence"—could not and should not control the present.[47]

Democratic-Republicans—focusing on free speech, small government and lower taxes, peace, religious freedom—won a resounding victory in 1800, capturing not only the presidency but both houses of Congress. Jefferson later called it the "Revolution of 1800." With the country run for thirty-two of the next thirty-six years by avowed Jeffersonians, it was easy to forget the crisis or to shape its memory. The earth, and governance, and the writing of history, all belong to the living. In the antebellum era, forgetting the details of the crisis of 1798–1799, southern leaders would broadly embrace the radical states' rights doctrines of the Kentucky and Virginia Resolutions that Madison and Jefferson belatedly sought to submerge, using nullification and compact theory in defense of the slavocracy and Native land dispossession. But for now, Jefferson had won, and the crisis faded. The task now was to govern, and to write the history.

Importantly, Jefferson won the presidency in a distinctly Henryesque manner: In a reversal of the elections of 1798–1799, and contra 1798 threats of state interventions, people went to the ballot box and voted for Jefferson and Democratic-Republicans in opposition to John Adams, Federalists, and the Alien and Sedition Acts. As Jefferson explained later in life, "The nation declared it's will by dismissing functionaries of one principle and electing those of another." Henry's final speech at Charlotte Courthouse spoke to the means of achieving this revolution: "it belonged to the people who held the reins . . . and to them alone, to say whether" the current government was "acceptable or otherwise."[48]

In the years between Jefferson's election and the Civil War, those defending states' rights inevitably embraced the Kentucky and Virginia Resolutions as fundamental constitutional doctrine and many equated the Resolutions to the Revolution of 1800. But in many respects, Jefferson's electoral victory and the Revolution of 1800 were the antithesis of the Resolutions. Jefferson won his election at the ballot box largely unaided by his radical states' rights statements and ruminations, certainly not by nullification or threats of secession. The peaceful transfer of power after an election became a hallmark of the United States for 220 years and an essential lesson of American history for which the election of 1800 is remembered, but it almost had not happened that way.[49]

Moreover, the principles that propelled Jefferson's success were largely the same as those articulated by Henry in his battle over ratification of the Constitution in 1788 and throughout his political career. Jefferson's campaign rested on a commitment to bring the people into a closer relationship with their government (albeit the relevant political community at the time was white and male). This close relationship between the government and American people is why Jefferson insisted in his inaugural address that his government would be the "strongest government on earth"; citizens would see an attack on the nation as an attack on themselves. Requiring government to be responsive to the people is exactly what Henry had put at the center of his political philosophy since his early legal and political career. "Jefferson appropriated the democratic mantle from Henry," Peter Onuf concludes, but then "cast[] the apostate into historical oblivion."[50]

Ironically, with Henry's death and Jefferson's election, the crisis that Jefferson had threatened to explode, and that Henry and Washington feared, evaporated. Had Henry lived and Jefferson lost the election, the Democratic-Republicans would likely have turned to more extreme measures and certainly returned to the threats of 1798–1799. How far this could have gone is unknown, but Jefferson himself had warned, if "disappointed" in their battle with the Alien and Sedition Acts, Democratic-Republicans were "determined . . . to sever ourselves from that union we so much value." The doctrine of nullification might have been more firmly embraced years before the nullification crisis. As Jefferson scholar Merrill Peterson wrote, the Kentucky and Virginia "Resolutions contained in embryo the idea of constitutional resistance by a single state to federal laws which in the view of that state transcended the compact of government. How far Jefferson meant to practice this idea would never be known (perhaps he never knew himself) largely because the election of 1800 made it unnecessary." With Jefferson rising to the presidency, Jeffersonians were relieved of the choice of whether the states would forcefully resist federal authority or secede, a choice they would face again sixty years later. A triumphant Jefferson might have (gratefully) forgotten the crisis, much as it quickly faded in the nation's historic memory.[51]

But perhaps the crisis affected Jefferson more than at first appears and in ways that historians have not fully appreciated. Perhaps he realized that he and his allies fueled the partisan politics that drove the new country precipitously close to the edge in the 1790s. As 1798 came to an end, Madison understood that and was seeking to pull back from that precipice. Perhaps too radical of an embrace of states' rights would endanger the federal government and the union to which Jefferson had devoted the better part of his life, "the sheet anchor of our peace at home, and safety abroad," he explained in his first inaugural address. President Jefferson is often accused of hypocrisy for failure to implement many of the policies that Democratic-Republicans promoted in the 1790s and for his broad use of federal power, his apparent turn from states' rights, but perhaps more was at play.[52]

Before turning to Jefferson's presidency, it is worth briefly considering one other circumstance that likely fueled Jefferson's recognition of the fragility of the union and his reconsideration of the hyperpartisanship and radicalism of the 1790s.

Before Jefferson could take office, the election posed a new conundrum: Jefferson and Aaron Burr, the Democratic-Republicans' erstwhile vice-presidential candidate, tied in the Electoral College vote. While no one doubted that the voters intended Jefferson to be president, the Constitution specified that in case of a tie the election was thrown into the House of Representatives with each state having one vote. The problem was that many state delegations in the lame duck Congress were still controlled by Federalists, and many of them seemed prepared to stop at nothing to deny Jefferson the presidency. Unfortunately for Jefferson, Burr did not help, apparently toying with the idea of encouraging his own election to the presidency and cooperating with Federalists in return. Federalists contemplated using the tie and congressional gridlock as an excuse to find a third option that might continue their hold on power.[53]

The dispute became dangerously heated. Alexander Hamilton, no political ally of Jefferson's, implored Federalist colleagues not to vote for the unscrupulous Burr who had "no principle, public or private" but was driven by an "extreme & irregular ambition." While Jefferson was "a contemptible hypocrite," Hamilton continued, he would not undermine the government. Warning of the "foolish game" that his own party was playing, Hamilton almost begged Federalist members of Congress to vote for Jefferson. Incredulous, Jefferson wrote to Madison that "even Hamilton" had become a "zealous partisan[] for us." After the heated political conflicts of the 1790s, Hamilton's effort must also have given Jefferson some pause.[54]

The volatile situation hung heavily over the young nation, and Jefferson. As the electoral dispute continued unabated, Jefferson happened upon John Adams in the streets of the new capital, the city of Washington; the intended new president warned the lame duck that any attempt "to defeat the Presidential election" threatened a violent reaction:

> I observed to him that a very dangerous experiment was then in contemplation, to defeat the Presidential election by an act of Congress declaring the right of the Senate by naming a President of the Senate, to devolve on him the govmt during any interregnum: that such a measure would probably produce resistance by force & incalculable consequences which it would be in his power to prevent by negativing such an act. he . . . observed it was in my power to fix the election by a word in an instant, by declaring I would not turn out the federal officers, not put down the Navy, nor spurge the National debt. finding his mind made up . . . I urged it no further.

There were reports that Democratic-Republicans were prepared to march on Washington with state militias if Federalists took the election from Jefferson; others were, again, openly discussing secession. With the nation watching and on edge, the House of Representatives went through thirty-six ballots over six days of almost uninterrupted sessions. Finally, in a complex arrangement, the details of which are still not fully understood, several Federalist members of Congress, led by James Bayard of Delaware, withheld their votes in a manner that guaranteed Jefferson's election. After the crisis was resolved, on the same day that Pennsylvania Governor McKean wrote to Jefferson that 20,000 militia men had been prepared to march if Federalists stole the election from Jefferson and Burr, Jefferson insisted that "there was no idea of force, nor of any occasion for it," but this was clearly not true.[55]

On March 4, 1801, Thomas Jefferson was inaugurated the third president under the U.S. Constitution.

President Jefferson

Volumes have been written about the election of 1800 and the Jefferson/Burr tie. An additional shelf of tomes dissects Jefferson's presidency, particularly how Jefferson "actually strengthened, rather than checked, the power of the executive and actually used the power of the state in ways that Hamilton could little imagine." Over time, the most radical of the states' rights Democratic-Republicans, led by John Randolph, revolted against Jefferson's apparent moderation, becoming the "tertium quids" (third thing), and started to oppose some Jeffersonian policies. Although historians and politicians have often seen hypocrisy in Jefferson's exercise of federal power, perhaps the more subtle effect of Patrick Henry's 1799 campaign and the crisis of union that had been avoided has been overlooked.[56]

The battles of 1799 and the election of 1800—Henry's and Washington's pointed opposition to the Resolutions (joined by a majority of the states), and the electoral battle over Burr—seemed to chasten Jefferson and Madison, to cause them to modify, abandon, or suppress somewhat the hyperpartisanship of the 1790s, including some of their states' rights positions. Jefferson and Madison seemed to recognize in retrospect that the still young nation was fragile; partisan politics had put the nation at risk. Perhaps more care was needed.

Jefferson was deeply committed to the success of the new nation, in many ways a nationalist, as Brian Steele points out. Yet the nation was almost driven to ruin over his desperate effort to encourage a radical response to the Alien and Sedition Acts, that themselves had tended to drive partisan wedges into the nation. With the Kentucky Resolutions, Jefferson "proposed a form of resistance to federal authority that after his election as president he would explicitly reject." With the crisis of the 1790s, combined with the vicious election campaign of 1800 itself, not to mention the tie with Burr, and the newfound responsibilities of actually being president, Jefferson seemed to change.[57]

Many historians point to the bitterness of the campaign of 1800, but more than name-calling was at play in a nation that was still learning how to run itself and grappling with the role of a loyal opposition. Both sides of the political dispute drove dangerously close to the precipice. Both saw the actions of their opponents as threatening the union, Federalists' alleged embrace of crypto-monarchy and Democratic-Republicans' flirting with nullification and secession. Jefferson's own wrestling with James Madison over the excesses of the Kentucky and Virginia Resolutions, not to mention the actions of ten states to reject the Resolutions' states' rights doctrines, must have caused even the headstrong Jefferson to pause. While he might claim to dismiss Henry's opposition, others would not, and while Jefferson was estranged somewhat from Washington, the first president's concerns must have weighed on the third. Jefferson knew that Henry's and Washington's deaths had paved the way for his election, making it more "*speedy,* as well as *certain.*" The Burr stalemate fed the sense of crisis, as Jefferson's almost desperate plea to John Adams about the risk of violence shows. While Jefferson insisted that "there was no idea of force," that was simply revisionist, an almost forced nonchalance, and he knew it. Even Hamilton's endorsement of Jefferson's election must have demanded careful thought and, perhaps, soul-searching from the new president. Our leading Jefferson scholar explains the election of 1800 "as Americans stood on the precipice and contemplated the prospect of disunion and war, they came to their senses and reaffirmed their national identity." Perhaps, too, Jefferson came to his senses.[58]

Not surprisingly, Jefferson publicly blamed the danger and crisis on the Federalists, but even he recognized that the partisanship of the 1790s, in which he was deeply engaged, stood behind the crisis. He told one correspondent that the Jay Treaty "produced a schism that went on widening and rankling till the years '98, '99, when a final dissolution of all bonds, civil and social, appeared imminent." What was left unsaid is that Jefferson, fearing the consequences of the Sedition Act and angry over the expansive views on government adopted by Federalists, was likewise thrown into the "phrenzy" that he described, indeed fed the frenzy that pushed the crisis, and the young nation, to the edge.[59]

In retirement, Jefferson returned to the dangerous, tumultuous nature of the political disputes of the 1790s and 1800, although insisting to John Adams, after their friendship was renewed in 1812, that only the Democratic-Republicans suffered in the convulsions. "None can concieve who did not witness them, and they were felt by one party only." Adams, never one to hold his tongue or his pen, was having none of it, reminding Jefferson of both the chaos and the threat faced by Federalists. "You never felt the Terrorism of Chaises [Shays's] Rebellion in Massachusetts. I believe You never felt the Terrorism of Gallatins Insurrection in Pensilvania [the Whiskey Rebellion]: You certainly never realized the Terrorism of Fries's, most outragious Riot and Rescue, as I call it, Treason, Rebellion as the World and great Judges and two Juries pronounced it." When Citizen Genet, revolutionary France's ambassador, caused 10,000 to take to the streets of Philadelphia, only yellow fever stopped the mobs, Adams declared.

> I have no doubt You was fast asleep in philosophical Tranquility, when ten thousand People, and perhaps many more, were parading the Streets of Philadelphia, . . . When even Governor Mifflin himself, thought it his Duty to order a Patrol of Horse And Foot to preserve the peace; . . . when I judged it prudent and necessary to order Chests of Arms from the War Office to be brought through bye Lanes and back Doors: determined to defend my House at the Expence of my Life, and the Lives of the few, very few Domesticks and Friends within it.

On which party caused more of the problem, Adams concluded, "Put Them in a bagg and shake them, and then see which comes out first." They both, Jefferson and Adams, remembered vividly partisan rancor that broke into violence; they "agreed . . . on one fundamental point," Joanne Freeman notes, in the 1790s, "the constitutional clock had almost run down."[60]

All of which is to say that historians perhaps have underrated the impact of the crisis of 1798–1799 and the dangerous confusion of the election of 1800 on Jefferson personally and on his presidency. Read in this light, Jefferson's first inaugural address takes on a more solemn and introspective tone. This address has long been seen as one of Jefferson's masterpieces. His reminder that "we are all republicans: we are all federalists," is well-known. The change in tone after the bitter election is evident, and is often attributed to the magnanimity of a winner, political magnanimity at that—reflecting more the spoils of victory and luxury of being generous, than a real concern for the defeated or shift in political philosophy.[61]

But perhaps more than political pablum was at work. Perhaps Jefferson, upon reflection, was seriously chastened by the crisis, by how close the nation came to open conflict or disunion (and by his own role in fueling the crisis, not to mention Madison's warnings that they may have gone too far). The new president told James Monroe that he hoped in his inaugural address to change "an incorrect idea of my views" and to focus on "conciliation, and adherence to sound principle." Even John Marshall, Jefferson's second cousin and bitter political enemy, saw the change, reporting to Charles Cotesworth Pinckney on the day of Jefferson's inauguration that "you will before this reaches you see his [Jefferson's] inauguration speech. It is in the general well judgd & conciliatory. It is in direct terms giving the lie to the violent party declamations which has elected him; but it is strongly characteristic of the general cast of his political theory." Benjamin Rush told Jefferson after the speech that "Old friends who had been separated by party names . . . shook hands with each Other."[62]

Having led the partisan battle cries of the 1790s, Jefferson now understood that the president, the one official who represented the entire nation, must speak for the entire nation and the people must "unite in common efforts for the common good." The hyperpartisan of the 1790s reminded the nation that while the majority must rule (as they had in passing the Alien and Sedition Acts), "the minority possess their equal rights, which equal laws must protect." While remembering the grievous injury caused by the Alien and Sedition Acts, he was promising Federalists, now in the minority, that their rights would be protected. Jefferson, having earlier called for secession, committed to banish "political intolerance." Having previously seen only Anglophone mischief in opponents' concerns over France, Jefferson now conceded that it was not surprising that Federalists feared that the European wars would reach "even this distant and peaceful shore." Making an effort to understand Federalists, he acknowledged that this fear would naturally "divide opinions as to measures of safety." Peter Onuf explains that "the specter of disunion and war became all too frighteningly visible in the presidential succession crisis immediately preceding Jefferson's inauguration. His rhetorical challenge was to distinguish American from European politics and convince his listeners and readers that they had been fighting over means, not ends." Perhaps he was also convincing himself.[63]

This was the context for Jefferson famous apologia: "every difference of opinion is not a difference of principle. we have called by different names brethren of the same principle. we are all republicans: we are all federalists." Jefferson assured skeptics that the U.S. government was the "strongest . . . on earth" because all the people, Federalists and Democratic-Republicans (or at least the white, male electorate), were invested in the government. (That need for a close relationship between the government and the people had led Henry to denounce British imperial actions in the Parsons' Cause and rally co-citizens to a Revolution.) While not mentioning that he had flirted with secession little more than a year earlier, Jefferson now insisted that any who would "wish to dissolve this Union, or to change its republican form," were in error. Assuring Joseph Priestley that, with the crisis behind, he was "much better satisfied now of it's [the nation's] stability, than I was before it was tried," what was not said was that Jefferson's actions had played a significant part in putting the system to the test. Recognizing that "decisions of the majority [are] the vital principle of republics," Jefferson may have been thinking of the crisis of 1798–1799 when he warned that there is "no appeal" from those decisions "but to force, the vital and immediate parent of . . . despotism."[64]

This was precisely Patrick Henry's final and damning point at Charlotte Courthouse (although acknowledging that openly was certainly too much for Jefferson). In the Revolution of 1800, Henry, or at least his argument on the proper role of a loyal opposition, won. With Jefferson's inauguration, the clouds receded. The threat of open conflict and disunion fled like morning mist on his Virginia mountaintop. After Jefferson's inauguration, America became, in many key respects, a Jeffersonian republic. The nation was committed to the peaceful transfer of power, meaning accepting electoral results even when one lost. Jefferson's and Madison's nullification and compact rhetoric of 1798 was abandoned, until it burst forth again in political discord after the Missouri Compromise, in the nullification crisis of the 1830s and the antebellum period, and on bloody American battlefields sixty years later.

It is true that Jefferson continued a strong partisan throughout his presidency. At times, he spoke as if he had been able to convince himself that all good Americans were Democratic-Republicans, and, unfortunately, as he aged, the memory of the danger of the crisis of 1798–1799 may have faded somewhat in his memory as well. This, though, is not inconsistent with the crisis having engendered added caution on his own part in his role as president, some moderation, resulting from a recognition of the danger from which the nation had, narrowly, escaped.[65]

Focusing on the election dispute with Burr, Joanne Freeman concludes that "by threatening to destroy the Union, the crisis of 1800 forced politicians to acknowledge their mutual commitment to it." The crisis of 1799—the opposition of Henry, Washington, and the majority of the states—was part of this realization. Even Jefferson, one of the most self-assured of the founders, seems to have gotten the message. Having espoused state nullification in 1798 and 1799 and openly toyed with secession, now Jefferson urged his fellow citizens, Democratic-Republicans and Federalists, "Let us, then, with courage and confidence, pursue . . . our attachment to union and representative government."[66]

Part of our failure to understand fully the crisis of union is, perhaps, our hesitancy to attribute partisan political motives to the founders, and our strong desire to find theoretical consistency in their actions, actions often taken over very long and rich and contentious political lives. In fact, even founders changed their views over time and adapted. In 1798–1799, Jefferson and Madison were engaged in a desperate political battle against repression of the free press with excessively strong rhetoric that, like political rhetoric throughout history, sometimes went too far. Madison realized that early. Jefferson's actions during the election of 1800 and as president suggest that, upon reflection, he did as well.

This explains in part why Jefferson's presidency did not produce the substantial structural reforms that seemed to be called for by the Kentucky and Virginia Resolutions and the partisan disputes of the 1790s. Other Democratic-Republicans complained about the lack of progress on the issues seen to be critical in 1798. In 1802, John Taylor of Caroline, who had played a leading role in the Kentucky and Virginia Resolutions, wrote that "I am fully convinced of the danger of the republican case at this time. We are too Idle." Taylor insisted that the principles of 1798 needed to be embedded in the Constitution. "Are not the paper systems, the Sedition and Alien law precedents, the executive patronage, and the influence of Congress by contracts capable of affecting our policy? If not why did we complain of them. If so, why do we neglect to provide against them?" Virginia scion (and Taylor's uncle) Edmund Pendleton took up the problem in a late 1801 pamphlet, *The Danger Not Over,* urging significant constitutional reform and enhancement of state power at the expense of the federal government (although, as in 1799, Pendleton did not argue that the Constitution was merely a compact). Pendleton warned against relying on the fact that Jefferson was president, "reposing on that wisdom and integrity, which has already softened even political malice." President Jefferson, for his part, seemed to moderate even on treatment of the federal (Federalist) judiciary, even after the much-despised Justice Chase was impeached on a resolution introduced by John Randolph. In fact, the rise of John Randolph's *tertium quids,* more radical Democratic-Republicans who sought more aggressive action from the Jeffersonians, was a response to Jefferson's apparent moderation. But efforts for fundamental or structural reform made almost no headway with Jefferson.[67]

Given the lack of fundamental constitutional reform, the question remains: Was the election of 1800 a "revolution," as Jefferson claimed in 1819, or not? Jefferson thought so, insisting that the "revolution of 1800. . . . was as real a revolution in the principles of our government as that of [17]76. was in it's form." The revolution, though, was not in the constitutional structure, but in the approach to government and its reliance on the voters exercising their rights as citizens to vote one party out and, peaceably, to introduce a new administration. It was equally essential that the "revolution," as Jefferson explained, was "not effected indeed by the sword, . . . but by the rational and peaceable instrument of reform, the suffrage of the people." Patrick Henry would have agreed.[68]

The same moniker, Revolution of 1800, has been warmly embraced by historians. For the first time, after an excessively noisy and rancorous election, and in the face of the threats of the 1790s political battles, the political party that controlled the presidency surrendered the reins of power to a different party. Before the election, either a peaceful transfer of power or even the peaceful retention of power was far from certain. Now, it is a hallmark of the U.S. constitutional system (albeit wildly and irresponsibly challenged in 2020 and 2021). Jefferson understood that the absence of a revolution was, perhaps, part of the revolution that he celebrated.[69]

Though history well remembers the "Revolution of 1800," that was not the revolution that had been feared by Henry, Washington, Hamilton, and Madison in 1798–1799. States did not refuse to implement federal laws. Federal officials enforcing federal statutes were not directly harassed and attacked. Neither state "nullification" of federal laws nor "interposition" between federal officials and state citizens came to pass. State judges did not issue writs of habeas corpus to free federal prisoners. Militia officers did not rally to a foreign banner. Military conflict between state militias and the federal government did not occur. The "revolution" was not the one presaged in the Resolutions of 1798.

In 1800, American voters—a rapidly expanding group as property and age qualifications were relaxed or eliminated (albeit still almost exclusively white men)—chose a charismatic Jefferson who seemed to embrace "everyman" over the grumpy and acerbic Adams who was the image of a New England elitist; they chose a commitment to democracy (and a free press) over the apparent aristocratic tendencies of Federalists. Not surprisingly, Jefferson's election was accomplished with a dramatic increase in voter participation. This was exactly what Henry had endorsed at Charlotte Courthouse and resonated with his political philosophy throughout his career.[70]

Of course, the election itself was much closer than the appellation of "revolution" might suggest; if a revolution, it was hardly a consensus. Jefferson received seventy-three votes in the Electoral College; Adams received sixty-five—which is to say that if five electoral votes were switched, Adams would have won the election. If four electoral votes were switched, the lame-duck Federalist House of Representatives would have resolved the tie between Adams, Jefferson, and Burr. With Henry (and Washington) alive and opposed to Jefferson's candidacy, this shift is easily imagined. Perhaps, too, Jefferson understood that. (Notably as we consider the appellation of "revolution," Jefferson's win in the Electoral College is also attributable to the extra electoral votes assigned to southern states because of their enslaved African American populations and the three-fifths rule.)[71]

Jefferson and States' Rights

Of course, the doctrine of states' rights has meant different things in different times and has been used to justify different actions over the nation's history. At the time, the states' alleged ability to nullify federal laws or interpose between the federal government and the people promoted by Jefferson and Madison in 1798 were not seen as essential for the continuation of slavery nor for the dispossession of Native Americans. While slavery was an omnipresent and critical issue in early America, and Native land dispossession had continued for centuries and would become a growing national concern, the political division in the 1790s was not focused on those issues. With respect to slavery, the issue of states' rights was not so clearly sectional, with Pennsylvania and New York, for example, supporting Jeffersonians and South Carolina maintaining a strong Federalist influence for many years. Nor did the states that opposed the Kentucky and Virginia Resolutions do so on abolitionist grounds. Nor was the opposition of Henry and Washington, both slaveholders, to Democratic-Republicans' states' rights agenda part of an antislavery movement. At the time, the institution of slavery did not seem to be fragile, and the implications of nullification and compact theory on the gruesome institution did not seem to be anyone's focus. After all, all four of the leading Virginia protagonists were slave owners. (Whether Jefferson and Madison at the time foresaw the long-term implications of their doctrine on the emerging defense of slavery in the antebellum era is less clear.) Similarly, while federal power, in the form of Supreme Court decisions, would come into conflict with states' rights in the nineteenth century over the issue of Native land dispossession, there is little evidence that these concerns motivated the political battles of 1798–1799.[72]

After the crisis of 1798–1799 receded, and after the moderation of his presidency (from whatever source), even in the 1810s, Jefferson was still able to write in his *Anas* that if "each state" was "sovereign and independent in all things" they would be "eternally at war with each other, & would become at length the mere partisans & satellites of the leading powers of Europe." Jefferson only returned to more radical states' rights rhetoric after the Missouri

Compromise of 1820, his "fire bell in the night," when he again believed that a political dispute over states' rights would tear the union asunder, this time over slavery. At about the same time, he used the threat of northern abolitionism and an appeal to state chauvinism to encourage reluctant (and stingy) Virginia legislators to fund the construction of the University of Virginia. Andrew O'Shaughnessy explains that "by appealing to the fear that northern abolitionists would indoctrinate southern students and by siding with opponents of the Missouri Compromise, Jefferson allowed himself to become complicit with the proslavery South."[73]

By 1825, with a North/South sectional difference rooted in slavery beginning to dominate the political environment, still fearing a sectional conflict that would rend the nation, an aging Jefferson again fixated on the division between federal and state power and the then-current proposals for the federal government to promote infrastructure as the nation approached the industrial age. Sending Madison a draft "Solemn Declaration and Protest" for the Virginia General Assembly, he grappled with the problem of what would happen if each state were to act independently on their views of the federal government's constitutional authority. Yet his tone, once again, smacked of a threat of secession. Jefferson would have the Virginia legislators declare that

> they respect too affectionately the opinions of those possessing the same rights under the same instrument, to make every difference of construction a ground of immediate rupture. They would indeed consider such a rupture as among the greatest calamities which could befall them; but not the greatest. There is yet one greater, submission to a government of unlimited powers. It is only when the hope of avoiding this shall become absolutely desperate, that further forbearance could not be indulged.

He demurred on immediate secession—"they do not mean to raise the banner of disaffection, or of separation from their sister-states, co-parties with themselves to this compact"—but obviously the draft implied the possibility. Awkwardly, Jefferson suggested that if the federal government adopted infrastructure policies that he believed exceeded constitutional authority, Virginia should avoid an immediate rupture by adopting into state law exactly the same actions, state laws mirroring the federal laws that he questioned. He would have the assembly declare that "to preserve peace . . . , we proceed to make it [federal policy] the duty of our citizens, until the legislature shall otherwise & ultimately decide, to acquiesce under those acts of the federal branch of our government which we have declared to be usurpations, and against which, in point of right, we do protest as null and void, and never to be quoted as precedents of right." Citizens could then abide by the state laws, rather than the identical but "unconstitutional" federal laws, without undermining Jefferson's views on states' rights.[74]

Madison, as he so often did, found a way to divert his headstrong colleague and avoid such a thinly veiled effort to assert state control over federal legislation while avoiding an open conflict.

> Should any strong interposition there be ultimately required, your paper will be a valuable resort. But I must submit to your consideration whether the expedient with which it closes of enacting Statutes of Congress into Virginia Statutes, would not be an anomaly without any operative character, besides the objection to a lumping and anticipating enactment. As the acts in question would not be executed by the ordinary functionaries of Virg[ini]a. and she could not convert the federal into State functionaries, the whole proceeding would be as exclusively under the federal authority as if the legislative interference of Virga. had not taken place: her interference amounting to nothing more than *a recommendation* to her Citizens to acquiesce in the exercise of the power assumed by Congress, for which there is no apparent necessity or obligation.

Twisting to avoid the danger and irrationality of 1798, Madison understood that Jefferson's proposal was both unworkable and, at base, silly.[75]

Madison's more mature moderation was evident in a letter that he had sent to Thomas Ritchie, the Jeffersonian editor of the *Richmond Enquirer*, a letter he now copied to Jefferson:

> Virginia has doubtless a right to manifest her sense of the Constitution, and of proceedings under it, either by protest or other equivalent modes. Perhaps the mode as well suited as any to the present occasion, if the occasion itself be a suitable one, would be that of instructions to her Representatives in Congs.; to oppose measures violating her constructions of the Instrument; with a preamble, appealing, for the truth of her constructions, to the cotemporary expositions by those best acquainted with the intentions of the Convention, which framed the Constitution; to the Debates & proceedings of the State Conventions which ratified it; to the universal understanding that the Govt. of the Union was a limited not an unlimited one; to the inevitable tendency of the latitude of Construction in behalf of internal improvements, to break down the barriers against unlimited power; it being obvious that the ingenuity which

deduces the authority for such measures, could readily find it for any others whatever.

In other words, Virginia should return to the type of protests that Henry had championed in the early 1790s, not attempting to interfere directly with federal laws, and count on electoral politics to address any federal usurpations. This was a far cry from what Jefferson and Madison had suggested in 1798. Jefferson again acquiesced, but his role in fomenting the radical states' rights movement was once more on display.[76]

Whatever its immediate electoral significance, and whatever the reason for President Jefferson's moderation, what is clear is that what Jefferson and Madison had done in 1798–1799 became powerful grist for nullification in the 1820s–1830s, secession in 1860s, and Lost Cause rhetoric in attacks on Reconstruction and federal power ever since. Even Aaron Burr saw the problem, saying that his Democratic-Republican colleagues "in the honest love of Liberty, had gone a little too far." The compact theory that Jefferson resurrected from the buried ruins of the Confederation became doctrine among nullifiers promoting the slave power and, continuing into the twentieth century, among those supporting massive resistance. Years later, as the sectional controversy concerning slavery heated up, and southern fire-eaters cited Jefferson and the "Spirit of '98" in support of their radical view of states' rights, Madison angrily, and not wholly successfully, sought to distance himself and his friend from nullification.[77]

With Jefferson's inauguration, the crisis was over, but the groundwork had been laid for disunion. Henry had correctly seen the danger.

Many historians have sought to avoid the extent to which the compact theory and nullification argument of the Kentucky and Virginia Resolutions, and the prestige of their authors, were used by secessionists in the run-up to the Civil War. Frank Anderson concludes simply that "neither the [Democratic-]Republican who asserted it nor the Federalist who denied it had any adequate conception of the results to which a logical development of the doctrine would lead." Bernard Weisberger states firmly that the Kentucky and Virginia Resolutions "were not the first step on the road to civil war except in Federalist editorials and in the historical hindsight that is never available to the generation actually living through a national experience." Other historians have similarly sought to sidestep the use to which the Kentucky and Virginia Resolutions were later put.[78]

Yet, while Anderson and Weisberger are correct that no one could see the full extent of what was to come in America's Civil War, many at the time did see the theory's implications, the nation torn apart, possibly civil war, a point made in several state responses and one that motivated opponents, including Henry and Washington. Rhode Island referred with "extreme concern and regret, [to] the many evil and fatal consequences that may flow from the very unwarrantable resolutions." A leading Massachusetts legislator insisted that if the Kentucky and Virginia Resolutions prevailed "State would be armed against State. The very Civil War, which had stalked before that gentleman's [an editor's] imagination in bloody and hideous visage [if the laws were not repealed], would in truth be realized." A widely reprinted letter from Virginia warned of "civil war."[79]

Abraham Lincoln recognized that the imprimatur provided by the Resolutions was critical to the support for the Confederacy offered by thousands of southerners. The impact on future secessionists was clear: "even as Madison [later] disowned the states' rights doctrines that he and his fellow Republicans had flirted with in 1798, Thomas Ritchie and the nullifiers of Virginia and South Carolina claimed Jefferson as their patron saint." While the 1798 Resolutions were not made in support of the slavocracy, as would be the case in South Carolina's arguments for nullification, the threat to the union was nonetheless clear. Henry saw it; it drove him out of retirement. After the Civil War, descendants of Patrick Henry made the point expressly: "Mr. Henry's effort was to calm the excited minds of the people and persuade them to use constitutional means to obtain redress of their grievances, and not to plunge, headlong, into civil war."[80]

Henry's understanding of a loyal opposition—taking disputes to the ballot box even when you disagree with government policy and seeking change in "a constitutional way"—has become foundational for the republic. Unfortunately, historic memory has not recognized Henry's role. In fact, his memory—largely limited to an anti-government radical screaming for "liberty or . . . death"— has been wrongly used to support just the type of extralegal actions that he had opposed.

Epilogue

"I Know of No Way of Judging of the Future but by the Past"

Henry's words from 1775—"I know of no way of judging of the future but by the past"[1]—are good advice, but the problem in knowing the past is that history is not simply recorded but is written, often by people who have an interest in the events discussed. In that process, much can be lost, misunderstood, or distorted. Of course, history is written by the living, and in the case of Henry's memory, largely by the Jeffersonians.

In the nineteenth century, the story of the Kentucky and Virginia Resolutions was also increasingly told by Democratic-Republicans as a triumphant, if not defiant, story of states' rights, a story embraced by defenders of slavery throughout the antebellum era and beyond. John Marshall lamented in 1833 that "the word 'State Rights,' as expounded in the resolutions of '98 and the [Madison] report of '99, has a charm against which all reasoning is vain. Those resolutions and that report constitute the creed of every politician who hopes to rise in Virginia, and to question them . . . is deemed political sacrilege." In 1852 and 1856, as the Civil War loomed, the Democratic party's platform declared that it "will faithfully abide by and uphold, the principles laid down in the Kentucky and Virginia resolutions of 1798, and in the report of Mr. Madison to the Virginia Legislature in 1799; that it adopts those principles as constituting one of the main foundations of its political creed, and is resolved to carry them out in their obvious meaning and import." The "Principles of '98" were kept almost as a sacred flame, as a rhetorical defense of slavery in the antebellum period, and continue to echo today in conservative, states' rights circles. Jefferson's very considerable prestige was used to bolster the proslavery argument of nullifiers and secessionists, and, in the twentieth century, "massive resistance."[2]

After his death in 1799, Patrick Henry's history was written by Jefferson and his acolytes. The result: Henry's memory was diminished, besmirched where possible, where it could not be erased, restricted to that of an orator, possibly a demagogue. His willingness to defend the Constitution that his fellow citizens adopted over his objections—his role in defining a loyal opposition—has been largely forgotten. In its place, a caricature was created of a Patrick Henry who believed only in personal "liberty, or . . . death"—a caricature abused by modern groups that ignore his demand that change must occur in "a constitutional way" and invoke Henry in efforts to undermine government authority in the name of a selfish individual liberty that Henry, a populist and communitarian, would find abhorrent.

In the antebellum era, Democratic-Republicans sought to dismiss or ignore Henry's 1799 campaign, an effort reinforced by Jefferson's personal loathing of Virginia's first state governor. If Henry's campaign was driven by jealousy of Jefferson, or if the old patriot was in his dotage, or if he was motivated by religious fanaticism (against French "atheists"), it would be so much easier to dismiss the inconvenient truth of why the leading antifederalist of 1788 and intellectual godfather of the states' rights movement was compelled to oppose the radical states' rights agenda of 1798–1799. The Jeffersonians vigorously sought to use each of these rationalizations to dismiss Henry's actions and, with Henry dead, spent decades seeking to recast him as no more than a demagogue.

Henry's alleged senility became a favorite trope; many Democratic-Republicans apparently deluded themselves that senility was the only possible explanation for his attack on the Kentucky and Virginia Resolutions. Judge John Tyler wrote to Henry's first biographer (another Jeffersonian) that Henry "might have been misled in founding his opinions by misrepresentations in his aged and infirm state." Even Henry's son-in-law, Spencer Roane, a devoted and rising Jeffersonian, argued that Federalist political opponents used "artfulness and misrepresentations" against Henry who suffered from "seclusion and debility, arising from the infirmity of age and disease." Roane added an equally damning argument, concluding that Henry must have been bribed with land to support the Federalists (speculating that his support for John Marshall's 1799 congressional campaign came from the same source).[3]

There is no serious evidence that Henry's admitted land speculation was anything other than commercial. With respect to his alleged senility, even a quick review of the Charlotte Courthouse speech disproves any suggestion that Henry was in his dotage.

Others argued that Henry was driven by a consuming hatred and jealousy of Jefferson and Madison. John Taylor wrote to Madison that Henry's actions, "his apostacy," could only be explained "by considering it as the issue of a personal enmity to Mr: Jefferson and yourself, to gratify which he has sacrificed his principles to a party, determined on your destruction." This was, he insisted, the only explanation for Henry's having "openly declared that Mr: Marshall, the inveterate enemy of Mr: Jefferson, is the *second* man in the union he would vote for."[4]

Or, it was argued, Henry was driven by his ambition for the public limelight and vanity.

Having embraced Henry as a devoted and discerning patriot in early 1799, the *Aurora,* the era's premier Democratic-Republican newspaper, led the charge alleging both vanity and senility shortly after Henry's Charlotte Courthouse speech (concluding with a rude scatological reference):

> the venerable *Patrick Henry,* in the wane of his proud course of years, has been assailed in this *weak place* of *vanity*—and offers have been actually made to support him in the race for the presidential chair—his mind no longer quick to the apprehension of worldly deceits, the insuspicious temper of *second-childhood* has made him a dupe—they promise him honor but they mean dishonor—they promise him support, but they mean only a disunion of the republican interest—he appears not to have a friend to tell him of their deceit, and his mind unstrung by age appears insensible to their purpose—while
>
>> Outrag'd reason cries with piercing voice
>> Loose from the rapid care your aged horse
>> Lest in the race derided—left behind,
>> He drag his aged limbs, and break his wind.[5]

Jealousy, pride, an imagined "bitter" old age are terribly weak explanations for the Charlotte Courthouse campaign. As a preliminary matter, Henry had repeatedly turned down high office—Supreme Court justice, secretary of state, senator, ambassador, a sixth term as governor—making his alleged thirst for fame a whisper-thin explanation for his opposition to the radical states' rights agenda. In terms of jealousy, Henry certainly had no great love for Jefferson by 1799, and he apparently joined in lighthearted poking fun at the future president. (There is the story that at Charlotte Courthouse Henry could not resist calling Jefferson "Frenchified" and making a snide reference to his French chef, as "he could no longer eat the vittles they were all fetcht up on.") But, while Jefferson seemed to be consumed by the abortive 1781 investigation of his governorship that he blamed on Henry, there is no evidence of similar vitriol from Henry directed at Jefferson nor Madison.[6]

These attacks on Henry and canards about his political sentiments did not stop with his death. After Henry's death, Jeffersonians propagated the story that the former governor had twice sought to assume dictatorial powers during the Revolution. But both accusations were flimsy and fell apart under scrutiny. Notably, no one connected Henry with either scheme to create a "dictator" until years after his death. William Wirt explored the issue with members of the 1781 Virginia assembly who were still living and concluded "that Henry was thought of for this office, has been alleged, and is highly probable; but that the project was suggested by him, or received his countenance, I have met with no one who will venture to affirm."[7]

While Jefferson was forced to concede both that Henry was perhaps the greatest speaker that ever lived and that he played a crucial role in "maintaining the spirit of the Revolution," everything else was an effort to belittle his role and reputation. But having dismissed Henry's political and legal abilities and having insisted that he was driven by jealousy and greed, Henry's undeniable oratorical abilities were twisted to an argument that he was a dangerous demagogue, feeding the equally thin claim that he had sought dictatorial powers. The demagogue fabrication never quite took hold, but it did serve further to reduce unfairly Henry's role in historic memory to that of only an orator.[8]

Historian Edmund S. Morgan perhaps more accurately explains the circumstances: "a man who values his historical reputation had better outlive his enemies."[9]

The campaign to besmirch Henry gained supporters among Democratic-Republicans (soon to be Democrats) for years. Martin van Buren, visiting Monticello in 1824, bought the Jefferson canard that Henry had embraced Hamilton's financial system, writing forty years later:

> In Virginia, which State has done so much to give a tone to national politics, Patrick Henry has been almost, if not quite, the only prominent man who abandoned the principles by which he had been governed during the Confederation, and embraced those of Hamilton at the coming in of the new government. Always admiring his character and conduct during the Revolutionary era, and strongly impressed by the vehemence and consistency with which he had, during the government of the Confederation, opposed every measure that savored

of English origin, I pressed Mr. Jefferson, as far as was allowable, for the reasons of his sudden and great change. His explanation was, "that Henry had been smitten by Hamilton's financial policy."

Jefferson's bitter portrayal of Henry is matched by Van Buren's credulous acceptance of whatever the third president reported in 1824 of the 1790s. This passage by Van Buren is also interesting in its effort to claim that Henry "abandoned the principles . . . which . . . governed during the Confederation"— principles of a compact among sovereign states. Of course, Henry did not abandon his principles, but the "government of the Confederation" was rejected by the American people when they ratified the Constitution over Henry's objections and vocal promotion of those principles, and Henry, a believer in the rule of law and decision of the community, acquiesced in their decision until changes could be made in "a constitutional way." That was the central demand upon a loyal opposition.[10]

Even after the Civil War, unrepentant Confederate and devoted Jeffersonian E. A. Pollard (author of the infamous *Lost Cause*) published an extended essay attacking Henry's political and legal abilities and arguing, ridiculously, that there was no evidence that he was even a very good speaker. The real cause for Pollard's vitriol is revealed in the conclusion of his extended essay in which he attacks Henry for questioning the "resolutions of 1798!"—Pollard's exclamation point.[11]

This was not all about Henry's "apostasy" in the crisis of 1799; Jefferson certainly had a longstanding feud with Henry. But regardless of the cause, the effect on history has been the same. It is not happenstance that Patrick Henry is the most important of the Founding Fathers about whom very little is known. This point has been made since at least 1815 when a Middlebury College student's commencement address praised Henry at length while noting that his "name has been too little the subject of eulogy." In 1817, the Edinburgh *Encyclopaedia* noted that "the chronicles of the provincial governments in North America, of the revolutionary war, and of the governments of Virginia and the United States since the year 1776, afford less satisfactory information of Mr Henry, and his specific services, than of any other man, at all distinguished in those several eras." Importantly, Henry is among the most prominent of the revolutionary generation for which a modern papers project has not been funded. It is equally noteworthy that Henry's 1799 campaign is dealt with in only a summary fashion in the dozen Patrick Henry biographies that are available.[12]

Beyond Henry, the net result of all of this was that two critical lessons from the battles of 1798–1799 have been largely lost or diminished: First, the

Founding era lesson on the central role of a free press to a functioning republic. Second, Henry's role in defining a loyal opposition and insisting upon change in a manner consistent with the Constitution, even when you lose, a lesson perhaps now more relevant than ever.

In 1798, before the Sedition Act was adopted, Jefferson lamented to his lieutenant that if the opposition papers failed, the hopes for the republic "will be entirely brow-beaten." The necessity of a free press for a functioning republic was at the root of the extreme measures that he proposed in the period that he termed a "reign of witches." Later in life, Jefferson would note that freedom of the press, by providing an effective check on government abuses, was critical in "produc[ing] reform peaceably, which must otherwise be done by revolution." Perhaps he was remembering the old battle. The problem in 1798–1799 was that with the free press under attack, what Jefferson perceived as government abuses—not only the attacks on the press itself and prosecution of scores of editors, but a large standing army (with Hamilton in effective command), a rabid prowar party against France, rising taxes, growing presidential power, use of religious leaders and religion to bolster the government in power, attacks on aliens, et cetera—might go unchecked. Unchecked, they would lead to tyranny and an end to a republic that was "the world's best hope." Jefferson chose a remedy very poorly, a "remedy" that threatened to destroy the nation even in his own time, but the crisis was real and has not been adequately appreciated. The extent to which this story has been submerged in what became in the nineteenth century a more convenient story for slave owners about states' rights is evident in history's failure to recognize the extent of the sedition prosecutions and the dangerous targeting of political opponents' access to the press.[13]

Jefferson's confidence in the suffrage of the people when properly informed was a cornerstone of American democracy. With the advantage of two hundred years of history, and given recent efforts to obscure government abuses by insisting that the free press is the "enemy of the people," the central necessity of a free press to support the electoral process in a democracy is even more clear. Jefferson and Madison were right about that. In fairness, though, "the democratic component of that liberal future" that they saw and espoused "owed far more to Jefferson's and Madison's longtime rival [Henry] than the two men were ever willing to admit."[14]

Then there is the matter of a loyal opposition.

From the Founding until today, few have questioned that the essence of a republic is rule of the majority (while protecting the equal rights of the minority). Jefferson trumpeted the idea in his first inaugural and often returned to it. He wrote in 1809, "where the Law of the majority ceases to be acknowledged, there government ends."[15]

Acknowledging the rule of the majority, though, was easy in many respects, especially after Jefferson's election, and tended to hide what was often a more difficult question: How should a minority behave when it lost an election, when the government adopted policies with which it fundamentally disagreed? It was to this question that Henry, and particularly his 1799 campaign, would speak most powerfully.

Central to understanding the whole episode is Henry's role as the leading antifederalist in opposition to ratification of the Constitution. One sees in the Charlotte Courthouse speech some anger, some disappointment, some incredulity. . . . "I warned you! I warned you!" Henry seemed to be repeating. Everyone, citizens of Virginia and citizens of the United States, had been well-warned of the dangers of an expansive authority in the national government. With a bit of "I told you so" creeping in, Henry reminded his listeners that he had led efforts to curb the power of the federal government and retain broad powers in the states.

But he had lost. "We, all of us, agreed," he seemed to be reminding the gathered throng. That he had opposed was not the point.

As on the evening of June 27, 1788, when Henry threw calming oil on the churning water generated by some of his antifederalist colleagues who insisted that they would not be reconciled to the newly ratified Constitution and would interfere with its implementation, Henry was reminding people that a republic only works when citizens accept their political disappointments, even what they see as serious political error in co-citizens, with magnanimity, with compromise, with a firm resolve to address problems in "a constitutional way."

Madison had made the same argument during debates over the Bill of Rights: "my idea of the sovereignty of the people is, that the people can change the constitution if they please, but while the constitution exists, they must conform themselves to its dictates." And this was a central theme of Washington's Farewell Address: "The basis of our political systems is the right of the people to make and to alter their constitutions of government. But the Constitution which at any time exists, until changed by an explicit and authentic act of the whole people, is sacredly obligatory upon all. The very idea of the power and the right of the people to establish government presupposes the duty of every individual to obey the established government."[16]

Henry's objections to the Kentucky and Virginia Resolutions were about how a republic had to operate if it was to survive. As the new nation was still grappling with how to be a self-created republic, it could not be that every time one "lost" an election or a policy debate, even when serious, it should beget refusal to comply with authority or a revolution.

On a larger scale, such power in a state to ignore or undermine national government action, a cornerstone of the Confederation, had been eliminated with the Constitution because the Confederation had proved wholly incapable of governing effectively. Henry, a believer in the rule of law, understood that the inability to abide by government decisions with which people disagreed spelled the doom of the republic, to be replaced with monarchy, tyranny. Similarly, each state deciding for itself which federal laws to permit to be implemented spelled internal conflict, doom for the republic, to be replaced with monarchy, tyranny. While political scientists note that the country grappled for many years to come to an understanding of a loyal opposition, this was the battle that Henry was fighting. His example continues to speak powerfully today.[17]

Henry's role also helps to highlight the fact that comparisons to 1776 that were made with such ease by the Democratic-Republicans in 1798–1799 (and by states' rights advocates throughout the antebellum period and still today) tend to ignore critical differences. For example, Jefferson's revolutionary rhetoric from the 1774 *Summary View of the Rights of British Citizens* has been used to explain the 1798 Resolutions, with William Watkins noting that in 1774 Jefferson said that acts of Parliament were "void," "inauthoritative." "Let no act be passed by any one legislature which may infringe on the rights and liberties of another."[18]

Henry understood as well as anyone, though, that such claims took the Revolution badly out of context and misstated its principles. The year 1798 was not 1776. In 1776, Americans were not represented in Parliament and had no prospects of being represented; they had no role in appointing a king or any effective way to respond legally to royal decisions with which they disagreed. As the Revolution approached, American petitions to the king were dismissed without being read. Even recourse to local courts and juries was being foreclosed as Britain moved critical cases out of the colonies. There was no "constitutional way" forward. As he explained in the Parsons' Cause when he lambasted the king for interfering in the will of the people through royal edict, the problem was not simply that a decision of the legislature was being challenged, but that those challenging it had no authority derived from the people. Although Henry had been deeply suspicious of some aspects of the Constitution, and continued to be so, in 1798, the American people had elected the Congress and the president and, critically, had a periodic opportunity at the ballot box to change their minds about how they wanted the country ruled. The central point was belief in the rights of the people, their sovereignty. In 1776, Henry correctly saw the alternative if the voice of the people was ignored when they had no control over their government, and in 1799, he saw the consequences if the people cannot live within the bounds of the government that they created and controlled.[19]

The same is true today. As often as not, then and now, those advocating revolution or a violent refusal to abide by lawful authority or an election are simply unwilling to live in a functioning republic when they do not get their way because they are in a minority (even temporarily) and the government, elected by their neighbors, adopts a policy with which they disagree. As John Nicholas argued in his angry letter denouncing his former Democratic-Republican colleagues, they are effectively challenging the very principle of majority rule, the very foundation of the republic. This is why Patrick Henry came out of retirement to defend the Constitution that he had originally opposed.

In spite of his central role in embracing the proper function of a loyal opposition, and arguably as an alternative to it, an image of the freedom-loving Patrick Henry as a supporter of a strong states' rights and individual liberty agenda was retained by some and occasionally replanted in the public mind by states' rights supporters. This image was promoted without any mention of his communitarianism, his deep concerns in 1799 with states interfering with the federal government, his demands that the will of the majority as expressed in the Constitution and the electoral process be respected, and his insistence that reforms be made in "a constitutional way." This effort to mischaracterize Henry continues today. Fed by the image of a fire-breathing radical demanding "liberty or death," the same distorted memory of Henry is evidenced in the warm embrace of Patrick Henry by the modern Tea Party, Proud Boys, Oath Keepers, Three-Percenters, and other extremists based on his alleged ideology of personal liberty *über alles* and opposition to government power. Today, as in the early nineteenth century, it is convenient for many to ignore Henry's stern warnings of incipient tyranny if we cannot abide by electoral results and the decisions of properly constituted authorities and respond to disagreements at the ballot box.

Finally, at the broadest level, the crisis of 1799 was a rich scene showcasing a complex shifting ideology of nation and citizenship that has long been a subject of historical inquiry. For years, historians have noted that around the end of the eighteenth century, there was an ideological shift from what is termed a "classic republican" model, focused on individuals of virtue sacrificing for the good of the community, to a "liberal" worldview focused on individual rights. Jefferson, in particular, is associated with that liberal idea of individual rights, personal pursuit of life, liberty, and happiness. Today, this view of the history is somewhat out of favor among historians, or at least viewed as simplistic, in part because changes in these types of societal values are never complete and always gradual. Moreover, no one is completely focused on the community to the exclusion of individual rights, and few are focused exclusively on personal freedom to exclusion of community interests.

Claims that the founders were committed to a republic run by a virtuous people are also called into question by the founders' continued support for slavery. Henry is not immune in this regard. Like Jefferson, Henry had strongly denounced slavery as immoral. Like Jefferson, he had urged those holding slaves to ameliorate their condition, to treat them more fairly. He, too, had recognized that the foul institution could not last. Jefferson reportedly told one inquirer that it was Henry, as governor, who led the 1778 efforts to ban slave imports to Virginia. Yet, Henry, when confronted by an abolitionist, confessed that he (like Jefferson) was "drawn along by the general inconvenience of living here without them." While Washington freed his own slaves upon his death, and the financially impaired Jefferson (at least after 1820) might have been blocked by creditors from doing so, Henry was a wealthy man who could have done far more for his enslaved, stating in his will only that his wife might free several if she so chose. The reality of slavery is central to the legacy of the founders. Henry himself owned ninety-eight people upon his death and rented others.[20]

Still, among themselves—white, male leaders of the young nation—and in trying to form a functioning republic, they continued to insist upon virtuous (that is, non-self-interested) leaders committed to the public weal.

Regardless of slavery, it does seem that a general and important shift in how people saw and interacted with the political world occurred around the turn of the eighteenth to nineteenth century. Liberalism, individual rights, a clear foundation for Jeffersonians, became a foundation for American society as the eighteenth century waned, and these principles continue to be central to American society today. Mark McGarvie makes the point in discussing how the shift impacted religious freedom and embraced a Jeffersonian separation of church and state: "Implicitly, law was reconceived in the Constitutional Convention—from supporting the social good through communitarian ideals consistent with Christian morality to serving ideals of individual liberty." (Ironically, success of Jeffersonian liberalism resulted in a short time in the success of Hamiltonian capitalism. Similarly, his advocacy of separation of church and state resulted in an explosion of religion freed from government oversight.) Henry, by comparison, led a public life centered on supporting the community, virtuous leadership, and public liberty more than an abstract or unlimited individual liberty. This was evident in his actions in 1799.[21]

As the curtain was falling on the eighteenth century, Henry (and Washington) continued to cling to what was quickly becoming an old-fashioned idea of classic republicanism, virtuous, non-self-interested service to the community and citizens' responsibilities being at least as important as individual rights. Such a worldview also included opposition to parties (or what they would term "factions"); such factions focused on advancing parochial interests rather than the interests of the community at large, reason enough for suspicion. As the nineteenth century progressed, partisanship became understood as a means to engage people who would otherwise feel dissociated from political developments, politically helpless. Perhaps that is true, but in 1799, partisanship and political parties were a way to divide.[22]

In more pejorative terms, we might say that for Henry (and Washington) country came before ideology; community came before party; the commonweal came before even individual interests. This is exactly why Henry and Washington were so outraged in their letter exchange as 1799 dawned: It seemed that Jefferson and Madison were putting party interests, and their personal quest for power, above the stability of the nation.[23]

In 1799, Henry was willing to lead by supporting a government under the Constitution with which he deeply disagreed because he believed in his community's right to choose, even when they chose contrary to his advice, even when they chose, he believed, poorly.

Such a renewed commitment to our shared community is desperately needed today.

Considering these changes gives a new way to understand the attacks on Henry as an apostate, a senile, jealous old man. It is not simply that some of his political opponents did not understand what Henry was doing, but they did not want to understand. Understanding might require them to consider carefully and critically their own behavior. Perhaps the same is true when today people focus only on Henry's call to "liberty, or . . . death." If, after all, Henry was right in 1799, then the entire radical states' rights agenda and a fixation on individual liberty without government authority and community responsibility, then and now, is seriously compromised. Modern attacks on government as "the enemy" must meet with Henry's insistence that it is our government; we created it; it is our responsibility. Perhaps the same is true when people so readily vilify political opponents without considering their real concerns or how deeply they rest on our shared principles, among the points that a chastened Jefferson made in his first inaugural address.

What about us? Can we draw some wisdom from this crisis of union and the leaders who confronted it? Of course, historians rightly object to a facile use of history from more than 200 years ago to address modern political problems, but if not relevant to our times, why are we studying it? Henry, in his 1775 "liberty, or . . . death" speech at Saint John's Church, told his colleagues that "I have no way of judging of the future but by the past." History gives us a lens not only into the past, but into the future.

Certainly, being periodically reminded of the tyranny latent in attacks on the free press is of lasting value. Jefferson was right, both about the danger of the Alien and Sedition Acts and about the need for a free press if government is to be prevented from abusing power for the few at the expense of the many. Any claim that the news media are the "enemy of the people" must be seen as a dangerous affront to the nation. For Jefferson, undermining the press undermined the political process itself and the nation.

This is also a strong story of "contingency" and individual "agency" as powerful forces in history. Had Henry (one man) lived, how different might American political history have been? While we can all be grateful that historians no longer focus so exclusively on the "great men" of history, undoubtedly there were those in our past who had enormous influence on the formation of our nation in ways that still affect us today. Today, there are undoubtedly individuals who will profoundly affect our history, and the power of individual actions should not be gainsaid.

So, in the end, I come back to Patrick Henry.

Henry was, in many respects, the leader of the movement to bring the common man into the polity (albeit white men in his time), initially more so than Jefferson (although Jefferson very effectively capitalized on the movement). Yet, Henry was not a libertarian. As Thomas Buckley explains, "For Patrick Henry, as for so many of the founders, liberty was purposeful. What some consider liberty today—the freedom to do whatever one wishes—Henry and the Revolutionary generation regarded as license." Henry fought not simply for himself, but for his community.[24]

More important, though, than such abstract questions of governmental philosophy, in an era when our system has been directly challenged by disingenuous efforts to reject electoral results and undermine constitutional procedures, we can recommit to share Patrick Henry's devotion to the community and nation—even when they act against our advice and wishes—recommit to his demand that differences be taken to the ballot box and to his admonition that change must occur in "a constitutional way."

· NOTES ·

ABBREVIATIONS

DHRC — Kaminski, John P., et al., eds., *Documentary History of the Ratification of the Constitution.* 42 vols. expected. Chicago: University of Chicago Press, 1976 to present.

Federalist — *The Federalist Papers,* November 22, 1787, to March 1, 1788.

Founders Online — *Founders Online,* National Archives, https://www.founders.archives.gov/.

Madison's Report — "Report of the Committee to whom was committed the proceedings of sundry of the other States, in answer to the Resolutions of the General Assembly" (1800). *Founders Online,* https://founders.archives.gov/documents/Madison/01-17-02-0202.

PGW — *Papers of George Washington Digital Edition.* Charlottesville: University of Virginia Press, Rotunda, 2008.

PJM — Stagg, J.C.A., et al., eds. *The Papers of James Madison Digital Edition.* Charlottesville: University of Virginia Press, Rotunda, 2010.

PTJ — Boyd, Julian P., et al., eds. *The Papers of Thomas Jefferson.* 45 vols. to date. Princeton, NJ: Princeton University Press, 1950 to present.

PTJ (RS) — Looney, J. Jefferson, et al., eds. *The Papers of Thomas Jefferson, Retirement Series.* 19 vols. to date. Princeton, NJ: Princeton University Press, 2004 to present.

INTRODUCTION

1. *Papers of George Washington Digital Edition* (Retirement Series) (hereinafter *PGW* [RS]), 3:317–18.
2. Ibid., 3:318–19.
3. Ibid., 3:371.
4. Bruce, *John Randolph*, 1:147.
5. Jefferson to Edward Carrington, December 21, 1787, *Papers of Thomas Jefferson* (hereinafter *PTJ*), 12:446.
6. Patrick Henry, June 25, 1788, *Documentary History of the Ratification of the Constitution* (hereinafter *DHRC*), 10:1537 ("a constitutional way"); Henry, *Henry*, 2:609 ("for a monarchy").
7. Gutzman, *Virginia's American Revolution*, 112n163 ("puzzle"). William Wirt to Thomas Jefferson, October 23, 1816, *PTJ* (RS), 10:487.

1. PATRICK HENRY'S POLITICAL PHILOSOPHY

1. There are a number of good general biographies of Henry. They include Jon Kukla, *Patrick Henry: Champion of Liberty*; Richard R. Beeman, *Patrick Henry: A Short Biography*; Robert Douthat Meade, *Patrick Henry: Patriot in the Making* and *Patrick Henry: Practical Revolutionary*; Henry Mayer, *A Son of Thunder: Patrick Henry and the American Republic*; Thomas Kidd, *Patrick Henry: First among Patriots*; the venerable Moses Coit Tyler, *Patrick Henry*; the first Henry biography, William Wirt, *Sketches of the Life and Character of Patrick Henry*; and the author's own, John A. Ragosta, *Patrick Henry: Proclaiming a Revolution*.
2. Letter from the Reverend James Maury to the Reverend John Camm, December 12, 1763, in Kennedy, ed., *Journals of the House of Burgesses of Virginia, 1761–1765*, lii. Henry's language was reported by Maury, who conceded that "I do not pretend to remember his words, but take this to have been the sum and substance . . . of his labored oration." While Maury was obviously an interested party, there is no indication from other sources that Henry's argument was misreported.
3. See, e.g., Ragosta, *Patrick Henry*, 29–33; Kukla, *Patrick Henry*, 80–97.
4. Notes of Daniel Webster, in Curtis, *Life of Daniel Webster*, 1:584–85. Ragosta, *Patrick Henry*, 4–6. *Richmond Enquirer*, September 2, 1815.
5. For a fuller discussion of Henry and slavery, see Ragosta, *Patrick Henry*, 37–39.
6. Henry to Jefferson, February 15, 1780, *PTJ*, 3:293.
7. The problems facing the new United States during the aptly named "Critical Period" are expertly explained in Van Cleve, *We Have Not a Government* and Klarman, *Framers' Coup*. See also Garmon, "Mapping Distress," 231–65.
8. Klarman, *Framers' Coup*, 20, citing Roger H. Brown, *Redeeming the Republic: Federalists, Taxation, and the Origins of the Constitution* (Baltimore: Johns Hopkins University Press, 1993), 25, 155. Klarman, *Framers' Coup*, 18–19.

9. Madison to Edmund Randolph, February 25, 1787, *Papers of James Madison Digital Edition*, Congressional Series (hereinafter *PJM* [CS]), 9:299.

10. E.g., Madison, "Vices of the Political System of the United States," *PJM* (CS), 9:350. Madison to Jefferson, January 22, 1786, *PJM* (CS), 8:476.

11. Washington to Benjamin Harrison Sr., March 4, 1783, *Founders Online*, https://founders.archives.gov/documents/Washington/99-01-02-10768. Madison to James Madison Sr., February 25, 1787, *PJM* (CS), 9:297.

12. Van Cleve, *We Have Not*, 10. See, e.g., secret instruction to Louis-Guillaume Otto, French charge d'affaires in the United States, August 30, 1787, Bancroft, *History of the Formation of the Constitution*, 2:438.

13. Madison to Jefferson, October 24, 1787, *PTJ*, 12:276. Richard Henry Lee to Francis Lightfoot Lee, July 17, 1787, Ballagh, ed., *Letters of Richard Henry Lee*, 2:424. On states' abuse of powers, see also Sloan, *Principle and Interest*, 38.

14. Madison to Washington, April 16, 1787, *PJM* (CS), 9:386. Madison to Edmund Pendleton, April 22, 1787, *PJM* (CS), 9:394. See generally Wood, *Power and Liberty*, 67–72.

15. Madison to Jefferson, October 24, 1787, *PTJ*, 12:276. See, e.g., Klarman, *Framers' Coup*, 74; Leonard and Cornell, *Partisan Republic*, 4. The classic volume on the Constitution as reactionary is Beard, *An Economic Interpretation of the Constitution of the United States*.

16. Henry, *Henry*, 2:175, Hening, ed., *Statutes at Large*, 11:66 (delaying half of taxes, accepting deer hides as payment). See generally Meade, *Practical Revolutionary*, 252.

17. Henry, *Patrick Henry*, 2:226–27. See also Meade, *Practical Revolutionary*, 275, quoting Irving Brant, *James Madison: The Nationalist, 1780–1787* (Indianapolis: Bobbs-Merrill, 1948), 2:316; *Journal of the House of Delegates of the Commonwealth of Virginia, Begun and Held in the City of Richmond, on Monday, the Third Day of May, in the Year of Our Lord Seventeen Hundred and Eighty-four,* May 19, 1784, 11–12. *DHRC*, 8:489–91.

   Jefferson made a similar argument, concluding that the Confederation had the inherent ability to enforce requisitions "by the law of nature." Thomas Jefferson Answers to Questions Propounded by M. de Meunier, January 24, 1786, *Founders Online*, https://founders.archives.gov/documents/Jefferson/01-10-02-0001-0002; Jefferson to Edward Carrington, August 4, 1787, *PTJ*, 11:678. See Mayer, *Constitutional Thought of Thomas Jefferson*, 93. Fortunately for Jefferson, this conclusion—inconsistent with his political position in the 1790s—did not become widely known until long after his political career ended. He appeared to abandon the position by 1818. Steele, "Thomas Jefferson, Coercion," 833.

18. William Short to Jefferson, May 14 [15], 1784, *PTJ*, 7:257; Madison to Jefferson, May 15, 1784, *PTJ*, 7:258.

19. Henry to Virginia Delegation, July 5, 1786, Henry, *Henry,* 3:363–64, 3:350–52 ("amongst the capital"). Ragosta, *Patrick Henry,* 73, see also 86–87; Van Cleve, *We Have Not,* 151–52. Henry's support for Native intermarriage (proposing to grant fifty acres to a couple that intermarried) was progressive for the period, but as with other founders who demanded assimilation (Jefferson and Washington among them), Natives had not been consulted and their sovereignty was largely ignored.

20. Nevins, *American States,* 346.

21. Morris, *Forging of the Union,* 234.

22. Ford, ed., *Journals of the Continental Congress,* August 25, 1785, 29:658. Van Cleve, *We Have Not,* 165.

23. Van Cleve, *We Have Not,* 165, citing Samuel Flagg Bemis, *Pinckney's Treaty: America's Advantage from Europe's Distress, 1783–1800* (New Haven, CT: Yale University Press, 1960), 62. See James Monroe to Henry, August 12, 1786, Henry, *Henry,* 2:293 (on exclusion of tobacco). Klarman believes that, in any case, the commercial benefits of the treaty were chimerical. Klarman, *Framers' Coup,* 60.

24. Charles Thomson's Notes of Debates, August 18, 1786, Smith, ed., *Letters of Delegates,* 23:496. James Monroe to Madison, May 31, 1786, *PJM* (CS), 9:69 (encoded text in italics). Van Cleve, *We Have Not,* 170–71. On the willingness of some frontiersmen, including a member of Congress from North Carolina, to join an enlarged Spanish empire, see Remini, "Northwest Ordinance of 1787," 20.

25. Jefferson to Madison, January 30, 1787, *PTJ,* 11:93. James Monroe to Henry, August 12, 1786, Henry, *Henry,* 2:295. See, e.g., Van Cleve, *We Have Not,* 174–75 (by the end of 1785, Rufus King and Theodore Sedgwick were advocating a northern confederacy); Kukla, *Patrick Henry,* 299–303.

26. James Monroe to Henry, August 12, 1786, Henry, *Henry,* 2:291, 297; see also James Monroe to Madison, September 3, 1786, *PJM* (CS), 9:112. Van Cleve, *We Have Not,* 174.

27. Madison to James Monroe, June 21, 1786, *PJM* (CS) 9:82 (footnote omitted) (encoded text in italics). Timothy Bloodworth to Richard Caswell, September 29, 1786, Smith, ed., *Letters of Delegates to Congress,* 23:573 (spelling as original).

28. John Marshall to Arthur Lee, Henry, *Henry,* 2:301. Charles Thomson's Notes of Debates, August 18, 1786, Smith, ed., *Letters of Delegates to Congress,* 23:496.

29. Madison to Edmund Randolph, February 25, 1787, *PJM* (CS), 9:299; Madison to George Nicholas, April 8, 1788, *PJM* (CS), 11:12. Wood, *Power and Liberty,* 64, quoting John Jay, Address before Congress on Spanish-American Diplomacy, August 3, 1786, in Ruhl J. Bartlett, ed., *The Record of American Diplomacy* (New York: Knopf, 1952), 56.

30. Henry Lee Jr., to Washington, August 7, 1786, *PGW* (CS), 4:200.

31. Madison to Washington, December 7, 1786, *PJM* (CS), 9:200. Edmund Randolph to Madison, March 1, 1787, *PJM* (CS), 9:301.

32. Van Cleve, *We Have Not*, 70, citing Jacob W. Price, *Capital and Credit in British Overseas Trade: The View from the Chesapeake, 1700–1776* (Cambridge, MA: Harvard University Press, 1980), 7, 9, tables 1 and 2. A modern value was calculated using https://www.measuringworth.com/calculators/ukcompare /relativevalue.php. See also Evans, "Private Indebtedness" (Virginians owed £2,000,000).

33. E.g., Evans, "Private Indebtedness," 353. *Virginia Gazette, or American Advertiser* (Richmond), June 7, 1783, quoted in ibid., 359.

34. Evans, "Private Indebtedness," 361 (failure to return slaves a "turning point in public opinion"). Edmund Pendleton thought that many Virginians saw British violations of the treaty simply as an excuse not to pay their debts. Edmund Pendleton to Madison, June 16, 1783, *PJM* (CS), 7:150. British officials, for their part, advised their military officers to retain the northwest forts even before King George's final ratification of the treaty. Jones, *Crucible*, 23. While it is difficult to say with certainty who "began" the violations, John Jay (apparently discounting removal of former slaves from New York in 1783) gave the Confederation Congress a legal opinion that American violations predated British, justifying British refusal to evacuate the forts. Van Cleve, *We Have Not*, 70–72.

35. Evans, "Private Indebtedness," 367–68. Van Cleve, *We Have Not*, 254. Henings, ed., *Statutes at Large* (October session 1787), 12:528. DHRC: 9:1138n10. DHRC: 8:xxvii. See Evans, "Private Indebtedness," 365.

36. Meade, *Practical Revolutionary*, 404; Evans, "Private Indebtedness," 355, 370.

37. Evans, "Private Indebtedness," quoting "Philo Decius," *Decius's Letters on the Opposition to the New Constitution in Virginia* (Richmond, 1789), 92. See Ford, ed., *Journals of the Continental Congress*, April 13, 1787, 32:177–84.

38. See *Ware v. Hylton*, 3 U.S. 199 (1796). See Evans, "Private Indebtedness," 371–72. Wirt, *Sketches*, 220 et seq., 228 ("salus populi"). See also Hobson, "Patrick Henry and John Marshall."

39. Wirt, *Sketches*, 256, 244.

40. Edmund Randolph to Madison, October 23 (ca. 29), 1787, *PJM* (CS), 10:230. Jefferson to Lewis Littlepage, May 9, 1789, *PTJ*, 15:106.

41. Ragosta, *Patrick Henry*, 85. Madison to Jefferson, March 19, 1787, *PTJ*, 11:221 (italics originally in cypher).

2. PATRICK HENRY, AMERICA'S LEADING ANTIFEDERALIST

1. James Madison, Notes on Origin of the Constitutional Convention, December 1835, *Founders Online* (early access), https://founders.archives.gov /documents/Madison/99-02-02-3189. For examples of states acting against states, see Van Cleve, *We Have Not*, 189 et seq.

2. Virginia General Assembly (January 21, 1786), in Kurland and Lerner, eds., *Founders' Constitution*, 1:185.

3. Ibid. at 1:187.

4. See *DHRC*, 8:xxviii. See also Madison to Jefferson, September 6, 1787, *PTJ*, 12:106.

5. See Richards, *Shays's Rebellion*; Gross, ed., *In Debt to Shays*.

6. Madison to Edmund Randolph, February 25, 1787, *PJM* (CS), 9:299. Washington to Madison, November 5, 1786, *PJM* (CS), 9:161, 162. See also Van Cleve, *We Have Not*, 238–42.

7. *DHRC*, 8:45.

8. Debates, May 28, May 29, 1787, Elliot, ed., *Debates in the Several State Conventions*, 1:40. Madison to Jefferson, June 6, 1787, *PTJ*, 11:400.

9. E.g., Klarman, *Framers' Coup*; Beeman, *Plain, Honest Men*; Bilder, *Madison's Hand*; Stewart, *Summer of 1787*; Waldstreicher, *Slavery's Constitution*; Van Cleve, *Slaveholders' Union*; Holton, *Unruly Americans*; Bowen, *Miracle at Philadelphia*; Wood, *Power and Liberty*. While no official transcript of the proceedings was kept, several delegates, most notably James Madison, kept notes, and there are a number of excellent primary sources. See, e.g., Madison, *Notes of Debates*; Elliot, ed., *Debates in the Several State Conventions*; Farrand, ed., *Records of the Federal Convention*; Yates, *Secret Proceedings*; Kurland and Lerner, ed., *Founders' Constitution*. A massive documentary source incorporating these and other relevant materials is being prepared at the University of Wisconsin, the *Documentary History of the Ratification of the Constitution* (*DHRC*) (42 volumes expected).

10. *DHRC*, 1:305–6.

11. *DHRC*, 1:318.

12. Madison to Jefferson, October 24, 1787, *PJM* (CS), 10:207. During ratification, Jefferson was ambivalent about the Constitution. He was skeptical of the power of the president and lack of term limits and insisted, among other things, that a bill of rights was needed. Interestingly, Madison was quick to suggest to Jefferson that Henry would likely oppose the Constitution; perhaps Madison understood that given Jefferson's strong personal antipathy toward Henry, the latter's opposition could encourage Jefferson's support. "The part which Mr. Henry will take is unknown here. Much will depend on it. I had taken it for granted from a variety of circumstances that he wd. be in opposition, and still think that will be the case. There are reports however which favor a contrary supposition." Ibid.

13. *Norfolk and Portsmouth Journal*, May 21, 1788, *DHRC*, 9:831.

14. Madison to Washington, October 18, 1787, *PGW* (CS), 5:383. Tobias Lear to John Langdon, October 19, 1787, *DHRC*, 8:80 (footnote omitted). Madison

to Washington, October 28, 1787, *PGW* (CS), 5:391 (footnote omitted). Edward Carrington to William Short, April 25, 1788, *DHRC*, 9:758.

15. Ragosta, *Patrick Henry,* 50; Kukla, *Patrick Henry,* 233–38.
16. Washington to Henry, September 24, 1787, *PGW* (CS), 5:339. Washington wrote the same letter at the same time to Benjamin Harrison and Thomas Nelson, both of whom also became important antifederalists.
17. Henry to Washington, October 19, 1787, *PGW* (CS), 5:384.
18. Washington to Benjamin Lincoln, April 1, 1788, *DHRC,* 9:636. Virginia's formal letter to the Confederation Congress providing notice of its ratification was agreed to on June 26, the date normally used for Virginia's ratification.
19. Edmund Randolph to Madison, February 29, 1788, *PJM* (CS), 10:542. E.g., Edward Carrington to Madison, January 18, 1788, *PJM* (CS), 10:383. Glover, *Fate of the Revolution,* 47. Madison to Jefferson, August 23, 1788, *PTJ,* 13:539–40 (North Carolina's actions attributed to Henry).
20. Edmund Randolph to Madison, December 27, 1787, *PJM* (CS), 10:347. Edmund Randolph, Debates, June 4, 1788, *DHRC,* 9:933, 1084.
21. Klarman, *Framers' Coup,* 541, quoting DeWitt Clinton Journal, July 18, 1788, *DHRC,* 23:2232.
22. Comte de Moustier to Comte de Montmorin, June 25, 1788, *DHRC,* 10:1679. At one point, Jefferson suggested just that: after nine states ratified, four should refuse to ratify, essentially holding the rest hostage until adequate amendments were made. See Jefferson to Madison, February 6, 1788, *PTJ,* 12:569.
23. Klarman, *Framers' Coup,* 548–49.
24. James Monroe, "Some Observations on the Constitution," ca. May 25, 1788, *DHRC,* 9:852, 858.
25. U.S. Const., Art. I, Sec. 8, cl. 18. Cassius II, *Virginia Independent Chronicle,* April 9, 1788, *DHRC,* 9:714. William Russell to William Fleming, January 25, 1788, *DHRC,* 8:324.
26. A Native of Virginia, "Observations upon the Proposed Plan of Federal Government," April 2, 1788, *DHRC,* 9:675. Randolph, June 17, 1788, *DHRC,* 10:1347–48.
27. Henry, June 14, 1788, *DHRC,* 10:1284. E.g., *Federalist* #9, 15, 39. Madison, June 6, 1788, *DHRC,* 9:995–96 (federal system avoids "the evils of absolute consolidation, as well as of a mere confederacy").
28. Henry, June 5, 1788, *DHRC,* 9:966. Theodrick Bland to Arthur Lee, June 13, 88, *DHRC,* 10:1617. Henry, June 14, 1788, *DHRC,* 10:1275.
29. Henry, June 12, 1788, *DHRC,* 10:1209–10.
30. *Federalist* #10. Madison repeated these arguments in the context of religious freedom during the ratification debates. Madison, June 12, 1788, *DHRC,* 10:1223 (protection of minority rights "arises from that multiplicity of sects,

which pervades America, and which is the best and only security for religious liberty in any society. For where there is such a variety of sects, there cannot be a majority of any one sect to oppress and persecute the rest").

31. Michael Klarman argues cynically that "it is impossible to know his [Henry's] real reasons for opposing [the Constitution], which might have been as trivial as his not having participated in its drafting." Klarman, *Framers' Coup*, 396. "That Henry and Madison were longtime political adversaries possibly played a role in Henry's decision to declare war on the Constitution." Ibid., 472n. Historians cannot know with certainty why any founder supported or opposed ratification, but Henry's objections were rooted in serious concerns and his well-established political philosophy.

32. Virginia's ratification convention had a reporter—David Robertson—giving historians one of the best-preserved archives of Henry's actual words; still, some caution is necessary. John Marshall critiqued the accuracy of the transcript: While most speakers were reported "not much worse than when delivered" (referring to William Grayson and James Monroe in particular), "Mr. Madison was badly reported,—Mr. Henry was reported worst of all,—no reporter could Correctly reporte him." Marshall added that he would not have recognized what was recorded as his own speeches. *DHRC*, 9:905. While lawyers are often displeased with stenographers, the speeches as recorded are still one of the best repositories of Henry's oratory.

33. Madison to Jefferson, December 9, 1787, *PTJ*, 14:410. On multiplicity of interests, see Kukla, "Spectrum of Sentiments."

34. Henry, June 7, 1788, *DHRC*, 9:1046–47. Henry, June 9, *DHRC*, 9:1052. Madison to Jefferson, July 24, 1788, *PJM* (CS), 11:197.

35. Henry, June 5, 1788, *DHRC*, 9:964. Henry, June 16, 1788, *DHRC*, 10:1329.

36. E.g., Meade, *Practical Revolutionary*, 392.

37. Henry, June 9, 1788, *DHRC*, 9:1064. Henry, June 5, 1788, *DHRC*, 9:962.

38. Henry, June 5, 1788, *DHRC*, 9:963, 964. Henry, June 23, 1788, *DHRC*, 10:1465.

39. William Grayson to William Short, November 10, 1787, *DHRC*, 8:151.

40. Edmund Randolph to Madison, December 27, 1787, *PJM* (CS), 10:346. George Nicholas to Madison, April 5, 1788, *DHRC*, 9:704.

41. Henry, June 7, 1788, *DHRC*, 9:1039, 1051.

42. Henry, June 18, 1788, *DHRC*, 10:1382.

43. Henry, June 19, 1788, *DHRC*, 10:1395. Madison, June 19, 1788, *DHRC*, 10:1396.

44. Grayson, June 13, 1788, *DHRC*, 10:1237. Henry, June 9, 1788, *DHRC*, 9:1051. Georgia began denouncing federal interference with state control (and displacement) of Native Americans by 1790. See Horsman, *Expansion*, 72.

45. John Pierce to Henry Knox, November 19, 1787, *DHRC*, 8:168. Archibald Stuart to John Breckinridge, June 19, 1788, *DHRC*, 10:1651. Mason did express some concern in this regard with the diversity of jurisdictions that the

Constitution vests in federal courts: a British creditor might demand a Virginia debtor travel to a federal court in another state to vindicate his interests. Mason, June 19, 1788, *DHRC*, 10:1405–6.

46. Henry, June 16, 1788, *DHRC*, 10:1322; June 7, 1788, *DHRC*, 9:1046–47. Mason, June 16, 1788, *DHRC*, 10:1326 (footnote omitted).

47. Henry, June 4, 1788, *DHRC*, 9:930. Henry, June 5, 1788, *DHRC*, 9:951. "Madison also argued that the choice of whether the Constitution would be ratified by state legislatures or by special conventions represented 'the true difference between a league or treaty and a constitution.'" Klarman, *Framers' Coup*, 415, quoting Madison, July 23, 1787, Farrand, ed., *Records of the Federal Convention*, 2:92–93.

48. In Philadelphia, Madison had argued that "some gentlemen are afraid that the plan is not sufficiently national, while others apprehend that it is too much so." Yates Notes, June 29, 1787, Farrand, ed., *Records of the Federal Convention*, 1:471. Pendleton, June 5, 1788, *DHRC*, 9:947, 948.

49. Henry, June 9, 1788, *DHRC*, 9:1059.

50. Edward Carrington to Henry Knox, February 10, 1788, *DHRC*, 9:606. Edward Carrington to Jefferson, April 24, 1788, *DHRC*, 9:755. George Nicholas to Madison, April 5, 1788, *DHRC*, 9:703. See also James Duncanson to James Maury, March 11, 1788: "Henry & his Minions, such as your friend French Strother, Tom Barbour &c. are hardy enough to declare that they would rather see the Union dissolved, than adopt the Constitution," *DHRC*, 8:479.

51. Glover, *Fate of the Revolution*, 54. Klarman, on the other hand, tends to accept federalist and later Democratic-Republican political attacks that Henry was "an enemy of the union" at face value. See Klarman, *Framers' Coup*, 554, quoting Edward Carrington to Madison, February 10, 1788, *PJM* (CS), 10:494; George Nicholas to Madison, April 5, 1788, *PJM* (CS), 11:9; Madison to Edmund Randolph, January 10, 1788, *PJM* (CS), 10:355.

52. Ragosta, *Patrick Henry*, 5. Henry, June 9, 1788, *DHRC*, 9:1057. Henry, June 5, 1788, *DHRC*, 9:967. Henry, June 9, 1788, *DHRC*, 9:1059. Edmund Randolph, June 10, 1788, *DHRC*, 9:1095.

53. Henry, June 5, 1788, *DHRC*, 9:954. Henry, June 16, 1788, *DHRC*, 10:1321. Henry, June 5, 1788, *DHRC*, 9:959.

54. Henry, June 5, 1788, *DHRC*, 9:959, 951–52, 966.

55. *Federal Republican* (Georgetown, DC), December 2, 1815.

56. Henry, June 7, 1788, *DHRC*, 9:1044. Henry, June 16, 1788, *DHRC*, 10:1322.

57. Klarman, *Framers' Coup*, 356, quoting Mason's Objections, *DHRC*, 8:43; Melancton Smith (at New York Convention) June 21, 1788, *DHRC*, 11:1740–50, 1753, 1754; Richard Henry Lee to Edmund Randolph, October 16, 1787, *DHRC*, 8:62; Brutus III, *New York Journal*, November 15, 1787, *DHRC*, 19:257.

58. Henry, June 5, 1788, *DHRC*, 9:967–68. See also *Pennsylvania Gazette*, June 18, 1788, *DHRC*, 10:1650.

59. Washington, September 17, 1787, Farrand, ed., *Records of the Federal Convention*, 2:644.

60. Bouton, *Taming Democracy*, 178–79 (footnote omitted), quoting Wilson, June 6 and 7, 1787, Farrand, ed., *Records of the Federal Convention*, 1:132–33, 154, and Madison, June 6, 1787, ibid., 1:134–35.

61. There are very limited instances of free Blacks and women voting before the Civil War (see, e.g., Leonard and Cornell, *Partisan Republic*), but these evidence very narrow exceptions to the general rule.

62. Klarman, *Framers' Coup*, 355–56. DHRC, 10:1553. The proposed amendment would have given Virginia twenty-three representatives rather than the ten initially provided for in the Constitution (using the 1790 census and the Constitution's three-fifths clause). While this amendment was not adopted, recognizing the antifederalists' concern, the first federal Congress increased the size of the House dramatically so that Virginia had nineteen representatives.

63. Henry, June 9, 1788, DHRC, 9:1072, June 24, 1788, 10:1477. Washington to Charles Cotesworth Pinckney, June 28, 1788: "in consequence of some conciliatory conduct and recommendatory amendments, a happy acquiescence it is said is likely to terminate the business here—in as favorable a manner as could possibly have been expected." DHRC, 10:1714.

64. Henry, June 24, 1788, DHRC, 10:1476–77. Klarman, *Framers' Coup*, 468. Letter from Edmund Randolph on the Constitution, published Richmond, December 27, 1787, DHRC, 8:269. Henry, June 24, 1788, DHRC, 10:1477. Henry's position on slavery is discussed further in Ragosta, *Patrick Henry*, 37–39; Kukla, *Patrick Henry*, 16–18.

65. Henry, June 24, 1788, DHRC, 10:1506. Wirt, *Sketches*, 209–10. Henry, June 24, 1788, DHRC, 10:1506. Several later accounts have the delegates running from the assembly as the roar of thunder echoed Henry's final words. E.g., Wirt, *Sketches*, 210 ("The scene became insupportable; and the house rose, without the formality of adjournment, the members rushing from their seats with precipitation and confusion"). While undoubtedly Henry's "Thunder Speech" was impressive, the record of continued proceedings puts the lie to that claim, at least for the convention as a whole.

66. Martin Oster to Comte de la Luzerne, June 28, 1788, DHRC, 10:1690.

67. Maier, *Ratification*, 305; DHRC, 10:1538–39. DHRC, 10:1540–41. (Had the vote on the resolution tied, the presiding officer—Edmund Pendleton, a federalist and a Henry opponent from before the Revolution—would have cast the deciding vote.)

68. DHRC, 10:1541. DHRC, 10:1551–56. (It was not until 1951 that the Twenty-second Amendment restricted the president to two terms.) While not going as far as Henry wanted, the fact that the Constitution as written requires a two-thirds majority of the Senate for adopting a treaty, rather than a mere

majority, has also been attributed to the Jay-Gardoqui episode. Hugh Williamson, a delegate to the Philadelphia Convention, wrote to Madison that "the Navigation of the Mississippi, after what had already happened in Congress, was not to be risqued in the Hands of a mere Majority." Hugh Williamson to Madison, June 2, 1788, *PJM* (CS), 11:71.

69. Richard Bland Lee to Leven Powell, March 29, 1789, in Veit and Bowling, eds., *Creating the Bill of Rights*, 225.

70. Henry, June 5, 1788, *DHRC*, 9:967. Main, *Antifederalists*, 249; 285. Ellis, "Persistence of Antifederalism," 295. Boyd, *Politics of Opposition*, 140.

71. Shortly after Virginia's ratification, Monroe told Jefferson, "Be assured, his [George Washington's] influence carried this government." James Monroe to Jefferson, July 12, 1788, *PTJ*, 13:352 (in cypher). *Pennsylvania Packet*, December 25, 1787: Nineteen of twenty of the yeomanry of Virginia supports the Constitution "on the side of General Washington, the *Man of the People.*" Reprinted in twenty other papers by February 11. *DHRC*, 8:259. See also *Virginia Gazette* (Winchester), February 29, 1788 (Washington and Franklin).

72. Mason, June 11, 1788, *DHRC*, 9:1163. Henry, June 24, 1788, *DHRC*, 10:1480.

73. Madison to George Nicholas, April 8, 1788, *PJM* (CS), 11:13. Henry Knox to Marquis de Lafayette, October 24, 1787 (GLC02437.03680, Gilder Lehrman Institute, New York City, NY).

74. Mason, June 23, 1788, *DHRC*, 10:1471. Henry Lee, June 23, 2788, *DHRC*, 10:1472. Madison to Washington, June 23, 1788, *PGW* (CS), 6:351.

75. Henry, June 24, 1788, *DHRC*, 10:1477–79.

76. Henry, June 24, 1788, *DHRC*, 10:1482. Henry, June 25, 1788, *DHRC*, 10:1537 (emphasis added).

77. Spencer Roane to Philip Aylett, June 26, 1788, *DHRC*, 10:1713.

78. *Virginia Independent Chronicle*, July 9, 1788, *DHRC*, 10:1560. *Massachusetts Centinel*, July 26, 1788, *DHRC*, 10:1561.

79. *Virginia Independent Chronicle*, July 9, 1788, reprinted in *Virginia Herald* and nine out-of-state newspapers. *DHRC*, 10:1562n1.

80. Campbell, "Invention of First Amendment Federalism," 547. David Meade Randolph, "Anecdote of Patrick Henry," likely after 1794 (see *DHRC*, 10:1562n5). *DHRC*, 10:1561–62. (Randolph references the "evening of the day of the final vote," apparently referring to the vote on proposed amendments that occurred on June 27.)

81. George Washington to Tobias Lear, June 29, 1788, *DHRC*, 10:1715–16. William Nelson Jr., to William Short, July 12, 1788, *DHRC*, 10:1701 (internal footnote omitted). See also Decius XVII, *Virginia Independent Chronicle*, April 1, 1789, *DHRC*, 10:1562n4, claiming that as a result of the meeting Mason "became as solitary and contemptible with his own party" as he had been with others. (Since Decius, John Nicholas Jr. of Albemarle County, had gone to

great lengths to criticize Henry in his essays on ratification, failure to mention him in this context is notable.) It is interesting that other newspaper accounts note Mason's leadership of the meeting prominently but do not discuss Henry's role. E.g., *Carlisle Gazette*, September 24, 1788, *DHRC*, 10:1561: letter from Charlottesville: Mason "wished to excite some confusion by a publication addressed to those who were adverse to the new government, but he was warmly opposed by the antifederalists."

82. See "Lesson to Men of All Parties," *Daily Advertiser* (New York), April 29, 1799; *Philadelphia Gazette and Universal Daily Advertiser*, April 30, 1799; *Albany Centinel*, May 3, 1799; *Commercial Advertiser* (New York), May 3, 1799; *Spectator* (New York), May 4, 1799; *Kline's Carlisle Weekly Gazette* (PA), May 8, 1799; *Federal Gazette and Baltimore Daily Advertiser*, May 15, 1799; *Independent Chronicle* (Boston), May 16, 1799; *Norwich Packet* (CT), May 16, 1799; *Times and District of Columbia Daily Advertiser* (Alexandria, VA), May 18, 1799; *Columbia Museum and Savanah Advertiser* (GA), May 21, 1799; *Federal Galaxy* (Brattleboro, VT), May 21, 1799; *South-Carolina State Gazette and Timothy's Daily Advertiser*, May 25, 1799; *New Hampshire Gazette*, May 28, 1799; *Columbian Courier* (New Bedford, MA), May 29, 1799; *Delaware Gazette*, May 29, 1799; *Amherst Village Messenger* (NH), June 1, 1799; *Herald of the United States* (RI), June 8, 1799 (from the *Reading Advertiser* [PA]); *Oracle of the Day* (Portsmouth, NH), June 8, 1799; *Connecticut Gazette*, June 26, 1799; *Maryland Herald and Hager's-Town Weekly Advertiser*, June 27, 1799. The dissemination of this essay seems only to have been arrested by news of Henry's death.

83. Madison to Alexander Hamilton, June 27, 1788, *PJM* (CS), 11:181–82 (footnote omitted). Madison to Alexander Hamilton, June 30, 1788, *PJM* (CS), 11:184. Madison to Jefferson, July 24, 1788, *DHRC*, 10:1707–8. See Rowland, *Life of George Mason*, 2:273–74. (Mason partisans, Rowland being a distant relative, later sought to link Mason to Henry's efforts to pacify the gathering.)

84. *Philadelphia Independent Gazetteer*, July 2, 1788, reprinted in the *New York Journal*, July 8, 1788, *DHRC*, 10:1698.

3. THE 1790S

1. Those opposing and supporting ratification are referred to as antifederalists and federalists (without capitalization); these loosely affiliated groups had no formal cohesion before or after ratification. In the mid-1790s, groups with opposing political views became more organized and formed what are generally understood as political parties. A large majority of antifederalists of ratification debates became Democratic-Republicans, and many ratification federalists became Federalists, but the groups did not align precisely (as James Madison, federalist and Democratic-Republican, demonstrates). The terms

will be used with this capitalization herein (unless different capitalization is used in a quotation).

2. E.g., Wood, *Friends Divided*, 246 ("no one as yet could conceive of a legitimate opposition in a republican government"). Washington to John Adams, August 20, 1795, *PGW* (PS), 18:566.

3. Compare Boyd, *Politics of Opposition*, 140: "Antifederalists had the support of a majority of the voters through the winter and spring of 1788. By fall [1788] the situation was changing. A majority of voters still supported amendments—both substantive and procedural—but some now looked to Federalists to implement the Constitution and obtain the promised amendments."

4. Henry, June 25, 1788, *DHRC*, 10:1537.

5. Washington to Madison, November 17, 1788, *PGW* (PS), 1:115. Henry Lee to Madison, November 19, 1788, *PJM* (CS), 11:357.

6. Virginia House of Delegates Resolution, October 20, 1788, *DHRC*, 10:1764.

7. Madison to Washington, July 27, 1788, *DHRC*, 10:1689. Washington to Madison, September 23, 1788, *PGW* (CS), 6:534.

8. Quoted in Edmund Randolph to Madison, September 12, 1788, *PJM* (CS), 11:251.

9. *DHRC*, 23:2335–36; *DHRC*, 10:1712. See also *DHRC*, 23:2504–5. *DHRC*, 23:2528–29.

10. Charles Lee to Washington, October 29, 1788, *PGW* (PS), 1:82. *DHRC*, 10:1712. Edward Carrington to Madison, November 15, 1788, *PJM* (CS), 11:345; *DHRC*, 10:1763. See, e.g., Labunski, *James Madison*, 131–32.

11. Beeman, *Old Dominion*, 56.

12. *DHRC*, 10:1551–58. Massachusetts, South Carolina, New Hampshire, Maryland, New York, and North Carolina, and later Rhode Island, also offered amendments. *DHRC:* 6 (MA): 1469–70; 10 (VA): 1551–56; 12 (MD-minority): 663–65; 23 (NY): 2304–8; 27 (SC): 392–93; 28 (NH): 377; 26 (RI): 976; Elliot, ed., *Debates* (1836), 4:243–47 (NC, while not ratifying at the time, proposed amendments). See Ellis, "Persistence of Antifederalism," 297. See also Jefferson to John Brown Cutting, July 8, 1788, *PTJ*, 13:315: "The argument is unanswerable that it will be easier to obtain amendments from nine states under the new constitution, than from thirteen after rejecting it."

13. Labunski, *James Madison*, 133, quoting *Virginia Centinel* (Winchester), July 16, 1788; see Denboer et al., eds., *Documentary History of the First Federal Election*, 2:257.

14. Edward Carrington to Madison, October 19, 1788, *PJM* (CS), 11:306.

15. Charles Lee to Washington, *PGW* (PS), 1:83. Henry Lee to Madison, November 19, 1788, *PJM* (CS), 11:356. See also Pasley, *First Presidential Contest*, 37. Henry to Richard Henry Lee, November 15, 1788, Henry, *Henry*, 2:429. See also Klarman, *Framers' Coup*, 557, 563.

16. Madison to Edmund Randolph, November 2, 1788, *PJM* (CS), 11:329. See generally *DHRC*, 10:1761–68. Labunski, *James Madison*, 134.

17. Labunski, *James Madison*, 139, citing Edward Carrington to Madison, November 15, 1788, *PJM* (CS), 11:345. The term "gerrymandering" came into use after Elbridge Gerry's 1812 manipulation of state senatorial districts in Massachusetts. E.g., Trickey, "Where did the Term 'Gerrymander' Come From?" Perhaps it is best for Patrick Henry's legacy that the process was not called "Henrymandering."

18. Madison to Edmund Randolph, October 17, 1788, *PJM* (CS), 11:305. Labunski, *James Madison*, 134. Ragosta, *Religious Freedom*, 111–12.

19. Madison to Jefferson, March 29, 1789, *PJM* (CS), 12:37. *Biographical Directory of the U.S. Congress.* E.g., Beeman, *Old Dominion*, 83; DenBoer, ed., *First Federal Elections*, 2:254. History, Art & Archives, U.S. House of Representatives, People Search, https://history.house.gov/People/Search. Compare "In Virginia, Antifederalists had constituted nearly half of the delegates to the state's ratifying convention in June 1788, and political observers had predicted that the legislature's gerrymandering of congressional districts would favor Antifederalists in the elections for the first House. Yet voters returned seven or eight Federalists—depending on how one of the representatives was counted—for the state's ten congressional seats." Klarman, *Framers' Coup*, 619, citing Edward Carrington to Madison, May 12, 1789; Madison to Jefferson, March 29, 1789; see also Labunski, *James Madison*, 176. Garland, *Life of John Randolph*, 1:40. As the 1790s proceeded, many members with federalist sympathies became disenchanted with the national government and, in an effort to support their Democratic-Republican bona fides, tended post hoc to "resort to Anti-federalist rhetoric" but, like Madison, they had been federalists during ratification. Beeman, *Old Dominion*, 115, 56.

20. Office of History, Art & Archives, https://history.house.gov/People/Search.

21. Klarman, *Framers' Coup*, 619 (footnote omitted). See also Madison to Jefferson, December 8, 1788, *PJM* (CS), 11:382 (discussing Senate/House composition).

22. Klarman, *Framers' Coup*, 568 (footnote omitted), 801n77. See also Bouton, *Taming Democracy*, 194.

23. Compare Bordewich, *First Congress*, 11: Federalists held twenty of twenty-two Senate seats, and forty-six of fifty-nine in the House. Other Senate and House sources show federalist dominance of eighteen of twenty-six in the Senate (after North Carolina and Rhode Island sent delegations) and thirty-seven of sixty-six in the House. U.S. Senate, https://www.cop.senate.gov/history/partydiv.htm; Office of History, Art & Archives, "Party Divisions of the U.S. House of Representatives: 1789 to present," https://history.house.gov/Institution/Party-Divisions/Party-Divisions/. Klarman, *Framers' Coup*,

568: "in the contests for seats in the first Congress, Antifederalists won only eleven out of the fifty-nine that were at stake in the House, and only two of the twenty-two at issue in the Senate," citing Boyd, *Politics of Opposition,* 88–89, 140–42, 144, 149–55; Jürgen Heideking, *The Constitution before the Judgment Seat* (Charlottesville: University of Virginia Press, 2012), 395–402; Veit and Bowling, *Bill of Rights,* xii; Maier, *Ratification,* 433.

24. Jefferson to Madison, December 20, 1787, *PTJ,* 12:440. Jefferson to Madison, March 15, 1789, *PTJ,* 14:660. Madison, June 8, 1789, *PJM* (CS), 12:207: "independent tribunals of justice will consider themselves in a peculiar manner the guardians of those rights; they will be an impenetrable bulwark against every assumption of power in the legislature or executive." See also Ragosta, "Jefferson, Madison, Adams," 164–70.

25. Madison to Jefferson, October 17, 1788, *PTJ,* 14:18. See generally Ragosta, *Religious Freedom,* 103–8. E.g., Madison to George Eve, January 2, 1789, *PJM* (CS), 11:404.

26. Madison, June 8, 1789, *PJM* (CS), 12:196–209, August 15, 1789, *PJM* (CS), 12:339.

27. Madison to Jefferson, December 8, 1788, *PJM* (CS), 11:383. Madison, June 8, 1789, Debates in Congress on Constitutional Amendments, *PJM* (CS), 12:199. Henry Lee to Washington, July 1, 1789, *PGW* (PS), 3:99. See generally Beeman, *Old Dominion,* 57.

28. See, e.g., Klarman, *Framers' Coup,* 567. Henry, *Henry,* 2:459.

29. Henry to Richard Henry Lee, November 15, 1788, Henry, *Henry,* 2:429. In addition to the ten amendments that we know as the Bill of Rights, Congress proposed two other amendments, the first of which was structural in nature. It would have increased the size of the House of Representatives, responding to antifederalist complaints that a small number of representatives tended to keep members of Congress aristocratic and distant from the people; much the same change was accomplished by legislation. The second proposed amendment provided that any increase in congressional salaries could not take effect until after a general election occurred; while not approved at the time, this became the Twenty-seventh Amendment in 1992 when it finally was approved by three-fourths of the (then much larger) number of states.

30. George Mason to John Mason, July 31, 1789, in Robert A. Rutland, ed., *The Papers of George Mason,* 3 vols. (Chapel Hill: University of North Carolina Press, 1970), 3:1164, quoted in Tarter, "George Mason and the Conservation of Liberty," 301. Tarter, "George Mason and the Conservation of Liberty," 301, quoting George Mason to Samuel Griffin, September 8, 1789, in Rutland, ed., *Papers of George Mason,* 3:1172. Mason still insisted that additional amendments requiring a supermajority for laws affecting commerce, restricting Senate power over treaties, etc., were essential. Bowling, "'A Tub to the Whale,'" 233.

31. E.g., *United States v. Darby*, 312 U.S. 100, 124 (1941).

32. *Federalist #21*. MA amendment, *DHRC*, 6:1469. NH, *DHRC*, 28:377. NY, *DHRC*, 23:2305; RI, *DHRC*, 26:976. See also SC, *DHRC*, 27:393 ("expressly relinquished"). Interestingly, amendments proposed by Virginia's convention dropped the term "expressly." *DHRC*, X:1553. The reasons for this are not clear; possibly antifederalists were despondent and unobservant at the late date when amendments were formulated. More likely, they believed that the term "expressly" was not necessary given Virginia's extensive list of structural amendments to constrain federal power, including a provision stating that express restrictions on federal power did not imply other powers. *DHRC*, 10:1555. See Feller, "Tenth Amendment Retires," 224 (footnote omitted): "Most significant was the use of the adjective 'expressly' or 'clearly' to qualify the powers of Congress in the proposals of all of the states, except Virginia and North Carolina."

33. This aspect of the Tenth Amendment has been discussed and analyzed ad nauseam. Hampden, "Rights of the States," *Enquirer* (Richmond), June 11, 1819 (Spencer Roane). E.g., Feller, "Tenth Amendment Retires," 224 (lack of "expressly" critical in *McCulloch v. Maryland*). Conservatives have argued that the Tenth Amendment, nonetheless, imposes a strict restriction on federal power. For example: "Perhaps the most important" of Bill of Rights was the Tenth Amendment; for Jefferson, this expressed " 'the foundation of the Constitution.' " Watkins, *Reclaiming the American Revolution*, 63, quoting Jefferson's Opinion on the Constitutionality of the Bill for Establishing a National Bank, February 15, 1791. Coleman, *American Revolution*, 6: "the Americans of the founding era considered the Tenth Amendment much more important than modern scholars do." But Justice Joseph Story and the Supreme Court saw the amendment as a mere "truism." *United States v. Darby*, 312 U.S. 100, 124 (1941). Feller, "Tenth Amendment Retires," 226–27.

34. *DHRC*, 23:2305; 24:976. See also Feller, "Tenth Amendment Retires," 225.

35. Fontaine, *Patrick Henry*, 18, 19–20. See also Beeman, *Old Dominion*, 11.

Kevin Gutzman argues that the Tenth Amendment, by stating that rights not vested in the federal government are retained by the people, proves that the Constitution created an interstate compact, rather than a "national charter." Gutzman cites Edmund Randolph's comment during ratification that "all rights therein declared to be completely vested in the people, unless *expressly* given away." Gutzman, "Virginia and Kentucky Resolutions Reconsidered," 476, quoting Randolph, June 24, 1788, *DHRC*, 10:1483. See also Steele, *Thomas Jefferson*, 245. But to say that the federal government does not have unlimited power does not make the Constitution a state compact. E.g., Onuf, *Jefferson and the Virginians*, 88. In any case, regardless of Randolph's passing comment, "expressly" is not included in either the Constitution or the Tenth Amendment. Henry's analysis, recognizing that the Tenth Amendment tended to undermine the ability of the states to enforce retained powers, seems more accurate. Given the addition of the "people" to the amendment, "no longer need the Court be assiduous to find that power resides somewhere; on the contrary the Court can rest comfortably in the assurance that the missing power is in the hands of the people who will amend the Constitution in due time." Feller, "Tenth Amendment Retired," 224, 225 (footnote omitted). See also Read and Allen, "Living, Dead, and Undead," 99: "All the text specifically affirms is that the federal government does not possess all political powers, only those powers vested in it by the Constitution. The amendment does not itself draw the line or specify who draws it."

36. Richard Henry Lee to Henry, September 14, 1789, Henry, *Henry,* 3:399. David Stuart to Washington, September 12, 1789, *PGW* (PS), 4:28. Richard Henry Lee to Henry, September 14, 1789, Henry, *Henry,* 3:399. William Grayson to Henry, September 29, 1789, Henry, *Henry,* 3:406.

37. See Labunski, *James Madison,* 247–48, 250. Beeman, *Old Dominion,* 65, citing Virginia House of Delegates Journal, December 5, 1789. Labunski, *James Madison,* 251.

38. See Beeman, *Old Dominion,* 65. Labunski, *James Madison,* 251, 246. Henry, *Henry,* 2:451. Labunski, *James Madison,* 252, quoting Henry, *Henry* 2:458. Labunski, *James Madison,* 253.

39. See, e.g., Klarman, *Framers' Coup,* 620 (footnote omitted) As much as 90 percent of federal tax revenue in the 1790s derived from import duties. Moreover, with the vast bulk of federal tax revenue coming from import duties and federal assumption of states' war-related debts (discussed below), states were able to reduce dramatically direct taxation, in some cases by as much as 85 or 90 percent. Substantial direct tax relief (in favor of indirect duties) helped reconcile rural America to the Constitution.

40. Henry to Robert Walker, November 12, 1790, Henry, *Henry,* 2:535. Beeman, *Old Dominion,* 66, citing Fisher Ames to George Minot, January 13, 1790, in Seth Ames, ed., *The Works of Fisher Ames,* 2 vols. (Boston, 1854), 1:72.

41. E.g., Miller, *Federalist Era,* 41; Wood, *Empire of Liberty,* 144–45.

42. June 17, 1788, DHRC, 10:1355–56. Bouton, *Taming Democracy,* 85.

43. E.g., Elkins and McKitrick, *Age of Federalism,* 121. Miller, *Federalist Era,* 41–42, 46. See also Resolution of Virginia House of Delegates, December 16, 1790: "A large proportion of the debt thus contracted by this state, has been already redeemed by the collection of heavy taxes levied on its citizens." Hening, *Statutes,* 13:237–38.

44. E.g., Miller, *Federalist Era,* 49. Wood, *Empire of Liberty,* 144–45. Henry, *Henry,* 2:454.

45. Henry Lee to Madison, April 3, 1790, *PJM* (CS), 13:136–37. Beeman, *Old Dominion*, 77.

46. Henry, *Henry*, 2:456. See Ellis, *Founding Brothers*, 76.

47. *Journal of the House of Delegates of the Commonwealth of Virginia, Begun and Held at the Capitol in the City of Richmond on Monday, the Eighteenth of October, in the Year of Our Lord One Thousand Seven Hundred and Ninety*, November 3, 1790, 36–37; Beeman, *Old Dominion*, 78. "Memorial of the General Assembly of Virginia to the Congress of the United States," *Journal of the House of Delegates*, December 16, 1790, 141–42.

48. *Journal of the House of Delegates*, November 8, 1790, 45. "Memorial of the General Assembly of Virginia to the Congress of the United States," *Journal of the House of Delegates*, December 16, 1790, 141–42. *Journal of the Senate of the Commonwealth of Virginia, Begun and Held in the City of Richmond, on Monday, the Eighteenth Day of October, in the Year of Our Lord 1790*, December 21, 1790, 77–78; *Journal of the House of Delegates*, December 22, 1790, 151. The House agreed to Senate amendments two days later. *Journal of the House of Delegates*, 156.

49. In Philadelphia (the nation's capital), multiple papers reported on the Virginia resolution calling assumption unconstitutional. *Federal Gazette and Philadelphia Advertiser*, November 16, 1790; *Gazette of the United States* (New York), November 17, 1790; *General Advertiser and Political, Commercial, Agricultural, and Literary Journal* (Philadelphia), November 18, 1790; *Pennsylvania Mercury and Universal Advertiser*, November 18, 1790; *Pennsylvania Packet*, November 18, 1790. See also *Albany Register*, November 25, 1790; *New York Daily Gazette*, November 30, 1790 (longer reprint); *New-Hampshire Spy*, December 1, 1790; *United States Chronicle* (Providence, RI), December 2, 1790; *City Gazette* (Charleston, SC), December 6, 1790.

50. See Jefferson's opinion on unconstitutionality of the bank, *Founders Online*, https://founders.archives.gov/documents/Jefferson/01-19-02-0051; Dellinger and Powell, "Constitutionality of the Bank Bill," 110–33; Madison, "Consolidation," *National Gazette*, December 3, 1791. John Taylor, *An Enquiry into the Principles*, 55, 56.

51. See, e.g., Gutzman, "Virginia and Kentucky Resolutions," 478; Kukla, *Patrick Henry*, 367–68. *Journal of the House of Delegates*, November 25, 1790, 82. Compare *Journal of the House of Delegates*, December 16, 1790, 141–42; *Journal of the House of Delegates*, December 22, 1790, 156.

52. Beeman, *Old Dominion*, 80–81.

53. Alexander Hamilton to John Jay, November 13, 1790, *Founders Online*, https://founders.archives.gov/documents/Hamilton/01-07-02-0166. Henry, *Henry*, 2:457, quoting William C. Rives, *History of the Life and Times of James Madison*, 3 vols. (Boston: Little, Brown, 1881), 3:151–52; *Federalist #26* and

28. *Federal Gazette* (Philadelphia), November 20, 1790; reprinted *New-York Packet,* November 25, 1790; *Independent Chronicle* (Boston), December 2, 1790; *Virginia Gazette and Alexandria Advertiser,* December 2, 1790; *Columbian Centinel* (Boston), December 4, 1790; *Connecticut Courant,* December 6, 1790; *Thomas's Massachusetts Spy* (Worcester, MA), December 9, 1790; *Connecticut Gazette,* December 10, 1790; *Middlesex Gazette* (CT), December 11, 1790.

54. Beeman, *Patrick Henry,* 175 (footnote omitted). Also Henry, *Henry,* 2:458.

55. Henry to James Monroe, January 24, 1791, Henry, *Henry,* 2:460–61. See also Beeman, *Patrick Henry,* 175–76.

56. Jefferson to Washington, May 23, 1792, *PTJ,* 23:539. Jefferson to Madison, October 1, 1792, *PTJ,* 24:432–33; see Bradburn, *Citizenship Revolution,* 74. On Jefferson and hyperbole, see, e.g., Ragosta, "Thomas Jefferson: Icon."

57. Jefferson Notes on Patrick Henry, before April 12, 1812, *PTJ* (RS), 4:604. Jefferson to Gouveneur Morris, November 26, 1790, *PTJ,* 18:82. See, e.g., Steele, *Thomas Jefferson,* 198n42 (Jefferson seemed to disagree with the Virginia General Assembly's conclusion that assumption was unconstitutional). Jefferson argued equally inaccurately to Henry's biographer that Henry, "From being the most violent of all anti-Federalists . . . was brought over to the new constitution by his Yazoo speculation . . . and abandoning the Republican advocates of the Constitution, the Federal government on Federal principles became his political creed." Henry, *Henry,* 2:616–17. Years earlier, Jefferson had suggested that Henry was involved in the Yazoo land controversy but at that time said it encouraged animosity to the government rather than support. Jefferson to Gouveneur Morris, November 26, 1790, *PTJ,* 18:82. Wirt, though, while a Jeffersonian, shows that Jefferson mischaracterized the Yazoo land controversy. See Ragosta, *Patrick Henry,* 113–16.

58. *National Gazette* (Philadelphia), June 18, 1792; *Dunlap's American Daily Advertiser* (Philadelphia), June 15, 1792; *Diary or Loudon's Register* (New York) June 18, 1792; *Carlisle Gazette* (PA), June 29, 1792; *City Gazette* (Charleston, SC) June 29, 1792; *Boston Gazette,* July 9, 1792. Garland, *Life of John Randolph,* 1:124.

59. Jefferson to Archibald Stuart, December 23, 1791, *PTJ,* 22:435. Jefferson to Archibald Stuart, September 9, 1792, *PTJ,* 24:351.

60. *Ware v. Hylton,* 3 U.S. (3 Dall.) 199 (1796). Wirt, *Sketches,* 256. See Ragosta, *Patrick Henry,* 121–23.

61. Henry, *Henry,* 2:472. Edmund Randolph to Washington, June 24, 1793, *PGW* (PS), 13:139. On Jefferson's position on the debt case, see Evans, "Private Indebtedness," 355.

62. *National Gazette* (Philadelphia), July 4, 1792. See Martin, *Government by Dissent,* 84.

63. Estes, "Shaping the Politics of Public Opinion," 411, quoting Resolutions of the Boston Chamber of Commerce, August 21, 1795. May, *Jefferson's Treasure,* 44.

64. Lurie, "Liberty Poles," 673–97, 679, 684, quoting *Baltimore Daily Intelligencer;* and William MacPherson, *Brigadier General in the Army of the United States, Commanding the Troops Destined to Act against the Insurgents in the Counties of Northampton, Montgomery, and Bucks, in the State of Pennsylvania* (Philadelphia: Library Company of Philadelphia, 1799). "For the Reading Eagle," *Aurora General Advertiser* (Philadelphia), May 13, 1799 (translated from *Reading Adler,* April 9, 1799), quoted in Lurie, "Liberty Poles," 679.

65. Washington to Burgess Ball, September 25, 1794, *PGW* (PS), 16:723. Washington to U.S. Senate and House of Representatives, November 19, 1794, *PGW* (PS), 17:181. Beeman, *Old Dominion,* 134. Washington Farewell Address, September 19, 1796, *PGW* (PS), 20:709. In contrast, Robert Martin concludes that very few members of Democratic-Republican Societies joined the Whiskey Rebellion, and many of the militia who marched to put the rebels down were members of such societies. Martin, *Government by Dissent,* 88. See also Madison to James Monroe, December 4, 1794, *PJM* (CS), 15:406 (Washington's denunciation of "self-created societies" was "the greatest error of his political life"). See also Halperin, *Alien and Sedition Acts,* 20.

66. Beeman, *Old Dominion,* 135n42. Jefferson to Madison, December 28, 1794, *PTJ,* 28:228–29.

67. Henry to Henry Lee, June 27, 1795, Henry, *Henry,* 2:551. Democratic Society of Pennsylvania, *Aurora General Advertiser* (Philadelphia), December 22, 1794.

68. See, e.g., Halperin, *Alien and Sedition Acts,* 25. Farnham, "Virginia Amendments of 1795," 78.

69. During debates over ratification of the Constitution, James Wilson had argued that the House "could effectively block treaties that it found objectionable by declining to enact legislation to implement them." Klarman, *Framers' Coup,* 366, citing Wilson at the Pennsylvania Convention, December 11, 1787, *DHRC,* 2:562–63.

70. Theodore Sedgwick, *Debates and Proceedings in the Congress* ("Annals of Congress"), 4th Cong., 1st Sess., March 11, 1796, 5:525. In an effort to quell Democratic-Republican opposition to the Jay Treaty, John Marshall, serving in the Virginia House of Delegates, made an argument oddly parallel to that made by Madison: Since the House of Representatives could control implementation of the treaty, Marshall argued, there was no need to denounce Washington's acceptance of the treaty. Thomas Mann Randolph (Jefferson's son-in-law) dubbed Marshall's argument (essentially the same being made by Madison) sophistry, "an uncandid artifice." Thomas Mann Randolph to Jefferson, November 22, 1795, *PTJ,* 28:534.

71. Washington to Charles Carroll, May 1, 1796, *PGW* (PS), 20:87. John Adams to Abigail Adams, May 3, 1796, *Founders Online*, https://founders.archives.gov/documents/Adams/04-11-02-0150.

72. See, e.g., Demmer, "Trick or Constitutional Treaty?" With the Jay Treaty, "Americans realized what the executive and Senate could accomplish through treaty-making for the first time." Ibid., 589. Of course, Henry and his allies had identified the danger during ratification.

73. E.g., Klarman, *Framers' Coup*, 336, citing Proposed Amendment 7, VA Convention, *DHRC*, 10:1554. Jefferson joined in Madison's argument. Farnham, "Virginia Amendments of 1795," 82; Jefferson to Edward Rutledge, November 30, 1795, *PTJ*, 28:541. Compare Bilder, *Madison's Hand*, 219–20: After the conflict over the Jay Treaty, Madison attempted to minimize the relevance of the Philadelphia Convention to the meaning of the treaty power because Hamilton argued the authority to bind the legislature was clear from the convention.

74. "Extract of a Letter from a gentleman, called to business in Richmond Virginia, to his friend in this city, dated June 9, 1796," *Gazette of the United States* (Philadelphia), June 19, 1796; reprinted *Columbian Herald* (Charleston, SC), July 26, 1796. Henry to Betsy Aylett, August 20, 1796, Henry, *Henry*, 2:568–69.

75. In November 1795, Virginia's General Assembly passed a resolution (on a vote of 100–50) approving Virginia's senators' opposition to the treaty. See Madison to Jefferson, January 31, 1796, *PJM* (CS), 16:209. See, e.g., Beeman, *Old Dominion*, 146; Risjord, "Virginia Federalists," 502. See Demmer, "Trick or Constitutional Treaty?" 593–95 (discussing proposals for amendments).

76. Edmund Randolph to Washington, June 24, 1793, *PGW* (PS), 13:139. Meade, *Practical Revolutionary*, 440. Henry, *Henry*, 2:200, 570.

77. See *Aurora General Advertiser* (Philadelphia), June 3, 1797 (Napoleon's great victories). Jefferson to Madison, June 1, 1797, *PTJ*, 29:422; Jefferson to Madison, June 15, 1797, *PTJ*, 29:433. Wirt, *Sketches*, 284 (Nathaniel Pope relating a conversation with Henry in 1798). As 1799 drew to a close, Jefferson was still voicing guarded optimism concerning Napoleon. For example, Jefferson expressed mild hope that after the coup of 18 Brumaire (November 1799) Napoleon might initiate reforms. Shulim, "Thomas Jefferson Views Napoleon," 289–90. By February or March of 1800, even Jefferson had given up on him. Ibid. Compare Jefferson to John Adams, July 5, 1814, *PTJ* (RS), 7:452 (rejected Napoleon as "scoundrel" after November 1799).

78. Henry to Washington, October 16, 1795, *PGW* (PS), 19:53.

79. One report adds, speculatively, that Henry declined in part because international relations, which were beyond the purview of the governor, were at the time the most important pending issues. Henry to Samuel Hopkins,

November 29, 1796, in Doubleday, *Atlantic Between*, 621–22. Spencer Roane to William Wirt [post-1796], Henry, *Henry*, 2:574–75.

80. *Gazette of the United States* (Philadelphia), August 12, 1794. Henry was offered the position of senator in 1790 after William Grayson died while in office. David Stuart to Washington, March 15, 1790, *PGW* (PS), 5:235–36.

81. Pasley, *First Presidential Contest*, 205. *Gazette of the United States* (Philadelphia). November 15, 1796, reprinting Patrick Henry letter of November 3, 1796; *City Gazette* (Charleston, SC), October 13, 1796. *Philadelphia Gazette and Universal Daily Advertiser*, June 30, 1796 (reprinted). John Marshall to Rufus King, May 24, 1796, *Founders Online*, https://founders.archives.gov/documents /Hamilton/01-20-02-0092-0002, n7. Pasley unfairly concludes that Henry, having "done a stint as governor," declined federal positions because he "seems to have sensed himself that he was more of a talker than an administrator." Pasley, *First Presidential Contest*, 205 (footnote omitted). This ignores Henry repeated and successful terms as governor, as well as his explanation that his family obligations (he had eight children sixteen or younger by the end of 1796) demanded his attention. See also Beeman, *Patrick Henry*, 110–20; Risjord, *Chesapeake Politics*, 464–67; Fischer, *Revolution of American Conservatism*, 374–75.

82. Beeman, *Old Dominion*, 161. E.g., Jefferson to Archibald Stuart, April 18, 1795, *PTJ*, 28:331–32.

83. On Jefferson's personal animosity to Henry, see Ragosta, *Patrick Henry*, 67–69; Ragosta, "Founding Rivals." Jefferson to James Monroe, May 20, 1782, *PTJ*, 6:185. Jefferson to Archibald Stuart, April 18, 1795, *PTJ*, 28:331. Jefferson to James Monroe, July 10, 1796, *PTJ*, 29:147–48.

84. Thomas Jefferson's Notes on Patrick Henry, before April 12, 1812, *PTJ* (RS), 4:604. Henry, *Henry*, 2:616–17. On the Yazoo land fraud, see Ragosta, *Patrick Henry*, 113–16. Henry's respect for Washington was often evident; for example, he wrote to one daughter that "if he [Washington], whose character as our leader during the whole war was above all praise, is so roughly handled in his old age, what may be expected of men of the common standard of character?" Henry to Elizabeth Aylett, August 20, 1796, Henry, *Henry*, 2:569–70.

85. Washington to Henry Lee, August 26, 1794, *PGW* (PS), 16:603.

86. On Henry's dislike of the levies, see David Stuart to Washington, June 2, 1790, *PGW* (PS), 5:462.

87. Henry Lee to Washington, August 17, 1794, *PGW* (PS), 16:572.

88. Washington to Henry Lee, August 26, 1794, *PGW* (PS), 16:602–3 (footnotes omitted). (Notably, Henry Lee's letter of August 17, 1794, to Washington also began a running dispute between Jefferson and Lee concerning the latter's comments about Washington's judgment.) Ragosta, *Patrick Henry*, 59–60.

89. Henry to Edmund Randolph, September 24, 1794, Henry, *Henry*, 2:549.

90. Henry to Henry Lee, June 27, 1795, Henry, *Henry*, 2:551, 553.

91. *Gazette of the United States* (Philadelphia), June 19, 1796; *Hampshire Gazette* (MA), July 6, 1796; *Columbian Herald* (Charleston, SC), July 26, 1796; *New Jersey Journal*, August 10, 1796; *North-Carolina Journal*, August 29, 1796. In at least one case, this quote was attributed to George Mason. *Albany Gazette*, July 8, 1796.

92. Edward Carrington to Washington, October 13, 1795, *PGW* (PS), 19:44–45.

93. Washington to Henry, October 9, 1795, *PGW* (PS), 19:36–37 (footnote omitted).

94. Henry to Washington, October 16, 1795, *PGW* (PS), 19:53–54.

95. Washington to Archibald Blair, June 24, 1799, *PGW* (RS), 4:150, reprinted in *Columbian Mirror* (Alexandria), June 3, 1800.

4. THE ALIEN AND SEDITION ACTS

1. Jefferson to Edward Rutledge, November 30, 1795, *PTJ*, 28:542. Weisberger, *America Afire*, 154.

2. Hartnett and Mercieca, "'Has Your Courage Rusted?'" 86 (over 330 U.S. ships seized from 1797 to 1798). Miller, *Federalist Era*, 205. Insurance rates on ships increased from about 6 percent to as much as 40 percent. Elkins and McKitrick, *Age of Federalism*, 645.

3. E.g., Miller, *Federalist Era*, 210–12.

4. Ferling, *Adams vs. Jefferson*, 108. Madison to Jefferson, April 22, 1798, *PTJ*, 30:289.

5. Risjord, *Old Republicans*, 12. Ferling, *Adams vs. Jefferson*, 109. Wood, *Friends Divided*, 306.

6. John Thayer, "A Discourse Delivered at the Roman Catholic Church in Boston" (1798), in Sandoz, ed., *Political Sermons*, 1358. Benjamin Rush, "Address to the People of the United States," *DHRC*, 13:47, quoted in Green, "'Focus of the Wills of Converging Millions,'" 441. See also Halperin, *Alien and Sedition Acts*, 67; Beeman, *Old Dominion*, 182; Carter, "Denouncing Secrecy," 411.

7. Beeman, *Old Dominion*, 175, citing Thomas Evans, reported in *Journal of the House Delegates of the Commonwealth of Virginia*, December 11, 1798. Also Declaration of Major General Richard Meade, Beeman, *Old Dominion*, 175, citing Governor James Wood to Captain Archibald McRae, July 16, 1798, Executive Letterbooks (Richmond). *City Gazette* (Charleston, SC) January 3, 1799. *Times and District of Columbia Daily Advertiser* (Alexandria, VA), December 18, 1798. Bird, *Criminal Dissent*, 146 (citing the *Washington Mirror*). *Times and District of Columbia Daily Advertiser* (Alexandria, VA), September 12, 1798; *New-York Gazette*, October 19, 1798 (July 24 meeting in Clark County, KY). *Times and District of Columbia Daily Advertiser* (Alexandria, VA), December 27, 1798 (Tazewell comment made in jest). *Gazette of the United States*

(Philadelphia), March 6, 1799 (Francis Bailey speaking to Daniel Morgan). *Porcupine's Gazette* (Philadelphia), March 8, 1799 (reprinted March 11, 1799) (opposition to Bailey as House of Representatives' printer because of treasonous comments). See also *Maryland Herald and Elizabeth-Town Advertiser,* September 13, 1798 (General Heister, Democratic-Republican running for Congress, "is in habits of electioneering intimacy with men who have declared if the French land an army in this country they will join them"). See Lurie, "Liberty Poles," 673–97.

8. John Quincy Adams to John Adams, April 3, 1797, Ford, ed., *Writings of John Quincy Adams,* 2:155. Bird, *Criminal Dissent,* 23.

9. Wood, *Friends Divided,* 304–5. John Adams to Jefferson, June 30, 1813, *PTJ* (RS), 6:254. Abigail Adams to Mary Cranch, April 26, 1798, *Founders Online,* https://founders.archives.gov/documents/Adams/04-12-02-0273. See also Smith, *Freedom's Fetters,* 96–97.

10. Wood, *Friends Divided,* 308. Halperin, *Alien and Sedition Acts,* 54–56. Bird, *Criminal Dissent,* 325 (footnote omitted): "By 1793, roughly 10,000–25,000 émigrés had reached the United States from France and from its most prosperous Caribbean colony, St. Domingue." Thousands more arrived in 1798. Bird, *Criminal Dissent,* 326.

11. Bird, *Criminal Dissent,* 361–62. Halperin, *Alien and Sedition Acts,* 75–76. Hartnett and Mercieca, "'Has Your Courage Rusted?'" 92, citing Smith, *Freedom's Fetters,* 161n6 ("15 shiploads"). Wood, *Friends Divided,* 309 ("many foreigners left before the act was enforced"). Anderson, "Enforcement of the Alien and Sedition Laws," 115–16 (one prosecution, but defendant fled). See Bird, *Criminal Dissent,* 37 (laws intended in part to discourage emigration).

12. "An Act in Addition to the Act, Entitled 'An Act for Punishment for Certain Crimes against the United States,'" Avalon Project, Yale Law School, https://avalon.law.yale.edu/18th_century/sedact.asp.

13. See, e.g., Ambuske and Flaherty, "Reading Law in the Early Republic," 237–40; Halperin, *Alien and Sedition Acts,* 68; Campbell, "Invention of First Amendment Federalism," 517–70. Jefferson to Madison, July 31, 1788, *PTJ,* 13:442. As president, Jefferson also urged use of state libel laws against political opponents and, on at least one occasion, seemed to acquiesce for a time in a federal common law sedition prosecution. See Levy, *Jefferson and Civil Liberties,* 58–66; Bird, *Criminal Dissent,* 364. For how freedom of the press expanded in the early republic, see generally Bird, *Press and Speech.*

14. Ferling, *Adams vs. Jefferson,* 109. Anderson, "Enforcement of the Alien and Sedition Laws," 119, 113–26.

15. E.g., Smith, *Freedom's Fetters,* 185; Bird, "New Light on the Sedition Act of 1798," 542. Slack, *Liberty's First Crisis,* 233; Elkins and McKitrick, *Age of Federalism,*

703; Dunn, *Jefferson's Second Revolution,* 112. Smith, "Beyond Strict Construction," 94. Jefferson to John Taylor, June 4, 1798, *PTJ,* 30:389.

16. See generally Bird, *Criminal Dissent, 7 et seq.;* Bird, *Press and Speech.* Bird, "New Light on the Sedition Act of 1798," 549, 571, 574, 584. See also Bouton, "'No Wonder the Times were Troublesome'"; Larson, *Magnificent Catastrophe,* 128–29. Bird, *Criminal Dissent,* 185, 189 (Fries prosecutions targeting editors).

17. Miller, *Federalist Era,* 90; Wood, *Friends Divided,* 262. Halperin, *Alien and Sedition Acts,* 73–74 (footnote omitted). Bird, *Criminal Dissent,* 7; Bird, *Press and Speech,* 330. Bird, "New Light on the Sedition Act of 1798," 591. E.g., Jefferson to Elbridge Gerry, January 26, 1799, *PTJ,* 30:650. Bird, *Criminal Dissent,* 137.

18. Bird, *Criminal Dissent,* 4, 288. Bird, "New Light on the Sedition Act of 1798," 579.

19. Anderson, "Contemporary Opinion . . . I," 62. Anderson, "Contemporary Opinion . . . II," 228. At the time, states, not bound by the First Amendment, had broad police powers to bring sedition cases. The First Amendment was made applicable to the states after Supreme Court decisions "incorporated" the protections of the First Amendment into the Due Process Clause of the post–Civil War Fourteenth Amendment in the twentieth century.

20. Jefferson to Madison, April 25, 1798, *PTJ,* 30:300. Madison, "Public Opinion," *National Gazette,* ca. December 19, 1791, *PJM* (CS), 14:170. Jefferson to William G. Munford, June 18, 1799, *PTJ,* 31:128. Bird, *Criminal Dissent,* 225–27. Jefferson to John Wayles Eppes, April 21, 1800, *PTJ,* 31:531.

21. Jefferson to Wilson Cary Nicholas, April 13, 1806, *Founders Online* (early access), https://founders.archives.gov/documents/Jefferson/99-01-02-3559. James Madison, "Notes for the *National Gazette* Essays," December 19, 1791–March 3, 1792, *PJM,* 14:160–61, quoted in Gibson, "Veneration and Vigilance," 26.

22. John Nicholas, July 5, 1798, *Debates and Proceedings in the Congress of the United States (Annals of Congress),* 8:2104. *Independent Gazetteer* (Worcester, MA), July 1, 1800. John Fowler's letter to his constituents was broadly reprinted, e.g., *Republican Watch-Tower* (New York), June 14, 1800; *Times and District of Columbia Daily Advertiser* (Alexandria, VA), June 16, 1800; *Constitutional Telegraph* (Boston), June 18, 1800; *Kline's Carlisle Weekly Gazette* (PA), June 18, 1800; *American Mercury* (Hartford, CT), June 26, 1800; *Independent Gazetteer* (Worcester, MA), July 1, 1800; *City Gazette* (Charleston, SC), July 9, 1800; *Impartial Observer* (Providence, RI), August 25, 1800. Madison's Report.

23. Campbell, "Invention of First Amendment Federalism," 556 (footnote omitted). Albert Gallatin, *Annals of Congress,* July 11, 1798, 8:2163–64, quoted in

Campbell, "Invention of First Amendment," 519. Jefferson to Madison, October 26, 1798, *PTJ*, 30:567–68. See also Hartnett and Mercieca, "'Has Your Courage Rusted?'" 96.

24. Gouveneur Morris, July 17, 1787, Farrand, ed., *Records of the Federal Convention*, 2:28. Jefferson to Madison, March 15, 1789, *PTJ*, 14:659. Henry Speech, June 12, 1788, *DHRC*, 10:1219. See also John Marshall, June 20, 1788, *DHRC*, 10:1431–32: "To what quarter will you look for protection from an infringement of the Constitution, if you will not give the power to the Judiciary?" Years later, when a proposal was made to create a separate tribunal to hear disputes between states and the federal government, Virginia responded: "a tribunal is already provided by the Constitution of the United States, to wit, the Supreme Court." Quoted in *North American Review* 31 (1830): 510.

25. Campbell, "Invention of First Amendment Federalism," citing Phillip I. Blumberg, *Repressive Jurisprudence in the Early American Republic: The First Amendment and the Legacy of English Law* (Cambridge: Cambridge University Press, 2010), 144–45. Bird, "New Light on the Sedition Act of 1798," 608. Bird, *Press and Speech*, 331 ("turned").

26. Sanford Levinson also points out that in 1798 there would have been issues with jurisdiction and the availability of a general injunction. Levinson, "21st Century Rediscovery of Nullification," 25.

27. E.g., Gutzman, "Virginia and Kentucky Resolutions Reconsidered," 473: "At the end of their collective rope (or at least imagining a gallows in the intermediate future)."

28. George Nicholas, June 4, 1788, *DHRC*, 9:926.

29. Madison to Nicholas P. Trist, May 15, 1832, *Founders Online* (early access) https://founders.archives.gov/documents/Madison/99-02-02-2567. Jefferson to Madison, October 1, 1792, *PTJ*, 24:433.

30. Campbell, "Invention of First Amendment Federalism," 543. Bird, *Criminal Dissent*, 107. Draft Petition to the Virginia House of Delegates, ca. August 3, 1797, *PTJ*, 29:495 ("leave"). Cabell was not silenced and proceeded to criticize federal judges for becoming "a band of political preachers, instead of a sage body to administer the law." Letter from Samuel Cabell, *Aurora General Advertiser* (Philadelphia), June 6, 1797.

31. James Monroe to Jefferson, September 5, 1797, *PTJ*, 29:524. Jefferson to James Monroe, September 7, 1797, *PTJ*, 29:526. See also Madison to Jefferson, August 5, 1797, *PTJ*, 29:505. See also Sharp, *American Politics*, 170; Campbell, "Invention of First Amendment Federalism," 551. Draft Petition to the Virginia House of Delegates, ca. August 3, 1797, *PTJ*, 29:496. Jefferson to Madison, August 3, 1797, *PTJ*, 29:490–91; James Monroe to Jefferson, October 27, 1797, *PTJ*, 29:566. Koch and Ammon, "Virginia and Kentucky Resolutions," 153, citing *Journals of the House of Delegates of the Commonwealth*

of Virginia for 1797, December 28, 1797, 55–58. See also Watkins, *Reclaiming,* 57; Halperin, *Alien and Sedition Acts,* 78.

32. John Taylor to Jefferson, before May 13, 1798, *PTJ,* 30:348. Jefferson to John Taylor, June 4, 1798, *PTJ,* 30:388.

33. Jefferson to Wilson Cary Nicholas, October 5, 1798, *PTJ,* 30:557. Koch and Ammon, "Virginia and Kentucky Resolutions," 155–56. Hartnett and Mer- cieca, "'Has Your Courage Rusted,'" 99. Watkins, *Reclaiming,* 69; *PTJ,* 30:532. Jefferson may have initially intended his draft for Virginia. See *PTJ,* 30:532. Compare the Kentucky Resolutions, *PTJ,* 30:529 *et seq.,* and the Virginia Resolutions, *PJM* (CS), 17:185 *et seq.* Jefferson's and Madison's authorship was not widely confirmed until 1814 when John Taylor published "An Inquiry into the Principles and Policy of the Government of the United States" (Fredericksburg, 1814). Mayer, *Constitutional Thought,* 360n34; *PTJ,* 30:530. Jefferson's first draft, mentioning "nullification," was published in 1832. *PTJ,* 30:530.

34. Jefferson to Madison, November 17, 1798, *PTJ,* 30:580. See also Powell, "Principles of '98," 717–18, 736 (ambiguity intentional).

35. *PTJ,* 30:543–44. Madison, July 23, 1787, *PJM* (CS), 10:112–13. Rufus King made the same point during Massachusetts's ratification convention: "The introduction to this constitution is in these words: 'We the people, &c.' The language of the confederation is, 'We the states, &c.' The latter is a mere federal government of states." January 21, 1788, *DHRC,* 6:1285. See, e.g., Leonard and Cornell, *Partisan Republic,* 75–76: The Kentucky and Virginia Resolutions "elaborated a theory of the Union as a compact among sovereign states rather than a government created by the American people as a whole." The term "compact" can be used loosely to describe any agreement, but Jef- ferson in the Kentucky Resolutions used the term to refer to an agreement in which each state maintains its sovereignty and, therefore, freedom to judge legality and enforcement and to withdraw. See also Lenner, "John Taylor," 421–42; "An Observor," *Genius of Liberty* (Morristown, NJ), March 7, 1799. The "compact" argument would feature prominently in antebellum disputes over states' rights. See, e.g., Stampp, "Concept of a Perpetual Union," 31: "The notion of a right of secession, [President Andrew] Jackson claimed, grew out of the mistaken belief that the Constitution is only a compact between states whose sovereignty was not diminished by the act of ratification."

36. Henry, June 4, 1788, *DHRC,* 9:930. Henry, June 5, 1788, *DHRC,* 9:951. See also Story, *Commentaries on the Constitution,* §358 (footnote omitted): "None of its advocates pretended to deny, that its design was to establish a national government, as contradistinguished from a mere league or treaty, however they might oppose the suggestions, that it was a consolidation of the states."

37. Jefferson to Edward Carrington, December 21, 1787, *PTJ*, 12:446. See Ellis, *Union at Risk*, 4 (footnote omitted). Cf. Story, *Commentaries*, §396: "to have left a final decision, in such cases [of controversy between state and federal governments], to each of the states, then thirteen, and already twenty-four, could not fail to make the constitution and laws of the United States different in different states, was obvious; and not less obvious, that this diversity of independent decisions must . . . speedily put an end to the union itself."

38. James Madison, Views of the Political System (1787), *PJM*, 9:353. Madison to Jefferson, October 24, 1787, *PTJ*, 12:271.

39. *Federalist* #43, #15, #21. "The States Soldier IV," *Virginia Independent Chronicle*, March 19, 1788, *DHRC*, 8:513.

40. Farrand, ed., *Records of the Federal Convention*, 1:122–23 (June 5). Madison, June 7, 1788, *DHRC*, 9:1028. Henry, June 9, 1788, *DHRC*, 9:1068. See also Madison, June 7, 1788, *DHRC*, 9:1029. *Federalist* #39. Madison to Nicholas P. Trist, February 15, 1830, *Founders Online*, https://founders.archives.gov /documents/Madison/99-02-02-1982. Compare Madison's notes from the Philadelphia Convention recognizing "the various defects in the federal system, the necessity of transforming it into a national efficient Government, and the extreme danger of delaying this great work." Bilder, *Madison's Hand*, 58. While Madison used the term "compact" in *Federalist* #39 in passing, that entire essay analyzes how the Constitution, formed by the people acting through their agent states, is contradistinguished from the confederacy formed by independent states. See also Bilder, *Madison's Hand*, 38: Madison's "notes emphasized the impossibility of using a confederation structure for national purposes."

41. Jefferson to Richard Price, January 8, 1789, *PTJ*, 14:420. Loring, *Nullification, Secession, Webster's Argument*, 45. In a compact, amendments operate differently. For example, while some provisions of the World Trade Organization can be amended by a vote of two-thirds of the members, the amendments only apply to nations accepting them. Marrakesh Agreement Establishing the World Trade Organization, 10:3. See generally Story, *Commentaries*, §§209–396, §351: compact: "contemplating the permanent subsistence of parties having an independent right to construe, control, and judge of its obligations."

William Watkins argues that "proponents of ratification . . . often described it," the Constitution, as a compact, but he cites only an obscure "Alfredus Essay I" by Samuel Tenney, a delegate to New Hampshire's ratification convention. Watkins, *Reclaiming*, 59. "Alfredus" made a passing reference to social compacts to form governments, a different matter altogether, and the federal government as a compact among political societies while discussing states' bills of rights. *DHRC*, 28:89. Kevin Gutzman argues that Jefferson's compact theory "corresponded closely to the explication of the Constitution offered" by federalists during Virginia's ratification debates, noting only that federalists agreed that the Constitution was a limited grant of powers, citing Edmund Randolph. Gutzman, "Virginia and Kentucky Resolutions," 474, 476. But a limited government does not necessarily imply that states are free unilaterally to interfere with federal laws in their states or withdraw when they believe that the "compact" has been breached. In fact, Randolph did not interpret that admonition as broadly as Gutzman. See, e.g., "I intend to shew the necessity of having a national Government in preference to the Confederation; . . . and that a Confederacy is not eligible, in our present situation." Edmund Randolph, June 6, 1788, DHRC, 9:976. See also Fritz, "Constitutional Middle-Ground," 178.

42. Lee, "Plain Truth," 14. Jaffa, *Conditions of Freedom*, 165 (quoting South Carolina convention's "Address to the People of the United States" [1832]).

To some extent, the argument over "compact" can be a semantic game: What is meant by "compact"? At ratification and through 1798, the Constitution was not understood to have the characteristics of a compact, i.e., the ability of a state to block action of the national government or to unilaterally declare a breach of the compact and act upon that breach.

43. See Stampp, "Concept of a Perpetual Union," 2: In 1798, "Madison and Jefferson formulated an ingenious doctrine of state sovereignty." Taylor, *Enquiry into the Principles*, 64–65. See also ibid. at 43 ("once sovereign individual States."). For example, Malone, *Jefferson and the Ordeal of Liberty*, 402: "this view of [the Constitution] was widely held" in the late eighteenth century. Tipton, *Nullification and Interposition*, 10 (not seriously challenged until 1830s). McDonald, *States' Rights*, 7–25. Pauline Maier cites nullification as a "Road Not Taken" that had legitimacy before the Civil War. Maier, "Road Not Taken." Gienapp, "How to Maintain a Constitution," 54 (footnote omitted).

44. *PTJ*, 30:544–45.

45. Jefferson's Kentucky Resolutions, *PTJ*, 30:544, 545, 546, 547 (emphasis added). Dumas Malone, Jefferson's highly sympathetic biographer, concludes that Jefferson's "impatience" at the serious crisis and "excess of zeal in defense of freedom" led him to this extremity. *PTJ*, 30:535, quoting Malone, *Jefferson and the Ordeal of Liberty*, 408. *PTJ*, 30:533, 550. James Read and Neal Allen lay out the traditional definition of nullification: "the theory that each state is fully sovereign and as such the final judge of its own constitutional rights and obligations; that consequently it may legitimately rule that any federal act . . . is unconstitutional; and most importantly that it may act on this judgment by blocking the implementation of that federal act within the state's boundaries." Read and Allen, "Living, Dead, and Undead," 96. Of course, states can affect federal actions through "uncooperative federalism," termed by some

"functional nullification," Levinson, "21st Century Rediscovery," 10, but "uncooperative federalism" is very distinct from legal nullification. In the former, "federal officials are not themselves estopped from enforcing federal law." Ibid., 11–12.

Like Malone, Brian Steele urges that Jefferson "seemed remarkably unconcerned with the theoretical implications of his use of the term" *nullify.* Steele, *Thomas Jefferson and American Nationalism,* 251. He and Madison "were perhaps less focused on articulating a general theory of union than they were on rectifying the political wrongs of the moment." Ibid., 249–50 (footnotes omitted). Steele is certainly correct that Jefferson did not oppose the federal government using broad powers when in proper hands (his). As Read and Allen explain, Jefferson could not "admit the legitimacy of a state's obstructing a federal law that [he] regarded as essential. This is not mere hypocrisy but connected with the very nature of nullification. Those who nullify federal law believing they possess the correct understanding of the Constitution are unlikely to accord equal legitimacy to those who nullify for what they perceive as constitutionally incorrect reasons." "Living, Dead, and Undead," 111–12.

46. *PJM* (CS), 9:352.
47. Quoted in Warfield, *Kentucky Resolutions,* 94, 95. *Stewart Kentucky Herald,* December 4, 1798; *Centinel of Freedom* (Newark, NJ), January 1, 1799. Warfield, *Kentucky Resolutions,* 88 (quoting William Murray), 93. See also *Herald of Liberty* (Washington, PA), August 27, 1798: Meeting here to discuss Alien & Sedition Acts, "It was currently said that the important questions of *Separation from the Union* would be agitated."
48. *Letter from George Nicholas of Kentucky to His Friend in Virginia* (reprinted Philadelphia 1799), 33–34. Jefferson to James Monroe, February 11, 1799, *PTJ,* 31:24. See generally Zemler, "'Conciliatory Declaration.'"
49. *Observations on a Letter from George Nicholas,* 29, 105.
50. Jefferson to John Taylor, November 26, 1798, *PTJ,* 30:589 (emphasis added).
51. Powell, "Principles of '98," 719. Madison to Edward Everett, August 28, 1830, *Founders Online* (early access), https://founders.archives.gov/documents/Madison/99-02-02-2138. In the early 1820s, Madison reminded Spencer Roane "that there must always be a provision for terminating disagreements between the federal and state governments about their respective spheres of authority, Madison vigorously denied that this trust—which he insisted the founders had correctly placed in the judicial branch of the general government—could be vested in the states in their individual capacity. The latter mechanism, he objected, would have the potential effect of rendering a different meaning for the Constitution in every state (and hence of reverting, he implied, to the chaos of the Articles of Confederation)." McCoy, *Last of the Fathers,* 131, citing Madison to Spencer Roane, June 29, 1821, *PJM* (RS),

2:347–48. See also Madison to Edward Everett, August 28, 1830, *Founders Online* (early access), https://founders.archives.gov/documents/Madison/99-02-02-2138.

52. *Country Porcupine*, April 3, 1799, quoted in Anderson, "Contemporary Opinion . . . I," 49.
53. *PJM* (CS), 17:186; *PTJ*, 30:5331.
54. *Virginia and Kentucky Resolutions of 1798 and 1799*, 6.
55. *PJM* (CS), 17:189 (footnote omitted).
56. Koch and Ammon, "Virginia and Kentucky Resolutions," 161n48; Stampp, "Concept of a Perpetual Union," 24. Madison to Alexander Rives, January 1, 1833, *Founders Online* (early access), https://founders.archives.gov/documents/Madison/99-02-02-2655. *PJM* (CS), 17:190. See also Madison to Nicholas P. Trist, February 15, 1830, *Founders Online* (early access), https://founders.archives.gov/documents/Madison/99-02-02-1982; Madison to Edward Everett, August 28, 1830, *Founders Online* (early access), https://founders.archives.gov/documents/Madison/99-02-02-2138 ("cannot be altered or annulled at the will of the States individually"). A similar argument was made by the Democratic-Republican *Richmond Enquirer* during the War of 1812 when Federalists threatened interference with federal action: "The same formality which forged the links of the Union, is necessary to dissolve it. . . . Until *that* consent has been obtained, any attempt to dissolve the *Union,* or obstruct the efficacy of its constitutional law, is Treason." *Richmond Enquirer*, November 1, 1814. The *Enquirer* made the same point in response to Federalist complaints about President Jefferson's exercise of power: "If it be at any time within the power of a state to evade the force of the general Government within that particular district, over which its own jurisdiction extends; . . . if the general government is thus compelled to consult the wishes of each state, before it dares to adopt any important law, the Union of these states will be like a rope of sand." *Enquirer,* February 14, 1809.
57. *PJM* (CS), 17:189.
58. Madison to Thomas Ritchie, December 18, 1825, *Founders Online*, https://founders.archives.gov/documents/Madison/04-03-02-0677. See, e.g., Fritz, "Interposition and the Heresy of Nullification."
59. Watkins, *Reclaiming*, 73.
60. Jefferson to Wilson Cary Nicholas, November 29, 1798, *PTJ*, 30:590. See, e.g., Beeman, *Old Dominion*, 191. *PJM* (CS), 17:187.
61. *Debates in the House of Delegates of Virginia, upon Certain Resolutions* (Richmond: Thos. Nicolson, 1818 [1798]), 78–79, quoted in Watkins, *Reclaiming*, 71. The front page of this publication lists MDCCCXVIII [1818], apparently through the transposition of X and C in the roman numeral dating.

62. McCoy, *Last of the Fathers*, 145, quoting Ralph Ketchum, *James Madison: A Biography* (Charlottesville: University of Virginia Press, 1990), 396–97. See also Lash and Harrison, "Minority Report," 448. Rakove, *James Madison and the Creation of the American Republic.*

63. Madison to Robert Young Hayne, April 3, 1830, *Founders Online* (early access), https://founders.archives.gov/documents/Madison/99-02-02-2016. See also McCoy, *Last of the Fathers*, 141. Madison to Robert Young Hayne, April 3, 1830, *Founders Online* (early access), https://founders.archives.gov /documents/Madison/99-02-02-2016. Madison to James Robertson Jr., March 27, 1831, *Founders Online* (early access), https://founders.archives.gov /documents/Madison/99-02-02-2310, discussed in Fritz, "Interposition and the Heresy of Nullification," 5.

64. *Federalist* #46. E.g., Koch and Ammon, "Virginia and Kentucky Resolutions," 160. See McGraw, "'To Secure These Rights,'" 57n8, 56: "nullification called for the states acting individually to declare unconstitutional federal legislation to be such and to be 'altogether void, and of no force.' Interposition only called for the states acting collectively to declare unconstitutional federal legislation to be just that, but nothing more."

65. Risjord, "Virginia Federalists," 505, quoting *Debates in the House of Delegates of Virginia, upon Certain Resolutions*, 110–17, 177. Risjord, "Virginia Federalists," 504, quoting Morgan to Benjamin Biggs, February 12, 1799, in Biggs Papers, Draper Manuscript Collection, Wisconsin Historical Society, Madison, WI. Lee, "Plain Truth," 15, 19, 21–22. See, e.g., *Porcupine's Gazette* (Philadelphia), April 1, 1799; *Commercial Advertiser* (New York), April 3, 6, 8, 16, 1799; *Spectator* (New York), April 6, 10, 17, 27, May 4, 8, 11, 1799; *Federal Gazette* (Baltimore), May 1, 11, 13, 14, 17, 21, 29, June 1, 1799. On secession being implicit in the compact theory, see, e.g., Story, *Commentaries*, §321. Patrick Henry to Henry Lee quoted in *Federal Gazette* (Baltimore), May 10, 1799; *Centinel of Liberty* (Georgetown, DC), May 10, 1799; *City Gazette* (Charleston, SC), May 18, 1799; *Albany Centinel*, May 24, 1799; *Connecticut Gazette*, June 26, 1799.

66. The Resolutions were not uniformly embraced in Virginia. Greenbrier County's court shred the Resolutions "to pieces and trampled [them] . . . underfoot." Koch and Ammon, "Virginia and Kentucky Resolutions," 164, quoting *Virginia Herald* (Fredericksburg), April 12, 1799. See also Beeman, *Old Dominion*, 200n45, quoting *Columbian Mirror*, April 23, 1799 (Staunton court, "without any deliberation, tore them to pieces and trampled them under foot").

67. *Virginia Argus* (Richmond), December 4, 1798; "Extra" *Virginia Argus*, December 5, 1798; *Stewart Kentucky Herald*, November 13, 1798; *Aurora General Advertiser* (Philadelphia), December 8, 1798; *Farmer's Register*

(Chambersburg, PA), December 12, 1798; *Centinel of Freedom* (Newark, NJ), December 18, 1798; *Maryland Herald and Hager's-Town Weekly Advertiser,* December 20, 1798; *Genius of Liberty* (Morristown, NJ), December 27, 1798; *Bee* (New London, CT), January 2, 1799; *Norwich Courier* (CT), January 2, 1799. *Times and District of Columbia Daily Advertiser* (Alexandria, VA), December 11, 1798. *Times and District of Columbia Daily Advertiser* (Alexandria, VA), December 18, 1798. *Federal Gazette and Baltimore Daily Advertiser,* December 13, 1798. *Bee* (New London, CT), December 19, 1798 ("The same may also be expected from the state of Tennessee, if not from some others").

68. *Virginia Argus,* December 25, 1798. Also *Independent Chronicle* (Boston), January 14, 1799 (amended Virginia Resolutions). Anderson, "Contemporary Opinion . . . II," 248 (MD responding to VA's null-and-void language). *PJM* (CS), 17:187, citing *Debates in the House of Delegates of Virginia, upon Certain Resolutions,* 148–50.

69. Extract of a Letter from Richmond gentleman to friend in Alexandria, *Federal Gazette* (Baltimore), January 26, 1799; *Gazette of the United States* (Philadelphia), January 29, 1799; *Porcupine's Gazette* (Philadelphia), January 29, 1799 (headlined "Civil War!"); *Philadelphia Gazette and Universal Daily Advertiser,* January 29, 1799; *New York Gazette,* January 31, 1799; *Daily Advertiser* (New York), February 1, 1799 (headlined "Civil War!"); *Commercial Advertiser* (New York), February 1, 1799; *Spectator* (New York) February 2, 1799; *Albany Centinel,* February 5, 1799; *New Jersey Journal,* February 5, 1799; *Columbian Centinel* (Boston), February 6, 1799; *Oracle of Dauphin* (Harrisburg, PA) February 6, 1799; *American Mercury* (Hartford, CT), February 7, 1799; *Genius of Liberty* (Morristown, NJ), February 7, 1799; *Russel's Gazette* (Boston), February 7, 1799; *Medley, or New Bedford Marine Journal,* February 8, 1799; *Newburyport Herald* (MA), February 8, 1799; *Salem Gazette* (MA), February 8, 1799 (headlined "Civil War"); *Columbian Courier* (New Bedford, MA), February 9, 1799; *Oracle of the Day* (Portsmouth, NH), February 9, 1799; *Providence Gazette,* February 9, 1799; *Weekly Companion* (Newport, RI), February 9, 1799; *Farmer's Weekly Museum* (Walpole, NH), February 11, 1799; *Gazette* (Portland, ME), February 11, 1799; *Impartial Herald* (Suffield, CT), February 12, 1799 (headlined "Civil War!"); *Political Repository* (Brookfield, MA), February 12, 1799; *Hampshire Gazette* (Northampton, MA), February 13, 1799; *Litchfield Monitor* (CT), February 13, 1799; *New-Hampshire Gazette* (Portsmouth, NH), February 13, 1799; *Norwich Packet* (CT), February 13, 1799; *Massachusetts Spy,* February 13, 1799; *Windham Herald* (CT), February 14, 1799; *Salem Gazette* (MA), February 15, 1799; *South-Carolina State Gazette and Timothy's Daily Advertiser,* February 18, 1799; *Rutland Herald* (VT), February 18, 1799; *Federal Galaxy* (Brattleboro, VT), February 19, 1799; *Maryland Herald and Eastern Shore Intelligencer,* February 19, 1799; *Sun*

(Dover, NH), February 20, 1799; *Columbian Museum* (Savannah, GA), February 22, 1799. *Sun* (Dover, NH), January 16, 1799 ("looks like"). Washington subscribed to the *Gazette of the United States* as well as the *Pennsylvania Gazette*. Hayes, *George Washington*, 308. See also *Albany Centinel*, February 5, 1799; *Salem Gazette* (MA), February 8, 1799; *Political Repository* (Brookfield, MA), February 12, 1799 (Virginia may precipitate a civil war).

70. *Massachusetts Mercury*, February 19, 1799; *Impartial Herald* (Suffield, CT), March 5, 1799. *Columbian Centinel* (Boston), February 9, 1799; *Commercial Advertiser* (New York), February 18, 1799; *Daily Advertiser* (New York), February 18, 1799; *Spectator* (New York), February 20, 1799; *Litchfield Monitor* (CT), February 27, 1799. Also Anderson, "Contemporary Opinion . . . II," 231, quoting *Federal Miscellany* (Exeter, NH), February 13, 1799.

71. See sources in note 69.

72. "To the People, No. I and No. II," *Virginia Argus* (Richmond), April 2, 1799. "To the People, No. III," *Virginia Argus* (Richmond), April 12, 1799. *Bee* (New London, CT), April 3, 1799. See Golladay, "Jefferson's 'Malignant Neighbor.'" See Malone, *Jefferson and the Ordeal of Liberty*, 416. Sharp, *American Politics*, 203 (footnote omitted) ("considerable credence"). This John Nicholas was a bit of a troublemaker; complicating the matter is that some of the sources, including Koch and Ammon, confuse the two John Nicholases. Notably, this John Nicholas was no friend of Patrick Henry: After ratification debates, he wrote the infamous Decius letters which, among other things, referred to Henry as a "political smellfungus." See Golladay, "Jefferson's 'Malignant Neighbor,'" 308.

With respect to Nicholas's claim concerning majority rule, some historians insist that Jefferson's Kentucky Resolutions were "grounded in . . . majoritarian sentiment." Ellis, *Union at Risk*, 4, quoted in Steele, "Thomas Jefferson, Coercion," 825n4. Madison did as well, distinguishing Kentucky's actions from the later actions of South Carolina in support of nullification because the former "was a defense of majority rule." Steele, *Thomas Jefferson and American Nationalism*, 262. But this assumes that opponents (and Jefferson and Madison), rather than Congress, were uniquely qualified to declare what the majority of Americans supported, a point made in congressional debates at the time. Compare *Claypoole's American Daily Advertiser* (Philadelphia), December 17, 1798; *New-York Gazette*, December 19, 1798; *Greenleaf's New York Journal*, December 19, 1798; *Federal Gazette and Baltimore Daily Advertiser*, December 21, 1798; *Spectator* (New York), December 21, 1798; *Connecticut Courant*, December 31, 1798; *South-Carolina State Gazette and Timothy's Daily Advertiser*, January 5, 1799; *City Gazette* (South Carolina), January 7, 1799.

73. *Annals of Congress*, January 1817, 798. Sharp, *American Politics*, 204, quoting Davidson, "Virginia and the Alien and Sedition Laws," 337 ("there was no

longer"). Randolph in debates, *Repertory* (Boston), February 15, 1817. Davidson, "Virginia and the Alien and Sedition Laws," 338. Compare Beeman, *Old Dominion*, 201–4 (Wilson Branch Giles insisted Virginia had peaceful intent). Howison, *History of Virginia*, 3:349.

74. William Heth to Alexander Hamilton, January 18, 1799, *Founders Online*, https://founders.archives.gov/documents/Hamilton/01-22-02-0240. Alexander Hamilton to Jonathan Dayton, October–November 1799, *Founders Online*, https://founders.archives.gov/documents/Hamilton/01-23-02-0526 (footnotes omitted). (This letter is almost certainly from December 1799 or later, after the Virginia Resolutions were adopted on December 10.) Alexander Hamilton to Theodore Sedgwick, February 2, 1799, *Founders Online*, https://founders.archives.gov/documents/Hamilton/01-22-02-0267. See Cunningham, *Jefferson vs. Hamilton*, 118. Theodore Sedgwick to Rufus King (ambassador to Britain), November 15, 1799, *Life and Correspondence of Rufus King*, ed. Charles King, 6 vols. (New York: G. P. Putnam's Sons, 1896), 3:147–48, quoted in Davidson, "Virginia and the Alien and Sedition Laws," 336. Also King, *Life and Correspondence of Rufus King*, 3:147–48, quoted in *Founders Online*, https://founders.archives.gov/documents/Hamilton/01-23-02-0526. See generally Sehat, *Jefferson Rule*, 28.

75. Koch and Ammon, "Virginia and Kentucky Resolutions," 163n55 citing Davidson, "Virginia and the Alien and Sedition Laws." Davidson, "Virginia and the Alien and Sedition Laws," noting that most of the measures had been approved years earlier. Sharp, *American Politics*, 188 ("although some"). See Beeman, *Old Dominion*, 201–4 (funding delayed for years until 1799 when a new effort to delay the purchase for a year was rejected on a partisan vote).

76. Such threats of military intervention were far more real at the end of the eighteenth century. For example, in the coming electoral crisis when Jefferson tied in the Electoral College with Aaron Burr, his ostensible vice-presidential candidate, there were again threats of states arming militia to march on Washington. Pennsylvania governor McKean declared that with "arms for upward of twenty thousand" Pennsylvania could arrest anyone involved in the "treason" of usurping intended electoral results. Thomas McKean to Jefferson, March 21, 1801, *PTJ*, 33:391. "Partisans were arming in Philadelphia, in Baltimore." Weisberger, *America Afire*, 273. McKean's threats resulted in some dangerous "smack talk" from Federalists who pointed out that "the militia of Massachusetts consist[s] of 60,000 (*regulars let us call them*) in arms—" and deriding southern military abilities, declaring that Virginia's militia "exercise[d] with corn stalks instead of muskets" and was burdened with an internal enemy (the enslaved). The warning ended: "Let those mad-men reflect on these things, let them forbear their menaces—let them respect the decision of the constituted authority." *Washington Federalist*, February 12, 1801;

Federal Gazette and Baltimore Daily Advertiser, February 16, 1801; *Daily Advertiser* (New York), February 18, 1801; *Hampshire Gazette* (MA), March 11, 1801.

77. Long term, use of the Sedition Act against Fries's participants was politically a significant negative for Federalists. On Fries's Rebellion and the Sedition Act, see Bird, *Criminal Dissent,* 185 *et seq.* See generally Bouton, "'No Wonder the Times Were Troublesome,'" 21–42.

78. *Sun* (Dover, NH), February 13, 1799. (This was a reprint of a small portion of the letter from Virginia that was broadly reprinted throughout the nation. See note 69.) William Heth to Alexander Hamilton, January 18, 1799, *Founders Online,* https://founders.archives.gov/documents/Hamilton/01-22-02-0240 (footnotes omitted).

79. Freeman, "Election of 1800," 1960.

5. "A CONSTITUTIONAL WAY"

1. Beeman, *Old Dominion,* 175. Elkins and McKitrick, *Age of Federalism,* 645–46 (Knox). Henry Knox to Washington, July 29, 1798, *PGW* (RS), 2:471. *Commercial Advertiser* (New York), April 6, 1799; *Spectator* (New York), April 10, 1799; *Hudson Gazette,* April 16, 1799 (from the *Salem Gazette,* March 29, 1799).

2. See Bouton, "'No Wonder the Times Were Troublesome." *J. Russell's Gazette* (Boston), April 29, 1799; *Massachusetts Mercury,* April 30, 1799; *Newburyport Herald* (MA), May 3, 1799; *New-York Gazette,* May 7, 1799; *Oracle of the Day* (Portsmouth, NH), May 11, 1799.

3. Henry to Archibald Blair, January 8, 1799, Henry, *Henry,* 2:591.

4. Henry, *Henry,* 2:590; Lash and Harrison, "Minority Report," 449; Wehtje, "Congressional Elections of 1799," citing John Marshall, *An Autobiographical Sketch by John Marshall,* ed. John Stokes Adams (Ann Arbor, MI: University of Michigan Press, 1937), 25, 26. Bird, *Criminal Dissent,* 104–9. Henry to Archibald Blair, January 8, 1799, Henry, *Henry,* 2:593 ("Scottish merchants"). Archibald Blair to Henry, December 28, 1798, Henry, *Henry,* 2:590.

5. Henry to Archibald Blair, January 8, 1799, Henry, *Henry,* 2:591–94. *Virginia Gazette,* October 2, 1799. Reprinted, e.g., *Columbian Mirror and Alexandria Gazette,* June 3, 1800; *Commercial Advertiser* (New York), October 14, 1800; *Federal Gazette and Baltimore Daily Advertiser,* October 18, 1800; *Newport Mercury* (RI), October 28, 1800; *Columbian Centinel* (Boston), November 5, 1800; *Washington Federalist* (DC), December 5, 1800; *Philadelphia Gazette and Daily Advertiser,* December 12, 1800 (from *Jenks' Portland Gazette*).

6. Henry to Archibald Blair, January 8, 1799, Henry, *Henry,* 2:592–93.

7. Henry, *Henry,* 2:597. Beveridge, *Life of John Marshall,* 2:413. Chief Justice Marshall would, among other things, reject the compact theory on which the

Kentucky and Virginia Resolutions were based. See, e.g., *McCulloch v. Maryland*, 17 U.S. 316 (1819).

8. See Henry, *Henry*, 2:599. *Gazette of the United States* (Philadelphia), May 2, 1799 (thirty-five votes). *Federal Gazette* (Baltimore), May 10, 1799; *Centinel of Liberty* (DC), May 10, 1799; *City Gazette* (Charleston, SC), May 18, 1799; *Fredericksburg Gazette* (VA), May 24, 1799, reprinted *Connecticut Gazette*, June 26, 1799. Lee, *Memoirs of the War*, 195. Jefferson to Archibald Stuart, May 14, 1799, *PTJ*, 31:110. Jefferson to Tench Coxe, May 21, 1799, *PTJ*, 31:113.

9. Archibald Blair to Henry, January 13, 1799, Henry, *Henry*, 3:427.

10. Washington to Henry, January 15, 1799, *PGW* (RS), 3:317.

It is intriguing that among Washington's many thousands of letters that were obviously carefully preserved, a January 1799 letter from David Stuart to Washington concerning this crisis is missing. The letter urged Washington to involve Henry, but what else it might have said about Jefferson and Madison, or what else it proposed, is unknown. Perhaps the letter was burned by Washington. See Washington to David Stuart, January 4, 1799, *PGW* (RS), 3:304 (referring to a letter "just received"). In his response, Washington laments: "It is not easy to predict the consequences which will result from the spirit which seems to pervade the Legislature of this State—and much indeed it is to be regretted, that at a crisis like the present, such men as Mr Henry—either from a love of ease—domestic enjoyments—or disinclination to oppose himself to a ruinous party—will not step forward. If in *principle* he is opposed to the measures of this Party, and his own apprehensions & Patriotism are not powerful enough to awaken him, I can hardly suppose that the sentiments of an individual would have much weight." Ibid., 305. Stuart wrote on the letter from Washington: "This letter was in answer to one in which I begged the Genl to urge Mr [Patrick] Henry to get into the Assembly." Ibid., 305n4. Washington may also have been pushed into action by a January 8 letter from John Marshall in which the congressional candidate, while regretting adoption of the Sedition Act, bemoaned the Virginia Resolutions: "it seems that there are men who will hold power by any means . . . and who would prefer a dissolution of the union to the continuance of an administration not of their own party." Marshall urged that while "I believe that no argument can moderate the leaders of the opposition—but it may be possible to make some impression on the mass of the people." The Democratic-Republicans "will risk all the ills which may result from the most dangerous experiments rather than permit that happiness to be enjoyed which is dispensed by other hands than their own. It is more than ever essential to make great exertions at the next election." Marshall to Washington, January 8, 1799, *PGW* (RS), 3:308.

11. Henry to Henry Lee, June 27, 1795, Henry, *Henry*, 2:551, 553. Henry to Washington, October 16, 1795, *PGW* (PS), 19:53.

12. Henry to Washington, February 12, 1799, *PGW* (RS), 3:370.

13. Spencer Roane to James Monroe, March 24, 1799, *Papers of James Monroe*, ed. Preston, DeLong, and Stello, 4:328 (footnote omitted). See Jefferson to Archibald Stuart, May 14, 1799, *PTJ*, 31:110.

14. Fontaine, "New Facts," 811 *et seq*. The "New Facts" account provides many personal observations by Henry's relatives and associates. Its provenance can be confusing. It was published in *DeBow's Review* in 1870, and lists the author as P. H. Fontaine, of LA (presumably Louisiana). But Patrick Henry Fontaine, the eldest grandson, had died in 1852, and there were several other Patrick Henry Fontaines in the nineteenth century, including at least one great-grandson and one great-great-grandson. Yet, posthumous publication of the manuscript of the eldest grandson, who knew Henry personally, seems the proper attribution (although the manuscript was apparently edited by his son, Edward Fontaine, living in New Orleans in 1870). First, the author is reported as being from Louisiana but mentions meeting in 1838 in Pontotoc, MS, with several people who had heard Henry's last speech, and the eldest grandson (Patrick Henry Fontaine) had moved to Pontotoc after receiving an appointment to a federal land office there in 1835. The author reports that his father told him of seeing Henry preparing cases at Red Hill, likely meaning John Fontaine, Patrick Henry Fontaine's father. Edward Fontaine, though, seems to have edited the piece, evident in the mention of an "article written by me . . . for the Southern Churchman," of which Edward Fontaine was the author. In addition, a number of particulars in this account match information attributed to Edward Fontaine's father (the eldest grandson, Patrick Henry Fontaine) in Edward's equally informative *Patrick Henry: Corrections of Biographical Mistakes*.

15. See Ragosta, *Patrick Henry*, Appendix: "Are Patrick Henry's Speeches Accurately Reported?"; Ragosta, "'Caesar Had His Brutus.'" See Wirt, *Sketches*, 274, *et seq*. Fontaine, "New Facts," 811 *et seq*. See also report of the Reverend Dr. James Alexander (another observer of the speech), *Wisconsin Democrat* (Madison), July 6, 1850. Randolph appeared that day in opposition to Henry's political position. Randolph later had a falling out with the Jeffersonians. In the early nineteenth century, as Jefferson seemed to moderate (see chapter 6), the most radical wing of the states' rights movement "rallied around former party lieutenant John Randolph, who had broken with Jefferson for political and personal reasons and who soon came to personify a narrow, states'-rights particularism—a literal devotion to a petrified version of the Republican creed of the 1790s." Jordan, *Political Leadership*, 18.

16. Fontaine, "New Facts," 811 *et seq.* Couvillon, *Demosthenes of His Age,* 80, quoting from Henry Howe, *Historical Collections of Virginia* (1852), 224.

17. Henry, *Henry,* 2:607–10. William Wirt Henry bases his account primarily on a paper in John Randolph's hand, dated March 1799, in William Wirt's papers. Henry, *Henry,* 2:611. Other accounts generally agree with this version, with a critical exception discussed below. See, e.g., Rev. Dr. James Alexander (another observer), *Wisconsin Democrat,* July 6, 1850 (crediting Wirt account as accurate, but less impressed than others by Henry's speech).

18. Henry, "Patrick Henry: A Vindication," 353. Henry was not saying that he had "erroneously opposed" the Constitution, as Longacre and Herring, *National Portrait Gallery of Distinguished Americans,* 2, "Patrick Henry," 8, argued. Rather, while he had opposed the Constitution on good grounds, it was adopted by his fellow citizens and needed to be accepted until reformed in "a constitutional way."

19. Henry, June 16, 1788, *DHRC,* 10:1299. Henry to Washington, October 16, 1795, *PGW* (PS), 19:53.

20. "Surgo ut Prosim," *Aurora General Advertiser* (Philadelphia), March 8, 1799. Reprinted *Vermont Gazette,* March 21, 1799; *Independent Chronicle* (Boston), March 21, 1799. Fontaine, *Patrick Henry: Corrections,* 22. Edward Fontaine was son of Patrick Henry Fontaine, Henry's eldest grandson and author of "New Facts." Some of Edward's information came directly from Dr. John Miller, the former Hampden-Sydney student, from whom he got information in 1838 in Pontotoc, MS, the same year that Patrick Henry Fontaine said that he met with Miller in Pontotoc. *Patrick Henry: Corrections,* 21. Edward Fontaine was living in Mississippi and Texas in the 1840s and 1850s and likely traveled with his father to Pontotoc in 1836 after the latter received an appointment to a federal land office in Pontotoc in 1835. Edward would have been twenty-four in 1838, and his account likely reflects family lore as well as what he heard from attendees at the Charlotte Courthouse speech.

21. Edward W. Johnston, "Jefferson—The Sage of Monticello," *New York Daily Times,* January 8, 1853.

22. Fontaine, *Patrick Henry: Corrections,* 22–23.

23. Ibid.

24. Henry, *Henry,* 2:610. Rice was an influential Presbyterian minister in the early republic, deeply involved in church-state issues and the founding of the University of Virginia.

25. Henry, *Henry,* 2:611. Several accounts suggest that Henry rose publicly to respond to Randolph, but other observers insist that this never occurred. See Fontaine, "New Facts" (disputing accounts by Wirt and Garland). See generally Rev. Dr. James Alexander, *Wisconsin Democrat* (Madison, WI), July 6,

1850: "All that is alleged in the Encyclopedia about Henry's returning to the platform and replying with extraordinary effect, is pure fabrication."

26. Howe, *Historical Collections of Virginia*, 224.

27. Wirt, *Sketches*, 275. Royster, *Light-Horse Harry Lee*, 81 (Royster also provides no citation and misreports that Henry was elected to Congress rather than the Virginia General Assembly).

28. Fontaine, *Patrick Henry: Corrections*, 22–23. See also Fontaine, "New Facts."

29. *Petersburg Index*, August 21, 1837, republished *Daily Dispatch* (Richmond), August 23, 1867. See also Henry, "Patrick Henry: A Vindication," 352–53.

30. Fontaine, "New Facts," 811. See also Note from John Henry, December 12, 1868. What Henry said, according to the note, was that "the Alien & Sedition laws were only the first fruit of that constitution the adoption of which he opposed." The author writes that Wirt's statement that Henry supported the Alien and Sedition Acts was "very incorrect[]." The note was apparently also a response, in part, to Howison's *History of Virginia* that, in a Jeffersonian voice, suggested that had Henry attended the General Assembly in 1799, he would have defended the Alien and Sedition Acts. Howison, *History of Virginia*, 2:337. John Henry, however, died on January 7, 1868, and would have been three years old when the Charlotte Courthouse speech occurred. One suspects that this is another family recollection and that the Virginia Museum has misdated the paper, as it appears upon inspection to have a date of 1864.

31. See also Bradburn, "Clamor in the Public Mind," 593 ("Henry and Marshall had made a point of publicly denouncing the Alien and Sedition Acts").

32. Address to Albemarle County citizens (1790), *PTJ*, 16:178 (footnote omitted).

33. Washington also made this point in his Farewell Address: "No alliances, however strict, between the parts can be an adequate substitute; they must inevitably experience the infractions and interruptions which all alliances in all times have experienced. Sensible of this momentous truth, you have improved upon your first essay [the Confederation], by the adoption of a Constitution of Government better calculated than your former for an intimate Union, and for the efficacious management of your common concerns."

34. Samuel Adams to the Massachusetts Legislature, January 16, 1795, *Writings of Samuel Adams*, ed. Cushing, 4:373.

35. Of seventy-three Virginia delegates who voted against ratification (excluding six from what became Kentucky), the political affiliation in the late 1790s is known of forty, and every one of them, excluding Patrick Henry, was a Democratic-Republican. Of the eighty-six Virginia delegates who voted to ratify (excluding three from Kentucky), the political affiliation in the late 1790s is known for sixty-one, of which almost two-thirds were Federalist. Risjord, "Virginia Federalists," 488. *Centinel of Liberty* (Georgetown, DC), June 21, 1799 ("Virginia may boast").

36. Longacre and Herring, *National Portrait Gallery of Distinguished Americans,* 2, "Patrick Henry," 7–8.

37. *Centinel of Liberty* (Georgetown, DC), May 10, 1799, extract letter from Patrick Henry to Henry Lee, printed *Fredericksburg Gazette,* May 7, 1799; reprinted *Albany Centinel,* May 24, 1799; *Connecticut Gazette,* June 26, 1799.

38. See "Lesson to Men of All Parties," *Daily Advertiser* (New York), April 29, 1799; *Philadelphia Gazette and Universal Daily Advertiser,* April 30, 1799; *Albany Centinel,* May 3, 1799; *Commercial Advertiser* (New York), May 3, 1799; *Spectator* (New York), May 4, 1799; *Kline's Carlisle Weekly Gazette* (PA), May 8, 1799; *Newburyport Herald* (MA), May 14, 1799; *Federal Gazette and Baltimore Daily Advertiser,* May 15, 1799; *Independent Chronicle* (Boston), May 16, 1799; *Norwich Packet* (CT), May 16, 1799; *Times and District of Columbia Daily Advertiser* (Alexandria, VA), May 18, 1799; *Columbian Museum & Savannah Advertiser* (GA), May 21, 1799; *Federal Galaxy* (Brattleboro, VT), May 21, 1799; *South-Carolina State Gazette and Timothy's Daily Advertiser,* May 25, 1799; *New Hampshire Gazette,* May 28, 1799; *Columbian Courier* (New Bedford, MA), May 29, 1799; *Delaware Gazette,* May 29, 1799; *Amherst Village Messenger* (NH), June 1, 1799; *Herald of the United States* (RI), June 8, 1799 (from *Reading Advertiser* [PA]); *Oracle of the Day* (Portsmouth, NH), June 8, 1799; *Connecticut Gazette,* June 26, 1799; *Maryland Herald and Hager's-Town Weekly Advertiser,* June 27, 1799.

39. *South-Carolina State Gazette and Timothy's Daily Advertiser,* June 26, 1799 (from Petersburg).

40. *Wisconsin Democrat,* July 6, 1850. Alexander's account responded to a report of the speech that claimed, Alexander insisted inaccurately, that Henry had risen to answer publicly Randolph's speech. Alexander generally credits Wirt's version of the speech, although he does not engage the question of Henry's views on the Alien and Sedition Acts. His account also appeared in the *Southern Literary Magazine* 16 (June 1850): 366 (reprinted from the *Princeton Magazine*). The letter is signed only "A.A.," but Alexander's son identified his father as the author. Hall, ed., *Forty Years' Familiar Letters,* 2:114. *Aurora General Advertiser* (Philadelphia), February 27, 1799; March 8, 1799; March 25, 1799; May 27, 1799, reprinted in part *Vermont Gazette,* June 6, 1799. Reprinting of this attack, too, may have been interrupted by Henry's death.

41. Jefferson to Archibald Stuart, May 14, 1799, *PTJ,* 31:110.

42. John Taylor to Madison, March 4, 1799, *PJM* (CS), 17:245.

43. Edward Carrington to Washington, October 13, 1795, *PGW* (PS), 19:45. Royster, *Light-Horse Harry Lee,* 153; Onuf, *Jefferson and the Virginians,* 52–53.

44. John Taylor to Madison, March 4, 1799, *PJM* (CS), 17:245. See also Sharp, *American Politics,* 222.

45. Jefferson to Tench Coxe, May 21, 1799, *PTJ,* 31:114.

46. Wood, *Friends Divided*, 314–15. The *Aurora's* February 27, 1799, endorsement of Henry was in this context. Ultimately, the delegation to France was made up of William Vans Murray, William Davie, and Oliver Ellsworth, but its departure was delayed by Adams administration officials who were more directly under the control of Alexander Hamilton than the president. This proved disastrous for Adams and the Federalists as the peace delegation successfully negotiated the Treaty of Mortefontaine in September 1800, but word of the treaty did not reach the United State in time to influence the presidential election. Weisberger, *America Afire*, 197–98, 249. Had news arrived earlier, it would likely have resulted in Adams's reelection. Jefferson, thinking as a party man, cynically believed the new peace delegation was more of a political gambit than a serious effort at peace. Jefferson to Madison, February 26, 1799, *PTJ*, 31:64.

47. See Howison, *History of Virginia*, 2:363.

48. Ragosta, *Patrick Henry*, 142; Tyler, *Patrick Henry*, 376–77.

49. Ralph Wormeley Jr. to Washington, May 12, 1799, *PGW* (RS), 4:68. Washington to Archibald Blair, June 24, 1799, *PGW* (RS), 4:150, printed in the *South-Carolina State Gazette and Timothy's Daily Advertiser*, October 24, 1800. William R. Davie to James Iredell, June 17, 1799, McKee, ed., *Life and Correspondence of James Iredell*, 2:578. *South-Carolina State Gazette and Timothy's Daily Advertiser*, June 26, 1799.

50. Bruce, *John Randolph*, 1:147. Edward J. Johnston, "Jefferson—The Sage of Monticello," *New York Daily Times*, January 8, 1853.

51. Madison to George Hay, August 23, 1823, *PJM* (RS), 3:109. Jefferson to Madison, January 1, 1797, *PTJ*, 29:247. The "winner-take-all" approach, along with the fact that each state receives two electors corresponding to its senators, regardless of the state's population, largely explain why the winner of the popular vote may not win the Electoral College. The "senator" votes increase the political power of states with below-average populations, generally more rural states. In 1790, the Electoral College "senator" votes accounted for 38 percent of the votes; now that percentage is down to 19 percent, still significant.

52. Cunningham, "Election of 1800," 1:101–34, 105. Virginia had over 15 percent of the electoral vote; by comparison, California had just over 10 percent in the 2020 presidential election.

53. *Journal of the House of Delegates . . . One Thousand Seven Hundred and Ninety-nine*, January 17, 1800, 91. *Statutes at Large of Virginia from October Session 1792, to December Session 1806*, 2:197–200. James Barbour to Jefferson, January 20, 1800, *PTJ*, 31:325–26. *Virginia Argus*, January 21, 1800, quoted in Cunningham, *Jeffersonian Republicans*, 145; *City Gazette* (Charleston, SC), February 3, 1800.

54. *Debates and Proceedings in the Congress of the United States* (*Annals of Congress*), 14th Cong., 2nd Sess., January 1817, 2:799; see also Bruce, *John Randolph*, 1:147.

55. *Columbian Mirror and Alexandria Gazette,* October 18, 1800, quoting Henry, June 12, 1788, DHRC, 10:1217. *Jenks' Portland Gazette* (ME), November 17, 1800. Beeman, *Old Dominion,* 216. The issue was still sufficiently contested in the summer of 1800 that an anonymous essayist wrote two long articles seeking to defend the change. See "Vindication of the General Ticket," *Times and District of Columbia Daily Advertiser* (Alexandria, VA), July 21, 1800 (including a backhanded reference to Madison's Report of 1800), July 26, 1800.

56. With party affiliation still somewhat fluid, the precise count of Virginia's 1799 Federalists varies by source. See, e.g., the *Bee* (New London, CT), May 29, 1799 (news from Fredericksburg). Beeman, *Old Dominion,* 209, citing Manning Julian Dauer, *The Adams Federalists* (Baltimore: Johns Hopkins University Press, 1953), 316–21. Steven Thomson Mason to Madison, January 16, 1800, PJM (CS), 17:356. Also Charles Pinckney to Madison, September 30, 1799, PJM (CS), 17:273.

57. Many consider Henry to be the reason that North Carolina initially refused to ratify the Constitution. Beeman, *Old Dominion,* 13; Madison to Jefferson, August 23, 1788, PTJ, 13:539–40 (attributable in part to opposition in Virginia and the "management of its leader").

58. "To the Electors of Virginia," *Jenks' Portland Gazette,* November 17, 1800, reprinted *Washington Federalist,* December 5, 1800; *Philadelphia Gazette and Daily Advertiser,* December 12, 1800.

59. *Federal Republican* (Baltimore), September 15, 1809. Benjamin Rush to Jefferson, March 12, 1801, PTJ, 33:262.

60. Garland, *Life of John Randolph,* 133–34. Loring, *Nullification, Secession, Webster's Argument,* iv–v.

61. Beeman, *Old Dominion,* 81.

62. Onuf, *Thomas Jefferson and the Virginians,* 15.

63. Gutzman, *Virginia's American Revolution,* 112n163. Henry, "Patrick Henry: A Vindication," 352–53.

6. THE CRISIS DISSOLVES

1. Jefferson to Archibald Stuart, February 13, 1799, PTJ, 31:35. Jefferson to Edmund Pendleton, February 14, 1799, PTJ, 31:36–37.

2. Ellis, "Persistence of Antifederalism," 303. Akhil Reed Amar, *America's Unwritten Constitution: The Precedents and Principles We Live By* (New York: Basic Books, 2012), 169, quoted in Campbell, "Invention of First Amendment Federalism," 521. Koch and Ammon, "Virginia and Kentucky Resolutions," 167.

3. Campbell, "Invention of First Amendment Federalism," 521n10.

4. Sharp, *American Politics,* 223 citing Risjord, *Chesapeake Politics,* 546–47; Beeman, *Old Dominion,* 204–11; Lisle Abbott Rose, *Prologue to Democracy: The Federalists in the South, 1789–1800* (Lexington: University of Kentucky

Press, 1968), 220–28; Editors' note, Alexander Hamilton to Jonathan Day-ton, October-November 1799, *Founders Online,* https://founders.archives.gov /documents/Hamilton/01-23-02-0526. Bell, *Party and Faction,* 58 ("The Vir-ginia and Kentucky Resolutions alarmed southwesterners, who turned to the Federalist party in large numbers"); Risjord, "Virginia Federalists," 503 (Vir-ginia House of Delegates). Wehtje, "Congressional Elections," 270 ("startled and unsettled"). *Virginia Gazette,* May 17, 1799. See *Commercial Advertiser* (New York) May 16, 1799 (from *Virginia Gazette*). Malone, *Jefferson and the Ordeal of Liberty,* 416 ("disunionist"). Later, some Federalists elected in 1798 switched affiliation to Democratic-Republican as Jeffersonians achieved he-gemony over southern politics. Risjord, "Virginia Federalists," 503n33. Some have sought to twist this debacle into a Jeffersonian triumph because results could have been worse. See Anderson, "Contemporary Opinion . . . II," 241: "The result of the elections in 1799 was a decided triumph for the Republi-cans, the slight gain made by the Federalists being not at all commensurate with the exertions which they put forth."

5. Wehtje, "Congressional Elections," 271, quoting Joseph C. Cabell to David Watson, "Letters to David Watson," *Virginia Magazine of History and Biog-raphy* 29 (July 1921): 263–64. Hartnett and Mercieca, "'Has Your Courage Rusted?'" 101, quoting Jeffrey Pasley, *"The Tyranny of Printers": Newspaper Politics in the Early American Republic* (Charlottesville: University of Virginia Press, 2001), 127 ("Jefferson's Resolutions 'were a political disaster that came closer to justifying and saving the Alien and Sedition Acts than stopping them'"). Halperin, *Alien and Sedition Acts,* 100 ("The resolutions generated a backlash against the Democratic-Republican cause"). Risjord, "Virginia Fed-eralists," 504 (success of Federalists "suggest also that the famous resolutions of 1798 had little immediate propaganda value, even in Virginia"). Wehtje, "Congressional Elections," 273.

6. Pendleton, *Address of the Honorable Edmund Pendleton,* 20 (emphasis added). Jefferson to Monroe, March 7, 1801, *PTJ,* 33:208.

7. Halperin, *Alien and Sedition Acts,* 108, 99. Hartnett and Mercieca, "'Has Your Courage Rusted?'" 102. Compare May, *Jefferson's Treasure,* 88 (footnote omit-ted) ("Prosecutions of several Republican newspaper editors under the Se-dition Act . . . provoked relatively little popular outcry, but they did cement the commitment of Republican partisans"). Jefferson to Archibald Stuart, May 14, 1799, *PTJ,* 31:110.

8. John Marshall to Joseph Story, July 31, 1833, Hobson, ed., *Papers of John Mar-shall,* 12:291. Broadwater, *Jefferson, Madison,* 204.

9. Loring, *Nullification, Secession, Webster's Argument,* 100. Anderson, "Contem-porary Opinion . . . II," 247. Anderson, "Contemporary Opinion . . . I," 51. *Virginia and Kentucky Resolutions of 1798 and 1799,* 9, 10, 14. E.g., *Gazette of*

the United States (Philadelphia), January 3, 1799 ("highly *improper*" "unwarranted"); *Virginia Gazette and Daily Advertiser* (Richmond), January 8, 1799; *Connecticut Gazette,* January 9, 1799.

10. See Bird, *Criminal Dissent,* 172 (repeal of Alien and Sedition Acts was "the grand issue"). Anderson, "Contemporary Opinion . . . I," 47 (MD). Bird suggests that when one house of a state legislature affirmatively rejected the Resolutions and the other house refused to consider them (as in Pennsylvania and New Jersey), that the state was split. But a refusal even to consider the appeal from Kentucky and Virginia is effectively a rejection. Compare *Commercial Advertiser* (New York), January 24, 1799 (New Jersey legislature felt "it would best express the abhorrence felt on the occasion, to dismiss them [Resolutions] from the files of the House"). Bird also reports that the New Jersey General Assembly opposition to Virginia and Kentucky was only decided by the speaker after a tie vote, but this is only true in the case of the milder Virginia Resolutions and, even in that case, legislators later switched votes to show stronger opposition to the Resolutions. Bird, *Criminal Dissent,* 175–76.

11. *Journals of the Senate and the House of the Second General Assembly of the State of Tennessee,* 355–56, 468–71. Bird, "Reassessing Responses," 534, quoting *Journal of the [Georgia] Senate* (November 22, 1799), 19. Bird, *Criminal Dissent,* 170.

12. Vermont, Anderson, "Contemporary Opinion . . . II," 233, quoting *Records of the Governor and Council of the State of Vermont,* 4:526–29. *Virginia and Kentucky Resolutions of 1798 and 1799,* 10. *Virginia and Kentucky Resolutions of 1798 and 1799,* 11 (MA).

13. *Virginia and Kentucky Resolutions of 1798 and 1799,* 9 (RI), 10 (MA), 13 (NY), 14 (NH), 15 (VT). Anderson, "Contemporary Opinion . . . I," 47 (MD), 51 (PA). Elliot, ed., *Debates in the Several State Conventions,* 4:539, quoted Watkins, *Reclaiming,* 75. "Replies of Vermont," 527. See also, e.g., *Farmer's Weekly Museum* (NH), March 25, 1799 (reporting on New Hampshire resolutions on judicial review).

Beeman seeks to minimize Jefferson's call for "nullification" by claiming that, unlike when John Calhoun resurrected nullification in the 1820s in the lead-up to the Civil War, in 1798, the Supreme Court "had not yet asserted its authority as final arbiter of the constitutionality of federal statutes." Beeman, *Old Dominion,* 200. In fact, judicial review was a well-established concept in 1798 (as seven states noted in their responses). By 1796, the Supreme Court had issued its decision in *Ware v. Hylton* overruling a state law that interfered with a federal treaty. 3 U.S. (3 Dall.) 199 (1796). See also Leonard and Cornell, *Partisan Republic,* 24. Beeman makes an equally weak argument that, absent precedent, it was not unreasonable to conclude that the power to review federal laws lay with the states, citing the Articles of Confederation "upon which the Constitution was based." Beeman, *Old Dominion*, 200. But the dramatic expansion of federal power in the Constitution and concomitant reduction in states' authority from the Confederation was one point on which everyone in the 1790s would agree.

14. Halperin, *Alien and Sedition Acts*, 107 (footnote omitted).

15. *Commercial Advertiser* (New York), July 4, 1799; *Spectator* (New York), July 6, 1799; *Philadelphia Gazette and Universal Daily Advertiser*, July 6, 1799; *Claypoole's American Daily Advertiser* (Philadelphia), July 8, 1799; *Albany Centinel*, July 9, 1799; *Albany Gazette*, July 12, 1799; *South-Carolina State Gazette and Timothy's Daily Advertiser*, July 25, 1799.

16. *Gazette of the United States* (Philadelphia), December 8, 1798; *Federal Gazette* (Baltimore), December 12, 1798; *Daily Advertiser* (New York), December 13, 1798; *Spectator* (New York), December 15, 1798; *Albany Centinel*, December 18, 1798; *Connecticut Courant*, December 24, 1798; *Connecticut Gazette*, December 26, 1798; *Hampshire Gazette* (MA), December 26, 1798; *Norwich Courier* (CT), December 27, 1798; *Otsego Herald* (NY), December 27, 1798; *Windham Herald* (CT), December 27, 1798; *Courier of New Hampshire*, January 12, 1799. See also *Porcupine's Gazette* (Philadelphia), December 12, 1798 (France seeking Kentucky's revolt). See Fritz, "Interposition and the Heresy of Nullification."

17. Madison to Jefferson, December 29, 1798, *PTJ*, 30:605.

18. Ibid. John Taylor had earlier made a similar argument to Jefferson but the point seemed to be ignored in Jefferson's drafting. John Taylor to Jefferson, June 25, 1798, *PTJ*, 30:434: "the people in state conventions, are incontrovertibly the contracting parties."

19. Madison to James Robertson, March 27, 1831, *Founders Online* (early access), https://founders.archives.gov/documents/Madison/99-02-02-2310.

20. Madison's Report, 6. See *Virginia and Kentucky Resolutions of 1798 and 1799*, 11 (MA) "state government"; 14 (NY) "legislatures of . . . states"; 14 (NH) "State legislature"; 15 (VT) "State legislatures"; Anderson, "Contemporary Opinion . . . II," 247 (CT) "Legislatures of the several states"; 248 (MD) "state government"; 245 (PA) "Legislatures of the several states." Rhode Island understood the same (*Virginia and Kentucky Resolutions of 1798 and 1799*, 9), noting that if a "state" party to the compact had authority to decide on the consistency of federal action, it would mix legislative and judicial authority. Rakove, *James Madison and the Creation*, 153 (Madison's letter of December 29, 1798, received January 5, 1799).

A number of historians accept Madison's post hoc redefinition. Compare Steele, *Thomas Jefferson and American Nationalism*, 257 ("state" left issue unresolved); Fritz, "Constitutional Middle-Ground," 160; Jaffa, *Conditions of*

Freedom, 175. Anderson criticizes Henry Lee by arguing that he "treated the term *states* in the resolution as if it was synonymous with the term *state governments,* whereas in the resolutions the term *states* means the people of each state." Anderson, "Contemporary Opinion . . . II," 240. Douglas Bradburn also seems to accept Madison's post hoc rationalization in an effort to deflect blame from Jefferson and Madison for the later use of the compact theory to defend slavery. "However later proponents of states' rights might change their concerns, the original proponents of the idea of the sovereignty of states grounded their arguments in the principles of popular constitutionalism, popular sovereignty, equality, and natural rights embodied in the most revolutionary sentiment of American Independence." Bradburn, "Clamor in the Public Mind," 596. But the Resolutions clearly relied on the authority of the state governments; the people's sovereignty was not at issue, although it later became a hallmark of Madison's 1800 Report in response to the other states' rejection of the Resolutions (discussed below).

21. *Massachusetts Mercury,* February 19, 1799 (Federalist House member). Powell, "Principles of '98," 718n117 ("virtually to eliminate"). See also Steele, *Thomas Jefferson and American Nationalism,* 226 ("No one in American politics denied the fundamental sovereignty of the people").

22. Koch and Ammon, "Virginia and Kentucky Resolutions," 168. Halperin, *Alien and Sedition Acts,* 115–16, citing John Breckinridge to Jefferson, December 13, 1799, *PTJ,* 31:266. Jefferson to Madison, August 23, 1799, *PTJ,* 31:173. *Gazette of the United States* (Philadelphia), March 28, 1799 (from *Virginia Gazette*) (Giles: "I am clearly for a separation, and hope it will take place"). See also Gutzman, "Troublesome Legacy," 580–81: "Pennsylvania's legislature decried them [the Virginia Resolutions] as part of a move toward disunion, and with good reason: John Taylor of Caroline, their sponsor in the House of Delegates, was privately advocating precisely such a move. William Branch Giles, who guided them through the Virginia Senate, avowed his secessionism publicly." Madison to Jefferson, August 28, 1799. This letter has not been found, but Madison's objections are made clear in Jefferson's September 5, 1799, letter to Wilson Cary Nicholas, *PTJ,* 31:178–79. What else was included in the letter is a mystery. Compare Steele, *Thomas Jefferson and American Nationalism,* 240 (Kentucky and Virginia Resolutions never "even broached" secession).

23. Jefferson to Wilson Cary Nicholas, September 5, 1799, *PTJ,* 31:179.

24. Ibid.

25. When historians refer to the Kentucky Resolutions, they are almost always referring to the 1798 resolutions. Herein, those Resolutions are capitalized throughout. The 1799 resolutions from Kentucky will not be capitalized. Virginia's response—"Report of the Committee to whom was committed the proceedings of sundry of the other States, in answer to the Resolutions of

the General Assembly" (1800), *PJM* (CS), 17:303 *et seq.*—is sometimes referred to as Madison's Report on the Virginia Resolutions, sometimes Virginia's Report of 1799, and sometimes Virginia's Report of 1800. Herein it is generally referred to as Madison's Report.

26. Kentucky resolutions of 1799 (December 3, 1799), quoted in Halperin, *Alien and Sedition Acts,* 116. John Breckinridge to Jefferson, December 13, 1799, *PTJ,* 31:266. Kenneth Stampp notes that as sectional battles over slavery erupted in the 1820s, the language of the 1798 Resolutions was increasingly used: "By the end of the 1820s, . . . the language of state sovereignty had become deeply embedded in the American vocabulary. Almost everyone spoke of the Union as 'our confederacy,' of the Constitution as a 'compact.'" Stampp, "Concept of a Perpetual Union," 28.

27. See Powell, "Principles of '98," 720 (1799 report suggests "states collectively" act).

28. Jaffa, *Conditions of Freedom,* 178.

29. Addison, *Analysis of the Report.* Gutzman, "Troublesome Legacy," 583 (Report of 1800 included "a touch of obfuscation"). Fritz, "Constitutional Middle-Ground," 201–2, citing Madison to Edward Everett, August 20 and 28, 1830, *Founders Online* (early access), https://founders.archives .gov/documents/Madison/99-02-02-2131 and https://founders.archives.gov /documents/Madison/99-02-02-2137 ("never claimed").

30. *Virginia and Kentucky Resolutions of 1798 and 1799,* 22. Madison's Report, *PJM* (CS), 17:309, 348. Madison would reiterate this argument in the 1830s. See Madison to James Robertson, March 27, 1831, *Founders Online* (early access), https://founders.archives.gov/documents/Madison/99-02-02-2310.

31. Madison's Report, *PJM* (CS), 17:309, 311.

32. McCoy, *Last of the Fathers,* 146 (footnote omitted).

33. Address of the Minority in the Virginia Legislature, 2, 5–6. Some have questioned Marshall's authorship of the minority report in 1799, but arguments for his authorship are strong. His role, however, was kept secret as, had it come to light, it would "have cost him his campaign for federal office." See Lash and Harrison, "Minority Report," 440.

34. Madison to Jefferson, February 8, 1825, *Founders Online,* https://founders .archives.gov/documents/Madison/04-03-02-0470. Meeting Minutes of University of Virginia Board of Visitors, March 4, 1825, *Founders Online* (early access), https://founders.archives.gov/documents/Jefferson/98-01-02-5019.

35. Jefferson to Edmund Pendleton, February 14, 1799, *PTJ,* 31:37.

36. William Heth to Alexander Hamilton, January 18, 1799, *Founders Online,* https://founders.archives.gov/documents/Hamilton/01-22-02-0240 (footnotes omitted) ("Martyrs").

37. *Richmond Examiner,* May 27, 1800; *Times and District of Columbia Daily Advertiser* (Alexandria, VA), May 31, 1800; *Political Mirror* (Staunton, VA), June 3, 1800; *American Citizen* (New York), June 4, 1800; *Republican Watch-Tower* (New York), June 7, 1800; *Albany Register,* June 10, 1800; *Constitutional Telegraph* (Boston), June 21, 1800.

38. James Monroe to Jefferson, January 4, 1800, *PTJ,* 31:290; Madison to James Monroe, May 23, 1800, *PJM* (CS), 17:390.

39. *Herald of Liberty* (Washington, PA), May 5, 1800 (from *Aurora*); *Stewart Kentucky Herald,* May 27, 1800 (from *Aurora*). *Republican Watch-Tower* (New York), April 23, 1800.

40. See Bird, *Criminal Dissent,* 167.

41. Jefferson to Edmund Pendleton, February 14, 1799, *PTJ,* 31:36–37 (footnote omitted). *Columbian Museum* (Savannah, GA), June 4, 1799 (reprinting letter from Petersburg). Bird, *Criminal Dissent,* 214 ("disaster for the Federalists").

42. *Aurora General Advertiser* (Philadelphia), March 8, 1799; *Independent Chronicle* (Boston), March 21, 1799; *Vermont Gazette* (Bennington), March 21, 1799.

43. See Callender, *Prospect before Us,* 1:46 (attack on Jay's Treaty), 1:83 (Adams squinting to monarchy about which Henry warned), 1:175 (Adams's actions what Henry warned about), 2:56 (Henry identified flaws in the Constitution), 2:125 (attack on bank notes). Jefferson to James Thomson Callender, October 6, 1799, *PTJ,* 31:201.

44. Henry to Timothy Pickering, Secretary of State, April 16, 1799, Henry, *Henry,* I2:623–24. *Claypoole's American Daily Advertiser* (Philadelphia), December 11, 1799; *Universal Gazette* (Philadelphia), December 12, 1799; *Constitutional Diary and Philadelphia Evening Advertiser,* December 13, 1799; *Commercial Advertiser* (New York), December 13, 1799; *Spectator* (New York), December 14, 1799; *Mercantile Advertiser* (New York), December 14, 1799; *American Mercury* (Hartford, CT), December 19, 1799; *Columbian Centinel* (Boston), December 21, 1799; *Political Repository* (Brookfield, MA), December 24, 1799; *Providence Journal,* December 25, 1799; *Providence Gazette,* December 28, 1799; *New-Hampshire Gazette,* January 1, 1800; *Norwich Courier* (CT), January 1, 1800. Fontaine, *Patrick Henry: Corrections,* 22.

45. *City Gazette* (Charleston, SC), August 18, 1800, reprinted *Carolina Gazette,* August 21, 1800; *Times and District of Columbia Daily Advertiser,* September 2, 1800. Perhaps in response, the local Federalist newspaper reprinted Washington's June 1799 letter to Archibald Blair lamenting Henry's death and suggested that people (read Jeffersonians) were "sowing the seeds of distrust" between Washington and Henry. *Carolina Gazette,* August 21, 1800; *South-Carolina State Gazette and Timothy's Daily Advertiser,* October 24, 1800.

46. Jefferson to Madison, January 30, 1799, *PTJ*, 30:666. See also Jefferson to Thomas Mann Randolph, January 30, 1799, *PTJ*, 30:668. Jefferson to Elbridge Gerry, January 26, 1799, *PTJ*, 30:649 (footnote omitted).

47. Jefferson to Madison, September 6, 1789, *PTJ*, 15:392 ("the earth belongs to the living"; "The earth belongs always to the living generation"; "the earth belongs in usufruct to the living"). Also Jefferson to John Wayles Eppes, June 24, 1813, *PTJ* (RS), 6:220. Jefferson to Henry Tompkinson (Samuel Kerchival), July 12, 1816, *PTJ* (RS), 10:226.

48. Jefferson to Spencer Roane, September 6, 1819, *PTJ* (RS), 15:16. Wirt, *Sketches*, 275. See also Taylor, *Thomas Jefferson's Education*, 65 (Jefferson also saw the election as "vindicating his character besmirched by the wartime crisis of 1781" and the attack on his character that he blamed on Henry). Simon, *What Kind of Nation*, 52–53, 57–62.

49. Powell, "Principles of '98," 694.

50. Steele, *Thomas Jefferson and American Nationalism*, 191–92. First Inaugural Address, March 4, 1801, *PTJ*, 33:149. Onuf, *Thomas Jefferson and the Virginians*, 77.

51. Jefferson to Madison, August 23, 1799, *PTJ*, 31:174. Peterson, *Jefferson Image*, 62.

52. On claims of Jefferson's hypocrisy, see, e.g., Freeman and Neem, eds., *Jeffersonians in Power*, 2, and materials cited therein, and Peterson, *Jefferson Image*, 59–60.

53. After the debacle of the 1800 electoral tie, the Twelfth Amendment was promptly adopted (1804) requiring electors to specify votes for president and vice president separately.

54. Alexander Hamilton to Gouverneur Morris, January 13, 1801, *Founders Online*, https://founders.archives.gov/documents/Hamilton/01-25-02-0165. Alexander Hamilton to James Bayard, January 16, 1801, *Founders Online*, https://founders.archives.gov/documents/Hamilton/01-25-02-0169. Jefferson to Madison, February 18, 1801, *PTJ*, 33:16.

55. Jefferson, "Notes on Aaron Burr," April 15, 1806, *Founders Online* (early access), https://founders.archives.gov/documents/Jefferson/99-01-02-3574. Samuel Tyler to James Monroe, February 11, 1801, "Original Letters," 104. Thomas McKean to Jefferson, March 21, 1801, *PTJ*, 33:391; Jefferson to Joseph Priestley, March 21, 1801, *PTJ*, 33:394.

56. Steele, *Thomas Jefferson and American Nationalism*, 190–91 ("actually strengthened"). See Larson, *Magnificent Catastrophe*; Dunn, *Jefferson's Second Revolution*; Ferling, *Adams vs. Jefferson*; Weisberger, *America Afire*; Sharp, *Deadlocked Election of 1800*; Freeman and Neem, eds., *Jeffersonians in Power*.

57. Steele, *Thomas Jefferson and American Nationalism*. Hoffer, *Free Press Crisis of 1800*, 54.

58. Jefferson to Madison, February 18, 1801, *PTJ*, 33:16 ("after seeing the impossibility of electing B[urr]. the certainty that a legislative usurpation would be resisted by arms, and a recourse to a Convention to reorganise & amend the government" if some legislative mechanism was used, "the whole body of Federalists, who being alarmed with the danger of a dissolution of the government" came to support the electoral victory). Benjamin Rush to Jefferson, March 12, 1801, *PTJ*, 33:262; Jefferson to Joseph Priestley, March 21, 1801, *PTJ*, 33:394 ("momentous crisis which lately arose"). Onuf, *Thomas Jefferson and the Virginians*, 19–20 ("as Americans stood").

59. Jefferson to Colonel Benjamin Hawkins, February 18, 1803, *PTJ*, 39:546.

60. Jefferson to John Adams, June 15, 1813, *PTJ* (RS), 6:193. John Adams to Jefferson, June 30, 1813, *PTJ* (RS), 6:254–55. Freeman, "Election of 1800," 1963.

61. Jefferson, First Inaugural Address, March 4, 1801, *PTJ*, 33:149.

62. Jefferson to Monroe, March 7, 1801, *PTJ*, 33:208 (footnote omitted). John Marshall to Charles Cotesworth Pinckney, March 4, 1801, Hobson, ed., *Papers of John Marshall*, 11:89–90. Benjamin Rush to Jefferson, March 12, 1801, *PTJ*, 33:261.

63. First Inaugural Address, March 4, 1801, *PTJ*, 33:149, unless otherwise noted. Onuf, *Thomas Jefferson and the Virginians*, 19 (footnote omitted): "he implicitly endorsed the prudential concerns of Federalists, who 'felt and feared' being sucked into the vortex of the Old World's wars."

64. First Inaugural Address, March 4, 1801, *PTJ*, 33:149, unless otherwise noted. Jefferson to Joseph Priestley, March 21, 1801, *PTJ*, 33:394. Interestingly, Judge John Tyler later wrote that Henry had earlier said, "Men might differ in ways and means, and not in principles." Judge John Tyler to William Wirt, in Henry, *Henry*, 2:622.

65. Jefferson wrote to one correspondent that after the election of 1800 "five sixths" of the people became "of one sentiment. . . . I think it will not be long before the whole nation will be consolidated in their antient principles, excepting a few who have committed themselves beyond recall, and who will retire to obscurity & settled disaffection." Jefferson to Benjamin Hawkins, February 18, 1803, *PTJ*, 39:546–47 (footnote omitted). See also Sehat, *Jefferson Rule*, 30–31, 37.

66. Freeman, "Election of 1800," 1989. First Inaugural Address, March 4, 1801, *PTJ*, 33:149.

67. Risjord, *Old Republicans*, 24, 37–38 (footnote omitted), quoting John Taylor to Wilson Cary Nicholas, September 16, 1802; and John Taylor to Wilson Cary Nicholas, June 10, 1806. Edmund Pendleton, *Danger Not Over* (1801), in Mays, ed., *Letters and Papers of Edmund Pendleton*, 2:695. See Ellis, *Jeffersonian Crisis*, 78–84, 84.

68. Jefferson to Spencer Roane, September 6, 1819, *PTJ* (RS), 15:16.

69. See, e.g., Horn, Taylor, and Onuf, eds., *Revolution of 1800*.

70. On voter turnout, see Leonard and Cornell, *Partisan Republic*, 79.

71. See, e.g., Gary Wills, *Negro President: Jefferson and the Slave Power* (New York: Houghton Mifflin, 2003).

72. See generally Bell, *Party and Faction*, 22. The issue of states' rights had come up in Georgia's protests against the federal government's New York Treaty with the Creeks but was not actively discussed in the context of 1798. Horsman, *Expansion*, 72, 81. On Native land claims generally, see issues surrounding *Worcester v. Georgia*, 31 U.S. 515 (1832), and, e.g., Lindsay G. Robertson, *Conquest by Law: How the Discovery of America Dispossessed Indigenous People of Their Land* (New York: Oxford University Press, 2005); Stuart Banner, *How the Indians Lost Their Land: Law and Power on the Frontier* (Cambridge, MA: Belknap Press, 2005).

73. Steele, "Thomas Jefferson, Coercion," 832, quoting *Anas*, February 4, 1818. O'Shaughnessy, *Illimitable Freedom*, 107.

74. Jefferson to Madison, December 24, 1825, *Founders Online*, https://founders .archives.gov/documents/Madison/04-03-02-0679.

75. Madison to Jefferson, December 28, 1825, *Founders Online*, https://founders .archives.gov/documents/Madison/04-03-02-0681. See, e.g., Wood, *Friends Divided*, 418–19 ("His friend Madison talked him out of submitting this extraordinary document, arguing that Virginia ought not any longer be taking leadership 'in opposing the obnoxious career of Congress, or, rather of their Constituents'").

76. Madison to Thomas Ritchie, December 18, 1825, *Founders Online*, https:// founders.archives.gov/documents/Madison/04-03-02-0677. Jefferson to Madison, January 2, 1826, *Founders Online*, https://founders.archives.gov /documents/Madison/04-03-02-0683.

77. Weisberger, *America Afire*, 223, quoting Burr from John Chester Miller, *Crisis in Freedom: The Alien and Sedition Acts* (Boston: Little, Brown, 1951), 179. On use of Jefferson and Madison in antebellum period, see, e.g., Sehat, *Jefferson Rule*, 81.

78. Anderson, "Contemporary Opinion . . . II," 237. Weisberger, *America Afire*, 223.

79. *Virginia and Kentucky Resolutions of 1798 and 1799* (RI), 10. See also Anderson, "Contemporary Opinion . . . II," 240. See above, chapter 4, note 69. Henry, "Patrick Henry: A Vindication," 353. Bird insists that the "Principles of '98" were "misused by advocates of nullification, slavery, and segregation," Bird, *Criminal Dissent*, 165 (footnote omitted), but as people saw at the time, this was their natural consequence.
    Nullification theory surfaced on several other occasions before the nullification crisis and the Civil War, e.g., in the Hartford Convention and Olmstead case, but it was always viewed as marginal and got little traction. When New Englanders opposed Jefferson's embargo "there was no declaration that the

embargo was 'void, and of no force' within the state's boundaries." Read and Allen, "Living, Dead, and Undead," 108. See also Samuelson, "Constitutional Statesmanship," 262: "the Hartford Convention, with its hints of secession, destroyed the Federalist Party." When Pennsylvania threatened to prevent enforcement of the Supreme Court's decision in *U.S. v. Peters* based on a compact theory, President Madison threatened to have state officials arrested, and a militia officer was prosecuted. See Treacy, "Olmstead Case, 1778–1809"; Douglas, "Interposition and the Peters Case." Jefferson supported that decision. Jefferson to Madison, May 22, 1809, *PTJ* (RS), 1:213.

80. Jaffa, *Conditions of Freedom*, 161–62 (Lincoln). Onuf, *Jefferson's Empire*, 144 ("even as"). See also Gienapp, "How to Maintain," 54 ("nullifiers and secessionists explicitly invoked the resolutions as inspiration and justification").

EPILOGUE

1. Patrick Henry's "Give me liberty" speech, Ragosta, *Patrick Henry*, 189.
2. John Marshall to Joseph Story, July 31, 1833, Hobson, ed., *Papers of John Marshall*, 12:291. The 1852 and 1856 Democratic Party Platform, American Presidency Project (ucsb.edu). Peterson, *Jefferson Image*, 39, 53–56.
3. Henry, *Henry*, 2:622. Tyler, *Letters and Times of the Tylers*, 183. Spencer Roane's Memorandum of Patrick Henry to William Wirt (1805) in *Patrick Henry in His Speeches and Writings*, 37.
4. John Taylor to Madison, March 4, 1799, *PJM* (CS), 17:245.
5. Compare *Aurora General Advertiser* (Philadelphia), February 27, 1799, March 8, 1799, May 27, 1799 ("the venerable"), reprinted *Vermont Gazette*, June 6, 1799. Further reprinting of this particularly nasty attack may have been arrested only by Henry's death.
6. Edward W. Johnston, "Jefferson—The Sage of Monticello," *New York Daily Times*, January 8, 1853. Jefferson to James Monroe, May 20, 1782, *PTJ*, 6:185, 187.

   When Jefferson's beloved University of Virginia opened, the first student organization formed was the Patrick Henry Debating/Literary Society. The Patrick Henry Society, though, was soon replaced by the Jefferson Society, formed a year before Jefferson's own death (and today the longest continuous student literary/debating organization in the country). Howard and Gallogly, *Society Ties*, 5–6. One might well wonder whether Jefferson, directly or indirectly, had some influence on the demise of the earlier organization honoring Henry.
7. E.g., Henry, "Patrick Henry: A Vindication," 346 *et seq.*, discussing the allegations exhaustively. Also Longacre and Herring, *National Portrait Gallery*, 2, "Patrick Henry," 5: "During the gloomiest period of the conflict for independence, a project was twice started to create a dictation, and whilst the most

satisfactory evidence exists that Mr. Henry had no participation in it, it is highly honorable to him, that the drooping spirits of his countrymen were turned to him as the safest depository of uncontrolled authority." In fact, when Henry's third term as governor was closing in 1779, some effort was made to enlist him for a fourth, in violation of Virginia's constitution (with proponents arguing that his first appointment was made by the convention that framed the constitution of 1776 rather than by the new legislature, thus not counting to the three-term limit). "He prevented this attempt by writing to the Speaker of the House of Delegates . . . that the constitution made him ineligible for office and he intended to retire." Meade, *Practical Revolutionary*, 219. Wirt, *Sketches*, 149.

8. See Ragosta, *Patrick Henry*, 69–71.

9. Morgan, *American Heroes*, 194.

10. Van Buren, *Inquiry into the Origin and Course of Political Parties*, 180.

11. Pollard, "Historical Doubts Concerning Patrick Henry," 327 *et seq.*

12. On the Jefferson-Henry feud generally, see, e.g., Ragosta, *Patrick Henry*, 67–69; Ragosta, "Founding Rivals," 22–23. *Vermont Mirror* (Middlebury), August 23, 1815; *American Magazine* (Albany) (1815), 402. Cummins, "Patrick Henry," 10:1:316. Perhaps demonstrating the point, the article in the *Edinburgh Encyclopaedia* has a number of significant biographical errors concerning Henry. Henry, *Henry*, 2:166.

13. Jefferson to Madison, April 26, 1798, *PTJ*, 30:300. Jefferson to Adamantios Coray, October 31, 1823, *Founders Online* (early access), https://founders.archives.gov/documents/Jefferson/98-01-02-3837. First Inaugural Address, March 4, 1801, *PTJ*, 33:149.

14. Beeman, "Democratic Faith," 316.

15. Jefferson to John Gassaway, February 9, 1809, *Founders Online* (early access), https://founders.archives.gov/documents/Jefferson/99-01-02-9817.

16. Madison, August 15, 1789, "Amendments to the Constitution," *PJM*, 12:341. Farewell Address, September 19, 1796, *PGW* (PS), 20:708–9.

17. E.g., Sharp, *American Politics*, 274.

18. Watkins, *Reclaiming*, 81, quoting *Summary View of the Rights of British North America* (1774).

19. Marshall made the same point during ratification when antifederalists sought to rely on the Spirit of '76: "We *were not* represented in Parliament. Here we are represented. Arguments which prove the impropriety of being taxed by Britain, do not hold against the exercise of taxation by Congress." John Marshall, June 10, 1788, *DHRC*, 9:1118. See also Ragosta, "What Would Patrick Henry Say?"

20. Thompson, "A Talk with Jefferson," 835 (Jefferson: "Henry was, at the time, even more determined in his opposition to slavery than the rest of us"). (This

source must be read with care. It reports on an 1822 conversation and the essay was clearly intended as a wartime response to Confederate efforts to show that slavery was embraced by Jefferson and other founders.) For Henry's views on slavery, see Ragosta, *Patrick Henry*, 37–39. See also Henry to Robert Pleasants, January 18, 1773, Henry, *Henry*, 1:152 (this important letter is often miscited as being to Anthony Benezet or miscited as a speech to the Virginia House of Burgesses on January 18, 1773). See also Samuel Allinson to Henry, October 17, 1774, in Gerlach, ed., *New Jersey in the American Revolution*, 87–89. Notably, most sources, including my biography of Henry, note that he enslaved sixty-seven individuals upon his death. In fact, the true figure is apparently considerably larger, at ninety-eight, with the sixty-seven only accounting for those enslaved on his Red Hill plantation, with others enslaved on other plantations that he owned.

21. McGarvie, "Disestablishing Religion," 77. See also Bouton, *Taming Democracy*, 74; Beeman, "Democratic Faith of Patrick Henry," 303, 305 (movement "toward a society in which values of the individual, of individual liberty, and of liberalism were much more prominently stressed") (footnote omitted).

22. Compare Sharp, *American Politics*, 285.

23. Describing this transition for Washington, Joseph Ellis writes of 1799, "At some level he [George Washington] recognized that political parties were transforming the shape of national politics, making character as he understood it irrelevant, even a liability. The new ground rules, soon to triumph in the new century, struck him as both alien and awful, a world in which he had no place." Ellis, *His Excellency: George Washington*, 267. On Henry's republicanism generally, see Beeman, "Democratic Faith of Patrick Henry."

24. Buckley, "Patrick Henry, Religious Liberty," 139.

· BIBLIOGRAPHY ·

PRIMARY SOURCES

Addison, Alexander. *Analysis of the Report of the Committee of the Virginia Assembly.* Philadelphia: Poulson, 1800.

Address of the Minority in the Virginia Legislature to the People of the State. Albany: Andrews, 1799.

Anderson, Frank Maloy. "Contemporary Opinion of the Virginia and Kentucky Resolutions I." *American Historical Review* 5:1 (October 1899): 49–63.

———. "Contemporary Opinion of the Virginia and Kentucky Resolutions II." *American Historical Review* 5:2 (December 1899): 225–52.

Ballagh, James Curtis, ed. *The Letters of Richard Henry Lee.* 2 vols. New York: Macmillan, 1914.

Callender, James. *The Prospect before Us.* Richmond, 1800.

Curtis, George Ticknor. *Life of Daniel Webster.* Vol. 1. New York: D. Appleton, 1889.

Debates and Proceedings in the Congress of the United States ("Annals of Congress"). 1st Cong., 1st Sess. (1789); 4th Cong., 1st Sess. (1796); 5th Cong., 2nd Sess. (1798); 14th Cong., 2nd Sess. (1817).

Denboer, Gordon R., et al., eds. *The Documentary History of the First Federal Election.* 4 vols. Madison: University of Wisconsin Press, 1984.

Elliot, Jonathan, ed. *Debates in the Several State Conventions on Adoption of the Federal Constitution.* 5 vols. Philadelphia: J. B. Lippincott, 1861.

Farrand, Max, ed. *The Records of the Federal Convention of 1787.* 4 vols. Reprint. New Haven: Yale University Press, 1966.

Ford, Worthington Chauncey, ed. *Writings of John Quincy Adams.* 7 vols. New York: Macmillan, 1913–17.

Ford, Worthington Chauncey, et al., eds. *Journals of the Continental Congress.* 34 vols. Washington DC: U.S. Government Printing Office, 1904–37.

Gerlach, Larry R., ed. *New Jersey in the American Revolution: A Documentary History.* Trenton: New Jersey Historical Commission, 1975.

Hening, William Waller, ed. *The Statutes at Large, Being a Collection of All of the Laws of Virginia.* 13 vols. Richmond: George Cochran, 1822.

Henry, William Wirt. *Patrick Henry: Life, Correspondence, and Speeches.* 3 vols. New York: Charles Scribner's Sons, 1891.

Hobson, Charles F., ed. *The Papers of John Marshall.* Vols. 11 and 12. Chapel Hill: University of North Carolina Press, 2014.

Journal of the House of Delegates of the Commonwealth of Virginia, Begun and Held in the City of Richmond, on Monday, the Third Day of May, in the Year of Our Lord Seventeen Hundred and Eighty-four. Richmond: Thomas W. White, 1828.

Journal of the House of Delegates of the Commonwealth of Virginia, Begun and Held at the Capitol in the City of Richmond on Monday, the Eighteenth of October, in the Year of Our Lord One Thousand Seven Hundred and Ninety. Early American Imprints, Series 1, no. 23944.

Journal of the House of Delegates of the Commonwealth of Virginia, Begun and Held at the Capitol in the City of Richmond, on Monday the Second Day of December, One Thousand Seven Hundred and Ninety-nine. Richmond: Meriwether Jones, 1799 [1800].

Journal of the Senate of the Commonwealth of Virginia, Begun and Held in the City of Richmond, on Monday, the Eighteenth Day of October, in the Year of Our Lord 1790. Richmond: Thomas W. White, 1828.

Journals of the Senate and the House of the Second General Assembly of the State of Tennessee held at Knoxville. Kingsport, TN: Southern Publishers, 1933.

Kennedy, John Pendleton, ed. *Journals of the House of Burgesses of Virginia, 1761–1765.* Richmond, 1907.

Kurland, Philip B., and Ralph Lerner, eds. *The Founders' Constitution.* 5 vols. Chicago: University of Chicago Press, 1987.

Lee, Henry. *Memoirs of the War in the Southern Department of the United States.* Washington, DC: Peter Force, 1827.

———. "Plain Truth: Addressed to the People of Virginia." Richmond, 1799.

Letter from George Nicholas of Kentucky to His Friend in Virginia. Lexington: John Bradford, 1798.

Madison, James. *Notes of Debates in the Federal Convention of 1787.* Athens: Ohio University Press, 1966.

Mays, David John, ed. *The Letters and Papers of Edmund Pendleton, 1734–1803.* 2 vols. Charlottesville: Virginia Historical Society, University of Virginia Press, 1967.

McKee, Griffith John, ed. *Life and Correspondence of James Iredell.* 2 vols. New York: D. Appleton, 1857.

McCulloch v. Maryland, 17 U.S. 316 (1819).

Note from John Henry, December 12, 1868. *Virginia Museum of History and Culture,* Manuscript Mss2 H39633.

Observations on a Letter from George Nicholas of Kentucky to His Friend in Virginia . . .
    by an Inhabitant of the Northwest Territory. Cincinnati: Edmund Freeman, 1799.

"Original Letters." *William and Mary Quarterly,* 1st ser., 1:2 (October 1892): 99–109.

Patrick Henry in His Speeches and Writings and in the Words of His Contemporaries.
    Compiled by James M. Elson. Lynchburg, VA: Warwick House, 2007.

Pendleton, Edmund. *An Address of the Honorable Edmund Pendleton, of Virginia,*
    to the American Citizens, on the Present State of Our Country. Boston: Benjamin
    Edes, 1799.

Pollard, Edward A. "Historical Doubts Concerning Patrick Henry." *The Galaxy*
    10:3 (September 1870), 327 *et seq.*

Preston, Daniel, Marlena C. DeLong, and Heidi C. Stello, eds. *The Papers of James*
    Monroe. 6 vols. (to date). Santa Barbara, CA: Greenwood, 2011.

"Replies of Vermont to the Kentucky and Virginia Resolutions of 1798." *Records of*
    the Governor and Council of the State of Vermont. Ed. E. P. Walton IV. Montpe-
    lier, VT: J. M. Poland, 1876.

Sandoz, Ellis, ed. *Political Sermons of the American Founding Era, 1730–1805.* Indi-
    anapolis: Liberty Press, 1991.

Smith, Paul H., ed. *Letters of Delegates to Congress.* 26 vols. Washington, DC:
    Library of Congress, 1976–2000.

Statutes at Large of Virginia from October Session 1792, to December Session 1806. 3
    vols. Richmond: Samuel Shepherd, 1835.

Taylor, John. *An Enquiry into the Principles and Tendency of Certain Public Measures.*
    Philadelphia, 1794.

Thompson, David Pierce. "A Talk with Jefferson." *Harper's New Monthly Magazine*
    (May 1863): 834–35.

Tyler, Lyon G. *The Letters and Times of the Tylers.* 3 vols. 1884. Reprint. New York:
    DaCapo Press, 1970.

United States v. Darby, 312 U.S. 100, 124 (1941).

U.S. Senate. "Party Division." https://www.cop.senate.gov/history/partydiv.htm.

Van Buren, Martin. *Inquiry into the Origin and Course of Political Parties in the*
    United States. New York, 1867.

The Virginia and Kentucky Resolutions of 1798 and 1799; with Jefferson's Original
    Draught Thereof, also, Madison' Report, Calhoun's Address, Resolutions of the
    Several States in Relation to State Rights. Reprint. Washington: Jonathan Elliot,
    1832.

Ware v. Hylton, 3 U.S. 199 (1796).

Writings of Samuel Adams. Ed. Harry Alonzo Cushing. 4 vols. New York: G. P.
    Putnam's Sons, 1904–1908.

Yates, Robert. *Secret Proceedings and Debates of the Convention Assembled at Phila-
    delphia in the Year 1787.* Albany: Websters and Skinners, 1821.

SECONDARY SOURCES

Ambuske, James P., and Randall Flaherty. "Reading Law in the Early Republic: Legal Education in the Age of Jefferson." In *The Founding of Thomas Jefferson's University*, ed. John A. Ragosta, Peter S. Onuf, and Andrew J. O'Shaughnessy. Charlottesville: University of Virginia Press, 2019.

Anderson, Frank Maloy. "Enforcement of the Alien and Sedition Laws." *Annual Report of the American Historical Association for the Year 1912* 18 (1914): 113–26.

Bancroft, George. *The History of the Formation of the Constitution of the United States of America*. 2 vols. 3rd ed. New York: D. Appleton, 1885.

Beard, Charles A. *An Economic Interpretation of the Constitution of the United States*. New York: Macmillan., 1913.

Beeman, Richard R. "The Democratic Faith of Patrick Henry." *Virginia Magazine of History and Biography* 95:3 (July 1987): 301–16.

———. *The Old Dominion and the New Nation, 1788–1801*. Lexington: University Press of Kentucky, 1972.

———. *Patrick Henry: A Short Biography*. New York: McGraw-Hill, 1974.

———. *Plain, Honest Men: The Making of the American Constitution*. New York: Random House, 2009.

Bell, Rudolph M. *Party and Faction in American Politics: The House of Representatives, 1789–1801*. Westport, CT: Greenwood Press, 1973.

Beveridge, Albert J. *The Life of John Marshall*. 4 vols. Boston: Houghton Mifflin, 1916.

Bilder, Mary Sarah. *Madison's Hand: Revising the Constitutional Convention*. Cambridge, MA: Harvard University Press, 2017.

Biographical Directory of the U.S. Congress, 1774 to Present. http://bioguide.congress.gov/biosearch/biosearch.asp.

Bird, Wendell. *Criminal Dissent: Prosecutions under the Alien and Sedition Acts of 1798*. Cambridge, MA: Harvard University Press, 2020.

———. "New Light on the Sedition Act of 1798: The Missing Half of the Prosecutions." *Law and History Review* 34:3 (August 2016): 541–614.

———. *Press and Speech under Assault: The Early Supreme Court Justices, the Sedition Act of 1798, and the Campaign against Dissent*. New York: Oxford University Press, 2016.

———. "Reassessing Responses to the Virginia and Kentucky Resolutions: New Evidence from the Tennessee and Georgia Resolutions and from Other States." *Journal of the Early Republic* 35:4 (Winter 2015): 519–51.

Bordewich, Fergus M. *The First Congress: How James Madison, George Washington, and a Group of Extraordinary Men Invented the Government*. New York: Simon & Schuster, 2017.

Bouton, Terry. "'No Wonder the Times Were Troublesome': The Origins of Fries Rebellion, 1783–1799." *Pennsylvania History: A Journal of Mid-Atlantic Studies* 67:1 (Winter 2000): 21–42.

———. *Taming Democracy: "The People," the Founders, and the Troubled Ending of the American Revolution.* New York: Oxford University Press, 2007.

Bowling, Kenneth R. "'A Tub to the Whale': The Founding Fathers and Adoption of the Federal Bill of Rights." *Journal of the Early Republic* 8:3 (Autumn 1988): 223–51.

Boyd, Steven R. *The Politics of Opposition: Antifederalists and the Acceptance of the Constitution.* Millwood, NY: KTO Press, 1979.

Bradburn, Douglas. *The Citizenship Revolution: Politics and the Creation of the American Union, 1774–1804.* Charlottesville: University of Virginia Press, 2009.

———. "A Clamor in the Public Mind: Opposition to the Alien and Sedition Acts." *William and Mary Quarterly* 65:3 (July 2008): 565–600.

Broadwater, Jeff. *Jefferson, Madison, and the Making of the Constitution.* Chapel Hill: University of North Carolina Press, 2019.

Bruce, William Cabell. *John Randolph of Roanoke: 1773–1833.* 2 vols. New York: G. P. Putnam's Sons, 1922.

Buckley, Thomas E. "Patrick Henry, Religious Liberty, and the Search for Civic Virtue." In *The Forgotten Founders on Religion and Public Life,* ed. Daniel L. Dreisbach, Mark David Hall, and Jeffry H. Morrison. Notre Dame, IN: University of Notre Dame Press, 2009.

Campbell, Jud. "The Invention of First Amendment Federalism." *Texas Law Review* 97 (2019): 517–70.

Carter, Katlyn Marie. "Denouncing Secrecy and Defining Democracy in the Early American Republic." *Journal of the Early Republic* 40:3 (Fall 2020): 409–33.

Coleman, Aaron N. *The American Revolution, State Sovereignty, and the American Constitutional Settlement, 1765–1800.* Lanham, MD: Lexington Books, 2015.

Couvillon, Mark. *The Demosthenes of His Age.* Dexter, MI: Thomas Shore, 2013.

Cummins, E. H. "Patrick Henry." *New Edinburgh Encyclopaedia.* 2nd American ed. New York: Whiting and Watson, 1817.

Cunningham, Noble E. Jr. "Election of 1800." In *History of American Presidential Elections: 1789–1968,* ed. Arthur M. Schlesinger, Jr. 4 vols. New York: Chelsea House, 1971.

———. *Jeffersonian Republicans: The Formation of Party Organization, 1798–1801.* Chapel Hill: University of North Carolina Press, 1957.

———. *Jefferson vs. Hamilton: Confrontations That Shaped a Nation.* Boston: Bedford/St. Martin's, 2000.

Davidson, Philip G. "Virginia and the Alien and Sedition Laws." *American Historical Review* 36 (1931): 336–42.

Dellinger, Walter, and H. Jefferson Powell. "The Constitutionality of the Bank Bill: The Attorney General's First Constitutional Law Opinion." *Duke Law Journal* 44: (October 1994): 110–33.

Demmer, Amanda C. "Trick or Constitutional Treaty? The Jay Treaty and the Quarrel over the Diplomatic Separation of Powers." *Journal of the Early Republic* 35:4 (Winter 2019): 579–98.

Doubleday, Rhoda van Bibber Tanner. *Atlantic Between.* New York: House of Field, Doubleday, 1947.

Douglas, William O. "Interposition and the Peters Case, 1787–1809." *Stanford Law Review* 9 (1956–57): 3–12.

Dunn, Susan. *Jefferson's Second Revolution.* Boston: Houghton Mifflin, 2004.

Elkins, Stanley M., and Eric L. McKitrick. *The Age of Federalism: The Early American Republic, 1788 to 1800.* New York: Oxford University Press, 1993.

Ellis, Joseph J. *Founding Brothers: The Revolutionary Generation.* New York: Vintage Books, 2000.

———. *His Excellency: George Washington.* New York: Vintage Books, 2004.

Ellis, Richard E. *The Jeffersonian Crisis: Courts and Politics in the Young Republic.* New York: Oxford University Press, 1971.

———. "The Persistence of Antifederalism after 1789." In *Beyond Confederation: Origins of the Constitution and American National Identity,* ed. Richard Beeman, Stephen Botein, and Edward C. Carter II. Chapel Hill: University of North Carolina Press, 1987.

———. *The Union at Risk: Jacksonian Democracy, States' Rights, and the Nullification Crisis.* New York: Oxford University Press, 1987.

Estes, Todd. "Shaping the Politics of Public Opinion: Federalists and the Jay Treaty Debate." *Journal of the Early Republic* 20:3 (Autumn 2000): 393–422.

Evans, Emory G. "Private Indebtedness and the Revolution in Virginia, 1776 to 1796." *William and Mary Quarterly* 28:3 (July 1971): 349–74.

Farnham, Thomas A. "The Virginia Amendments of 1795: An Episode in the Opposition to Jay's Treaty." *Virginia Magazine of History and Biography* 75:1 (January 1967): 75–88.

Feller, A. H. "The Tenth Amendment Retires." *American Bar Association Journal* 27:4 (April 1941): 223–27.

Ferling, John E. *Adams vs. Jefferson: The Tumultuous Election of 1800.* New York: Oxford University Press, 2004.

Fischer, David Hackett. *The Revolution of American Conservatism: The Federalist Party in the Era of Jacksonian Democracy.* New York: Harper & Row, 1965.

Fontaine, Edward. *Patrick Henry: Corrections of Biographical Mistakes, . . .* Ed. Mark Couvillon. 1872. Reprint, Brookneal, VA: Patrick Henry Memorial Foundation, 2011.

Fontaine, Patrick Henry. "New Facts in Regard to the Character and Opinions of Patrick Henry." *DeBow's Review* (October 1870).

Freeman, Joanne B. "The Election of 1800: A Study in the Logic of Political Change." *Yale Law Journal* 108:8 (June 1999): 1959–94.

Freeman, Joanne B., and Johann N. Neem, eds. *Jeffersonians in Power: The Rhetoric of Opposition Meets the Realities of Government*. Charlottesville: University of Virginia Press, 2019.

Fritz, Christian G. "A Constitutional Middle-Ground Between Revision and Revolution: A Reevaluation of the Nullification Crisis and the Virginia and Kentucky Resolutions through the Lens of Popular Sovereignty." In *Law as Culture and Culture as Law: Essays in Honor of John Phillip Reid,* ed. Hendrik Hartog and John Phillip Reid. Madison, WI: Madison House, 2000.

——. "Interposition and the Heresy of Nullification: James Madison and the Exercise of Sovereign Constitutional Power." *First Principles* (Heritage Foundation) 41 (February 21, 2012): 1–17.

Garland, Hugh A. *Life of John Randolph*. 9th ed. New York: D. Appleton, 1854.

Garmon, Frank W. Jr. "Mapping Distress: Taxation and Insolvency in Virginia, 1782–1790." *Journal of the Early Republic* 40:2 (Summer 2020): 231–65.

Gibson, Alan. "Veneration and Vigilance: James Madison and Public Opinion, 1785–1800." *Review of Politics* 67:1 (Winter 2005): 5–35.

Gienapp, Jonathan. "How to Maintain a Constitution: The Virginia and Kentucky Resolutions and James Madison's Struggle with the Problem of Constitutional Maintenance." In *Nullification and Secession in Modern Constitutional Thought,* ed. Sanford Levinson. Lawrence: University Press of Kansas, 2016.

Glover, Lorri. *The Fate of the Revolution: Virginians Debate the Constitution*. Baltimore: Johns Hopkins University Press, 2016.

Golladay, V. Dennis. "Jefferson's 'Malignant Neighbor': John Nicholas, Jr." *Virginia Magazine of History and Biography* 86:3 (July 1978): 306–19.

Green, Nathaniel C. "'The Focus of the Wills of Converging Millions': Public Opposition to the Jay Treaty and the Origins of the People's Presidency." *Journal of the Early Republic* 37:3 (Fall 2017): 429–69.

Gross, Robert A., ed. *In Debt to Shays: The Bicentennial of an Agrarian Rebellion*. Charlottesville: University of Virginia Press, 1993.

Gutzman, Kevin R. C. "A Troublesome Legacy: James Madison and 'The Principles of '98.'" *Journal of the Early Republic* 15:4 (Winter 1995): 569–89.

——. "The Virginia and Kentucky Resolutions Reconsidered: 'An Appeal to the Real Laws of Our Country.'" *Journal of Southern History* 66:3 (August 2000): 473–96.

——. *Virginia's American Revolution: From Dominion to Republic, 1776–1840*. Lanham, MD: Lexington Books, 2007.

Hall, John, ed. *Forty Years' Familiar Letters of James W. Alexander*. 2 vols. New York: Charles Scribner, 1870.

Halperin, Terri Diane. *Alien and Sedition Acts of 1798: Testing the Constitution*. Baltimore: Johns Hopkins University Press, 2016.

Hartnett, Stephen J., and Jennifer Rose Mercieca. "'Has Your Courage Rusted?': National Security and the Contested Rhetorical Norms of Republicanism in Post-Revolutionary America, 1798–1801." *Rhetoric & Public Affairs* 9:1 (Spring 2006): 79–112.

Hayes, Kevin J. *George Washington: A Life in Books.* New York: Oxford University Press, 2017.

Henry, William Wirt. "Patrick Henry: A Vindication of His Character, as an Orator and a Man." *Historical Magazine* (November–December 1873).

Hobson, Charles F. "Patrick Henry and John Marshall, the 18th Century Legal Dream Team." *Newsletter of the Patrick Henry Memorial Foundation* (Summer 2005).

Hoffer, Peter Charles. *The Free Press Crisis of 1800: Thomas Cooper's Trial for Seditious Libel.* Lawrence: University Press of Kansas, 2011.

Horn, James J., Jan Ellen Taylor, and Peter S. Onuf, eds. *The Revolution of 1800: Democracy, Race, and the New Republic.* Charlottesville: University of Virginia Press, 2002.

Horsman, Reginald. *Expansion and American Indian Policy: 1783–1812.* Norman: University of Oklahoma Press, 1992.

Howard, Thomas L. III, and Owen W. Gallogly. *Society Ties: A History of the Jefferson Society and Student Life at the University of Virginia.* Charlottesville: University of Virginia Press, 2017.

Howe, Henry. *Historical Collections of Virginia.* Charleston: W. R. Babcock, 1849.

Howison, Robert R. *A History of Virginia.* 2 vols. Richmond: Drinker and Morris, 1848.

Jaffa, Harry V. *The Conditions of Freedom: Essays in Political Philosophy.* Baltimore: Johns Hopkins University Press, 1975.

Jones, Howard. *Crucible of Power: A History of American Foreign Relations to 1913.* Lanham, MD: Rowman & Littlefield, 2009.

Jordan, Daniel P. *Political Leadership in Jefferson's Virginia.* Charlottesville: University of Virginia Press, 1983.

Kidd, Thomas. *Patrick Henry: First among Patriots.* New York: Basic Books, 2011.

Klarman, Michael J. *The Framers' Coup: The Making of the United States Constitution.* New York: Oxford University Press, 2016.

Koch, Adrienne, and Harry Ammon. "The Virginia and Kentucky Resolutions: An Episode in Jefferson's and Madison's Defense of Civil Liberties." *William and Mary Quarterly* 5:2 (April 1947): 145–76.

Kukla, Jon. *Patrick Henry: Champion of Liberty.* New York: Simon & Schuster, 2017.

———. "A Spectrum of Sentiments: Virginia's Federalists, Antifederalists, and 'Federalists Who Are for Amendments,' 1787–1788." *Virginia Magazine of History and Biography* 96:1 (July 1988): 276–96.

Labunski, Richard E. *James Madison and the Struggle for the Bill of Rights.* New York: Oxford University Press, 2008.

Larson, Edward J. *A Magnificent Catastrophe: The Tumultuous Election of 1800, America's First Presidential Campaign.* New York: Free Press, 2007.

Lash, Kurt T., and Alicia Harrison. "Minority Report: John Marshall and the Defense of the Alien and Sedition Acts." *Ohio State Law Journal* 68:2 (2007): 435–516.

Lenner, Andrew C. "John Taylor and the Origins of American Federalism." *Journal of the Early Republic* 17 (Autumn 1997): 399–423.

Leonard, Gerald, and Saul Cornell. *The Partisan Republic: Democracy, Exclusion, and the Fall of the Founders' Constitution, 1780s–1830s.* Cambridge: Cambridge University Press, 2019.

Levinson, Sandford. "The 21st Century Rediscovery of Nullification and Secession in American Political Rhetoric." In *Nullification and Secession in Modern Constitutional Thought,* ed. Sandford Levinson. Lawrence: University Press of Kansas, 2016.

Levy, Leonard W. *Jefferson and Civil Liberties: The Darker Side.* Cambridge, MA: Belknap Press, 1963.

Longacre, James B., and James Herring. *The National Portrait Gallery of Distinguished Americans.* 4 vols. Philadelphia: Henry Perkins, 1835.

Loring, Caleb William. *Nullification, Secession, Webster's Argument, and the Kentucky and Virginia Resolutions: Considered in Reference to the Constitution and Historically.* New York: G. P. Putnam's Sons, 1893.

Lurie, Shira. "Liberty Poles and the Fight for Popular Politics in the Early Republic." *Journal of the Early Republic* 38 (Winter 2018): 673–97.

Maier, Pauline. *Ratification: The People Debate the Constitution, 1787–1788.* New York: Simon & Schuster, 2010.

———. "The Road Not Taken: Nullification, John C. Calhoun, and the Revolutionary Tradition in South Carolina." *South Carolina Historical Magazine* 82 (January 1981): 1–19.

Main, Jackson Turner. *The Antifederalists: Critics of the Constitution, 1787–1788.* New York: W. W. Norton, 1961.

Malone, Dumas. *Jefferson and the Ordeal of Liberty.* Boston: Little, Brown, 1962.

Martin, Robert W. T. *Government by Dissent: Protest, Resistance, and Radical Democratic Thought in the Early American Republic.* New York: NYU Press, 2013.

May, Gregory. *Jefferson's Treasure: How Albert Gallatin Saved the New Nation from Debt.* Washington, DC: Regnery History, 2018.

Mayer, David Nicholas. *The Constitutional Thought of Thomas Jefferson.* Charlottesville: University Press of Virginia, 1995.

Mayer, Henry. *A Son of Thunder: Patrick Henry and the American Republic.* New York: Franklin Watts, 1986.

McCoy, Drew R. *Last of the Fathers: James Madison and the Republican Legacy.* Cambridge: Cambridge University Press, 1989.

McDonald, Forrest. *States' Rights and the Union: Imperium in Imperio, 1776–1876.* Lawrence: University Press of Kansas, 2000.

McGarvie, Mark D. "Disestablishing Religion and Protecting Religious Liberty in State Laws and Constitutions (1776–1833)." In *No Establishment of Religion: America's Original Contribution to Religious Liberty,* ed. T. Jeremy Gunn and John Witte Jr. New York: Oxford University Press, 2012.

McGraw, Joseph. "'To Secure These Rights:' Virginia Republicans on the Strategies of Political Opposition, 1788–1800." *Virginia Magazine of History and Biography* 91:1 (January 1983): 54–72.

Meade, Robert Douthat. *Patrick Henry: Patriot in the Making.* Philadelphia: J. B. Lippincott, 1957.

———. *Patrick Henry: Practical Revolutionary.* Philadelphia: J. B. Lippincott, 1969.

Miller, John C. *The Federalist Era 1789–1801.* New York: Harper & Row, 1960.

Morgan, Edmund S. *American Heroes: Profiles of Men and Women Who Shaped Early America.* New York: W. W. Norton, 2009.

Morris, Richard B. *The Forging of the Union, 1781–1789.* New York: Harper & Row, 1987.

Nevins, Allan. *The American States, during and after the Revolution, 1775–1789.* New York: A. M. Kelley, 1969.

Onuf, Peter S. *Jefferson and the Virginians: Democracy, Constitutions, and Empire.* Baton Rouge: Louisiana State University Press, 2018.

———. *Jefferson's Empire: The Language of American Nationhood.* Charlottesville: University of Virginia Press, 2000.

O'Shaughnessy, Andrew J. *The Illimitable Freedom of the Human Mind: Thomas Jefferson's Idea of a University.* Charlottesville: University of Virginia Press, 2021.

Pasley, Jeffrey L. *The First Presidential Contest: 1796 and the Founding of American Democracy.* Lawrence: University Press of Kansas, 2016.

Peterson, Merrill D. *The Jefferson Image in the American Mind.* New York: Oxford University Press, 1960.

Powell, H. Jefferson. "The Principles of '98: An Essay in Historical Retrieval." *Virginia Law Review* 80:3 (April 1994): 689–743.

Ragosta, John A. "'Caesar Had His Brutus': What Did Patrick Henry Really Say?" *Virginia Magazine of History and Biography* 126:3 (2018): 282–97.

———. "Founding Rivals." *Monticello Magazine* (Summer 2022).

———. "Jefferson, Madison, Adams: Conversations on Religious Liberty." In *Rival Visions of the Early American Republic,* ed. Andrew Bibby and Dustin Gish. Charlottesville: University of Virginia Press, 2021.

———. *Patrick Henry: Proclaiming a Revolution.* New York: Routledge, 2017.

——. *Religious Freedom: Jefferson's Legacy, America's Creed.* Charlottesville: University of Virginia Press, 2013.

——. "Thomas Jefferson: Icon." In *Thomas Jefferson: Critical Insights,* ed. R. Evans. Pasadena, CA: Salem Press, 2020.

——. "What Would Patrick Henry Say?" *Richmond Times Dispatch,* January 18, 2021.

Rakove, Jack N. *James Madison and the Creation of the American Republic.* 2d ed. New York: Longman, 2002.

Read, James H., and Neal Allen. "Living, Dead, and Undead: Nullification Past and Present." In *Nullification and Secession in Modern Constitutional Thought,* ed. Sanford Levinson. Lawrence: University Press of Kansas, 2016.

Remini, Robert V. "The Northwest Ordinance of 1787: Bulwark of the Republic." *Indiana Magazine of History* 84:1 (March 1988): 15–24.

Richards, Leonard L. *Shays's Rebellion: The American Revolution's Final Battle.* Philadelphia: University of Pennsylvania Press, 2002.

Risjord, Norman K. *Chesapeake Politics, 1781–1800.* New York: Columbia University Press, 1978.

——. *The Old Republicans: Southern Conservatism in the Age of Jefferson.* New York: Columbia University Press, 1965.

——. "The Virginia Federalists." *Journal of Southern History* 33:4 (November 1967): 486–517.

Rowland, Kate Mason. *Life of George Mason.* 2 vols. New York: G. P. Putnam's Sons, 1892.

Royster, Charles. *Light-Horse Harry Lee and the Legacy of the American Revolution.* New York: Alfred A. Knopf, 1981.

Samuelson, Richard. "The Constitutional Statesmanship of James Madison." In Freeman and Neem, *Jeffersonians in Power,* 262–81.

Sehat, David. *The Jefferson Rule: How the Founding Fathers Became Infallible and Our Politics Inflexible.* New York: Simon & Schuster, 2015.

Sharp, James Roger. *American Politics in the Early Republic: The New Nation in Crisis.* New Haven: Yale University Press, 1993.

——. *The Deadlocked Election of 1800: Jefferson, Burr, and the Union in the Balance.* Lawrence: University Press of Kansas, 2018.

Shulim, Joseph I. "Thomas Jefferson Views Napoleon." *Virginia Magazine of History and Biography* 60:2 (1952): 288–304.

Simon, James F. *What Kind of Nation: Thomas Jefferson, John Marshall, and the Epic Struggle to Create a United States.* New York: Simon & Schuster, 2002.

Slack, Charles. *Liberty's First Crisis: Adams, Jefferson, and the Misfits Who Saved Free Speech.* New York: Atlantic Monthly Press, 2015.

Sloan, Herbert E. *Principle and Interest: Thomas Jefferson and the Problem of Debt.* Charlottesville: University of Virginia Press, 1995.

Smith, James Morton. *Freedom's Fetters: The Alien and Sedition Laws and American Civil Liberties.* Ithaca, NY: Cornell University Press, 1956.

Smith, Mark. "Beyond Strict Construction: Jeffersonians in the 1790s." In Freeman and Neem, *Jeffersonians in Power,* 80–102.

Stampp, Kenneth M. "The Concept of a Perpetual Union." *Journal of American History* 65:1 (June 1978): 5–33.

Steele, Brian. *Thomas Jefferson and American Nationalism.* New York: Cambridge University Press, 2015.

———. "Thomas Jefferson, Coercion, and the Limits of Harmonious Union." *Journal of Southern History* 74:4 (November 2008): 823–54.

Stewart, David O. *The Summer of 1787: The Men Who Invented the Constitution.* New York: Simon & Schuster, 2007.

Story, Joseph. *Commentaries on the Constitution of the United States.* Boston: Hillard, Gray, 1833.

Tarter, Brent. "George Mason and the Conservation of Liberty." *Virginia Magazine of History and Biography* 99:3 (July 1991): 279–304.

Taylor, Alan. *Thomas Jefferson's Education.* New York: W. W. Norton, 2019.

Tipton, Diane. *Nullification and Interposition in American Political Thought.* Albuquerque: University of New Mexico Press, 1969.

Treacy, Kenneth W. "Olmstead Case, 1778–1809." *Western Political Quarterly* 10 (1957): 675–91.

Trees, Andrew. "Apocalypse Now: Thomas Jefferson's Radical Enlightenment." In Freeman and Neem, *Jeffersonians in Power,* 199–221.

Trickey, Erick. "Where did the Term 'Gerrymander' Come From?" *Smithsonian Magazine,* July 20, 2017. https://www.smithsonianmag.com/history/where-did-term-gerrymander-come-180964118/.

Tyler, Moses Coit. *Patrick Henry.* 1887. Reprint. Langhorne, PA: Chelsea House, 1980.

Van Cleve, George William. *We Have Not a Government: The Articles of Confederation and the Road to the Constitution.* Chicago: University of Chicago Press, 2017.

Veit, Helen E., and Kenneth R. Bowling, eds. *Creating the Bill of Rights.* Baltimore: Johns Hopkins University Press, 1991.

Warfield, Ethelbert Dudley. *The Kentucky Resolutions of 1798: An Historical Study.* 1894. Reprint. Freeport, NY: Books for Libraries Press, 1969.

Watkins, William J. Jr. *Reclaiming the American Revolution: The Kentucky and Virginia Resolutions and Their Legacy.* New York: Palgrave Macmillan, 2004.

Wehtje, Myron F. "The Congressional Elections of 1799 in Virginia." *West Virginia History* 29:4 (July 1968): 251–73.

Weisberger, Bernard A. *America Afire: Jefferson, Adams, and the Revolutionary Election of 1800.* New York: William Morrow, 2000.

Wirt, William. *Sketches of the Life and Character of Patrick Henry.* Ithaca, NY: Andrus, Gauntlett, 1850.

Wood, Gordon S. *Empire of Liberty: A History of the Early Republic, 1789–1815.* New York: Oxford University Press, 2009.

——. *Friends Divided: John Adams and Thomas Jefferson.* New York: Penguin Books, 2017.

——. *Power and Liberty: Constitutionalism in the American Revolution.* New York: Oxford University Press, 2021.

Zemler, Jeffrey Allen. "'A Conciliatory Declaration': George Nicholas, the Virginia Ratification Convention, and the Misuse of History." *Register of the Kentucky Historical Society* 112:2 (Spring 2014): 179–97.